A Guide to the
Companies Act 1989

A Guide to the Companies Act 1989

Christopher Swinson, MA, FCA,
National Managing Partner,
BDO Binder Hamlyn

Butterworths
London, Dublin and Edinburgh
1990

United Kindom	Butterworth & Co (Publishers) Ltd., 88 Kingsway, LONDON WC2B 6AB, and 4 Hill Street, EDINBURGH EH2 3JZ
Australia	Butterworths Pty Ltd, SYDNEY, MELBOURNE, BRISBANE, ADELAIDE, PERTH, CANBERRA and HOBART
Canada	Butterworths (Canada) Ltd, TORONTO and VANCOUVER
Ireland	Butterworth (Ireland) Ltd, DUBLIN
Malaysia	Malayan Law Journal Sdn Bhd, KUALA LUMPUR
New Zealand	Butterworths of New Zealand Ltd, WELLINGTON and AUCKLAND
Puerto Rico	Equity de Puerto Rico, Inc, HATO REY
Singapore	Malayan Law Journal Ptd Ltd, SINGAPORE
USA	Butterworth Legal Publishers, ST PAUL, Minnesota; SEATTLE, Washington; BOSTON, Massachusetts; AUSTIN, Texas; Equity Publishing, ORFORD, New Hampshire; and D & S Publishers, CLEARWATER, Florida

Typeset by Phoenix Photosetting, Chatham, Kent
Printed and bound by Mackays of Chatham PLC, Chatham, Kent

Foreword

In the past fifteen years, developments in company law have provided plenty of opportunities for the production of new books. The continued progress of the European Community's programme of company law harmonisation promises that there will be more opportunities in future.

This book aims to provide an introduction to the Companies Act 1989 which owes its existence to two European Community company law directives (the Seventh and Eighth) but deals with a great many other matters in addition. My purpose has been to provide a guide to the structure of the Act's provisions and an indication of their effect.

In preparing the book, I have been greatly assisted by Butterworths' editorial staff who readily assumed the task of preparing an index, by Christine, my wife, and Timothy, my son, who on occasion played some of his games softly to help me.

January 1990   Christopher Swinson

Contents

Contents

Contents

Table of statutes

('New' section numbers inserted or substituted by the 1989 Act are denoted by ★)

Chapter 1

Introduction

1.1 Introduction

The Companies Act 1989 comprises a pot pourri of provisions involving changes
to the laws relating to companies, competition, financial services and insolvency.
Introduced into the House of Lords in December 1988, the original bill consisted
of 148 clauses and 17 Schedules. By Royal Assent, the Act grew to 218 sections
and 24 Schedules.

The result is an Act which has no single objective but a number of principal
themes:

(1) To implement the Seventh and Eighth European Community Company Law
    Directives relating to group accounts and the regulation of auditors.
(2) To extend deregulation and to simplify administrative requirements for
    smaller companies.
(3) To improve existing regulatory powers by the extension of existing powers of
    investigation, and the introduction of procedural reforms for merger control.
(4) To improve market efficiency through the clarification of the law relating to
    insolvency and financial markets and amendment of the Financial Services
    Act 1986.

1.2 Group accounts (Chapters 2–4)

The Act implements the Seventh European Community Company Law Directive
relating to consolidated accounts. European Community member states were
required to implement the directive for financial years commencing on or after
1 January 1990 as part of a broader plan to harmonise European company law.

Under existing law, holding companies may prepare group accounts in any one
of several ways, although in each case subject to an overriding requirement that
the accounts should give a true and fair view. The Act requires that all group
accounts should be consolidated accounts in the form specified in Schedule 2
although the overriding principle that consolidated accounts must give a true and
fair view remains.

Under the existing definition of a 'subsidiary', contained in section 736 of the
1985 Act, a company is a subsidiary of another if the investing company either
holds more than half the subsidiary's equity share capital or is both a member of it
and controls the composition of its board of directors. Group accounts need take
account of the balance sheets and profit and loss accounts only of the holding
company and its subsidiaries. A number of techniques have been devised to
ensure that companies which are under a company's de facto control do not fall

within the technical definition of subsidiary and thus that they can be excluded from group accounts. It was hoped that implementation of the Seventh Directive would provide an opportunity to reduce the scope for creative accounting of this type.

The result is a new concept of 'subsidiary undertaking' which, unlike the old 1985 Act definition of a 'subsidiary', is based more on control than on ownership. Subsidiary undertakings are widely defined to include all companies, unincorporated associations and partnerships where a parent undertaking either holds or controls a majority of the whole voting rights or exercises control over the board of directors. Also included are entities in respect of which the parent undertaking either has the right to direct the operating and financial policies, or holds a 'participating interest' and exercises a continuing 'dominant influence' or manages the two companies on a 'unified basis'.

At first sight, these changes would appear to spread much more widely the net for entities which are to be included in a holding company's group accounts. Certainly the status of existing off-balance sheet companies will need to be reconsidered and many of them will have to be brought on balance sheet if no other steps are taken. However, long detailed definitions are notoriously vulnerable to ingenious manipulation, and the 1989 Act seems to be no exception.

As well as introducing a new definition of 'subsidiary' for accounting purposes, the Act introduces a revised definition for non-accounting purposes. These new provisions focus on control through voting rights and influence over the board and thus are a contrast with the existing 1985 Act definition of subsidiary which focuses on ownership through the size of equity share capital held or the ability to control the composition of the board of directors.

The effect of these provisions is that a number of companies which were not previously subsidiaries will become 'subsidiary undertakings' for consolidation purposes and 'subsidiaries' for other Companies Act purposes. There will no longer be congruence between the two definitions.

Apart from changing the definition of groups and the requirements for preparation of group accounts, the 1989 Act substantially re-enacts the provisions of the 1985 Act relating to the preparation, approval, delivery and publication of accounts and reports. As part of this a number of significant changes is made:

(1) The period allowed for a company's initial election of its accounting reference period is extended to nine months.
(2) Listed public companies will no longer be required to send full financial statements to members but instead summary financial statements will suffice.
(3) New provisions are introduced for banking and insurance companies and groups.
(4) New disclosure requirements are introduced to improve the presentation of mergers and acquisitions in company accounts.
(5) The required disclosure in respect of related undertakings is materially extended.
(6) The disclosure of compensation for loss of office of directors in future must include any benefits in kind. 'Golden hellos' will in future be disclosed.
(7) Companies will be required to state in their annual accounts that they have been prepared in accordance with applicable accounting standards and any material departures must be highlighted.

1.3 Regulation of auditors (Chapter 5)

The 1989 Act also implements the Eighth European Community Company Law Directive by specifying minimum requirements for auditors' education, training and regulation and seeks to ensure that company audits are carried out by competent people with integrity and independence.

The accountancy bodies will have primary responsibility for the regulation of auditors provided that their rules and practices meet new statutory specifications so that they qualify as recognised supervisory bodies (RSBs).

Only those individuals and firms eligible under the rules of an RSB may be appointed to the office of auditor. The present prohibition on corporate companies acting as auditors is removed.

In addition to RSBs, the Act provides for the recognition of qualifying bodies (RQBs). An RQB will be a body established in the U.K. offering a recognised professional qualification in accountancy. The Act thus separates the functions of authorisation and supervision from examination and training although the established professional bodies will probably apply for recognition in respect of both functions. Whilst they may achieve greater harmonisation within the European Community, the effect of these measures is to give the Government much greater influence and control over the accounting profession.

1.4 Investigations (Chapter 6)

The Department of Trade and Industry (DTI) recently carried out a review of its investigation powers. Its recommendations are implemented in the Act. Defects were identified in the system of powers to order investigations in cases of suspected fraud, unreasonable withholding of information from shareholders and other cases of misconduct justifying enquiry in the public interest.

The Act extends the Secretary of State's power to appoint inspectors and to direct or terminate their inspections. For example, the Act grants the Secretary of State power for the first time to appoint inspectors even where he has expressly declared an intention not to publish their report.

The powers of inspectors are extended. For example, inspectors are to have powers to order that any person who has information relevant to an investigation must make full disclosure. Inspectors will have back-up search and entry powers. Where there are grounds for believing that a serious offence has been committed and that relevant documents may have been interfered with, a new power of pre-emptive search and entry will be available.

1.5 Company charges (Chapter 7)

In 1962, the Jenkins Committee recommended a major overhaul of the system of registration of company charges in the United Kingdom. The recommendations were embodied in the Companies Bill 1973 which was lost when Parliament was dissolved in readiness for the 1974 election. More recently, the Diamond Report has recommended urgent reform of the system of registration of company charges.

The existing system is based on the duty of a company to deliver prescribed particulars of a charge together with the instruments creating the charge to the Registrar of Companies within 21 days of its creation. Breach of this duty is an offence. Companies House first checks the accuracy of the particulars of the charge against the instrument creating the charge. The Registrar then issues a certificate that the statutory provisions have been complied with. If inaccurate particulars of a charge are mistakenly entered on the register a person who suffers loss as a result will nevertheless be bound by the Registrar's certificate since that certificate is conclusive evidence of registration of the charge.

A number of important changes are made to this system. Firstly, in future the sole duty of Companies House will be to file on the register particulars of a charge in the form in which they are received. Secondly, the Registrar's certificate will cease to be conclusive evidence that the requirements of the Companies Acts have been complied with. Charges will be waived against third parties if and to the extent that particulars of the charge are inaccurate or understate any security right. Thirdly, the duty to file prescribed particulars of a charge within 21 days of its creation will continue. However, new safeguards protect persons searching the register during the intervening period. Finally, a new procedure allows late registration of particulars and correction of particulars previously delivered without the need to apply to the court in circumstances where both the chargor and chargee consent.

1.6 A company's objects (Chapter 8)

The 1989 Act seeks to reform the ultra vires rule. In future, the validity of an act done by a company will not be capable of being called into question on the grounds of anything in the company's memorandum. Directors will however continue to be liable for any breach of their powers flowing from the memorandum. The company in general meeting may by special resolution ratify the acts of the directors but such ratification will not affect the question of the liability of the directors or of any other person, although relief from such liability may be agreed in a special resolution.

1.7 Deregulation of private companies (Chapter 9)

As part of a general policy to remove 'red tape' and to simplify administrative requirements, the Act recognises that many Companies Act requirements are unnecessary for small private companies. Two major steps are taken in this respect by the Act. Firstly, the Act prescribes a procedure for private companies to agree business by unanimous written resolutions instead of resolutions passed at general or class meetings. Secondly, private companies are empowered to decide by unanimous resolution (referred to as an 'elective resolution') to disapply certain provisions of the Companies Acts including those relating to holding an annual general meeting and authorising short notice of meetings.

1.8 Appointment and removal of auditors (Chapter 10)

To reflect the possibility that private companies may not hold annual general meetings, the rules concerning the appointment and removal of auditors are revised.

4

1.9 Mergers (Chapter 11)

The 1989 Act seeks to promote competition by removing certain obstacles to mergers and by introducing measures to facilitate those mergers deemed to be in the public interest. The effect of these changes is to shift the balance of power between the regulatory authorities from the Monopolies and Mergers Commission (MMC) to the Office of Fair Trading (OFT).

The Act introduces a system of voluntary pre-notification of mergers. Companies which pre-notify a merger should know in most cases within 20 working days thereafter whether or not they can proceed. If the OFT does not refer the matter to the MMC within the specified period the merger cannot thereafter be referred provided that certain other conditions are fulfilled.

The OFT is required to advise the Secretary of State whether a proposed merger or takeover bid should be referred to the MMC. The Secretary of State may respond to that advice either by allowing the transaction to proceed or referring it immediately or seeking legally binding undertakings from the parties.

The Secretary of State will then publish the advice given by the OFT and details of relevant undertakings.

1.10 Financial markets and insolvency (Chapter 12)

The Act seeks to safeguard the integrity and continuing operation of financial markets by making special provision for the insolvency of and enforcement of charges against members of certain financial markets. The Act provides that the default procedures of recognised investment exchanges and recognised clearing houses will override general insolvency law to protect the integrity of the financial market concerned. A defaulting member will be allowed to resolve his market commitments in an orderly fashion, to minimise the possibility that an isolated default could result in a collapse of confidence in that market.

1.11 Financial Services Act (Chapter 13)

The Act makes a number of significant amendments to the Financial Services Act with the objectives of reducing the complexity and diversity of existing rule books and of leading to a system that is better understood and more effectively policed. The Act will enable a new three-tier approach to be taken to rule books. Firstly, at the top level, a set of principles will focus on the main elements of the conduct and financial standing expected of persons engaged in investment business. Secondly, there will be a set of designated core rules common to all self-regulating organisations. These will relate specifically to the conduct of business, financial resources, clients' money and unsolicited calls. Thirdly, there will be detailed support in the form of rules, codes of practice or other means which will be chosen by the relevant regulator and which thus might differ between SROs.

1.12 Miscellaneous amendments (Chapter 14)

As is often the case with government legislation, the DTI, the department sponsoring the Companies Bill, added to the bill a large number of minor measures dealing with detailed changes to the Companies Acts. Among other matters, these provisions abolish the requirement for companies to have a company seal, ease the creation of employee share ownership plans, stiffen the requirements for disclosure of interests in shares, simplify the requirements for annual returns, abolish the doctrine of deemed notice and vary the rights of members to damages in certain circumstances.

Chapter 2

Group accounts

2.1 Background

The preparation of group accounts has been a requirement of the U.K. company law since 1947. Before that many companies had voluntarily chosen to publish consolidated accounts and since the early 1940s the Stock Exchange had required newly listed companies to do this. Since 1947 the legal requirements for the publication of group accounts and their preparation have remained virtually unchanged. However, in recent years, there has been growing concern about some of the characteristics of these provisions and these concerns might in any case have led to reform in due course. On 13 June 1983, the Council of the European Communities adopted the Seventh Company Law Directive which deals with requirements for the publication of consolidated accounts and with the manner of their preparation. Irrespective of purely domestic concerns, therefore, the implementation of this directive required a reconsideration of the provisions which were already in force in the United Kingdom.

In August 1985, the Department of Trade and Industry (DTI) published a consultative paper on the implementation of the Seventh Directive and identified four main changes to United Kingdom legislation which would be required as a result. These were: the situations in which consolidated accounts must be prepared, the definition of parent and subsidiary undertakings, the rules by which the process of preparing consolidated accounts must be carried out and the treatment of associated companies and undertakings.

Consideration of the situations in which consolidated accounts must be prepared is dominated by the definition of 'parent' and 'subsidiary', relationships. These matters are the primary subject for this chapter whilst the basis on which consolidated accounts are to be prepared is described in the next chapter.

2.2 Existing definitions

The definitions of a holding company, subsidiary and wholly owned subsidiary are set out in section 736 of the Companies Act 1985. The heart of the definition is set out below:

'For the purposes of this Act, a company is deemed to be a subsidiary of another if (but only if):

(a) that other either:

   (i) is a member of it and controls the composition of its board of directors, or
   (ii) holds more than half in nominal value of its equity share capital, or

(b) the first mentioned company is a subsidiary of any company which is that other's subsidiary.'

This definition appears in section 736(1) which is augmented by a further subsection which deals with circumstances in which the composition of the company's board of directors is deemed to be controlled by another company and circumstances in which share holdings are to be included or excluded from the calculations for the purposes of the section.

Equity share capital is defined in section 744 of the 1985 Act as follows:

' "Equity share capital" means, in relation to a company, its issued share capital excluding any part of that capital, which neither as respects dividends nor as respects capital, carries any right to participate beyond a specified amount in a distribution.'

Equity shares are therefore those which are not limited to a known fixed monetary amount of either dividends or assets on a winding up. These entitlements are treated as not being fixed if their calculation involves use of any unspecified figure (e.g. dividends as a percentage of profits over a pre-determined level.

In practice this definition of the holding company-subsidiary relationship has caused two main areas of difficulty.

Firstly, the definition emphasises the level of equity holding rather than control of activities through the voting rights which attach to any shares held. This means that one company can hold all the ordinary shares of another company, without that other company being treated as a subsidiary because other shares held by a third party qualify as equity capital and amount to 50% or more of the company's equity shares. Assuming that the other party does not control the composition of the board, the company owning the ordinary shares may exert control because these shares have superior voting rights to the other classes of shares in issue and may effectively be entitled to virtually all of the profits of the 'subsidiary'. This problem stems from the definition of equity which makes it very easy for a class of share to be designed to qualify as equity within the 1985 Act definition whilst having only limited voting rights and dividend rights.

The second area of difficulty arising from the definition of the holding company-subsidiary relationship concerns the reference in the definition to control of the composition of the board of directors of a company. This is not necessarily the same as control of the company's activities through the board. Under the 1985 Act, a company is deemed to control the composition of a board of directors if it can appoint or remove the holders of all or a majority of the directorships. In the circumstances described above, it is possible for the company owning the ordinary shares to be entitled to appoint or remove only half of the number of directors and therefore be unable to control the composition of the majority of the board. In practice, the company owning the ordinary shares may still achieve control of the business by ensuring that the directors it can appoint have more voting rights than the other directors. Thus although there would be practical control over the activities of the investee company, for the purposes of the 1985 Act it would not be a subsidiary of the company and there would be no requirement for the investee company to be included in group accounts published by the investor company.

As a result of these difficulties, it is possible that a controlled non-subsidiary can be created. Most of the structures commonly used are combinations of the following elements:

(1) An investor holds no more than 50% of the investee's equity shares capital. The holding may be as low as zero. A friendly third party may be used to hold the remaining if not all of the equity share in the investee. This role may be taken by the investor's bank.

(2) The investor cannot control the composition of the investee's board of directors. Whilst controlling the election of only up to one half of the directors it may actually control the investee's activities through the structure of the directors' voting rights.

(3) The investor and a third party shareholder may have put or call options on shares held by each other.

(4) The investor may receive the majority of the investee's profits through the structure of shareholder rights on distribution or management charges.

(5) The investor company may have indirect share holdings which can be structured so that the investee is a member of the investor's group for tax purposes but not a member of the group for Companies Act purposes.

The possibility of creating controlled non-consolidated companies led to consolidation becoming to a large extent optional. Scope for creativity has been considerable as a parent company has been able to use this approach to exclude as many activities as it wished from its group accounts. As the purpose of introducing the requirement for group accounts in 1947 was to allow readers of financial statements to form an overall picture of a group's activities and affairs, these techniques have tended to undermine the purpose for which the group accounts requirement was originally introduced.

Controlled-subsidiary companies have been used for a number of different purposes. For example, companies may sell assets to a controlled non-subsidiary to transfer assets and related borrowings to that other company to reduce the gearing ratio shown in the group accounts. It may also be done so a company can report profits on the transfer of assets to a controlled non-subsidiary company. Controlled non-subsidiary companies have been used as vehicles to acquire companies or assets especially where the company to be acquired is expected to make losses for a certain time after acquisition. This mechanism would avoid post-acquisition losses affecting the group's results.

2.3 Seventh Directive

Article 1 of the directive sets out six situations in which a parent-subsidiary relationship is to be regarded as existing and in which the parent company would be required to present consolidated accounts. Article 1 also describes one further situation requiring consolidation even though such a relationship does not exist. The first four of these situations must be incorporated in member state law while the remaining three are optional. The seven situations are as follows.

(1) MAJORITY OF VOTING RIGHTS

A company will be regarded as a subsidiary of another if the latter company holds a majority of its shareholders' or members' voting rights. This is the principal definition of the parent-subsidiary relationship based on the power of one entity to control another through the exercise of shareholder voting. Unlike the existing definition of a subsidiary in U.K. law, this definition concentrates on those shares which can exercise voting power rather than those which are defined in terms of their rights to participate beyond a specified amount in a distribution. Voting rights are not defined as such by the directive.

(2) CONTROL OF THE BOARD OF DIRECTORS

A company will be regarded as a subsidiary of another if the latter company is a shareholder or member of it and has the right to appoint or remove a majority of the members of its administrative, management or supervisory board (in other words, the board of directors in the United Kingdom). This is similar to the requirement in section 736 of the 1985 Act. In essence, it is an anti-avoidance measure which extends the control concept from control of the company through the exercise of shareholder voting rights to control of the board to cover situations where the latter exists but not the former.

(3) CONTROL BY CONTRACT

A company will be regarded as a subsidiary of another if the latter company can exercise a dominant influence over it under a contract with it or under a provision in its memorandum or articles of association. Such a contract which is a feature of German business organisations is not usually possible under U.K. company law because it would conflict with the directors' fiduciary duty to conduct the affairs of the company in accordance with its own best interests. It is permitted only where the memorandum and articles specifically envisage the arrangement. The directive provides that this definition of the parent-subsidiary relationship only applies where it is consistent with the company law of the country concerned.

(4) CONTROL BY AGREEMENT

A company will be regarded as a subsidiary of another if the latter company is a shareholder or member of it and controls alone under an agreement with other shareholders or members a majority of the voting rights in the subsidiary. This is a more stringent application of the concept of de facto control by a minority investor, as it requires there to be an agreement with other shareholders rather than merely tacit acceptance that control can be exercised. The directive provides that member states may introduce more particular requirements for the form and content of such agreements.

(5) DE FACTO CONTROL OVER APPOINTMENT OF THE BOARD

A company is the subsidiary of another company if the latter company is a shareholder or member of it and a majority of the members of the board who have held office throughout the year, the previous year, and up to the time of the issue of the consolidated accounts have in fact been appointed solely as a result of the exercise of the parent company's voting rights. This provides for the situation in which the majority of a company's shares are so widely dispersed that a minority shareholder can exercise de facto control. The directive provides that this criterion will not apply if the investee company is already the subsidiary of another company under one of the earlier definitions. It also allows member states not to implement this part of the definition or to make it conditional on the holding of at least 20% of the voting rights.

(6) PARTICIPATING INTEREST

A company is the subsidiary of another company if the latter company holds a participating interest in it and either exercises a dominant influence over it or manages the two entities on a unified basis. For this purpose the definition of a participating interest in the Fourth Directive applies. There is no definition of the concept of either dominant influence or managed on a unified basis.

(7) HORIZONTAL GROUPS

Consolidated accounts must be prepared for companies which have no shareholding relationship in either of two sets of circumstances. The first situation arises where companies are managed on a unified basis under the terms of a contract or provisions in their memoranda or articles of association. The second situation arises where the same people form the majority of the members of the board of both companies during the year and for the period up to the preparation of the accounts.

2.4 New definitions

Section 21 of the 1989 Act inserts a new section, 258, in the 1985 Act. This section defines the expressions 'parent undertaking' and 'subsidiary undertaking' and also the expression 'parent company' which is simply a parent undertaking which is a company.

There are six circumstances in which an undertaking is to be regarded as the parent undertaking in relation to another undertaking (i.e. the subsidiary undertaking). These circumstances are as follows.

(1) VOTING RIGHTS

The first undertaking holds a majority of the voting rights in another undertaking (the subsidiary undertaking) – new section 258(2)(a).

(2) BOARD APPOINTMENTS

The parent undertaking is a member of another undertaking and has the right to appoint or remove a majority of its board of directors – new section 258(2)(b). For these purposes an undertaking is to be regarded as a member of another if any of its subsidiary undertakings is a member of that undertaking or if any shares in that other undertaking are held by a person acting on behalf of the undertaking or any of its subsidiary undertakings – new section 258(3).

(3) DOMINANT INFLUENCE

An undertaking has the right to exercise a dominant influence over the undertaking by virtue of provisions contained in that undertaking's memorandum or articles of association or by virtue of a control contract – new section 258(2)(c).

(4) CONTROL OF VOTING RIGHTS

An undertaking is a member of another undertaking and a majority of the voting rights in that undertaking are controlled by it alone under an agreement with other shareholders or members – new section 258(2)(d). Again an undertaking is to be treated as a member of another undertaking if any of its subsidiary undertakings is a member of it or if any shares in it are held by a person acting on behalf of the undertaking or any of its subsidiary undertakings – new section 258(3).

(5) PARTICIPATING INTEREST

An undertaking has a participating interest in another undertaking and actually exercises a dominant influence over that other undertaking or it and the other undertaking are managed on a unified basis – new section 258(4).

(6) SUB-SUBSIDIARY UNDERTAKINGS

A parent undertaking's subsidiary undertakings themselves have subsidiary undertakings – new section 258(5).

These basic provisions are supplemented by a number of definitions of particular terms.

2.5 What is an undertaking?

For these purposes, an undertaking means a body corporate or partnership, or an unincorporated association carrying on a trade or business with or without a view to profit – new section 259(1), section 22 of the 1989 Act.

References to shares are to be construed flexibly to take account of the range of entities included within the term 'undertaking'. For example, in relation to an undertaking with a share capital, references to shares relate to allotted shares. If an undertaking has capital but no share capital, references to shares relate to right to share in the capital of the undertaking. In relation to an undertaking without capital, references to shares relate to interests conferring any right to share in the profits or any liability to contribute to the losses of the undertaking or giving rise to an obligation to contribute to the debts or expenses of the undertaking in the event of a winding up – new section 259(2), section 22 of the 1989 Act.

Other expressions which are appropriate for companies are to be construed in relation to an undertaking which is not a company as references to the corresponding persons, officers, documents or organs which are appropriate to the undertaking of that description – new section 259(3), section 22 of the 1989 Act.

The effect of this definition is that the range of entities which the law requires to be included within consolidated accounts is considerably extended.

2.6 What are voting rights?

References to the voting rights in an undertaking are to rights conferred on shareholders in respect of their shares. In the case of an undertaking not having a share capital, voting rights are those rights conferred on members to vote at general meetings of the undertaking on all or substantially all matters. If an undertaking does not have general meetings at which matters are decided by the exercise of voting rights, references to holding a majority of the voting rights in the undertaking are to be construed as references to having the right under the constitution of the undertaking to direct the overall policy of the undertaking or to alter the terms of its constitution – 1989 Act, Schedule 9 paragraph 2.

2.7 What is a right to exercise a dominant influence?

In the third situation in which a parent-subsidiary undertaking relationship is presumed to exist, an undertaking is not to be regarded as having the right to exercise a dominant influence over another undertaking unless it has a right to give directions with respect to the operating and financial policies of that other undertaking which its directors are obliged to comply with whether or not they are for the benefit of that other undertaking – 1989 Act, Schedule 9 paragraph 4(1).

The 1989 Act specifically excludes this definition from affecting the construction of the expression 'actually exercises a dominant influence' in the fifth situation in which a parent-subsidiary undertaking relationship is to be presumed to exist – 1989 Act, Schedule 9 paragraph 4(3). No definition of this expression is provided by the Act.

2.8 What is a control contract?

A control contract is a contract in writing conferring such a right of a kind authorised by the memorandum or articles of the undertaking in question and permitted by the law under which that undertaking is established – 1989 Act, Schedule 9 paragraph 4(2).

2.9 What is a right to appoint or remove a majority of the directors?

The second situation in which a parent-subsidiary relationship is to be presumed to exist refers to the right to appoint or remove a majority of the directors. This refers to the right to appoint or remove directors holding a majority of the voting rights at meetings with the board on all or substantially all matters. An undertaking is to be regarded as having the right to appoint to a directorship if a person's appointment to it follows necessarily from his appointment as a director of the undertaking or the directorship is held by the undertaking itself. If a right to appoint or remove a director is exercisable only with the consent or concurrence of another person, it is to be left out of account unless no other person has a right to appoint or remove in relation to that directorship – 1989 Act, Schedule 9 paragraph 3.

2.10 What is a participating interest?

In the fifth situation in which a parent-subsidiary relationship is to be presumed to exist, a participating interest means an interest held by an undertaking in the shares of another undertaking which it holds on a long-term basis for the purpose of securing a contribution to its activities by the exercise of control or influence arising from or relating to that interest. It is to be presumed that a holding of 20% or more of the shares of an undertaking constitutes a participating interest unless the contrary is shown – new section 260(1),(2), section 22 of the 1989 Act.

For these purposes, a reference to an interest in shares includes an interest which is convertible into an interest in shares and an option to acquire shares or any such interest. Further, an interest or option is to be included even though the shares to which it relates will remain unissued until the conversion or the exercise of the option – new section 260(3), section 22 of the 1989 Act.

13

In assessing the interest held by an undertaking in the shares of another, account has to be take of any interest held on its behalf and by any of the undertaking's subsidiary. References to the purpose and activities of an undertaking include the purposes and activities of any of its subsidiary undertakings and of the group as a whole – new section 260(4),(5), section 22 of the 1989 Act.

2.11   What rights are to be taken into account?

The 1989 Act deals with four circumstances in which rights are to be taken into account when determining whether a parent-subsidiary relationship exists. These circumstances are as follows.

(1)   RIGHTS EXERCISABLE ONLY IN CERTAIN CIRCUMSTANCES

If a right may only be exercised in certain circumstances, it shall only be taken into account when those circumstances have arisen and for so long as they continue to obtain or when the circumstances are within the control of the person having the right – 1989 Act, Schedule 9 paragraph 5(1).

(2)   RIGHTS TEMPORARILY INCAPABLE OF EXERCISE

If a right is normally exercisable but is only temporarily incapable of exercise, then it is still to be taken into account – 1989 Act, Schedule 9 paragraph 5(2).

(3)   FIDUCIARY CAPACITY

If rights are held by a person in a fiduciary capacity they are to be regarded as not being held by him – 1989 Act, Schedule 9 paragraph 6.

(4)   NOMINEES

Rights which are held by a person as a nominee for another are to be treated as held by that other person. Rights are to be regarded as being held as nominee for another person if they are exercisable only on his instructions or with his consent or concurrence – 1989 Act, Schedule 9 paragraph 7.

(5)   SECURITY

Rights attached to shares held by way of security are to be treated as held by the person providing the security. This applies where apart from the right to exercise them for the purpose of preserving or realising the value of the security the rights are exercisable only in accordance with that person's instructions and where the shares are held in connection with the granting of loans as part of normal business activities and apart from the right to exercise them for the purpose of preserving or realising the value of security if the rights are exercisable only in his interests – 1989 Act, Schedule 9 paragraph 8.

(6)   PARENT UNDERTAKING

Rights are to be treated as held by a parent undertaking if they are held by any of its subsidiary undertakings. Nothing in the provisions concerning nominee holdings or shares held by way of security is to be construed as requiring rights held by a parent undertaking to be treated as held by any of its subsidiary undertakings. In considering shares held by way of security, rights should be treated as being exercisable in accordance with the instructions or in the interests of an undertaking if they are exercisable in accordance with the instructions of or as the case may be in the interest of any group undertaking – 1989 Act, Schedule 9 paragraph 9.

(7)   DISREGARDED RIGHTS

The voting rights in an undertaking are to be reduced by any rights held by the undertaking itself – 1989 Act, Schedule 9 paragraph 10.

2.12   Effect of the new legislation

It is obvious that the new legislation has the potential for producing in practice a significant change in the formal definition of groups of companies for which the preparation of group accounts is required. To what extent will that potential be realised?

The first point to make is that a large number of entities which are at present off-balance sheet will need to be reconsidered and may well have to be included within future group accounts if no action is taken. This is achieved by the inclusion within the new definitions of undertakings which are not incorporated together with the references to various rights and practical control mechanisms. The effect of these changes on some controlled non-subsidiary companies can be seen in an example:

EXAMPLE

Group structure
Company A sets up Company B which has the following share structure:

Shares	*Owner*
1000 ordinary shares of £1	Company A
1000 6% voting convertible preference shares of £1	Friendly third party

On a winding up the preference shares receive 10% of the balance of Company B's share premium account together with the return of the amount originally subscribed. The conversion rights entitle the holder of the preference shares to convert into 10000 ordinary shares in ten years' time.

Options
The friendly third party has a put option on Company A on Company B's preference shares which can be exercised in six years' time. Company A has a call option which can be exercised at any time within five years.

Under the definition set out in section 736 of the 1985 Act, Company B would probably not be a subsidiary of Company A. In a winding up the preference shares confer a right to participate in a distribution beyond a specified amount so that they would be regarded as equity share capital. As a result, Company A owns exactly 50% of Company B's equity share capital. Unless Company A controlled the composition of Company B's board of directors, Company B would not be a subsidiary.

Under the new definitions introduced by the 1989 Act, the position would be changed. Company A would probably have a participating interest in Company B. Its actual holding (50%) already exceeds the 20% presumption in new section 260(2), but new section 260(3) requires the actual holding to be increased by shares covered by an option to acquire (i.e. a further 50%). Assuming that Company A is a long-term investor in Company B and that it actually exercises a dominant influence over Company B, then Company B would be a subsidiary of Company A – new section 238(4).

This does not mean, however, that the new definitions leave no scope for the creation of controlled non-subsidiary companies. For example, it might be possible to create a structure in which the investor company is not a member in an investee company, does not hold a majority of the voting rights with that company and has no right to exercise a dominant influence over the investee company although in practice it does. Avoidance of being a member of the investee company and of any conversion or option rights might mean that there is no participating interest and that the question of actual dominant influence does not arise. In such a case, the investee company might not be regarded as a subsidiary although the investigating company may have considerable control over it.

2.13 Alternative definition

The definition of the parent-subsidiary relationship in section 736 of the 1985 Act was effective for many purposes other than the inclusion of companies in group accounts. With the revision of the definition for accounting purposes, the general definition is revised for other purposes. This is done by the replacement of old section 736 by two new sections, 736 and 736A – section 144.

The new section 736 provides that a company is a subsidiary of another company (its holding company) if that company:

(1) holds a majority of the voting rights in it,
(2) is a member of it and has the right to appoint or remove a majority of its board of directors,
(3) is a member of it and alone controls a majority of the voting rights in it pursuant to an agreement with other shareholders or members, or
(4) is a subsidiary of a company which is itself a subsidiary of that other company – new section 736(1).

New section 736A explains certain terms used in new section 736 and in particular references to rights and voting rights. In effect, these terms are extended in ways similar to the construction of rights in the definitions for accounting purposes.

This new definition applies for all purposes other than the accounting provisions of the Companies Acts.

2.14 Commencement

The new definition for accounts purposes is expected to be brought into force together with most of the other accounting requirements of the 1989 Act (i.e. for financial years starting on or after 1 January 1990). However, the revised form of section 736 for other purposes is not expected to be brought into force before June 1990.

Chapter 3

Preparation of group accounts

3.1 Introduction

Having specified at some length the entities which should be included within group accounts, the 1989 Act describes how these accounts are to be prepared. This represents the completion of a departure from the traditional approach of U.K. law to these subjects. Before the U.K. joined the European Community, company law did not deal with detailed questions relating to the preparation of accounts, the valuation of assets and liabilities and the calculation of profit and loss. These were matters which the law left for decision by those preparing and auditing accounts according to what in their opinion would show a true and fair view. Any standardisation was dealt with through standards issued by professional bodies. The European Community's company law directives require however that these matters should be dealt with in member states' public law. For the accounts of individual companies, this was achieved in the U.K. in the 1981 Act which implemented the Fourth Directive. For group accounts, this is achieved in the 1989 Act which has implemented the Seventh Directive.

3.2 Requirement for group accounts

The new requirements are set out in a series of new sections inserted in the 1985 Act.

If at the end of a financial year, a company is a parent company, it is required to prepare group accounts as well as individual accounts. These accounts are to take the form of a consolidated balance sheet dealing with the state of affairs of the parent company and its subsidiary undertaking and a consolidated profit and loss account – new section 227(1), (2) of the 1985 Act, section 5. This represents a significant change. The old legislation permitted several other forms to be used for group accounts. For example, they might consist of more than one set of consolidated accounts dealing with separate groupings of subsidiaries, or they could consist of separate accounts dealing with each subsidiary. These options will no longer exist.

The group accounts are to give a true and fair view of the state of affairs at the end of the year and the profit and loss for the year of the undertaking included in the consolidation. They are however to comply with new Schedule 4A to the 1985 Act (Schedule 2 to the 1989 Act) although where compliance with that Schedule and other provisions of the 1985 Act would not show a true and fair view, the necessary additional information is to be given in the accounts or the notes to the accounts. If in special circumstances compliance with any of these provisions is inconsistent with the obligation to show a true and fair view, the company is to depart from these provisions to show a true and fair view – new section 227(3)–(6) of the 1985 Act, section 5.

3.3 Exemption for parent companies

The 1985 Act provided an exemption from the requirement to prepare group accounts for any parent company which at the end of a financial year was the wholly-owned subsidiary of a company incorporated in Great Britain – old section 229(2) of the 1985 Act.

This exemption is revised by the 1989 Act. Section 5(3) introduces a new section 228 in the 1985 Act. In future an unlisted parent company, which is itself a subsidiary undertaking and whose immediate parent undertaking is established with the European Community, may be exempt if one of two circumstances applies:

(1) the company is a wholly-owned subsidiary of the immediate parent undertaking, or
(2) the parent undertaking owns more than 50% of the shares in the company and the shareholders have not required the preparation of group accounts. To be effective for this purpose a shareholders' notice must be supported by more than half of the remaining shares in the company or 5% of the total shares in the company and must be served within six months of the beginning of the financial year to which it relates – new section 228(1) of the 1985 Act.

Use of the exemption also depends upon complying with a number of conditions:

(1) the company must be included in consolidated accounts for a larger group drawn up to the same date (or to an earlier date in the same financial year) by a parent undertaking established under the law of a member state of the European Community,
(2) these group accounts and the parent undertaking's annual report must be drawn up according to the provisions of the Seventh Directive,
(3) the company must disclose in its individual accounts that it is exempt from the obligation to prepare group accounts,
(4) the company must state in its individual accounts the name of the parent undertaking drawing up the group accounts referred to in (1) above and, if it is incorporated, the country in which it is incorporated (or if in Great Britain, the country in which it is registered), and if it is unincorporated, the address of its principal place of business,
(5) the company must deliver to the Registrar of Companies, within the period normally allowed for delivering its individual accounts, a copy of the group accounts, the parent undertaking's annual report and the relevant auditors' report. If any of these documents is in a language other than English, a certified translation must also be delivered to the Registrar – new section 228(2) of the 1985 Act.

3.4 Exclusions from consolidation

Apart from defining the parent-subsidiary relationship which would normally lead to an entity being included in the consolidation accounts, the 1985 Act provides that in certain circumstances group accounts need not deal with a subsidiary. This option is available if the company's directors hold one of the opinions stated in (1)–(4) below.

(1) IMPRACTICABILITY

It was impracticable to include the subsidiary or would be of no real value to the company's members in view of the insignificant amounts involved.

(2) EXPENSE OR DELAY

It would involve expense or delay out of proportion to the value to members.

(3) MISLEADING OR HARMFUL RESULT

The result would be misleading, or harmful to the business of the company or any of its subsidiaries provided that the Secretary of State agreed with this view.

(4) DIFFERENT BUSINESSES

The business of the holding company and that of the subsidiary are so different that they cannot reasonably be treated as a single undertaking – section 229 of the 1985 Act.

The 1985 Act also provides that if the directors were of that opinion about each of the company's subsidiaries, group accounts would not be required. The discretion of directors is somewhat limited by the 1985 Act's requirement that a proposal not to deal with a subsidiary in group accounts either on the ground that the result would be harmful or on the ground of the difference between the business of the holding company and that of the subsidiary, would require the approval of the Secretary of State.

The 1989 Act describes different circumstances in which the inclusion in group accounts of a subsidiary undertaking would not be required, set out below.

(1) IMMATERIALITY

A subsidiary undertaking may be excluded if its inclusion is not material for the purpose of giving a true and fair view. Two or more undertakings may only be excluded if they are immaterial taken together.

(2) LONG-TERM RESTRICTION

A subsidiary undertaking may be excluded where severe long-term restrictions substantially hinder the exercise of the rights of the parent over the assets or management of that undertaking.

(3) DISPROPORTIONATE EXPENSE

A subsidiary undertaking may be excluded from consolidation where the information necessary for the preparation of group accounts cannot be obtained without disproportionate expense or undue delay.

(4) RESALE

A subsidiary undertaking may be excluded where the parent company interest is exclusively with a view to subsequent resale and the undertaking has not previously been included in consolidated group accounts prepared by the parent company.

(5) DIFFERENT ACTIVITIES

Where the activities of one or more subsidiary undertakings are so different from those of other undertakings to be included in the consolidation that their inclusion would be incompatible with the obligation to give a true and fair view, those undertakings are to be excluded from consolidation. However this exclusion does not apply merely because some of the undertakings are industrial, some commercial and some provide services or because they carry on industrial or commercial activities involving different products or providing different services – new section 229 of the 1985 Act.

Reference in these provisions to the rights of the parent company and to the interest of the parent company are respectively to rights and interests held by or attributed to the company for the purposes of the definition of 'parent undertaking' in the absence of which it would not be the parent company – new section 229(2) of the 1985 Act.

No group accounts are required where all the subsidiary undertakings of a parent company fall within these exclusions – new section 229(5) of the 1985 Act.

There are two particular changes worthy of note. Firstly, the new provisions seek to restrict the applicability of the 'different activities' ground for exclusion of a subsidiary. Some cases in which this ground has been used in the past (e.g. customer credit subsidiaries for retail groups) should be more problematical in future. Secondly, the new provisions do not have any equivalent to the 'misleading or harmful result' ground in the old provisions.

3.5   Parent company's individual accounts

As before, parent companies preparing group accounts under these provisions are not required to publish a separate profit and loss account for the parent company itself and need not disclose certain information which would ordinarily supplement the company's profit and loss account (see paragraphs 52–57 of Schedule 4 to the 1985 Act). A number of conditions must be satisfied, however:

(1) the notes to the company's individual balance sheet must show the company's profit or loss for the year,
(2) the individual profit and loss account must be approved by the directors in the normal way (i.e. as required by new section 233(1)),
(3) the company's annual accounts must disclose that this exemption applies – new section 230 of the 1985 Act.

3.6   Form and content of group accounts

The remaining paragraphs of this chapter deal with the new requirements relating to the form and content of group accounts. These requirements are set out in Schedule 2 to the 1989 Act which is inserted in the 1985 Act as new Schedule 4A. In the remainder of this chapter, reference will be made to this Schedule as new Schedule 4A.

3.7 General rules

New Schedule 4A starts by specifying a series of general rules.

(1) SCHEDULE 4

Group accounts are to comply as far as practicable with Schedule 4 (the requirements for individual accounts) as if the group were a single company – paragraph 1(c) of new Schedule 4A.

(2) TREATMENT OF INFORMATION

Consolidated accounts are to incorporate in full the information contained in the individual accounts of the undertakings included in the consolidation subject to the adjustments permitted or required by new Schedule 4A and subject to any other adjustments which may be appropriate in accordance with generally accepted accounting principles or practice – paragraph 2(1) of new Schedule 4A.

(3) FINANCIAL YEARS

In practice, the financial year of a subsidiary undertaking may differ from that of the parent company. When this happens, the group accounts are to be based on either:

(a) the subsidiary undertaking's accounts for its financial year last ending before the end of the parent company's reporting date provided that it ended no more than three months before the parent company's reporting date, or
(b) interim accounts prepared by the subsidiary undertaking as at the end of the parent company's financial year – paragraph 2(2) of new Schedule 4A.

This provision is more restrictive than the previous requirement (in old section 230(7) of the 1985 Act) which did not contain the 'three months' condition for use of the subsidiary's last accounts. The previous requirements permitted the Secretary of State to vary the old requirements for particular cases. There is no equivalent to this power in the new provisions.

(4) CONSISTENT VALUATION BASES

In practice, entities to be included in group accounts may have valued assets and liabilities according to accounting rules which differ from those used for the group accounts. Where this happens, the values or amounts involved are to be adjusted on consolidation to accord with the rules used for group accounts. Immaterial differences are to be ignored for this purpose. Where the directors of a company consider that there are special reasons for departing from these requirements for consistency, they may do so, but particulars of the departure, the reasons for it and its effect are to be set out in a note to the accounts – paragraph 3 of new Schedule 4A.

This is substantially an enactment of the requirement for uniform accounting policies appearing in paragraph 16 of Statement of Standard Accounting Practice Number 14 (SSAP14): Group Accounts.

(5) DIFFERENCES IN ACCOUNTING RULES

If any differences exist between the accounting rules applying to the parent

21

company's individual accounts for a financial year and its group accounts, they are to be disclosed and the reasons for them given in a note to the group accounts – paragraph 4 of new Schedule 4A.

3.8 Elimination of group transactions

Paragraph 6 of new Schedule 4A sets out the adjustments which are to be made during the preparation of consolidated accounts to remove the effect of intra-group transactions. Firstly, debts and claims between undertakings and income and expenditure relating to transactions between undertakings included in the consolidation are to be eliminated in preparing the group accounts. Secondly, where profits and losses result from transactions between undertakings and are included in the book value of assets, they are to be eliminated in preparing the group accounts. This elimination, however, may be calculated by reference to the proportion of the group's interest in the shares of the undertakings concerned. These adjustments need not be made if the amounts concerned are not material for the purpose of showing a true and fair view – paragraph 6 of new Schedule 4A.

3.9 Acquisition and merger accounting

New Schedule 4A starts by setting out the conditions in which a company may use either acquisition or merger accounting, continues by describing each of these two methods of accounting for business combinations and then prescribes the information which is to be provided in accounts in respect of business combinations.

In the past, the classification of business combinations has been a matter dealt with in SSAP23: Accounting for Acquisitions and Mergers. Paragraph 11 of that accounting standard reads as follows:

'A business combination may be accounted for as a merger if all of the following conditions are met:

(a) the business combination results from an offer to the holders of all equity shares and the holders of all voting shares which are not already held by offeror; and

(b) the offeror has acquired, as a result of the offer, a holding of (i) at least 90% of all equity shares (taking each class of equity separately), and (ii) the shares carrying at least 90% of the votes of the offeree; and

(c) immediately prior to the offer, the offeror does not hold (i) 20% or more of all equity shares of the offeree (taking each class of equity separately), or (ii) shares carrying 20% or more of the votes of the offeree; and

(d) not less than 90% of the fair value of the total consideration given for the equity share capital (including that given for shares already held) is in the form of equity share capital; not less than 90% of the fair value of the total consideration given for voting non-equity share capital (including that given for shares already held) is in the form of equity and/or voting non-equity share capital.'

In new Schedule 4A the event of an undertaking becoming a subsidiary undertaking of a parent company, is referred to as an 'acquisition'. The undertaking which has become a subsidiary undertaking is referred to as the 'undertaking acquired' – paragraph 7(2) of new Schedule 4A. Such an acquisition is to be accounted for by the acquisition method of accounting unless the conditions for using the merger method of accounting are met and the merger method of accounting is adopted – paragraph 8 of new Schedule 4A.

The conditions for accounting for an acquisition as a merger are to be as follows:

(1) at least 90% of the nominal value of the relevant shares in the undertaking acquired is held by or on behalf of the parent company and its subsidiary undertakings,
(2) the parent company's proportion of the nominal value of the relevant shares in the undertaking acquired was attained as a result of an arrangement providing for the issue of equity shares by the parent company or one or more of its subsidiary undertakings,
(3) the fair value of any consideration other than the issue of equity shares given under that arrangement did not exceed 10% of the nominal value of the equity shares issued,
(4) adoption of the merger method of accounting is in accordance with generally accepted accounting principles or practice – paragraph 10(1) of new Schedule 4A.

For these purposes, relevant shares is a reference to shares carrying unrestricted rights to participate both in distributions and in the assets of the undertaking upon liquidation – paragraph 10(2) of new Schedule 4A.

There are some significant differences between these new conditions and those originally set out in SSAP23. Firstly, the SSAP23 requirement that the business combination must result from an offer to the holders of all equity shares and of all voting shares not already held by the offeror disappears. Secondly, whereas SSAP23 required that the offeror must have secured as a result of his offer a holding of at least 90% of all equity shares and of shares carrying at least 90% of the votes of the offeree, new Schedule 4A makes no reference to voting rights. All that is necessary is a holding of at least 90% of the nominal value of the relevant shares of the undertaking. Thirdly, the SSAP23 requirement in respect of the prior holding of shares by the offeror is not reproduced in new Schedule 4A. Finally, the requirement in respect of the proportion of the consideration which is to be in the form of equity is stiffened. Whereas in the past the non-equity element of the total consideration given could not exceed 10% of the fair value of the total consideration, in future that portion of the consideration may not exceed 10% of the nominal value of the equity shares issued under the arrangement.

Following the implementation of the 1989 Act, SSAP23 will have to be reconsidered by the Accounting Standards Committee and it is possible that some of the SSAP23 conditions which are not reproduced in new Schedule 4A will reappear. As set out above, the fourth condition for merger accounting being available to a company is that its adoption must accord with general accounting principles or practice.

The acquisition method of accounting as described in new Schedule 4A requires that the identifiable assets and liabilities of the undertaking acquired are to be included in the consolidated balance sheet and to their fair values as at the date of acquisition. For this purpose, identifiable assets or liabilities are those assets or liabilities of an undertaking which can be disposed of separately without disclosing of a business of the undertaking. There is little difference between this requirement and a provision of paragraph 16 of SSAP23 and SSAP14 in this respect – paragraph 9(2) of new Schedule 4A.

Income and expenditure of an undertaking acquired are to be brought into the group accounts only from the date of acquisition. Finally, the acquisition cost of the interest in the shares of the acquired undertaking held by the parent company and its subsidiary undertakings is to be matched against the interest of the parent company and its subsidiary undertakings in the adjusted capital and reserves of the undertaking acquired. For this purpose, acquisition cost means the amount of any cash consideration and the fair value of any other consideration together with any amount in respect of fees and other expenses of the acquisition as the company may determine. Adjusted capital and reserves of the undertaking acquired means its capital and reserves at the date of the acquisition after adjusting identifiable assets and liabilities of the undertaking to fair values as at that date. Any resulting amount which is positive is to be treated as goodwill and any negative amount resulting as a negative consolidation difference – paragraph 9(3)–(5) of new Schedule 4A.

Under the merger method of accounting as described in new Schedule 4A, assets and liabilities of the acquired undertaking are to be included in the group accounts at the figures appearing in the undertaking's accounts, subject of course to the general adjustments required by new Schedule 4A. Income and expenditure of the acquired undertaking are to be included in the group accounts for the entire financial year including the period before acquisition. The corresponding amounts shown in the group accounts and relating to the previous financial year are to include the acquired undertaking as if it had been included in the consolidation throughout that period. Finally, the nominal value of the issued share capital of the acquired undertaking held by the acquiring group is to be set off against the appropriate amount in respect of qualifying shares issued by the parent company or its subsidiary undertakings in consideration for the acquisition of shares in the acquired undertaking and the fair value of any other consideration for the acquisition of shares determined as at the date when those shares were acquired. For these purposes qualifying shares means shares in relation to which merger relief (see section 131 of the 1985 Act) applies. In these cases the appropriate amount is the nominal value or shares in relation to which group reconstruction relief (see section 132 of the 1985 Act) applies, in respect of which the appropriate amount is the nominal value together with any minimum premium value as defined in that section. The resulting amount is to be shown as an adjustment to the consolidated reserves – paragraph 11 of new Schedule 4A.

Where an acquisition is made during a financial year, certain information must be given in a note to the group accounts as follows:

(1) the name of the undertaking acquired or of the parent undertaking of a group acquired, and
(2) whether the acquisition has been accounted for by the acquisition or the merger method of accounting – paragraph 13(2) of new Schedule 4A.

Where an acquisition significantly affects the figures shown in the group accounts, the following further information is to be given:

(1) The composition and fair value of the consideration for the acquisition given by the group.
(2) The profit or loss of the undertaking or group acquired for the period from the beginning of the financial year of the undertaking or of the parent undertaking of the group up to the date of the acquisition, and for the previous financial year of that undertaking or parent undertaking. The date on which the financial year referred to above began must also be shown.
(3) Where the acquisition method of accounting has been adopted, the book

values immediately prior to the acquisition and the fair values at the date of acquisition of each class of assets and liabilities of the undertaking or group acquired are to be stated in tabular form. This is to include a statement of the amount of any goodwill or negative consolidation difference arising on the acquisition together with an explanation of significant adjustments made.

(4) Where the merger method of accounting has been adopted, there is to be an explanation of any significant adjustments made in relation to the amounts of the assets and liabilities of the undertaking or group acquired. There must also be a statement of any resulting adjustment to the consolidated reserves (including the restatement of opening consolidated reserves) – paragraph 13(3)–(6) of new Schedule 4A.

When, for the purposes of these disclosures, a company is determining the profit or loss of a group, the book values and fair values of assets and liabilities of a group or the amount of the assets and liabilities of a group, the set-offs and other adjustments required generally in respect of group accounts are to be made – paragraph 13(7) of new Schedule 4A.

The notes to group accounts must show the cumulative amount of goodwill resulting from acquisitions in the financial year and earlier years which has been written off. This figure is to be shown net of any goodwill attributable to subsidiary undertakings or businesses disposed of before the balance sheet date – paragraph 14 of new Schedule 4A.

Where during a financial year there has been a disposal of an undertaking or group which significantly affects the figures shown in the group accounts, there is to be shown in a note to the accounts the name of that undertaking and the extent to which the profit or loss shown in the group accounts is attributable to the profit or loss of that undertaking or group – paragraph 15 of new Schedule 4A.

None of these disclosures in respect of acquisitions or disposals needs be made in respect of an undertaking which is established under the law of a country outside the United Kingdom or which carries on business outside the United Kingdom if the directors of the parent company believe that the disclosure would be seriously prejudicial to the business of that undertaking or to the business of the group. Any proposal not to disclose information under this provision must be agreed by the Secretary of State – paragraph 16 of new Schedule 4A.

3.10 Minority interests

New Schedule 4A amends the balance sheet and profit and loss formats set out in Schedule 4 to the 1985 Act to make provision for the disclosure of minority interests – paragraph 17 of new Schedule 4A.

Under the new heading for minority interests in the balance sheet formats, companies are to show the amount of capital and reserves attributable to shares in subsidiary undertakings included in the consolidation held by or on behalf of persons other than the parent company and its subsidiary undertakings. Under the heading for minority interests in the profit and loss account formats, parent companies are to show the amount of any profit or loss on ordinary activities attributable to shares in subsidiary undertakings included in the consolidation held by or on behalf of persons other than the parent company and its subsidiary undertakings – paragraph 17 of new Schedule 4A.

3.11 Exclusion from consolidation – disclosure

As explained in paragraph **3.4** above, it is possible for subsidiary undertakings to be excluded from consolidation. The interest of the group in such subsidiary undertakings and the amount of profit or loss attributable to that interest are to be shown in the consolidated balance sheet and consolidated profit and loss account by the equity method of accounting – paragraph 18 of new Schedule 4A.

3.12 Joint ventures

New Schedule 4A permits proportional consolidation to be used in respect of joint ventures. For this purpose a joint venture means an undertaking managed by the parent undertaking preparing the group accounts jointly with one or more undertakings which are not included in the consolidation. Proportional consolidation may be used in respect of such a joint venture if it is not a body corporate or a subsidiary undertaking of the parent company – paragraph 19 of new Schedule 4A.

There is no description within new Schedule 4A of proportional consolidation. This provision reflects the recognition in paragraph 10 of SSAP1 (Accounting for Associated Companies) that: 'in some cases partnerships or non-corporate joint ventures can have features which justify accounting for a proportionate share of individual assets and liabilities as well as profits or loss.'

3.13 Associated undertakings

For these purposes an 'associated undertaking' means an undertaking in which an undertaking included in the consolidation has a participating interest and over whose operating and financial policy it exercises a significant influence and which is not a subsidiary undertaking of the parent company or a joint venture accounted for by using proportional consolidation. A participating interest is defined in new section 260 of the 1985 Act and described in Chapter 2. Where an undertaking holds 20% or more of the voting rights in an undertaking, it is to be presumed that it exercises a significant influence over that other undertaking unless the contrary is shown. For this purpose, the voting rights in an undertaking means the rights conferred on shareholders in respect of their shares or, in the case of an undertaking not having a share capital, or members, to vote at general meetings of the undertaking on all or substantially all matters. Paragraphs 5–11 of new Schedule 10A apply in determining whether an undertaking holds 20% or more of the voting rights in another undertaking. The requirements of new Schedule 10A are also described in Chapter 2 – paragraph 20 of new Schedule 4A.

The interest of an undertaking in an associated undertaking and the amount of profit and loss attributable to such an interest is to be shown according to the equity method of accounting. Where the associated undertaking is itself a parent undertaking, the net assets and profit or losses to be taken into account are those of the parent and its subsidiary undertakings after making any consolidation adjustments. The equity method of accounting need not be applied if the amounts in question are not material for the purpose of showing a true and fair view – paragraph 20 of new Schedule 4A.

Amendments are made to the format set out in Schedule 4 to the 1985 Act to require the separate disclosure of interests in associated undertakings and other participating interests.

3.14 Commencement

It is expected that these provisions will be effective for accounting purposes beginning on or after 1 January 1990.

Chapter 4

Miscellaneous accounting provisions

4.1 Introduction

Apart from implementing the Seventh EC Company Law Directive, the 1989 Act makes a large number of changes to the law concerning the preparation of accounts in general. Indeed much of that law is completely replaced by revised provisions. The more significant changes made in this process are reviewed in this chapter.

4.2 Accounting records

The requirements relating to the maintenance of accounting records which until now have been set out in old sections 221 and 222 of the 1985 Act are largely re-stated in new sections 221 and 222 – section 2.

An additional requirement is introduced however. With the introduction of the concept of a subsidiary undertaking which need not be a limited company, parent companies may be obliged to include within consolidated accounts the accounts of entities which are not subject to the provisions of the Companies Acts. To deal with this, new section 221 provides that where a parent company has a subsidiary undertaking which is not subject to the accounting records requirements of section 221, the parent company's directors are to take reasonable steps to prove that the subsidiary undertaking maintains accounting records adequate to ensure that any accounts are prepared in accordance with the Companies Acts – new section 221(4).

4.3 Accounting reference periods

The existing provisions determining a company's financial year and accounting reference period (old sections 224–226 of the 1985 Act) remain broadly the same – new sections 223–225 of the 1985 Act inserted by section 3.

However, the Act extends from six to nine months the period which is allowed for a newly incorporated company's initial election of its accounting reference period. If such a company did not make an election, its accounting reference date was, by default, 31 March. This too is changed for companies incorporating after implementation of these provisions. In the absence of an election by the company, the accounting reference date will automatically be the last day of the month in which the anniversary of the company's incorporation falls – new section 224(3)(b).

4.4 Related undertakings

The requirements for disclosure in accounts of information about subsidiaries and parent companies has been entirely recast – section 6 inserting new section 231 in the 1985 Act.

Firstly, the disclosure requirements now refer to subsidiary undertakings (i.e. the new widened definition) irrespective of whether the preparation of group accounts is required by the Act. Of itself, this provision widens the scope of disclosure.

Secondly, the information to be provided is considerably extended – particularly in the case of parent companies required to prepare group accounts.

A limited exemption from disclosure is provided in respect of an undertaking which is established outside the United Kingdom and which carries on business outside the United Kingdom. Information about such an undertaking need not be disclosed if, in the company's directors' opinion, disclosure would be seriously prejudicial to that undertaking's business, the company's business, or to the business of any of the company's subsidiary undertakings. The Secretary of State must agree to the non-disclosure and where advantage is taken of this exemption, that fact is to be stated in the notes to the company's accounts – new section 231(3),(4).

The detailed disclosure requirements are set out in Schedule 3 to the 1989 Act.

4.5 Approval and signing of accounts

The existing provisions concerning the approval and signing of accounts remain broadly the same save that in future accounts need only be signed by one director on behalf of the board (i.e. not two) – new section 233(1) of the 1985 Act, section 7.

4.6 Defective accounts

Under old section 245 of the 1985 Act, it has been an offence to lay before a company in general meeting or to deliver to the Registrar of Companies accounts which do not comply with the requirements of the Act. Every person who, at the time the accounts were laid or delivered, is a director of the company is also guilty of an offence.

Apart from this provision, there have been no other provisions dealing with defective accounts. In particular, the 1985 Act provides no mechanism by which a company can be obliged to correct accounts which are believed to have been defective.

In practice, of course, it happens from time to time that the directors of a company or its professional advisers become aware that it has issued defective accounts. In a number of cases, companies have chosen to withdraw the original accounts and to issue replacement accounts, particularly where the defect in the original accounts is so material that the accounts were grossly misleading. This happens rarely, however.

The Companies Act 1985 deals with this lacuna by providing a mechanism by which companies can revise their accounts and by which third parties can require that a company's accounts should be revised.

A new section 245 is inserted in the 1985 Act by section 12 of the 1989 Act permitting directors of a company to prepare revised accounts or a revised directors' report if it appears to them that the company's annual accounts or directors' report fail to comply with the requirements of the 1985 Act – new section 245(1). Where copies of the previous accounts or report have been laid before the company in general meeting or delivered to the Registrar, the revisions permitted by new section 245 are confined to the correction of respects in which the accounts or report did not comply with the 1985 Act and to the making of any necessary consequential adjustments – new section 245(2).

Power is given to the Secretary of State to make regulations about the application of the 1985 Act to revised annual accounts or a revised directors' report. In particular, these regulations may deal with the following matters:

(1) Whether annual accounts or reports are to be replaced or supplemented by documents indicating the corrections to be made.
(2) The auditors' functions in relation to the revised accounts or report.
(3) The directors' obligations to take certain specified steps where the previous accounts or report have been sent to members and others or laid before the company in general meeting or delivered to the Registrar. They may also deal with the situation in which a summary financial statement based on the previous accounts has been sent to members under new section 251 of the 1985 Act – new section 245(3), (4).

Where it appears to the Secretary of State that a company has published accounts which may not comply with the requirements of the 1985 Act, he may issue a notice to the directors indicating the respects in which it appears to him that there is doubt about the accounts' compliance. The notice must specify a period of not less than one month for the directors to give an explanation of the accounts or to prepare revised accounts. If at the end of this period the Secretary of State considers that no satisfactory explanation of the accounts has been given and the accounts have not been revised to comply with the Act, he may apply to the court – new section 245A. On application, the court may declare that the annual accounts in question do not comply with the 1985 Act and order the directors of the company to prepare revised accounts – new section 245B. The court may also require the revised accounts to be audited and related reports to be revised – new section 245B(3).

If the court finds that the accounts did not comply with the 1985 Act, it may require that the costs of the application and any reasonable expenses incurred by the company in the preparation of revised accounts are to be borne by those directors who were party to the approval of the defective accounts. For this purpose every director at the time the accounts were approved is to be taken to have been a party to their approval unless he shows that he took all reasonable steps to prevent their being approved – new section 245B.

The 1989 Act enables the Secretary of State to authorise other parties to apply to the court in respect of defective accounts. To qualify for this authorisation, a person must be interested in ensuring that accounts comply with the 1985 Act and have appropriate monitoring procedures – new section 245C.

4.7 Small and medium-sized companies

Small and medium-sized companies will continue generally to be able to file modified accounts with the Registrar of Companies. Some categories of company have been unable to make use of these exemptions in the past, however; these categories will in future be:

(1) public companies whether U.K. or overseas companies,
(2) banking and insurance companies,
(3) companies authorised under the Financial Services Act 1986, and
(4) companies which are members of groups including companies in any of these categories – new section 246 of the 1985 Act, section 13.

Previously shipping companies were also included as an additional category.

4.8 Summary of financial statements

Section 15 of the 1989 Act inserts a new section 251 in the 1985 Act which permits the Secretary of State to issue regulations enabling listed companies to circulate to shareholders a summary financial statement rather than the full statutory accounts normally required by section 238 – new section 251(1). The 1989 Act itself does not define either the circumstances in which public companies may use this approach or the contents of summary financial statements. However, if companies take advantage of these provisions and circulate summary financial statements to shareholders there will remain an obligation to send the full statutory accounts to any member of the company who wishes to receive them. It is envisaged that the Secretary of State will also make regulations concerning the way in which shareholders are to make their wishes known – new section 251(2).

Although the Act does not specify the form and content of summary financial statements, it specifies that they are to be derived from the company's annual accounts and that they should:

(1) state that the summary financial statement is only a summary of information in the annual accounts and the directors' report,
(2) contain a statement by the company's auditors of their opinion as to whether the summary financial statement is consistent with the annual accounts and the directors' report and that it complies with the Act, and
(3) state whether the auditors' report on the annual accounts was unqualified or qualified and if it was qualified set out the report in full together with any further material needed to understand the qualification – new section 251.

4.9 Private companies

The 1989 Act introduces an element of de-regulation by permitting private companies to elect that some standard procedures are not to apply to them. As part of this, private companies are enabled to dispense with the laying of accounts and reports before the company in general meeting. This can be done by passing an elective resolution under the provisions of new section 279A (see Chapter 9) – new section 252 of the 1985 Act, section 16.

When such an elective resolution has been passed, although accounts need not be laid before the company in general meeting they must still be sent to shareholders (not less than 28 days before the end of the normal period for laying accounts – 10 months from the end of the financial year). Such accounts are to be accompanied by a notice informing the shareholders that they still have the right to require the accounts and reports to be laid before the company in general meeting. Any shareholder (or auditor) wishing to require this must do so within 28 days of the date on which the accounts are sent out. The requisition, in writing, must be deposited at the company's registered office. Upon receipt the company's directors must convene the necessary meeting within certain specified deadlines – new section 253 of the 1985 Act, section 16.

4.10 Unlimited companies

Although unlimited companies are subject to the normal requirements for the preparation of annual accounts and their circulation to members, they have not generally been required to deliver copies of their accounts to the Registrar of Companies. Filing of accounts has been required, however, if an unlimited company either was or was potentially the subsidiary of a limited company or was the holding company of a limited company – section 241(4) of the 1985 Act.

In principle, these provisions remain unchanged. However, the conditions are now expressed in terms of 'subsidiary undertakings'. Thus an unlimited company must deliver its accounts and reports for a financial year to the Registrar of Companies if at no time during the relevant accounting reference period:

(1) it was to its knowledge a subsidiary undertaking of an undertaking which was then limited,
(2) there have been to its knowledge rights which were exercisable by two or more undertakings which were then limited which if exercisable by one of them would have made the company a subsidiary undertaking of it, or
(3) it was a parent company of an undertaking which was then limited – new section 254 of the 1985 Act, section 17.

4.11 Banking and insurance companies and groups

Under section 257 of the 1985 Act, banking companies, shipping companies and insurance companies were 'special category companies' for which special accounting rules were provided. Essentially, these accounting rules were similar to those which had applied in U.K. company law before the implementation of the Fourth EC Company Law Directive in the 1981 Act.

In the case of shipping companies, they were included as special category companies because the Fourth Directive allowed member states of the European Community to take advantage of an extended transitional period for such companies in implementing the Fourth Directive. In the case of the United Kingdom, this enabled shipping companies to continue for a further period to avoid the disclosure of certain items. Historically, these exemptions sprang from a concern over the strategic importance of the shipping industry to the United Kingdom. The extended transitional period is now coming to an end and shipping companies will be required to comply with the general requirements in respect of the preparation of accounts.

The European Community has for many years been developing separate accounting requirements in respect of banking and insurance companies. Pending the implementation of these requirements in the United Kingdom, such companies may continue to use the separate accounting provisions set out in Schedule 9 to the 1985 Act – new section 255(1) of the 1985 Act, section 18. Since the old legislation required such companies to use the separate accounting provisions, the change in the law opens the way for banking and insurance companies to use the accounting provisions applying to companies in general if they so wish.

Similar provisions apply in respect of the preparation of group accounts by banking groups and by insurance groups. For these purposes a banking group is either a group whose parent company is a banking company or a group in which at least one of the undertakings is an authorised institution under the Banking Act 1987 and whose predominant activities make it inappropriate to prepare group accounts in accordance with the general provision of Schedule 4 to the 1985 Act. An insurance group is similarly defined – new section 255A of the 1985 Act, section 18.

Additional powers are given to the Secretary of State enabling him to extend these accounting requirements to banking partnerships (i.e. partnerships which are authorised institutions under the Banking Act 1987) – new section 255D of the 1985 Act, section 18(2).

4.12 Accounting standards

In response to concern about the effectiveness of the process for setting accounting standards, a review committee was established under Sir Ron Dearing in 1987 and reported in 1988.

Apart from a number of recommendations about the way in which standards are developed and improvement in the quality of standards, the committee recommended that a Financial Reporting Council should be created representing a wide range of interests. The objectives of the new council would be to guide the body responsible for setting accounting standards on work programmes and issues of public concern, to see that the work on accounting standards is properly financed and to act as a powerful influence for securing good accounting practice.

The existing Accounting Standards Committee would be reconstituted into an Accounting Standards Board which would be able to issue accounting standards on its own authority. Companies would be required by law to state in their accounts that they had complied with the relevant accounting standards. To encourage compliance with accounting standards, the Dearing Committee further recommended the creation of a review panel to examine any identified or alleged material departures from accounting standards. The findings of the review panel would spell out what revisions to the financial statements or what additional information it considered should be made available to users to provide an acceptable set of accounts giving a true and fair view. In a further recommendation, the Dearing Committee suggested that there should be a statutory power for certain authorised bodies or the Secretary of State to apply to the court for an order requiring the revision of accounts which do not give a true and fair view.

The Dearing Committee report was welcomed by the Department of Trade and Industry, and at the end of October 1989 Sir Ron Dearing was appointed with a small team to take the steps necessary to establish the new bodies.

The 1989 Act assists in the process by implementing a number of the recommendations of the Dearing Committee.

(1) The Secretary of State is empowered to make grants to or for the purposes of bodies concerned with issuing of accounting standards, overseeing their issue and securing compliance – new section 256 of the 1989 Act, section 19.

(2) Companies will be obliged to state in their accounts whether the accounts have been prepared in accordance with applicable accounting standards and to give particulars of a material departure – new paragraph 36A of Schedule 4 to the 1985 Act, Schedule 1 paragraph 7 to the 1989 Act.

(3) The new defective accounts (see paragraph **4.6** above) provisions reflect the Dearing Committee recommendations.

4.13 Preparation of individual company accounts

Schedule 4 to the 1985 Act which sets out the detailed framework for the preparation of individual company accounts is revised by the 1989 Act in a number of detailed ways:

(1) Consistency – old paragraph 11 of Schedule 4 has required that a company must apply accounting policies consistently from one financial year to the next. This rule remains but is augmented by a requirement that accounting policies are also to be applied consistently within the same accounts – new paragraph 11 of Schedule 4 to the 1985 Act, Schedule 1 paragraph 5 to the 1989 Act.

(2) Revaluation reserve – the rules concerning the use of the revaluation reserve are tightened to prevent the reserve from being used for transactions other than capitalisation issues and transfers in respect of depreciation or realised profit. In other words, goodwill cannot be written off against the revaluation reserve – new paragraphs 34(3), (3A), (3B) of Schedule 4 to the 1985 Act, Schedule 1 paragraph 6 to the 1989 Act.

4.14 Directors' remuneration

The 1989 Act amends the requirements for the disclosure in accounts of the emoluments of a company's chairman and directors.

Firstly, the requirements are altered to refer throughout to subsidiary undertakings in conformity with the changes to the description of a 'group'. Thus the amount to be shown as directors' emoluments will include amounts paid or receivable in respect of services by directors as directors of a company's subsidiary undertakings or otherwise in connection with the management of any of the company's subsidiary undertakings. This change is consistent with the changing definition of a group and reduces the scope for avoiding disclosure of remuneration.

Secondly, for these purposes, the emoluments of a person are to include any emoluments in respect of a person's accepting office as director. Under the previous legislation, 'golden hellos' were thought not to be included within the definition of emolument which had to be disclosed.

Thirdly, it is made clear that in disclosing the aggregate amount of any compensation to directors or past directors in respect of loss of office, benefits otherwise than in cash are to be included. The amount to be included is the estimated money value of the benefit.

Fourthly, companies will be required to disclose the total amount paid to or receivable by third parties for making available the services of any person as a director of the company or while a director as a director of any of its subsidiary undertakings. The amount to be disclosed is to include the value of any benefits otherwise than in cash and the nature of these benefits is to be disclosed.

Fifthly, additional disclosure is required in cases where the legal status of payments to directors is changed. Payments to a director may be omitted from disclosure on the ground that the director has a liability to account to the company or its subsidiary for those payments. If the liability is not enforced the effect is that the director has received money without any disclosure of the amount so received. In future, if the liability is wholly or partly released or is not enforced within a period of two years the sums concerned are to be disclosed separately in a note to the next accounts of the company. This disclosure requirement also applies in the case of sums paid by way of expense allowances which are charged to U.K. income tax after the end of the relevant financial year.

All these amendments are included in the restated provisions which take the place of Schedule 5 Part V to the 1985 Act – Schedule 4 to the 1989 Act.

4.15 Commencement

It is expected that these provisions will be implemented on the following dates:

Summary financial statements – April 1990
Accounting standards – September 1990
Other provisions – for financial years beginning after 1 January 1990.

Chapter 5

Auditors

5.1 Background

Part II of the Act implements the European Community's Eighth Company Law Directive which was approved in 1984. This directive fits into a series of company law directives, two of which deal with the format and content of company accounts. These two directives, the Fourth and Seventh, specify that accounts drawn up in accordance with Community Law must be audited. The purpose of the Eighth Directive was to regulate the authorisation, training and conduct of those people who undertake statutory audits.

For many years there have been United Kingdom regulations concerning people who may accept audit appointments. The Companies Act 1985 (section 389) provides that such appointments may only be accepted by members of a small number of professional accounting bodies:

The Institute of Chartered Accountants in England and Wales,
The Institute of Chartered Accountants of Scotland,
The Institute of Chartered Accountants in Ireland, and
The Chartered Association of Certified Accountants.

Provision is made for the Secretary of State to recognise individuals who are not members of these bodies, and this route is used to approve members of certain overseas bodies.

Detailed regulation of the qualifications and conduct of auditors is a matter on which the law is largely silent and is thus left to the professional bodies themselves through the publication of their own standards and the operation of their own disciplinary procedures.

The directive requires that statutory audits may only be undertaken by approved persons. Both natural persons and companies can be approved, but where a company is to be approved for auditing, conditions are laid down concerning the ownership and management of the company. Any natural persons wishing to be approved to act as auditor, must be of good repute and have completed a certain programme of education. This education is to be of university level and to cover a certain number of specified subjects although provision is made for natural persons qualified by long experience rather than by examination to gain access to the approval process. In addition to a formal education a person wishing to be approved must have completed a period of supervised practical training which is required not to be shorter than three years. Anticipating the introduction of a system for mutual recognition of professional qualifications, member states may choose to recognise qualifications gained in other member states as the basis for approval for auditing.

The directive goes beyond these requirements by making provision in respect of the conduct of auditors. Approved auditors are required to display professional integrity in the discharge of their function. They are also required to demonstrate independence although the directive does not itself lay down detailed rules in respect of independence. Member states are required to ensure that approved persons are liable to appropriate sanctions when they do not carry out audits with appropriate professional integrity and independence.

It is envisaged in the directive that in each country there will be appropriate authorities to deal with the detailed implementation of the directive. It is specifically provided however that these authorities may be professional associations provided that the national law of the member state permits the associations to grant approval within the terms of the directive.

The directive was to be incorporated in national laws by 1 January 1988 with a view to implementation by 1 January 1990.

In the summer of 1986, the Department of Trade and Industry published a Consultative Document outlining the implications of the Eighth Directive and seeking views on the way in which the directive should be put implemented. In as far as the directive lays down minimum requirements regarding the qualifications of persons wishing to train as auditors and the form, length and content of their theoretical and practical training, the DTI took the view that compliance with such minimum rules and requirements would not in itself involve any significant changes in the United Kingdom. The Department also considered that the directive's rules on the conduct of auditors should cause no difficulty in the United Kingdom.

However, the DTI saw the implementation of the directive as an opportunity for a general review of the regulation of auditors and the Consultative Document raised three basic issues. Firstly, the DTI asked whether the regulation of auditors should remain a responsibility of the existing professional bodies or should be transferred to a quasi-governmental board or council. Secondly, the DTI sought views on the rules which should be applied to guarantee the independence of auditors and in particular asked whether the existing requirements and regulations were adequate to the task. Finally, the DTI solicited views on the advisability of permitting auditing firms to incorporate.

In implementing the Eighth Directive through the Companies Act 1989, the Government has dealt with each of these issues.

5.2 Structure of the legislation

Part II of the Act is intended to ensure that only persons who are properly supervised and appropriately qualified are appointed company auditors and that audits carried out by company auditors are carried out properly and with integrity and with a proper degree of independence – section 24(1). For this purpose, a 'company auditor' is simply a person appointed to act as an auditor under section 384 of the Companies Act 1985 (i.e. to audit the accounts of a company) – section 24(2).

This Part of the Act has eight principal elements:

(1) ELIGIBILITY (SECTIONS 25–29)

The Act specifies conditions which must be fulfilled for a person to be eligible to act as a company auditor. It further specifies certain circumstances in which a person will be ineligible and then deals with the consequences of acting as a auditor whilst ineligible.

(2)   RECOGNITION OF SUPERVISORY BODIES (SECTION 30)

One of the principal conditions of eligibility to act as a company auditor is membership of a recognised supervisory body. The Act sets out the circumstances in which a body may be recognised as a supervisory body for these purposes, and the circumstances in which that initial recognition can be revoked.

(3)   APPROPRIATE QUALIFICATIONS (SECTIONS 31–32)

One of the conditions which must be satisfied by a body seeking recognition as a supervisory body, is that its rules should ensure that only persons with appropriate qualifications are recognised as auditors. The Act defines the conditions which must be satisfied if a professional qualification is to be recognised for this purpose.

(4)   OVERSEAS QUALIFICATIONS (SECTION 33)

The Act then specifies the circumstances in which overseas qualifications may be regarded as appropriate qualifications.

(5)   DUTIES OF RECOGNISED BODIES (SECTIONS 35–40)

The Act specifies the duties of recognised supervisory bodies.

(6)   OFFENCES (SECTIONS 41–44)

The Act describes certain acts which are to be regarded as offences.

(7)   DELEGATION OF FUNCTIONS (SECTION 46)

The Act provides that the functions of the Secretary of State under Part II of the Act may be delegated by him to a body corporate established for the purpose.

(8)   RESTRICTIVE PRACTICES (SECTION 47)

Rules and guidance issued by regulatory bodies are to be subject to review by the Director General for Fair Trading who is to examine the extent to which they limit competition.

The overall effect of this legislation is to create a system of regulation of the activity of auditing which is completely within the control of the Secretary of State, although it may retain some of the appearance of self-regulation. It may always have been inevitable that implementing the Eighth Directive would produce this effect, but the change represents a significant departure from previous practice. In this sense, there is some similarity in approach between the 1989 Act and the Government's white paper proposals for reform of the legal profession.

5.3   Eligibility

A person will only be eligible for appointment as statutory auditor of a company (i.e. as a company auditor) if he is:

(1) a member of a recognised supervisory body, and
(2) eligible for appointment as a company auditor under the rules of that body –
    section 25(1).

It will be possible for either an individual or a firm to be appointed a company auditor – section 25(2). Since for these purposes, 'a firm' includes both a partnership and a body corporate, the long-standing statutory rule that companies may not act as auditors is removed. Whether this change in the law proves useful in practice will depend upon whether the professional bodies change their own rules which at present tend to repeat the old statutory restriction.

There has been a long-standing anomaly because the Companies Acts only spoke of individuals being appointed as auditors although in practice partnerships are commonly appointed. This anomaly is resolved by the Act.

Where a partnership is constituted under the law of England and Wales and Northern Ireland that partnership's appointment as a company auditor is to be regarded as an appointment of that partnership. This will also apply to any partnership constituted under the law of any other country in which a partnership is not a legal person – section 26(1). This rule is extended to any eligible partnership which succeeds to the practice of a partnership which ceases and any eligible person who succeeds to that practice having previously carried it on in partnership – section 26(3). This resolves the technical difficulty caused by changes in the identity of a partnership. A partnership will be treated as succeeding to the practice of another partnership only if the partners of the successor and predecessor firms are substantially the same. A partnership or other person (i.e. including a company) may only be regarded as succeeding to the practice of a partnership if it or he succeeds to the whole or substantially the whole of the business of the former partnership – section 26(4). Where the partnership ceases and no person is treated under section 26(3) as having succeeded to the audit appointment, the company being audited may consent to the appointment being extended to a partnership or other eligible person succeeding to the former business or to part of it – section 26(5).

Having set out the basic conditions for eligibility to be appointed as a 'company auditor', the Act turns to defining situations in which people may be ineligible.

Firstly, the Act restricts the eligibility of those individuals who retain only 1967 Companies Act authorisation – section 25(3). Some individuals are only qualified to act as auditors because they retain an authorisation granted by the Board of Trade or the Secretary of State under section 13(1) of the Companies Act 1967. Essentially such authorisation was granted as a transitional measure to people adversely affected by a narrowing of the qualifications for auditors in the 1967 Act and authorised such people only to audit private companies. Their eligibility under the 1989 Act is limited to appointment as auditor of an unquoted company – section 34(1). A company is unquoted for this purpose if at the time the person is appointed auditor neither it nor its parent undertaking has offered any shares or debentures for public subscription or purchase or has shares or debentures which have been quoted on a stock exchange anywhere – section 34(2).

Secondly, a person may be ineligible for appointment as company auditor:

(1) If he is an officer or employee of the company, or a partner or employee of such a person, or of a partnership of which such a person is a partner.
(2) If he is ineligible for appointment as company auditor of any associated
    undertaking, i.e. a parent undertaking or subsidiary undertaking of the company, or a subsidiary undertaking of any parent undertaking of the company – sections 27(1) and (3).

The phrases 'parent undertaking' and 'subsidiary undertaking' have the meanings introduced by the 1989 Act in implementing the Seventh Directive (see Chapter 2) – section 50.

Power is given to the Secretary of State to issue regulations specifying other types of relationships with a company which would lead to a person being ineligible for appointment as a company auditor – section 27(2).

In principle these rules on ineligibility may appear to go little further than the existing statutory requirements (see section 389 of the 1985 Act). In practice, however, the new definitions of parent and subsidiary undertakings are considerably wider than the old definitions of holding and subsidiary companies so that the effect of these rules will also be wider.

The effect of ineligibility for appointment as company auditor is that no ineligible person shall act as a company auditor. A company auditor may become ineligible for appointment during his term of office. If this happens, the Act requires that he should thereupon vacate his office and give notice in writing to the company that he has vacated his office by reason of ineligibility. Any person who acts as company auditor even though he is ineligible or who fails to give the required notice of vacating his office is guilty of an offence. If an auditor continues in office improperly he will be liable to continuing default fines. In proceedings concerning such offences, it will be a defence to show that the person concerned did not know and had no reason to believe that he was or had become ineligible for appointment as a company auditor – section 28.

If a person undertakes a company audit but was, for any part of the period during which the audit was conducted, ineligible for appointment as a company auditor, the Secretary of State may direct the company concerned to retain a person eligible for appointment as auditor of the company:

(1) to arrange for the relevant accounts to be audited again, or
(2) to review the first audit and to report, giving his reasons, whether a second audit is needed – section 29(1).

Where the Secretary of State gives such a direction, the company must comply within twenty one days – section 29(1). If a second audit is recommended as a result of a review of the first audit, the company must immediately comply with that recommendation – section 29 – and that audit is to be undertaken, under the statutory and other provisions which applied to the first audit – sections 29(2) and (4).

The Secretary of State must send a copy of any direction he makes to the Registrar of Companies, and, when it has received any report from the person retained to review the first audit, within twenty one days of receiving it the company is to send that report to the Registrar of Companies – section 29(3).

A company failing to comply with these requirements is to be guilty of an offence – section 29(5). However, where a person accepts an appointment or continues to act as company auditor at a time when he knows he is ineligible, the company concerned may recover from him any costs incurred by it in complying with the requirements of section 29 – section 29(7).

5.4 Recognition of supervisory bodies

To be eligible for appointment as a company auditor a person must be a member of a recognised supervisory body – section 25(1). For these purposes, a supervisory body is a body established in the United Kingdom which operates rules concerning both the eligibility of persons to seek appointment as company auditors, and also the conduct of company audit work. These rules must be binding on people seeking appointment or acting as company auditors either because they are members of that body or because they are subject to the control of that body for some other reason – section 30(1). References in the Act to members of a supervisory body include people who although they are not members are subject to the body's rules in seeking appointment or acting as company auditor – section 30(2).

References in the Act to the rules of a supervisory body relate to those rules which the body has power to enforce in relation to eligibility for appointment and the conduct of company audit work irrespective of whether the rules have been specified by the body itself. They include rules relating to the admission and expulsion of members of the body – section 30(3). References in the Act to guidance issued by such a body include any guidance or recommendations which would, if they were rules, fall within the rules mentioned above – section 30(4).

In order to be recognised for these purposes, a supervisory body may apply for an order declaring it to be a recognised supervisory body. The Secretary of State is to specify the form of each application which is to be accompanied by any information that the Secretary of State reasonably requires. The applicant body can be required subsequently to provide further information – Schedule 11 paragraph 1.

In response to an application, the Secretary of State may make or refuse to make an order declaring the applicant body to be a recognised supervisory body, although he may only make a recognition order if he considers that the requirements of Schedule 11 are satisfied by that body. A recognition order may be refused if the Secretary of State considers that recognition of the body concerned is unnecessary in view of the existence of one or more other bodies which maintain and enforce rules as to the appointment and conduct of company auditors – Schedule 11 paragraph 2.

Any recognition order may be revoked by the Secretary of State if at any time it appears to him:

(1) that any requirements of Schedule 11 are not satisfied by the body concerned, or
(2) that the recognised body has failed to comply with an obligation imposed on the body by Part II of the Act, or
(3) that the continued recognition of the body is undesirable in view of the existence of one or more other bodies – Schedule 11 paragraph 3.

Schedule 11 requires the Secretary of State to warn the body concerned of his intention to make a revocation order and to allow members of that body to make representations both orally and in writing. In reaching his decision, the Secretary of State must have regard to any representations made to him. If a revocation order is made nonetheless, it must not have effect for at least three months after it is issued. However, if it is thought essential in the public interest that there should be no delay in implementing a revocation order, the Secretary of State may issue an order with immediate effect without either notice period or delay in implementation – Schedule 11 paragraph 3.

To be recognised, a supervisory body must satisfy a number of conditions under the following heads:

(1) Holding of appropriate qualification.
(2) Auditors to be fit and proper persons.

(3) Professional integrity and independence.
(4) Technical standards.
(5) Procedures for maintaining competence.
(6) Monitoring and enforcement.
(7) Membership eligibility and discipline.
(8) Investigation of complaints.
(9) Meeting of claims arising out of audit work.
(10) Register of auditors.
(11) Costs of compliance.
(12) Promotion and maintenance of standards.

The effect of these requirements is that the Secretary of State is able to control the way in which any recognised supervisory body regulates the auditing profession. Under each head, the Act requires that a body should have rules to ensure certain matters. Whether rules are adequate will be a matter for the Secretary of State to decide. He will also decide whether monitoring arrangements are adequate and whether arrangements for investigating complaints are effective.

5.4.1 *Holding of appropriate qualification*

To be recognised, a supervisory body's rules must ensure that persons are not considered eligible for appointment as a company auditor unless they are either individuals holding an appropriate qualification or firms satisfying the following conditions:

(1) individuals responsible for company audit work on behalf of the firm must hold appropriate qualifications, and
(2) the firm is controlled by qualified persons – Schedule 11 paragraph 4.

For these purposes, an individual is qualified if he holds an appropriate qualification and a firm is qualified if it is eligible for appointment as a company auditor – Schedule 11 paragraph 5(2).
   A firm is to be regarded as controlled by qualified persons only if a majority of the firm's members are qualified persons. Where the firm's constitution provides that decisions are made through the exercise of voting rights, qualified persons must hold a majority of the rights to vote on all or substantially all matters. Otherwise, under the firm's constitution qualified persons must have rights enabling them to direct the firm's overall policy or alter its constitution – Schedule 11 paragraph 5(3) and (4).
   If the firm's affairs are managed by a board of directors, committee or another management body, a majority of the members of that body must be qualified persons. If there are only two members, at least one of them must be a qualified person. Where the management body makes decisions by the exercise of voting rights, qualified persons must hold a majority of the rights to vote on all or substantially all matters. Otherwise, qualified persons must have rights enabling them to direct the management body's overall policy or to alter its constitution – Schedule 11 paragraph (3) and (5).
   The effect of these provisions is to remove the statutory requirement for partnerships to consist solely of persons qualified for appointment as statutory auditors. In practice, the usefulness of this change in the law will depend upon changes in the rules and requirements of professional bodies. Schedule 11 expressly empowers recognised supervisory bodies to impose more stringent

rules – Schedule 11 paragraph 4(2). At present the accounting bodies' policy is that they will only allow non-qualified persons to hold up to a 25% interest in an authorised firm.

5.4.2 *Fit and proper persons*

The applicant body's rules must ensure that persons eligible for appointment as a company auditor are fit and proper persons. The matters to be taken into account in assessing this must include:

(1) any matter relating to any person who is or will be employed by or associated with him for the purposes of or in connection with the company audit work,
(2) in the case of a body corporate, any matter relating to any director or controller of the company,
(3) in the case of a partnership any matter relating to any of the partners, any director or controller of any of the partners, any body corporate in the same group as any of the partners and any director or controller of any such body – Schedule 11 paragraph 6.

In relation to a body corporate, a controller means a person who either alone or with any associate or associates is entitled to exercise or control the exercise of 15% or more of the voting rights at any general meeting – Schedule 11 paragraph 6(3).

5.4.3 *Professional integrity and independence*

The body's rules must ensure that company audit work is conducted properly and with integrity and that persons are not appointed company auditors in circumstances where they have any interest likely to conflict with the proper conduct of the audit. No firm may be eligible under the body's rules for appointment as a company auditor unless the firm has arrangements to prevent individuals who do not hold an appropriate qualification or who are not members of the firm exerting influence over the way in which an audit is conducted, in circumstances where the integrity of the audit would thereby be affected – Schedule 11 paragraph 7.

5.4.4 *Technical standards*

The body is obliged to specify the technical standards to be applied in company audit work and the manner of their application in practice – Schedule 11 paragraph 8.

5.4.5 *Procedures for maintaining competence*

The body's rules must ensure that persons eligible to be company auditors maintain their competence in undertaking audits – Schedule 11 paragraph 9.

5.4.6 *Monitoring and enforcement*

The body must have adequate arrangements for the effective monitoring and enforcement of compliance with its rules. Arrangements for monitoring may make provision for these functions to be performed on behalf of the body by another body – Schedule 11 paragraph 10.

5.4.7 *Membership, eligibility and discipline*

The body's rules concerning admission and expulsion of members, eligibility for appointment as a company auditor and discipline are to be fair and must make provision for appeals – Schedule 11 paragraph 11.

5.4.8 *Investigation of complaints*

There must be arrangements for the investigation of complaints against persons eligible for appointment as company auditors and against the supervisory body itself. These investigations may be carried out by a body or person independent of the supervisory body itself – Schedule 11 paragraph 12.

5.4.9 *Meeting of claims*

The body's rules must ensure that company auditors are reasonably able to meet claims against them arising out of company audit work. This may be achieved by professional indemnity insurance or other appropriate arrangements – Schedule 11 paragraph 13.

5.4.10 *Register of auditors*

The body's rules must require compliance with the Act's requirements in respect of the register of auditors – Schedule 11 pararaph 14.

5.4.11 *Cost of compliance*

The body must have arrangements adequate to ensure that when rules are framed, proper account is taken of the costs which would be incurred by people subject to the body's rules in complying with its rules – Schedule 11 paragraph 15.

5.4.12 *Standards*

Finally, the body must promote and maintain high standards of integrity in company audit work – Schedule 11 paragraph 16.

A recognised supervisory body, its officers, employers and governing body's members are not to be held liable in damages for acts done or not done in good faith under Part II of the Act – section 48.

5.5 Appropriate qualification

One of the conditions for recognition as a supervisory body is that a body's rules must ensure that those of its members who are company auditors have 'an appropriate qualification'. For these purposes a person has such a qualification if:

(1) immediately before the implementation of section 25 (which deals with eligibility for appointment as an auditor) the person was qualified for appointment as an auditor by virtue of being a member of a body listed in section 389(1)(a) of the 1985 Act (see paragraph **5.1**), or

(2) he holds a recognised professional qualification obtained in the U.K., or

45

(3) he holds an 'approved overseas qualification' and satisfies any additional educational requirements which the Secretary of State may impose upon applicants with such qualifications – section 31(1).

Transitional arrangements cover those who were qualified under the 1985 Act to act as auditors, but not by section 389(1)(a) i.e. those persons recognised individually by the Secretary of State. This recognition will enable such persons who were recognised in this way before 1 January 1990 to continue in practice as auditors for twelve months from the date on which section 25 is implemented. They will continue to be recognised thereafter if during that period of twelve months they notify the Secretary of State that they wish to retain the benefit of that recognition – section 31(1) and (2). There is a fail-safe procedure for people given such authorisation under the 1967 Act and who can show good reason for failing to apply for recognition within the period allowed by the 1989 Act and demonstrate that they genuinely intend to practise as an auditor in Great Britain – section 31(3).

A further transitional provision relates to students who on 1 January 1990 had begun a course of study or practical training leading to a U.K. professional accountancy qualification. Students will be treated as holding an appropriate qualification if they gain the qualification before 1 January 1996 and the qualification has been recognised for this purpose by the Secretary of State – section 31(5).

5.6 Recognised professional qualification

For the purposes of section 31, a 'recognised professional qualification' is a professional qualification recognised by the Secretary of State and offered by a 'qualifying body' (i.e. a body established in the U.K. and offering a professional qualification in accountancy) – section 32.

The administrative arrangements for recognition of a professional qualification are similar to those prescribed for the recognition of supervisory bodies – Schedule 12 paragraphs 1–3.

Apart from these administrative arrangements, the Act specifies various detailed conditions for recognition of a qualification. These conditions largely reflect the requirements of the Eighth Directive and concern:

(1) *entry requirements* – either a university level qualification or a sufficient period of professional experience is required,
(2) *theoretical instruction* – either a course of theoretical instruction or a sufficient period of professional experience is required,
(3) *professional experience* – to suffice, a period of professional experience must consist of at least several years in a professional capacity in the fields of finance, law and accountancy,
(4) *examination* – the Secretary of State may specify the subjects to be covered and the standard to be achieved is to be equivalent to that of a university degree,
(5) *practical training* – a period of at least three years is required of which a substantial part must be spent being trained in company audit work,
(6) *the qualifying body* – the qualifying body must monitor its compliance with the Act, the standard of its examination and the adequacy of its students' practical training – Schedule 12 paragraphs 4–9.

5.7 Approved overseas qualifications

Under the Eighth Directive (Article 11) persons may be regarded by member states as eligible for appointment as company auditors, if they are appropriately qualified in other member states. In permitting such migration, member states may require that applicants should have appropriate knowledge of their domestic law insofar as it is relevant to the audit of accounts.

The Act makes use of these provisions by empowering the Secretary of State to declare that persons should be regarded as holding an approved professional qualification if they are:

(1) qualified to audit accounts under the law of a specified country outside the U.K., or
(2) hold a specified professional qualification in accountancy recognised under the law of such a country – section 33(1).

This power may only be used, however, if the Secretary of State is satisfied that the qualification offers assurance of professional competence equal to that of a recognised professional qualification – section 33(2).

In exercising his powers, the Secretary of State may have regard to questions of reciprocity, i.e. whether people eligible under the Act for appointment as a company auditor or holding a recognised professional qualification are recognised by the law of the country in question to audit accounts there – section 33(3). He may also require applicants holding the overseas qualification to obtain certain additional qualifications to ensure that they have adequate knowledge of the law and practice of the U.K. relating to the audit of accounts – section 33(4).

5.8 Duties of recognised bodies

The Act empowers the Secretary of State to make regulations requiring the maintenance of a register of persons eligible for appointment as company auditors and of individuals holding an appropriate qualification who are responsible for company tax or company audit work on behalf of eligible firms – section 35. Regulations may also cover the availability to the public of information about eligible firms – section 36.

The Secretary of State may require a recognised supervisory body or a qualifying body:

(1) To notify him of the occurrence of such events as he may specify, giving such information as he may require – section 37(1)(a).
(2) To provide him at such times or in respect of such periods as he may specify, with the information which he prescribes – section 37(1)(b).
(3) To provide him with any information which he needs to discharge his functions under Part II of the Act and which is specified in a notice. The Secretary of State may specify a time limit for the provision of such information and the way in which it should be verified – section 38.

If the Secretary of State considers that a recognised supervisory or qualifying body is not satisfying the Act's requirements for recognition or discharging its obligations under Part II of the Act, he may decide not to revoke the body's recognition order, and instead may make an application to the court under section 39. If satisfied, the court may make an order that the body concerned should take the steps specified by the court to ensure that the requirement is satisfied or the obligation discharged – section 39. Further the Secretary of State may direct such a body either to take or not to take certain action, if he considers that:

(1) any proposed action by such a body would be incompatible with European Community or other international obligations of the U.K. or
(2) any action within the body's powers is required for the purpose of implementing such obligations – section 40.

5.9 Offences

It will also be an offence:

(1) for a person to furnish information which he knows is false or misleading in a material particular for any purpose under Part II of the Act,
(2) for such purposes to furnish recklessly information which is false or misleading in a material particular,
(3) for a person whose name is not included in the register of auditors to describe himself as a registered auditor, and
(4) for a body which is not a recognised supervisory or qualifying body to describe itself as such a body – section 41.

Where an offence under Part II of the Act is committed by a body corporate, and is shown to have been committed with the consent of an officer of the body corporate (or a person purporting to act as an officer) he also is guilty of an offence. If a body corporate is managed by its members, they also are caught by these provisions. In the case of a partnership, a partner who consented to or connived at the offence is caught by these provisions as well as the partnership itself – section 42.

5.10 Delegation of functions

If he wishes, the Secretary of State may by order (a 'delegation order') create a body corporate to exercise his functions under Part II of the Act. A delegation order has the effect of transferring to that body all of the Secretary of State's functions apart from:

(1) deciding whether a recognition order should be refused on grounds related to competition,
(2) powers which can be exercised in consequence of a competition report – section 46.

In addition, the Secretary of State may confer on the body appropriate supplementary or incidental functions. Even if such powers are delegated, the Secretary of State would remain empowered to call for information and to give directions to ensure compliance with international obligations. Detailed provisions are set out in Schedule 13 to the Act concerning the constitution, financing, functions and reports of such a body – section 46.

5.11 Restrictive practices

Before the Secretary of State decides to recognise either a supervisory or a qualifying body, the Director General of Fair Trading is to review the rules and guidance of the body concerned and to report whether the rules and guidance would significantly restrict, distort or prevent competition. If such an effect on competition is identified, the Secretary of State may only recognise the body concerned if he considers that the effect is reasonably justifiable in view of the purposes of Part II of the Act – section 47(1) and Schedule 14. This presumably allows for rules to be retained even if they are anti-competitive provided that they are required to ensure, for example, the independence or integrity of company auditors.

Subsequently, the Director General is to keep the rules and guidance of recognised bodies under review, and must report to the Secretary of State any circumstances which may have the effect of significantly restricting competition. The Director General may also from time to time consider the effects on competition of a body's rules concerning eligibility for appointment as a company auditor and the conduct of company auditors. To assist him in discharging these obligations, the Director General is empowered to require the production of documents and other information. In response to a report from the Director General, the Secretary of State may either revoke a body's recognition order, direct it to take certain specified steps or make alterations to the body's rules – section 47, Schedule 14.

5.12 Commencement

The DTI expect that the first commencement date will fall between January and March 1990 and intend to recognise supervisory bodies and bring the whole scheme into operation by March 1991.

Chapter 6

Investigations

6.1 Background

Various statutes provide that in appropriate circumstances the Department of Trade and Industry is to investigate a company's affairs (sections 431, 432 of the 1985 Act), the ownership of shares of a company (sections 442, 444 of the 1985 Act), dealings in options in shares or debentures of a company or failure to disclose share holdings (section 446 of the 1985 Act) or insider dealing (section 177 of the Financial Services Act 1986). In each case, the investigation is generally carried out by one or several inspectors appointed by the DTI although the ownership of the shares of a company may be investigated by the DTI directly without the appointment of an inspector (see section 444 of the 1985 Act).

In addition, sections 447–451 of the 1985 Act give the Secretary of State powers to call for the production of books and documents by all companies regulated by the Companies Act (or one of its predecessors) and certain other bodies. These powers to commission investigations and to obtain information are revised and generally extended by the 1989 Act.

6.2 Section 432: Investigations – reports

Section 432 of the 1985 Act empowers the Secretary of State to appoint inspectors to investigate the affairs of the company if there are circumstances which suggest misconduct. In the past the inspectors' reports have been public documents but in the future the Secretary of State will be able to appoint inspectors on terms that their report is not for publication. In such a case, the provisions of section 437 concerning the availability into publication of inspector's reports do not apply – section 55 of the 1989 Act, new section 432(2A) of the 1985 Act.

This new section was vigorously attacked during the House of Commons committee debates on the grounds that it may allow the Secretary of State to avoid the publication of information which he considers would be embarrassing. In dealing with this criticism during debate, assurances were given that the intention of the new section was merely to ensure that investigations could be speeded up with the result that information needed to bring criminal charges against offenders could be collected more quickly. A further assurance was given that if information comes to light during an investigation which in the public interest should be published, the Secretary of State would reappoint the inspectors on the basis that their report should be published in due course.

6.3 Sections 431 and 432: Investigations – powers

Section 431 of the 1985 Act empowers the Secretary of State to appoint inspectors to investigate the affairs of a company in response to an application either by the company itself or by a significant group of shareholders. This power complements the Secretary of State's powers under section 432 of the 1985 Act to appoint inspectors of his own volition. The powers of such inspectors, particularly with regard to obtaining information, are set out in section 434 of the 1985 Act and have been amended by the 1989 Act.

The amendments to section 434 are intended to clarify the extent to which inspectors can obtain access to documents and information. Firstly it is made clear that the inspectors can require the production of documents or information relating to a matter which they believe to be relevant to the investigation – section 56(3), new section 434(2) of the 1985 Act. Previously, inspectors could only require the production of information relating to the affairs of the company under investigation or of books and documents relating to the company's affairs. Judicially, the phrase 'the affairs of a company' has been taken to comprise 'all its business affairs, interests or transactions, all its investments or other property interests, all its profits and losses or balance of profits or losses and its goodwill' (*R v Board of Trade ex parte St Martin Preserving Co Ltd* (1965) 1 QB 603 at 618).

Secondly, 'documents' are defined to include information recorded in any form. Where information is recorded otherwise than in legible form, the inspectors' power to require the production of that information includes the power to require the production of a copy of the information in legible form – section 56(5), new section 434(6) of the 1985 Act.

6.4 Inspectors' reports

Section 56 of the 1989 Act deals with the conflict which can arise between the conduct of an investigation and the desire to lay criminal charges against offenders. The Government believes that it is desirable to commence criminal prosecution wherever possible and that this can be more difficult where both inspectors and police are investigating the same matters. Accordingly the Secretary of State is now given powers to bring a DTI investigation to an early close.

The powers can be used where matters have come to light in the course of the investigation which suggest that criminal offences have been committed and have been referred to the appropriate prosecuting authority. In such circumstances, the Secretary of State may direct the inspectors to take no further steps in the investigation or alternatively to take only such further steps as he specifies. Where such a direction is made by the Secretary of State, the inspectors shall only make a final report where they owe their appointment to an order of the court under section 432(1) of the 1985 Act or where the Secretary of State directs them to do so – section 57, new section 437(1B) and (1C) of the 1985 Act.

6.5 Investigations – expenses

Section 439 of the 1985 Act provides that the Secretary of State is in the first instance to meet the expenses (both direct and incidental) of an investigation. In future the expenses of the investigation are to include such reasonable sums as the

Secretary of State may determine in respect of general staff costs and overheads, thus broadening the DTI's ability to recover its own costs – section 59, new section 439(1) of the 1985 Act.

6.6 Winding up petitions

Section 440 of the 1985 Act gives the Secretary of State powers to petition for the winding up of a company in the public interest following the publication of an inspectors' report or on obtaining information from the company. Section 60 of the 1989 Act inserts a new section 124A in the Insolvency Act 1986 and extends the Secretary of State's powers. As well as using Companies Act inspectors' reports, the Secretary of State will also be able to petition for a winding up on the basis of investigations under the Financial Services Act, investigations under the Insurance Companies Act, investigations by the Serious Fraud Office and on the basis of information obtained from overseas regulatory authorities under the new powers granted by section 83 of the 1989 Act – section 60.

6.7 Company ownership – investigations

By section 442 of the 1985 Act the Secretary of State has discretion to appoint inspectors to investigate the true ownership and control of a company but only if requested by sufficient members of the company and if he is satisfied that the application is not vexatious and that it is unreasonable for the matter to be investigated. Section 61 of the 1989 Act amends the section in two ways. Firstly, the Secretary of State may, before appointing inspectors, require the applicant or applicants to give security, to an amount not exceeding £5,000, or such other sum as he may specify, for payment of the costs of the investigation. Secondly, the Secretary of State is now to have the option of responding to an application from shareholders by using the powers which he has under section 444 of the 1985 Act to investigate the ownership of particular shares or debentures of a company rather than by using his powers under section 442. Section 444 of the 1989 Act deals with situations in which the Secretary of State believes that there is good reason to investigate the ownership of any share or debentures of the company but that it is unnecessary to appoint inspectors for the purpose. These changes provide some flexibility to the Secretary of State so that by making in-house enquiries he can avoid the potential damage to a company which can result from the public appointment of inspectors. The expense and delay of such a process can also be avoided.

6.8 Entry and search of premises

Section 448 of the 1985 Act deals with the entry and search of premises. It is repealed and replaced by a new section 448 set out in section 64 of the 1989 Act.

The original power granted by old section 448 is retained in the new section. A justice of the peace may issue a warrant if satisfied by information on oath that there are reasonable grounds for believing that there are on any premises documents whose production has been required under a provision in Part XIV of the 1985 Act and which have not been produced. Old section 448 referred only to documents whose production had been requested by the Secretary of State using his power in section 447 to require production of documents. In the future, since the new section 448 refers to the whole of Part XIV of the Act, inspectors appointed by the Secretary of State will have these powers extended to them – new section 448(1).

The new section 448 also provides that a justice of the peace may issue a warrant if satisfied by information on oath that there are reasonable grounds for believing that an offence has been committed for which the penalty is imprisonment for not less than two years, and that there are on any premises documents relating to whether the offence has been committed. The justice of the peace must also be satisfied that the person making the application (whether the Secretary of State or someone appointed by him) has power to require the production of the documents concerned and that, if production of the documents was required, the documents would not be produced but removed from the premises, hidden, tampered with or destroyed – new section 448(2).

This represents a considerable increase in the powers of the Secretary of State and DTI inspectors. Under the old legislation, to obtain a warrant for the entry and search of premises, it was first necessary to show that documents had been withheld in spite of a requirement for their production. Now it will be possible for the Secretary of State and for DTI inspectors to arrange surprise raids to obtain documents thought to be at risk.

A warrant issued under this section may authorise a constable, any other person named in the warrant and any other constables:

(1) To enter the premises specified using such force as is reasonably necessary for the purpose.
(2) To search the premises and to take possession of any documents appearing to be the documents required to be produced or take in relation to such documents any other steps which may appear to be necessary for preserving or preventing interference with them.
(3) To take copies of any such documents.
(4) To require any person named in the warrant to provide an explanation of them or to state where they may be found – new section 448(3).

In granting a warrant, the justice of the peace may extend authorisation beyond specified documents to other documents thought relevant to the investigation – new section 448(4).

Any documents of which possession is taken under new section 448 may be retained for a period of three months. If within that period proceedings to which the documents are relevant are commenced against any person for any criminal offence, then the documents may be held until the conclusion of those proceedings – new section 448(6).

6.9 Security of information

Section 449 of the 1985 Act sets out the ways in which information obtained by the Secretary of State and DTI inspectors may be used and thus provides for its security. Effectively that section provides that information and documents relating to a body must not be disclosed without that body's prior consent unless the disclosure is made to a competent authority or the disclosure is required for a number of specified purposes. These purposes include the exercise by the Secretary of State of his functions under various Acts, the initiation of various criminal proceedings and so on.

A number of additional purposes are now added to this list:

- To assist any inspector appointed under section 94 or 177 of the Financial Services Act.
- To assist a recognised supervisory body or a qualifying body in discharging its functions in the new scheme for the regulation of auditors.
- To assist in disciplinary proceedings relating to the discharge by a public servant of his duties.
- To assist an overseas regulatory authority in its regulatory functions – section 65(2).

6.10 Destruction of documents

Section 450 of the 1985 Act provides that destruction or mutilation of a document relating to a company's affairs or making a false entry in such a document or dealing with it fraudulently constitutes an offence. These provisions are now extended by the new definition of 'documents' – section 66. Thus wiping a computer file or otherwise tampering with a computer file would constitute an offence.

6.11 Disclosure of information

Section 451A was inserted in the 1985 Act by the Financial Services Act 1986 and empowered the Secretary of State if he thought fit to disclose any information obtained under the powers in Part XIV of the 1985 Act to any of the competent authorities listed in section 449. This list consists of a number of regulatory and legal authorities.

Section 67 of the 1989 Act substitutes a new section 451A which in addition enables the Secretary of State to authorise or require a DTI inspector appointed under Part XIV of the 1985 Act to make disclosures in the same way. Such inspectors will also be permitted to disclose information in their possession to another DTI inspector or to inspectors appointed under other measures such as the Financial Services Act 1986, the Insurance Companies Act 1982 – new section 451A (2),(3).

Finally, the new section empowers the Secretary of State to disclose information obtained under section 444 (the section by which he may arrange for in-house investigations of the ownership of shares or debentures in the company). In particular, this information may be disclosed to the company whose ownership is the subject of the investigation, any member of the company, any person whose conduct was investigated in the course of the investigation, the company's auditors or any person whose financial interests appear to be affected by matters covered by the investigation – new section 451A(5).

6.12 Privileged information

Section 452 of the 1985 Act maintains the doctrine of privilege in relation to certain information. In particular section 452(1)(b) ensures that bankers cannot be requested to disclose information as to the affairs of any customer other than the company being investigated.

The confidentiality of banking information is now dealt with in two new subsections (452(1A) and (1B)). New subsection (1A) provides that nothing in sections 434 (production of documents and evidence to inspectors), 443 (investigations under section 442) or 446 (investigation of share dealings) requires a person to disclose information or produce documents in respect of which he owes an obligation of confidence by virtue of carrying on the business of banking unless:

(1) the person to whom the obligation of confidence is owed is the company under investigation,
(2) the person to whom the obligation of confidence is owed, consents to the disclosure or production, or
(3) the making of the requirement is authorised by the Secretary of State – section 69(3).

In other words, these provisions extend the existing powers in two significant respects. Firstly, DTI inspectors can now require bankers to disclose banking information about a company being investigated without that company's permission to breach an obligation of confidence. DTI inspectors can also require bankers to disclose banking information in respect of which an obligation of confidence is owed to someone other than the company being investigated, but only with that person's agreement. Secondly, the Secretary of State may require a banker to disclose information in breach of an obligation of confidence.

Subsection (1A) does not apply where the obligation of confidence is owed by the company or other body corporate which is under investigation under sections 431, 432 or 433 – new section 452(1B). Thus, where a bank is being investigated, there is no protection for banking information which it holds and in respect of which it would normally be under a duty of confidence – section 69(3).

6.13   Financial Services Act 1986

The effect of sections 72–76 of the 1989 Act is simply to include within the investigation provisions of the Financial Services Act 1986 changes which are similar to those effected in the investigations provisions of the 1985 Act. In particular these amendments:

(1) change the law in respect of the confidentiality of banking information;
(2) enable the Secretary of State to direct an inspector not to continue with investigation or to take a certain number of specified steps;
(3) require a person convicted on a prosecution instituted as a result of an investigation to pay the expenses of the investigation to the extent specified in the order;
(4) revise the rules on the purposes for which information may be disclosed and the bodies to which it may be disclosed;
(5) revise the rules concerning the entry and search of premises.

6.14   Insurance Companies Act 1982

The Insurance Companies Act 1982 is amended to incorporate rules concerning entry and search of premises which are similar to those introduced by the 1989 Act in respect of DTI investigations – section 77.

6.15 Overseas regulatory authorities

The effect of sections 82–91 is to enable the Secretary of State to assist an overseas regulatory authority which has requested his assistance in connection with enquiries being carried out by it or on its behalf.

For these purposes an overseas regulatory authority is an authority in a country outside the United Kingdom which in that territory exercises any functions corresponding to those of a designated agency or competent authority under the Financial Services Act 1986, or to functions of the Secretary of State under the Insurance Companies Act 1982, the Companies Act 1985 or the Financial Services Act 1986 or to functions of the Bank of England under the Banking Act 1987. It would also include a body in another country which exercises regulatory functions in connection with insider dealing. Finally, the Secretary of State may by regulations specify any other functions relating to companies or financial services which would qualify an overseas regulatory authority under these provisions – section 82(2).

The Secretary of State is not simply given a general power to assist overseas regulatory authorities. He must first be persuaded that the assistance which is sought is required for the purpose of the overseas authority's regulatory functions in respect of companies or financial services – section 82(3). In deciding whether this is the case, the Secretary of State may take a number of issues into account:

– Reciprocity – would the country concerned give equivalent assistance to a U.K. regulatory authority?
– Equivalence – do the enquiries relate to a breach in the law or a jurisdiction which either has no close parallel or would not be recognised in the U.K.?
– Significance – is the subject of the enquiries sufficiently serious? Is the U.K. information sought important to the enquiries? Could the assistance be obtained by other means?
– Appropriateness – is it appropriate in the public interest to give the assistance sought? – section 82(4).

Two other matters must also be considered by the Secretary of State. Where his assistance is sought by an overseas banking supervisor, the Secretary of State is obliged to consult the Bank of England – section 82(5). Finally the Secretary of State may decline to give the assistance sought if the overseas regulatory authority refuses to make an appropriate contribution to the related costs – section 82(6).

The powers given to the Secretary of State in assisting overseas regulatory authorities are that he may require any person:

(1) to attend before him at a specified time and place and answer questions or otherwise furnish information with respect to any matter relevant to the enquiries;
(2) to produce specified documents which relate to any matter relevant to the enquiries;
(3) otherwise to give such assistance in connection with the enquiries as he is reasonably able to give – section 83(1).

6.16 Commencement

The DTI expects that these provisions will be implemented with effect from March 1990.

Chapter 7

Company charges

7.1 Introduction

Under the Companies Act 1985 there are two systems of registration of company charges: the first is in the register kept by the company itself and the second is in the register kept by the Registrar of Companies.

The 1985 Act obliges every limited company to keep a register of charges at its registered office in respect of all specific mortgages and charges secured on its property and of all floating charges secured on its undertaking or on any of its assets. This register shows the sum secured, the property charged and the names of the persons entitled to the charge, and is open to inspection. Failure by the company to register a mortgage or charge in its register of charges does not affect the mortgagee's security, unless the failure to register was procured or connived at by the mortgagee with the intention of concealing his mortgage from subsequent creditors of the company.

The second duty of registration, the duty of a company to deliver to the Registrar of Companies particulars of certain charges created by it over its assets, is more important than the first. Failure to file particulars of a charge at Companies House may result in the invalidity of the charge.

Only charges created by a company over its property need to be registered at Companies House (e.g. charges created by the operation of law such as a vendor's lien for unpaid purchase money are not registrable). There are nine classes of charges created by a company which must be registered, comprising most but not all of the charges which a company may create over its assets (see section 395 of the 1985 Act).

A company is required to deliver particulars of a registrable charge and the instrument creating the charge to the Registrar of Companies within 21 days of its creation. If the company fails to do this, any other interested party may register the charge within the permitted time. A charge which is not registered within 21 days of its creation is void against the liquidator and any creditor of the company so far as any security on the company's property or undertaking is conferred by the charge. Under section 401 of the 1985 Act, the Registrar of Companies is required to issue a certificate of registration and this constitutes conclusive evidence of compliance with the requirements of the Act as to registration. This applies even if the particulars registered are defective. For example, an error in the particulars about the date of creation or the amount secured would not result in the certificate of registration being treated as not conclusive.

By a mechanism prescribed in section 404 of the 1985 Act, an accidental failure to register a charge can be rectified by the court ordering an extension of the normal registration period. Omissions or misstatements of any particulars can be rectified if the court so orders but only if certain conditions are satisfied. The court is not empowered to order deletion of the whole of the entry or to alter the date of registration of a charge which has been wrongly backdated.

This system of registration has long been regarded as deficient. For example, the Jenkins Committee on Company Law, reporting in 1962, stated:

> 'We understand that the Registrar has been advised that the effect of these provisions is to impose upon him an absolute duty to enter on the register the effect of every instrument of charge delivered to him under section 95 [now section 395]. Thus, he may receive an instrument of charge which is extremely complicated or is obscurely drafted, but in fact creates both a specific charge on land and a floating charge over the remaining assets of the company, although the prescribed particulars furnished to him may mention only the fixed charge; if he fails to detect the existence of the floating charge and therefore omits any reference to it from his register, he may be liable to anyone who suffers loss in consequence of the omission.' (Jenkins Committee report, Cmnd 1749, paragraph 302)

In December 1985, Professor A. L. Diamond was asked by the Government to examine the need for alteration of the law relating to security over property other than land. In his final report which was published during 1989, Professor Diamond dealt with this subject in general but in particular made proposals for changes in the system of registration of the company charges which would deal with the principal criticisms levelled against the existing system. The 1989 Act takes account of Professor Diamond's recommendations and reforms the system of registration of company charges.

7.2 Charges requiring registration

Section 93 of the 1989 Act replaces old sections 395 and 396 of the 1985 Act with new sections specifying charges requiring registration.

For the purposes of these provisions, a charge means any form of security interest (fixed or floating) over property other than an interest arising by operation of law and property including future property – new section 395(2). The charges requiring registration are to be as follows:

(1) A charge on land or in the interest in land (other than a charge for rent or any other periodical sum issuing out of the land in England and Wales and in Scotland a charge for any rent, ground, annual or any other periodical sum payable in respect of the land) – new section 396(1)(a).

(2) A charge on goods or any interest in goods other than a charge under which the chargee is entitled to possession either of the goods or of the document of title to them – new section 396(1)(b). For this purpose, goods means any tangible movable property (in Scotland, corporeal movable property) other than money – new section 396(2)(d). A charge is not excluded from this category of registrable charge because the chargee is entitled to take possession in case of default – new section 396(2)(c).

(3) A charge on intangible movable property (in Scotland incorporeal movable property) of the following descriptions: goodwill, intellectual property, book debts (whether book debts of the company or assigned to the company), uncalled share capital of the company or calls made but not paid – new section 396(1)(c). For this purpose, intellectual property means any patent, trademark, service mark, registered design, copyright or design right or any licence under or in respect of any such right – new section 396(2)(d). A

debenture which is part of an issue or series is not to be treated as a book debt – new section 396(2)(e). Neither a shipowner's lien on subfreights nor the deposit by way of security of a negotiable instrument given to secure the payment of book debts are to be treated as a charge on book debts – new section 396(2)(f), (g).

(4) A charge for securing an issue of debentures – new section 396(1)(d).

(5) A floating charge on all or part of the company's property – new section 396(1)(e).

7.3 Companies charges register

The Registrar of Companies is to keep for each company a register of charges on property of the company. The register is to consist of a file containing for each charge the particulars and other information delivered to the Registrar under the provisions of the 1985 Act. Any person may require the Registrar to provide a certificate stating the date on which any specified particulars of or other information relating to a charge was delivered to him. This certificate is to be conclusive evidence that the particulars specified were delivered to the Registrar no later than the date stated in the certificate. Unless the contrary is proved, it is to be presumed that the particulars were not delivered earlier than the date stated on the certificate – new section 397 of the 1985 Act, section 94 of the 1989 Act. In other words the significance of the certificate is to be reduced and the Registrar has a duty only to register those particulars which are delivered to him. No longer will he be obliged to check those particulars against the original documents creating the charge.

7.4 Delivery of particulars for registration

Any company which creates a charge or acquires property subject to a charge is to be under a duty to deliver the prescribed particulars of the charge in the prescribed form to the Registrar for registration. This must be done within 21 days after the date of the charge's creation or, if appropriate, the date of the acquisition of the property subject to the charge. Although the company is under a duty to deliver the particulars of the charge to the Registrar for registration, the particulars may be delivered for registration by any person interested in the charge. Where such a person delivers the particulars for registration, that person is entitled to recover from the company the amount of fees paid by him to the Registrar in connection with his own registration – new section 398(1), (2) of the 1985 Act, section 95 of the 1989 Act. In practice, no doubt charges will continue to be registered by the person who benefits from the charge.

On receipt, the Registrar is to send to the company and any person appearing from the particulars to be the chargee and, if the particulars were delivered by another person interested in the charge, to that person, a copy of the particulars filed by him and of the note made by him as to the date on which they were delivered – new section 398(3)–(5) of the 1985 Act, section 95 of the 1985 Act. This provides information for those concerned that the charge has been appropriately registered.

Where a charge is created and no prescribed particulars are delivered for registration within the specified period of 21 days, the charge is void against an administrator or liquidator of the company and any person who for value acquires an interest in or right over property subject to the charge. This applies where insolvency proceedings begin or that interest or right is acquired after the creation of the charge whether before or after the end of the 21 day period – new section 399 of the 1985 Act, section 95 of the 1989 Act.

Where particulars of a charge are delivered for registration more than 21 days after the date of the charge's creation, new section 399(1), which deals with the effects of a failure to deliver particulars for registration, does not apply in relation to events occurring after the particulars are delivered. However, the charge is void as against the administrator or liquidator if at the date of delivery of the particulars, the company is unable to pay its debts, or if it subsequently becomes unable to pay its debts in consequence of the transaction under which the charge is created and insolvency proceedings begin within a certain period of the date of delivery of the particulars. The specified period is as follows:

(1) two years in the case of a floating charge created in favour of a person connected with the company,
(2) one year in the case of a floating charge created in favour of any other person,
(3) six months in any other case – new section 400 of the 1985 Act, section 95 of the 1989 Act.

Further particulars of a charge supplementing or varying particulars which have already been registered may be delivered to the Registrar for registration at any time – new section 401 of the 1985 Act, section 96 of the 1989 Act. The effect of these provisions is to allow late registration of the particulars of a charge subject to a number of safeguards.

7.5   Effect of omissions and errors

Where the registered particulars of a charge are not completed accurately, the charge is void to the extent that rights are not disclosed by the registered particulars which would have been disclosed if particulars had been completed accurately. To that extent, the charge is void as against an administrator or liquidator of the company and any person who for value acquires an interest in or right over property subject to the charge. This only applies however if insolvency proceedings began or the interest was acquired at a time when the particulars were incomplete or inaccurate in a material respect. Nonetheless the court may order that the charge is effective as against an administrator or liquidator of the company if it is satisfied that the omission or error is unlikely to have misled materially to his prejudice any unsecured creditor of the company or that no person became an unsecured creditor of the company at the time when the registered particulars of the charge were incomplete or inaccurate in a relevant respect. The court may also order that the charge is effective as against a person acquiring an interest in or right over property subject to the charge if it is satisfied that in connection with the acquisition he did not rely on registered particulars which were incomplete or inaccurate in a relevant respect – new section 402 of the 1985 Act, section 97 of the 1989 Act.

7.6   Cessation

Where a charge of which particulars have been delivered to the Registrar ceases to affect the company's property a memorandum to that effect may be delivered to the Registrar for registration. The memorandum must be in a prescribed form signed by or on behalf of both the company and the chargee. Where a memorandum is delivered to the Registrar and it appears to him to be duly signed he is to file it in the register and note in such form as he thinks fit the date on which it was delivered to him – new section 403(1)–(3) of the 1985 Act, section 98 of the 1989 Act.

The Registrar must send to the company and any person appearing from the memorandum to be the chargee and, if the memorandum was delivered by another person interested in the charge, to that person, a copy of the memorandum filed by him and of the note made by him as to the date on which it was delivered. If a duly signed memorandum is delivered in a case where the charge in fact continues to affect the company's property, the charge is void as against an administrator or liquidator of the company and any person who for value acquires an interest in or right over property subject to the charge. This only applies where insolvency proceedings began or the interest was acquired after the registration of the memorandum – new section 403 of the 1985 Act, section 98 of the 1989 Act.

7.7 Voidness of charges

No charge is to be void by virtue of these provisions as against a subsequent charge unless some or all of the relevant particulars of that charge are duly delivered for registration within 21 days after the date of its creation or before complete and accurate relevant particulars of the earlier charge are duly delivered for registration. Where the particulars of the subsequent charge are incomplete or inaccurate the earlier charge is void as against that charge only to the extent that the rights of the subsequent charge are disclosed by registered particulars duly delivered for registration before the corresponding relevant particulars of the earlier charge – new section 404 of the 1985 Act, section 99 of the 1989 Act.

A charge is not to be void as against a person acquiring an interest in or right over property where the acquisition is expressly subject to the charge. Nor is a charge to be void in relation to any property simply because insolvency proceedings begin or another interest is acquired after the company which created the charge has disposed of the whole of its interest in that property – new section 405 of the 1985 Act, section 99 of the 1989 Act.

Where a charge becomes void to any extent by virtue of these provisions, the whole of the sum secured by the charge is payable forthwith on demand even though the sum secured by the charge is also the subject of other security – new section 407 of the 1985 Act, section 99 of the 1989 Act.

7.8 Additional information

Where particulars of a charge for securing an issue of debentures have been delivered for registration, it is the duty of the company to deliver to the Registrar particulars of the date on which any debentures of the issue are taken up and the amount taken up and to do so before the end of the period of 21 days after the date on which they are taken up – new section 408 of the 1985 Act, section 100 of the 1989 Act.

If a person obtains an order for the appointment of a receiver or manager of the company's property, or appoints such a receiver or manager under powers contained in an instrument he shall within seven days of the order or of the appointment under those powers give notice of that fact in the prescribed form to the Registrar for registration – new section 409 of the 1985 Act, section 100 of the 1989 Act.

The Secretary of State may also require other information to be given. For example regulations may require notice of the occurrence of events affecting the nature of the security under a floating charge of which particulars have been registered and exercise of powers conferred by a fixed or floating charge of which particulars have been registered – new sections 409 and 410 of the 1985 Act, section 100 of the 1989 Act.

7.9 Copies to be held by company

Each company is to keep at its registered office a copy of every instrument creating or evidencing a charge over the company's property. In the case of a series of uniform debentures, a copy of one debenture of the series is sufficient. Each company is also to keep at its registered office a register of all such charges containing entries for each charge giving a short description of the property charged, the amount of the charge and, except in the case of bearer securities, the names of the persons entitled to it. This applies to any charge whether or not particulars are required to be delivered to the Registrar for registration. The copies and register kept by each company are to be open to inspection. The company may be asked to provide a copy of any interest creating or evidencing a charge over the company's property or any entry in the register of charges kept by the company on payment of such fee as may be prescribed. The requirement for provision of copies applies to any charge whether or not particulars are required to be delivered to the Registrar of Companies for registration – new sections 411 and 412 of the 1985 Act, section 101 of the 1989 Act.

7.10 Commencement

It is expected that these provisions will be implemented with effect from March 1991.

Chapter 8

A company's objects

8.1 Background

Since the introduction in the nineteenth century of the system of incorporation by registration, it has been a statutory requirement that a company's Memorandum of Association should state the objects of the company or, in other words, the purposes for which the company is formed. The effect of a company entering into a contract with respect to a matter not authorised by its objects clause was considered by the courts in 1875 in *Ashbury Rly Carriage and Iron Co Ltd v Riche* (1875) LR 7 HL 653. Lord Cairns LC described the effect of the objects clause in the following way:

'It states affirmatively the ambit and extent of vitality and power which by law is given to the corporation, and it states, that if it is necessary so to state, negatively, that nothing shall be done beyond that ambit, and that no attempt shall be made to use the corporate life for any other purpose than that which is so specified.'

Accordingly, anything outside a company's objects clause will be beyond that company's capacity and therefore ultra vires. Such a transaction is void and could not be rectified even by the unanimous agreement of all members.

In the years since the *Ashbury Rly Carriage* case in 1875, the effect of the doctrine of ultra vires has been gradually eroded as a result both of developments in practice and of legislative action. The courts have been prepared to assume that, depending on the nature of the objects set out in its Memorandum of Association, a company has a wide range of implied powers to enable it to conduct its business more effectively. Further, the practice has developed of including within Memoranda of Association objects clauses which contain a profusion of objects effectively enabling directors to carry on any business which they consider can be advantageously carried on by the company. In practice, the effect of the requirement for an objects clause can largely be vitiated by good drafting.

As for erosion of the effect of the objects clause by legislative action, companies have long since been given the power to alter their objects clauses by special resolution. This effectively gives companies the power to render intra vires a class of transactions or activities which was previously ultra vires. The scope of the doctrine was further limited as a result of the First Company Law Directive of the European Community which obliges member states to provide safeguards for third parties dealing with a company. In particular, the directive sought to ensure that 'acts done by the organs of the company shall be binding upon it even if these acts are not within the acts of the company' – article 9(1). Member states may derogate from this requirement and may provide that a transaction is not to be binding on a company if a third party knew or ought to have known that the act concerned is outside the company's objects. This requirement is reflected in section 35 of the Companies Act 1985. The effect of this section is that a company is bound by decisions of its directors even with respect to matters outside its objects clause unless the third party dealing with a company is not acting in good faith. It is presumed that a third party is acting in good faith unless the contrary is proven.

Although section 35 represented a considerable erosion of the doctrine of ultra vires, the position remained unsatisfactory for a number of reasons. Firstly, the language of section 35 has proved difficult to interpret. For example, the section refers to a person dealing with a company in good faith in a transaction decided on by the directors. There is some doubt over the exact meaning of 'dealing', 'good faith' and 'decided on by the directors'. Secondly, a third party is deprived of the protection of section 35 where it is shown that he did not act in good faith. Thirdly, since section 35 commences with the words 'in favour of a person dealing with a company in good faith' it would appear that the doctrine of ultra vires continues to operate against the company. In other words, it may be possible that a company which has performed its part of the transaction would be unable to compel a third party who had benefited from the company's performance to perform his part of the transaction.

These difficulties have long been recognised. Both the Cohen Committee, which reported in 1945, and the Jenkins Committee, which reported in 1962, recommended that the situation should be reformed. The Companies Bill 1973 followed the suggestions of the Jenkins Committee and provided for the virtual abolition of the doctrine of ultra vires but lapsed with the dissolution of Parliament in 1974. The 1980 Act did not adopt the reforms proposed in the lapsed bill. In 1985, the Department of Trade and Industry commissioned Dr Dan Prentice of Oxford University to carry out a study into the legal and commercial implications of abolishing the ultra vires doctrine in companies law. Dr Prentice's report was published in July 1986 and recommended that a company should have the option of not registering an objects clause. Companies would, however, be required to file an annual activities and business statement as part of their annual return and this statement would be treated, at least for public companies, as a part of the Memorandum of Association. It would remain possible for companies to register objects clauses.

The 1989 Act includes legislation intended to deal with these difficulties.

8.2 A company's capacity

Section 35 of the Companies Act 1985 is replaced by section 108 of the Companies Act 1989.

Under new section 35 it would not be possible to call into question the validity of an act by a company by reason of anything in its Memorandum of Association – new section 35(1). Members of the company will still be able to bring proceedings to restrain the doing of an act which, but for the effect of new section 35(1), would be beyond the company's capacity as defined in its object clause. Members may not take such action, however, where the act to be done fulfils a legal obligation arising from a previous act of the company – new section 35(2). In spite of these changes, directors remain under an obligation to respect any limitations on their powers which are imposed by the company's Memorandum of Association. Any action which, but for new section 35(1) would be beyond the company's capacity, may only be ratified by the company by special resolution. Any such ratification would not affect the liability incurred by the directors or any other person. A separate special resolution is required in order to give relief from any such liability – new section 35(3).

A person dealing with a company in good faith may assume that the power of the board of directors to bind the company is free of any limitation under the company's constitution – new section 35A(1). For this purpose, a person deals with a company if he is a party to any transaction or other act to which the company is a party – new section 35A(2)(a). A person is not to be regarded as acting in bad faith simply because he knows that an act is beyond the powers of the directors under the company's constitution – new section 35A(2)(b). Unless the contrary is proved, a person is to be presumed to have acted in good faith – new section 35A(2)(c). For this purpose, the limitations on the powers of directors under a company's constitution include limitations which derive from a resolution of the company in general meeting or a meeting of any class of shareholders or an agreement between shareholders or of any class of shareholders – new section 35A(3).

These provisions do not affect the right of a member of the company to bring proceedings to restrain the doing of an act which is beyond the powers of the directors. However, proceedings may not be brought in respect of an act which fulfils a legal obligation arising from a previous act of the company – new section 35A(4). Nor do these provisions affect any liability incurred by the directors or any other person which arises because the directors have exceeded their powers – new section 35A(5).

No party to a transaction with the company need enquire whether it is permitted by the company's Memorandum of Association whether there is any limitation on the powers of the board of directors to bind the company or to authorise others to do so – new section 35B.

Section 680 of the 1985 Act envisages that certain companies not formed under that Act may nonetheless register. The effect of registration is set out in Schedule 21 to that Act. That Schedule provides that in some cases the company would not be allowed to change its constitution by special resolution, e.g. where its objects are specified in an Act of Parliament. The 1989 Act provides that where this is the case, such a company does not have the power to ratify acts of the directors which contravene the relevant provision – section 108(2).

All these provisions are applied equally to unregistered companies subject to any regulations which may be made by the Secretary of State – section 108(3).

8.3 Invalidity of transactions

Section 109 of the 1989 Act inserts in the 1985 Act a new section 322A which is intended to limit the possibility of unscrupulous directors abusing the new liberation of the ultra vires doctrine.

The provisions apply to transactions which satisfy two conditions. Firstly the parties to the transaction must include either a director of the company or of its holding company or a person connected with such a director or a company with which such a director is associated. Secondly, in approving the transaction, the board of directors must have exceeded any limitation on their powers under the company's constitution – new section 322A(1).

Any such transaction is voidable at the instance of the company – new section 322A(2). Even if the transaction is not avoided certain parties are obliged to account to the company for any direct or indirect gain which they have made as a result of the transaction and to indemnify the company for any loss or damage incurred as a result of the transaction. The parties concerned are those mentioned in new section 322A(1) and any director of the company who authorised the transaction – new section 322A(3). A person who is not a director is not liable if he shows that he was not aware that the directors were exceeding their powers – new section 322A(6).

In certain situations the transaction ceases to be voidable. This happens if restitution of any money or other asset which was the subject of the transaction ceases to be possible, if the company is indemnified for loss or damage arising from the transaction, if rights acquired bona fide and without actual notice of the directors exceeding their powers would be affected by the avoidance or if the transaction is ratified by the company in general meeting – new section 322A(5).

8.4   Statement of company's objects

Section 2 of the 1985 Act requires that the Memorandum of Association of every company must state the objects of the company. The 1989 Act does not amend that section so that it will remain a requirement that the Memorandum of Association should include an objects clause.

Section 4 of the 1985 Act which dealt with the mechanism by which the objects clause be changed is repealed, however, and replaced with two new sections – 3A and 4 – section 110.

New section 3A provides that a company's Memorandum may state that the object of the company is to carry on business as a general commercial company. Such a statement will mean that the object of the company is to carry on any trade or business whatsoever and that the company has power to do all such things as are incidental or conducive to the carry on of any trade or business by it – new section 3A.

Alterations of a memorandum with respect to the statement of the company's objects will still have to be made by way of special resolution – new section 4(1). This resolution will be subject to the procedures for objecting to alteration of a company's objects which are set out in section 5 of the 1985 Act.

8.5   Charitable companies

Section 111 of the 1989 Act replaces section 30 of the Charities Act 1960 with new sections 30, 30A, 30B and 30C of that Act. New section 30 simply restates section 30(1) of the Charities Act 1960 which provided that the Attorney General is to be one of the persons authorised by the Insolvency Act 1986 who may petition the High Court for a charitable company to be wound up by the court.

The remaining new sections deal with the objects of charitable companies.

Firstly, the ability of a charity which is a company to alter the instruments establishing or regulating it are subject to two restrictions. The first restriction renders invalid any exercise of the power to change the body's instruments which has the effect of the body ceasing to be a charity and which might affect the application of any property acquired under any charitable disposition or agreement other than for full consideration or any property representing property in this way, any property representing income accrued before the alteration is made or the income from any such property – new section 30A(1). This restriction is effectively a restatement of section 30(2) of the Charities Act 1960.

The second restriction renders ineffective any alteration of a charitable company's objects clause without the prior written consent of the Charity Commissioners. When an alteration in a charitable company's objects clause is delivered to the Registrar of Companies under section 6 of the 1985 Act, a copy of the Commissioners' consent must also be delivered – new section 30A(2).

New sections 35 and 35A of the 1985 Act do not apply except in favour of a person who either does not know at the time that the company is a charity or who gives full consideration in money or money's worth in relation to the act in question and does not know at the time that the act is done that it is not permitted by the Memorandum of Association or that it is beyond the directors' powers – new section 30B(1). However, if the charitable company is attempting to transfer or grant an interest in property, these provisions do not affect the title of a person who subsequently acquires the property or an interest in it for full consideration without actual notice of the circumstances affecting the validity of the company's act – new section 30B(2). In any proceedings which arise from these provisions, the burden of proof that a person did not know that an act was beyond the objects of the company or that a person did know that a company was a charity lies on the person making that allegation – new section 30B(3).

Both new sections 35(3) and 322A of the 1985 Act provide that acts by boards of directors exceeding limitations on their powers may be ratified by the company. In the case of a company which is a charity, such a ratification would be ineffective without the prior written consent of the Charity Commissioners – new section 30B(4).

Any company which is a charity and whose name does not include the word charity or charitable must state on its correspondence and on other documents the fact that it is a charity. This applies to all the company's business letters, all its notices and other official publications, bills of exchange, cheques and orders purporting to be signed by or on behalf of the company and so on – new section 30C.

8.6 Commencement

The DTI expects that these provisions will be introduced with effect from November 1990.

Chapter 9

Deregulation of private companies

9.1 Background

There has long been an argument about the extent to which private companies should be expected to comply with rules originally intended for the regulation of public companies. Accounting and auditing requirements provide a good example of this. Until the Companies Act 1908, no companies were required to file accounts with the Registrar of Companies. That Act introduced the distinction between public and private companies and required the former but not the latter to file a statement in the form of a balance sheet. The Companies Act 1948 introduced the further distinction between exempt and non-exempt private companies and required all companies other than exempt private companies to file accounts. The Companies Act 1967, following the recommendations of the Jenkins Committee, abolished the distinction between exempt and non-exempt private companies. Indeed the Jenkins Committee had recommended that there should be no distinction in the Companies Acts between the treatment of public and private companies.

The political attitude of governments to regulation of business has changed in the past 20 years. In the 1980s the Government has been concerned to ensure that the regulatory burden borne by smaller businesses is reasonable. This policy was described in the White Paper, 'Lifting the Burden' (see Cmnd 9571, July 1985):

'. . . for the best of motives, regulations have grown over the years to a stage where many of them are too heavy a drain on our national resources. To the extent that regulations go further than necessary, there were lower profits for firms or raised prices, or both. Output and employment will tend to be lower. Regulations can also stifle competition and deter new firms from entering the market or prevent others from expanding. Too many people in central and local Government spend too much of their time regulating the activities of others. Some regulations were framed a century and more ago, have been added to or amended, and now bear little relevance to the modern business world. Other regulations are too complex and confusing even to professional advisors (and sometimes to the people who administer them, too). Many regulations are necessary and it is, of course, Government's responsibility to ensure that flexibility and freedom are not abused by those who would flout the proper interests of customers, consumers and employees. We must maintain our quality of life, but we have to strike the right balance.'

In response to the Government's initiatives, a large number of organisations have made representations concerning the need to reduce the burden of company law on smaller companies. In particular, the Institute of Directors commissioned Dr L. S. Sealy, fellow of Gonville and Caius College Cambridge, to produce a comprehensive report on existing problems and opportunities for reform. Subsequently, the Institute of Directors published its recommendations for deregulation for small private companies. It recommended that legislation should be introduced to provide for an elective regime by which companies could opt out of provisions of the Companies Act 1985 and related legislation which do not affect the interests of parties external to the company and which are redundant to its internal purposes. It further recommended that the most effective initial step towards an elective regime would be to clarify the law to ensure the full equivalence of a unanimous resolution in writing to any other form of resolution required by the Companies Act 1985.

It is ideas of this sort which are reflected in that portion of the 1989 Act which deals with the deregulation of private companies.

9.2   Written resolutions

Section 113 of the 1989 Act inserts three new sections (381A, 381B, 382A) in the Companies Act 1985.

New section 381A provides that, in the case of a private company, anything which may be done by resolution of the company in general meeting or by resolution of a meeting of any class of members may be done by written resolution without a meeting and without any previous notice. This resolution in writing must be signed by or on behalf of all the members of the company who at the date of the resolution would be entitled to attend and vote at such a meeting. The signatures themselves need not be on a single document provided that each is on a document which accurately states the terms of the resolution. The date of the resolution is the date on which the resolution is signed by or on behalf of the last member to sign. A resolution in writing agreed in this way is to have effect as if it has been passed by the company in general meeting or by the relevant class of members at a meeting. Any reference in any enactment to the date of passing of a resolution in respect of a resolution in writing applies to the date of the resolution as defined above except in the case where the special arrangement concerning auditors set up in section 381B (see below) applies. A resolution may be agreed in writing even though the Companies Acts require it to be passed as a special extraordinary or elective resolution – new section 381A.

There are however two specific exemptions from the power to resolve matters in writing. These are resolutions under section 303 of the Companies Act 1985 to remove a director before the expiration of his period of office and resolutions under section 391 of the Companies Act 1985 removing an auditor before the expiration of his term of office – section 114 inserting new Schedule 15A in the 1985 Act.

As a result of recognising the possibility of resolutions in writing, a number of adaptations are made to general procedural requirements. These are also set out in the new Schedule 15A which is inserted in the 1985 Act. They deal in the main with cases in which the Companies Act 1985 requires that statements or other documents should be made available to members attending meetings to consider particular types of resolutions – Part II of new Schedule 15A.

9.3   Rights of auditors

New section 381B provides that a company's auditors are to be provided with a copy of any written resolution which it is proposed should be agreed to in accordance with new section 381A. If the resolution concerns the auditors, they may within seven days from the date on which they receive the copy of the written resolution give notice to the company stating their opinion that the resolution should be considered by the company in general meeting or, if appropriate, by a meeting of the relevant class of members of the company – new section 381B(1), (2).

A written resolution shall not have effect unless the auditors notify the company that in their opinion the resolution does not concern them as auditors or that, although it does concern them, it need not be considered by the company in general meeting or by a meeting of a class of members. Alternatively, if the period during which the auditors may give this notice expires without any notice having been given, the written resolution will have effect. Any written resolution previously agreed to in accordance with new section 381A is not to have effect until the notification is given or the period expires – new section 381B(3), (4).

These provisions have effect in spite of any provision of the company's memorandum or articles of association. Further, they do not affect any provision of law concerning things done other than by passing a resolution or cases in which a resolution is treated as having been passed or a person is precluded from alleging that a resolution has not been duly passed – new section 381C.

When a written resolution has effect as if agreed by the company in general meeting, a record of the resolution is to be entered in the company's minute book in the same way as minutes of the proceedings of general meetings of the company. Any such record, if signed by a director or by their company secretary is to be evidence of the proceedings, and until the contrary is proved, it will be deemed that the requirements of sections 381A and 381B have been complied with. The normal penalties relating to failures to comply with rules concerning minutes of meetings and a section of minutes will apply in respect of records of written resolutions – new section 382A.

9.4 Elective regime

Section 116 of the 1989 Act inserts a new section (379A) in the Companies Act 1985. This new section provides that the members of a private company may elect by resolution in general meeting to dispense with certain of the requirements of company law. Such a resolution is called an 'elective resolution' – new section 379A(1).

An elective resolution does not have effect unless at least twenty one days' notice in writing is given of the meeting. The notice must state that an elective resolution is to be proposed and set out its terms. The resolution must be agreed to at the meeting in person or by proxy by all the members entitled to attend and vote at the meeting. An elective resolution may be revoked by the company at any time by means of an ordinary resolution and, in any case, an elective resolution ceases to have effect if the company is re-registered as a public company. Elective resolutions may be passed notwithstanding any contrary provision in the company's articles of association – new section 379A(2)–(5).

Elective resolutions must be registered with the Registrar of Companies in accordance with section 380 of the 1985 Act – section 116(3).

At present, elective resolutions may only deal with the following general provisions of the 1985 Act:

– Election concerning the duration of authority to allot shares.

- Election to dispense with the laying of accounts and reports before general meetings.
- Election to dispense with holding of annual general meetings.
- Election as to majorities required to authorise short notice of meetings.
- Election to dispense with appointment of auditors annually.

Section 115 of the 1989 Act defines the extent of these elections in greater detail.

Section 115 of the 1989 Act introduces a new section (80A) into the 1985 Act dealing with elections by private companies as to the duration of authority to allot shares. Section 80 of the Companies Act 1985 provides that directors may not allot securities of the company unless they are authorised to do so by the company in general meeting or by the company's articles. Any such authority must state the maximum amount of relevant securities that may be allotted under it and the date on which it would expire, which is subject to a maximum of five years.

New section 80A provides that a private company may pass an elective resolution authorising the directors to allot shares to a maximum amount but stating that the authority is for either an indefinite period or a fixed period. The period under new section 80A may be longer than five years (the maximum period allowed by section 80) but must state the date on which it expires. An authority given in this form may be revoked or varied by the company in general meeting. Authority is given for a fixed period to be renewed by the company in general meeting. Any such renewal resolution must state the amount of the relevant securities which may be allotted under the authority or the amount remaining to be allotted under the authority. It must also state whether the authority is renewed for an indefinite period or for a fixed period, in which case the date on which the renewed authority expires must be stated – new section 80A(1)–(5).

If an election under new section 80A ceases to have effect (for example if the company is re-registered as a public company) then any authority in force at that time which was given for an indefinite period or for a fixed period of more than five years shall have effect as if it had been given for a fixed period of only five years. In effect, any authority given five years or more before the election ceases to have effect and expires forthwith – new section 80A(7).

As far as Annual General Meetings are concerned, a new section (366A) is introduced in the 1985 Act enabling private companies to elect to dispense with the holding of Annual General Meetings. Such an election is effective for the year in which it is made and subsequent years but does not affect any existing liability as a result of a default in holding an Annual General Meeting. In any year in which an Annual General Meeting would be required to be held but for the election and in which no such meeting has been held, any shareholder of the company may by notice not later than three months before the end of the year require the holding of an Annual General Meeting in that year. If the election ceases to have effect (for example, if the company is re-registered as a public company) and less than three months of the year remain, the company is not under an obligation to hold an Annual General Meeting in that year. This would not affect any obligation of the company to hold an Annual General Meeting in accordance with a notice given by a shareholder in accordance with new section 366A(3) – new section 366A.

As for elections concerning majorities required to authorise short notice of meetings, section 115 of the 1989 Act provides that the normal percentage for approving short notice (95%) may be reduced by a private company by an elective resolution to any percentage not lower than 90% – section 115(3).

Finally, as far as the appointment of auditors is concerned, new section 386 of the Companies Act 1985 (inserted by section 119) provides that a private company may elect to dispense with the obligation to appoint auditors annually. When such an election is in force, the auditors are deemed to be re-appointed for each succeeding financial year unless a resolution is passed under section 250, as a result of which the company is exempt from the obligation to appoint auditors, or a resolution is passed under section 393 to the effect that the appointment of the auditors should be brought to an end. If the election ceases to be in force (perhaps because the company is re-registered as a public company) the auditors then holding office continue to hold office until the next date on which the appointment of auditors would be considered in accordance with the normal rules. These rules are described in greater detail in Chapter 10.

Section 117 of the 1989 Act gives the Secretary of State power to make regulations enabling private companies to pass elective resolutions dispensing with compliance with further requirements of the Act.

9.5 Commencement

The DTI expects that these provisions will be implemented with effect from March 1990.

Chapter 10

Appointment and removal of auditors

10.1 Background

The principal purpose of the changes which are effected by sections 113–117 of the 1989 Act in respect of the appointment and removal of auditors is threefold. Firstly, the changes implement the consequential amendments necessary following the introduction of an elective regime for private companies. Secondly, a number of changes are made in respect of the disclosure of the remuneration of firms acting as auditors. Thirdly, changes are made to deal with comments made in various Department of Trade and Industry inspectors' reports on the procedures applying to auditors leaving office.

10.2 Appointment of auditors

Section 119 of the 1989 Act inserts a number of new sections (384, 385, 385A, 386, 387) in the 1985 Act in place of old section 384. These new sections became necessary with the introduction of powers by which private companies may dispense with Annual General Meetings and the formal recognition of written resolutions.

New section 384 repeats the requirement for every company to appoint an auditor or auditors subject to section 250 of the 1985 Act by which a dormant private company may make itself exempt from the obligation to appoint auditors. In general auditors are to be appointed at general meetings at which accounts are laid (under new section 385) except in the case of private companies which have elected to dispense with the laying of accounts, in which case the provisions in new section 385A apply – new section 384.

At each general meeting at which accounts are laid, any public company and any private company which has not elected to dispense with the laying of accounts must appoint an auditor or auditors to hold office from the conclusion of that meeting until the conclusion of the next general meeting at which accounts are laid. The first auditors of such a company may be appointed by the directors at any time before the first general meeting of the company at which accounts are laid and hold office until the end of that first general meeting. If the directors fail to appoint the first auditors of a company, the appointment may be made by the company in general meeting – new section 385.

Any company which has dispensed with the laying of accounts in general meeting must appoint auditors before the end of the period of 28 days beginning with the day on which copies of the company's annual accounts for the previous financial year are sent to members. Alternatively, if notice is given under section 253(2) requiring the laying of the accounts before the company in general meeting, the auditors must be appointed before the conclusion of that meeting. Once appointed the auditors are to hold office either from the end of the period for appointing them or the conclusion of the meeting at which they are appointed until the end of the time for appointing auditors for the next financial year – new section 385A(1), (2).

The first auditors of a company which has dispensed with the laying of accounts in general meeting may be appointed by the directors at any time before the end of the period of 28 days beginning with the day on which copies of the company's first annual accounts are sent to members under section 238, or if notice is given requiring the laying of accounts before the company in general meeting, the beginning of that meeting. Once appointed the auditors are to hold office until the end of the period of 28 days or the end of that meeting – new section 385A(3). If directors fail to appoint the first auditors, these powers may be exercised by the company in general meeting – new section 385A(4).

Auditors who hold office at the time an election is made to dispense with the laying of accounts before the company in general meeting, are to continue to hold office until the end of the time for appointing auditors for the next financial year. The company in general meeting may however decide otherwise. Auditors holding office when such an election ceases to have effect are to continue to hold office until the conclusion of the next general meeting of the company at which accounts are laid – new section 385A(5).

Although the general rule for companies is that auditors are to be appointed on an annual basis, as explained in Chapter 9 a private company may elect (by elective resolution in accordance with new section 379A) to dispense with the obligation to appoint auditors annually. When such an election is in force, the company's auditors are deemed to be re-appointed each year, unless a resolution is passed under section 250 of the 1985 Act so that the company is exempt from the obligation to appoint auditors (i.e. because it is dormant), or a resolution is passed under section 393 of the 1985 Act bringing their appointment to an end. If the election ceases to be in force, the auditors in post either continue in office to the end of the next general meeting at which accounts are laid or, if the company has dispensed with the laying of accounts, until the end of the time for appointing auditors for the next financial year (under new section 385A) – new section 386.

If no auditors are appointed, re-appointed or deemed to be re-appointed before the end of the time for appointing auditors, the Secretary of State may appoint a person to fill the vacancy. Within one week of the end of the time for appointing auditors, the company must give notice to the Secretary of State of his power having become exercisable. New section 387 provides for the penalties which may be applied if a company fails to comply with this.

A casual vacancy in the office of auditor may be filled by the directors or by the company in general meeting. While such a vacancy continues, any surviving or continuing auditors may continue to act. Special notice is required for a resolution at a general meeting of the company filling a casual vacancy in the office of auditor or re-appointing as auditor a retiring auditor who was appointed by the directors to fill a casual vacancy. If the company receives notice of such an intended resolution, the company is obliged to send a copy of it forthwith to the person proposed to be appointed and if the casual vacancy was caused by the resignation of an auditor, to the auditor who resigned – new section 388.

Special provisions apply to the appointment of auditors in cases where the exemptions for dormant companies under section 250 of the 1985 Act cease to apply – new section 388A.

10.3 Rights of auditors

Section 120 of the 1989 Act inserts new sections 389A and 390 in the Companies Act 1985 replacing a number of old sections.

New section 389A brings together material from several old sections of the 1985 Act:

– A right of access at all times to the company's records and a right to require information and explanations to be provided by the company's officers – old section 237(3).
– A right to attend general meetings of the company – old section 387.
– The offence of an officer providing false or misleading information to the auditor – old section 393.
– The obligation of U.K. subsidiaries and their auditors to provide information and explanations to the holding company's auditors – old section 392(1)(a).
– The holding company's obligation to obtain from an overseas subsidiary information required by the holding company's auditors – old section 392(1)(b).

New section 390 entitles a company's auditors to see all notices of and other communications relating to any general meeting which a member of the company is entitled to receive. They may also attend any general meeting of the company and be heard at any general meeting which they attend on any part of the business of the meeting which concerns them as auditors – new section 390(1).

Where it is proposed that a private company should agree to a written resolution under new section 381A the company's auditors are entitled to receive all such communications relating to the resolution as are required to be supplied to a member of the company and to give notice, in accordance with new section 381C, of their opinion that the resolution concerned them as auditors and should be considered by the company in general meeting or by a meeting of the relevant class of members. When such a meeting is held, the auditors are entitled to attend it and, if they attend, to be heard at it on any part of the business which concerns them as auditors. The auditors' right to attend or be heard at a meeting is exercisable in the case of a body corporate or partnership by an individual authorised by it in writing to act as its representative – new section 390.

10.4 Remuneration of auditors

Section 121 of the 1989 Act inserts two new sections (390A and 390B) in the 1985 Act in place of old section 385.

Section 390A provides that the remuneration of auditors appointed by the company in general meeting including their expenses shall be fixed by the company in general meeting or in such manner as the company in general meeting may determine. The remuneration of auditors appointed by the directors or by the Secretary of State may be fixed by the directors or by the Secretary of State. The amount of the remuneration of the company's auditors as such is to be stated in a note to the company's annual accounts. Where this remuneration includes benefits in kind, the nature of such benefits is to be disclosed together with their estimated money value – new section 390A.

There has been some controversy surrounding the DTI's proposal that accounts should disclose to shareholders the amount of all fees paid to their company's auditors irrespective of the nature of the services provided. New section 390B empowers the Secretary of State to make regulations to require the disclosure of the amount of any remuneration received or receivable by a company's auditors or their associates in respect of services other than those of auditors in their capacity as such. The regulations may specify the definition of associates and associated undertakings and may also require the disclosure of remuneration in respect of services rendered to associated undertakings of the company. Auditors may be obliged to disclose this information in their report or alternatively the relevant information may be disclosed in a note to the company's accounts. In such cases, the regulations may require the auditors to supply the directors of the company with such information as is necessary to enable the disclosure to be made – new section 390B.

10.5   Removal and resignation of auditors

Section 122 of the 1989 Act inserts five new sections (391, 391A, 392, 392A, 393) in the Companies Act 1985, in place of old sections 386, 390 and 391.

At any time, a company may remove an auditor from office by ordinary resolution in spite of anything in any agreement between the company and the auditor. Within fourteen days of the general meeting at which such a resolution is passed, the company is required to give notice of that fact in the prescribed form to the Registrar. Notwithstanding his removal, an auditor who has been removed retains the right conferred by new section 390 in relation to any general meeting of the company at which his term of office would have otherwise expired or at which it is proposed to fill the vacancy caused by his removal. In such a case, the references in new section 390 to matters concerning the auditors as auditors are to be construed as references to matters concerning him as a former auditor – new section 391.

Special notice is required for a resolution at a general meeting of a company removing an auditor before the expiration of his term of office or appointing as auditor a person other than a retiring auditor. On receiving notice of such a resolution, the company must send a copy forthwith to the person proposed for removal or the person proposed for appointment and to the retiring auditor. The auditor proposed for removal or the retiring auditor may make representations in writing about the resolution to the company. Unless the representations are received too late, any notice of the resolution given to members of the company must state that the representations have been made and a copy of the representations must be sent to every member of the company to whom notice of the meeting is sent. If a copy is not sent as required the auditor may require that the representations should be read out at the meeting. This does not prejudice the auditor's general right to be heard at the meeting itself. The representations need not be circulated or read at the meeting if the court agrees that the rights conferred by new section 391A are being abused to secure needless publicity for defamatory matter. The court may then order that the company's costs on the application should be paid in whole or part by the auditor – new section 391A.

An auditor may resign his office by depositing a notice in writing at the company's registered office. To be effective, the notice must be accompanied by the statement required by new section 394. An effective notice of resignation brings the auditor's term of office to an end on the date on which the notice is deposited unless the notice specifies a later date – new section 392.

New section 392A deals with what is to happen when an auditor's resignation notice is accompanied by a statement of circumstances which the auditor considers should be brought to the attention of members or creditors of the company. In such cases, the auditor may deposit with the resignation notice a signed requisition calling on the directors of the company to convene an extraordinary general meeting of the company to receive and consider his explanation of the circumstances connected with his resignation. The auditor may also request the company to circulate a statement of these circumstances to its members before the meeting convened on his requisition or before any general meeting at which his term of office would otherwise have expired or at which it is proposed to fill the vacancy caused by his resignation. Unless the statement is received too late, any notice of a meeting given to members of the company must state that the statement has been made and a copy must be sent to every member of the company to whom notice of the meeting is sent. Within 21 days from receiving a requisition the directors must convene a meeting for a date not more than 28 days after the date of the notice convening the meeting – new section 392A(1)–(5).

If the auditor's statement is not circulated, the auditor may require that the statement should be read out at the meeting. The statement need not be circulated or read out if the court agrees that the statement represents an abuse of the provisions of new section 392A to secure needless publicity for defamatory matter – new section 392A(6)–(8).

Where a private company has elected to dispense with the annual appointment of auditors, any member of the company may deposit a written notice at the company's registered office proposing that the auditors' appointment should be brought to an end. No member may deposit more than one such notice in any financial year. On receipt of the notice, the directors must convene a general meeting of the company within 28 days of the date on which the notice was given. At the meeting the directors must propose a resolution enabling the company to decide whether the appointment of the company's auditors should be brought to an end. If the appointment is brought to an end in this way, the auditors shall be deemed not to be re-appointed when next they would be. If the notice is deposited within the period of 14 days immediately following the distribution of the annual accounts, any deemed re-appointment which has already occurred for the financial year following that to which those accounts relate shall cease to have effect. If the directors do not convene a meeting within 14 days from receiving the notice the member who deposited the notice may himself convene the meeting. The meeting is then to be convened as nearly as possible in the same manner as that in which meetings are convened by directors – new section 393.

10.6 Statement on cessation of office

Section 123 of the 1989 Act inserts two new sections (394, 394A) in the 1985 Act.

Where an auditor ceases for any reason to hold office, he is to deposit at the company's registered office a statement of any circumstances connected with his ceasing to hold office which he considers should be brought to the attention of the members or creditors of the company. If he considers that there are no such circumstances, he must deposit a statement that there are none – new section 394(1).

Where an auditor resigns, his notice of resignation must be accompanied by such a statement. Where the auditor fails to seek re-appointment, the statement is to be deposited not less than 14 days before the end of the time allowed for next appointing auditors. In any other case, the statement is to be deposited not later than the end of the period of 14 days beginning with the date on which the auditor ceases to hold office. If the statement indicates circumstances which should be brought to the attention of the members or creditors of the company, the company is within 14 days to send a copy of the auditor's statement to every person who under section 238 is entitled to be sent copies of the accounts. Alternatively the company may apply to the court notifying the auditor of the application. If the auditor does not receive notice of such an application within 21 days, he shall within a further 7 days send a copy of the statement of the Registrar. If the court is satisfied that the auditor is using the statement to secure needless publicity for defamatory matter, it shall order that copies of the auditor's statement need not be sent out. Within 14 days the company is to send a statement setting out the effect of the order to every person who under section 238 is entitled to be sent copies of the accounts. Where the court is not satisfied with the company's application, the company must within 14 days send copies of the auditor's statement to everyone entitled to receive it and must notify the auditor of the decision. Within 7 days the auditor must send a copy of the statement to the Registrar – new section 394.

Failure to comply with new section 394 will render the auditor guilty of an offence and liable to a fine – new section 394A.

10.7   Commencement

The DTI expects that these provisions will be implemented with effect from March 1990.

Chapter 11

Mergers

11.1 Background

In June 1986, the Government launched a review of U.K. competition law and policy, including mergers policy and the merger control provisions of the Fair Trading Act 1973. The period from the beginning of 1984 to the launch of the review in June 1986 had been one of high acquisition and merger activity and there were no signs that the level of activity would decline. Although the numbers of acquisitions and mergers were not exceptionally high, there were a few large acquisitions and total expenditure by U.K. industrial and commercial companies in 1986 had reached £14.9 billion. In constant price terms this exceeded the peaks of the previous acquisition and merger booms of 1968 and 1972 and this high level of merger activity aroused considerable controversy. In recognition of this, the Government decided that it was right to carry out a thorough review of the policy. It was also decided to examine the procedures involved in statutory merger controls and in particular to enquire whether there was scope for shortening the time taken to investigate and reach decisions on individual cases.

Provision for the control of mergers as such was first made in the Monopolies and Mergers Act 1965. That Act was repealed and re-enacted with modifications in the Fair Trading Act 1973. The general scheme of the provisions on mergers is that the Secretary of State for Trade is empowered to refer certain executed and prospective mergers to the Monopolies and Mergers Commission (MMC) which investigates the facts and assesses the effects of the merger against public interest criteria. In the event of the MMC concluding that the merger operates or would operate against the public interest, sanctions are available to terminate or prevent the merger. To assist the Secretary of State in the exercise of his powers, one of the functions of the Director General of Fair Trading established under the 1973 Act is to keep himself informed about actual and prospective mergers and to make recommendations on these matters to the Secretary of State.

The key features of the merger control provisions of the 1973 Act are as follows.

(I) SCOPE

There is a wide definition of the mergers to which statutory merger control applies. Controls apply not simply to public bids for shares but also to transfers of subsidiaries and other enterprises between companies, mergers between private companies, and acquisitions of substantial shareholdings.

(2) QUALIFYING MERGERS

Actual or proposed mergers (including partial shareholdings) qualify for

83

consideration under the Act if they create or enhance a 25% market share or if the value of the assets taken over exceed £30 million. This limit can be varied by statutory instrument.

(3) NOTIFICATION

There is no obligation to notify qualifying mergers to the authorities but the Director General of Fair Trading (the Director General) has a duty to keep himself informed about mergers which may qualify for investigation and to advise the Secretary of State on the steps which should be taken under the Act and in particular a qualifying merger should be referred to the MMC.

(4) REFERENCE

It is the Secretary of State who decides whether to refer a qualifying merger to the MMC, and the 1973 Act gives him a very wide discretion in exercising this power.

(5) INVESTIGATIONS

When a merger is referred, the MMC is required to investigate and report whether the merger operates or may be expected to operate against the public interest. In its investigation, the MMC must take into account 'all matters which appear to them in the particular circumstances to be relevant'. The 1973 Act also specifies a number of matters which the MMC must consider (e.g. the desirability of promoting competition). The MMC are not asked to consider whether the merger would be positively in the public interest, and there is no obligation on the parties to demonstrate the positive benefits arising from the merger (although in practice the parties often seek to do so).

(6) FURTHER ACTION

Unless the MMC concludes that the merger operates or may be expected to operate against the public interest, there are no powers under the Act to prevent the merger or to impose conditions. If the MMC concludes that the merger may be expected to operate against the public interest, the Secretary of State may prohibit the merger, or allow it to proceed subject to conditions. He may also allow the merger to proceed unconditionally despite an adverse MMC finding but, generally, the Secretary of State accepts an adverse finding by the MMC.

As a result of the review, the Government decided that the broad thrust of current merger policies should remain unchanged. Many of those submitting views to the review believed that intervention by the Government should be possible on a number of different grounds other than competition. Such additional grounds included effects on employment, on the regional economic development, on research and on development spending. The Government's view is that none of these additional grounds is one in which the public interest diverges materially from the interests of private sector decision-makers, although in exceptional cases there may be some divergence. Thus the Government sees no case for intervening on a regular basis to prevent firms from carrying through their business decisions on the grounds that those plans may have adverse implications for such matters as employment or research and development.

Nonetheless the Government accepted that there was room for improvement in the procedures of statutory merger control. The main objectives for these improvements are a shortening in the length of time taken by the control procedures and also an improvement in the flexibility and efficiency of their operation. The two major improvements which were proposed by the review and are implemented by the 1989 Act are the introduction of a pre-notification system and a provision for parties to a merger to give statutory undertakings thus obviating a reference to the MMC.

Many other countries have mandatory pre-notification systems, at least for the more important mergers. Such systems are justified by the difficulty of unscrambling a merger once it has been effected.

The review concluded that such a mandatory pre-notification system would be inappropriate in the U.K. It was recognised that a number of potentially qualifying mergers, particularly smaller ones, are not brought to the attention of the Office of Fair Trading by the parties themselves. Subsequently, many of these un-notified mergers come to the notice of the Office of Fair Trading (OFT) as a result of references in the press and by other means. Such cases are investigated and many prove not to qualify under the criteria laid down in the Fair Trading Act. Of those which do, a great majority are found to be straightforward cases with no grounds for reference to the MMC. In practice, it has been comparatively rare for completed mergers to raise issues which justify reference to the MMC. Nevertheless, the review suggested that there was a case for a non-mandatory pre-notification arrangement to facilitate the more rapid and efficient handling of those cases (well over 95%) by enabling the OFT to establish at an early stage that there was no serious ground for contemplating a reference.

The second proposal concerned statutory undertakings. The review recognised that though a proposed merger may pose an obvious threat to competition the parties may be willing to promise to modify the arrangement in such a way that the threat to competition is removed. In fact, the 1973 Act does nothing to prevent parties to a proposed merger from approaching the OFT with possible variants on a merger proposal. The Director General merely has a statutory duty to advise the Secretary of State on any proposal put to him. Indeed the review found that in a few cases, the Director General has advised and the Secretary of State decided against a reference to the MMC explicitly on the understanding, backed by legally binding agreements between the parties, that certain of the assets or activities involved in a merger would be divested. However, the existing legislation is not well designed for this purpose. There is no explicit provision for the Director General to discuss divestments with the parties as an alternative to an MMC reference, nor is there any provision for binding undertakings to be given so that the planned divestments can be carried out. As a result it is not clear what the Secretary of State's sanction would be if divestments were promised but not performed. The merger policy review therefore proposed a change to the 1973 Act to enable the Director General to discuss proposed mergers and accept statutory undertakings in the place of a reference to the MMC.

11.2 Prior notice arrangements

The Companies Act 1989 introduces provisions restricting the power of the Secretary of State to refer a merger to the MMC where prior notice has been given. These provisions are introduced by way of inserting new sections (75A–75F) into the 1973 Act – section 146.

These new sections provide that notice may be given to the Director General of proposed arrangements which might result in the creation of a merger situation qualifying for investigation – new section 75A(1) of the 1973 Act. Such a situation is already defined by section 64 of the 1973 Act as a merger which:

(1) either produces a situation in which at least one quarter of all the goods or services of a particular description which are supplied in the United Kingdom or as a substantial part thereof will be supplied by or to the same person,
(2) or involves a transfer of assets exceeding £30 million in value.

For these purposes, the 1973 Act provides that the determination of when goods or services can be treated as being of a separate description shall be a matter for the Secretary of State to decide in the light of the circumstances of the case.

The person giving the notice of the proposed arrangement is to be specified by regulation as is the prescribed form for the notice. To be effective, the notice must state that the existence of the proposal has been made public – new section 75A(2) of the 1973 Act.

The merger policy review envisaged that the power to specify the form of the notice of a proposed arrangement would be used to require the submission of answers to a standard questionnaire setting out basic information about the transactions and about the businesses involved. Major items of information likely to be required include:

(1) names of companies, all subsidiaries and associated companies,
(2) details of the proposed transaction and its financing,
(3) latest annual accounts of the companies concerned,
(4) statement of the reasons for the proposal and any expected changes in the businesses involved,
(5) main products of the companies, identifying those which compete in the same U.K. market, and of those which are inputs for or bought by the other company,
(6) main competitors in overlapping product markets,
(7) main customers in overlapping product markets,
(8) estimates of U.K. market shares for overlapping products or of products that are inputs for or bought by the other company including the share of imports.

Once the merger notice has been properly given, the Director General is given a period in which to consider the notice. If the proposed arrangements are not referred to the MMC during that period, then no reference may be made after that period in respect of those arrangements or of any qualifying merger situation created as a result of putting those arrangements into effect – new section 75A(3) of the 1973 Act.

The period during which the Director General is to consider the merger lasts for 28 days, beginning on the first working day after he receives the notice and any fee payable has been paid. If the last of these days is not a working day the period ends with the end of the first subsequent working day – new section 75B(2) of the 1973 Act.

When the period begins the Director General is to take appropriate action to bring the following information to the knowledge of those who he believes could be affected if the arrangements are carried into effect:

(1) the existence of the proposal,
(2) the fact that the merger notice has been given, and
(3) the date on which the period for considering the notice may expire – new section 75B(1) of the 1973 Act.

The Director General is provided with three steps which he can take. Firstly, he may extend the period for considering the merger notice by further periods of 14 days. This is to be done by giving notice to the person who originally gave the merger notice. There appears to be no limit to the number of 14-day extensions which may be ordered – new section 75B(3) of the 1973 Act. To be effective, notice of an extension must be given before the end of the period for consideration of the merger notice – new section 75B(5) of the 1973 Act.

Secondly, the Director General may require the person who submitted the merger notice to provide such further information as he specifies within a period that he may also specify – new section 75B(4) of the 1973 Act. To be effective, any such notice must be given to the person who gave the merger notice before the end of the period for considering that notice – new section 75B(5) of the 1973 Act.

Finally, at any time before the period for consideration expires, the Director General may reject the merger notice if:

(1) he suspects that any information given in respect of the notified arrangements by the person who gave the notice is in any material respect false or misleading, or
(2) any prescribed information is not given in the merger notice or in response to a subsequent notice within the period specified in that notice – new section 75B(6) of the 1973 Act.

If the period for consideration of the notice expires without any reference being made to the MMC, then no reference may be made to the MMC with respect to the notified arrangements or to the creation of a qualifying merger situation as a result of putting those arrangements into effect. However, a reference to the MMC may still be made if:

(1) before the end of the period for consideration of the merger notice the merger notice is rejected by the Director General under new section 75B(6) – new section 75C(1)(a) of the 1973 Act,
(2) before the end of the period for consideration of the merger notice, any of the enterprises to which the notified arrangements relate cease to be distinct from each other – new section 75C(1)(b) of the 1973 Act. In general terms enterprises are regarded as ceasing to be distinct enterprises if either they are bought under common ownership or common control or one of them ceases to be carried on at all in consequence of an arrangement or a transaction entered into to prevent competition between them – section 65 of the Fair Trading Act 1973,
(3) any information material to the arrangements (whether it had been prescribed or not) is not disclosed to the Secretary of State or the Director General before the end of the period for considering the merger notice – new section 75C(1)(c) of the 1973 Act,
(4) at any time after the merger notice has been given but before the enterprises to which the notified arrangements relate cease to be distinct from each other, any of those enterprises ceases to be distinct from any enterprise other than an enterprise to which those arrangements relate – new section 75C(1)(d) of the 1973 Act,
(5) within a period of six months beginning with the end of the period for considering the merger notice the enterprises to which the merger notice relates do not cease to be distinct from each other (i.e. the proposed arrangements are not put into effect) – new section 75C(1)(e) of the 1973 Act,

(6) the merger notice is withdrawn – new section 75C(1)(f) of the 1973 Act,
(7) any information given by the person who gave the original merger notice is in any material respect false or misleading. This applies irrespective of whether the information concerned was given in the merger notice or otherwise – new section 75C(1)(g) of the 1973 Act.

It may also be possible to make a reference to the MMC in respect of certain linked transactions. Under existing legislation the Secretary of State may refer a merger to the MMC within six months of the merger taking place (i.e. of the enterprises ceasing to be distinct) – section 64(4) of the Fair Trading Act 1973. For this purpose, the Secretary of State may treat successive events within a two-year period as having all happened on the date of the latest of them – section 66(1) of the Fair Trading Act 1973. In circumstances where section 66(1) applies, and the latest of the transactions concerned could have been the subject of a reference to the MMC notwithstanding new section 75A(3), a reference to the MMC can be made in respect of any of the transactions which actually occurred less than six months before:

(1) the date of the latest transactions (i.e. the date on which all transactions are to be regarded under section 66(1) as having occurred), or
(2) the actual occurrence of another of those transactions with respect to which such a reference may be made – new section 75C(2) of the 1973 Act.

In determining when a transaction occurred, account shall only be taken of options or other conditional rights when the option is exercised or the condition satisfied – new section 75C(3) of the 1973 Act.

Extensive powers are given to the Secretary of State to specify the practical implementation of these procedures by way of regulation – new section 75D of the 1973 Act. He may also amend new sections 75B to 75D by regulations to determine the effect of giving a merger notice and the steps to be taken by any person in connection with such a notice – new section 75F of the 1973 Act.

11.3 Statutory undertakings

The Companies Act 1989 introduces provisions enabling the Secretary of State to accept undertakings in place of a reference to the MMC. These provisions are introduced by way of new sections (75G–75K) in the Fair Trading Act 1973 – section 106. Provisions concerning the enforcement of such undertakings are also introduced as a new section (93A) of the 1973 Act – section 107.

The Secretary of State's new power to accept statutory undertakings instead of making a reference to the MMC will apply where:

(1) he has a power to make reference to the MMC under section 64 or 75 of the Fair Trading Act 1973,
(2) the Director General has made a recommendation that such a reference should be made, and
(3) the Director General has either at the time of that recommendation or subsequently advised the Secretary of State that the creation of the merger situation qualifying for investigation would have particular effects adverse to the public interest – new section 75G(1) of the 1973 Act.

In these circumstances, instead of making a merger reference to the MMC, the Secretary of State will be empowered to accept from the parties concerned undertakings that they will take the steps which the Secretary of State considers appropriate to remedy or prevent the effects adverse to the public interest – new section 75G(1) of the 1973 Act.

To be effective, the undertakings must provide for one or more of the following:

(1) the division of a business by the sale of any part of the undertaking or assets or otherwise. For this purpose, all the activities carried on by way of business by any one person or by any two or more bodies corporate may be treated as a single business – new section 75G(2)(a) of the 1973 Act,

(2) the division of a group of interconnected bodies corporate – new section 75G(2)(b) of the 1973 Act,

(3) the separation by the sale of any part of the undertaking or assets concerned or by other means, of enterprises which are under common control even though they are not enterprises of interconnected bodies corporate – new section 75G(2)(c) of the 1973 Act.

Apart from these essential matters, the undertakings may also provide for:

(1) the prevention or restriction of actions which might prevent or impede the division or separation – new section 75G(3)(a) of the 1973 Act,

(2) the carrying on of any activities or the safeguarding of assets until that division or separation is effected – new section 75G(3)(b) of the 1973 Act,

(3) any matters necessary to affect or take account of the division or separation – new section 75G(3)(c) of the 1973 Act,

(4) enabling the Secretary of State to ascertain whether the undertakings are fulfilled – new section 75G(3)(d) of the 1973 Act.

If he accepts undertakings under these provisions the Secretary of State may not make a reference of the MMC in respect of a merger situation which was the subject of those undertakings – new section 75G(4) of the 1973 Act. This restriction does not apply, however, if material facts about the arrangements or proposed arrangements were not notified to the Secretary of State (or the Director General) or made public, before the undertakings were accepted – new section 75G(5) of the 1973 Act. For this purpose 'made public' means so publicised as to be generally known or readily ascertainable – section 64(9) of the Fair Trading Act 1973.

Once he has accepted undertakings in place of a reference to the MMC, the Secretary of State is required to arrange for their publication together with the advice given by the Director General for the purpose of new section 75G(1)(c), and any variation or release of the undertakings – new section 75H(1) of the 1973 Act. In arranging for such publication, the Secretary of State is required by new section 75H(3) to exclude from the advice published under new section 75H(1):

(1) any matter relating to the private affairs of an individual where the Secretary of State or the Director General considers that individual's interest would or might be seriously and prejudicially affected by publication – new section 75H(4)(a) of the 1973 Act,

(2) any matter relating specifically to the affairs of a particular body of persons whether corporate or unincorporate where the Secretary of State or the Director General considers that those persons' interests would or might be seriously and prejudicially affected by publication unless in the view of the Secretary of State or the Director General the inclusion of this matter is

essential for the purposes of the advice – new section 75H(4)(b) of the 1973 Act,

(3) any other matter if the Secretary of State is satisfied that its publication would be against the public interest – new section 75H(3)(b) of the 1973 Act.

In giving his advice for the purposes of new section 75G(1)(c), the Director General is to have regard to the need for excluding, as far as practicable, any of the matters mentioned above relating to the affairs of individuals or a body of persons corporate or unincorporate – new section 75H(2) of the 1973 Act.

Once an undertaking has been accepted by the Secretary of State, the Director General is required to keep under review the carrying out of that undertaking and to consider from time to time whether changes in circumstances have rendered the undertaking no longer appropriate. In such an event he is to consider whether the parties may be released from the undertaking or whether it should be varied or superseded by a new undertaking – new section 75J(a) of the 1973 Act. If the Director General believes that the undertaking has not been fulfilled, that a person can be released from the undertaking or that the undertaking needs to be varied or superseded, the Director General is to give the appropriate advice to the Secretary of State – new section 75J(b) of the 1973 Act. If an undertaking has not been fulfilled, the Secretary of State may take steps to remedy or prevent the adverse effects of the merger which were identified in the original advice given by the Director General – new section 75K(1)–(2) of the 1973 Act. In doing this, the Secretary of State is to take into account any advice he has received from the Director General under section 75J(b) on the fulfilment of the undertakings – new section 75K(3) of the 1973 Act. The provisions contained in any order made by the Secretary of State may be different from those contained in the original undertaking which has not been fulfilled – new section 75K(4) of the 1973 Act. Any such order has the effect that the undertaking which has not been fulfilled and any other relevant undertaking accepted under section 75G of the 1973 Act are released – new section 75K(5) of the 1973 Act.

The next steps which can be taken by the Secretary of State are set out in Schedule 20 to the 1989 Act as new paragraphs to be inserted in Schedule 8 to the Fair Trading Act 1973. These powers enable the Secretary of State to make an order by statutory instrument by which:

(1) a person supplying goods or services may be required to publish accounting information relating to the supply of the goods and services. He may also be required to publish information relating to the quantities of goods or services supplied or the geographical areas in which they are supplied. The exact nature of the information to be published is to be specified or described in the order. The term 'accounting information' relates to the costs of the supply including fixed costs and overheads, the manner in which fixed costs and overheads are calculated and apportioned for accounting purposes and the income attributable to the supply – new paragraph 9A of Schedule 8 to the 1973 Act,

(2) any person is required to provide any information to the Director General as may be specified by the order – new paragraph 12A of Schedule 8 to the 1973 Act,

(3) any activities are required to be carried on separately from any other activities – new paragraph 12B of Schedule 8 to the 1973 Act,

(4) the exercise of any right to vote exercisable by virtue of the holding of any shares, stocks or securities is prohibited or restricted – new paragraph 12C of Schedule 8 to the 1973 Act.

Any failure to fulfil an undertaking under new section 75G may become the subject of civil proceedings which may be brought by any person (i.e. not merely the Secretary of State or the Director General). For this purpose, an undertaking is to be regarded as if any obligation had been imposed by an order under section 90 of the Fair Trading Act 1973 – new section 93A(2) of the 1973 Act.

These enforcement provisions are extended to undertakings accepted after the commencement of the new section 93A:

(1) under section 88 of the 1973 Act (which deals with undertakings accepted by the appropriate minister after the MMC has produced a negative report on a monopoly or merger reference),
(2) under section 4 of the Competition Act 1980 (this concerns undertakings accepted by the Director General after he has reported on an anti-competitive practice), and
(3) under section 9 of the Competition Act 1980 (i.e. undertakings accepted by the Director General after an MMC report on a competition reference) – new section 93A(1) of the 1973 Act.

11.4 Restrictions on share dealings

The Companies Act 1989 introduces restrictions on share dealings in the context of a merger situation by way of inserting new subsections (4A)–(4L) into section 75 of the Fair Trading Act 1973 – section 149.

Share dealings are restricted temporarily where a reference to the MMC is made. This restriction applies to anyone carrying on an enterprise to which the reference to the MMC relates or having control of such an enterprise or to any subsidiary of his or to any person associated with him or to any subsidiary of such a person. The restriction is that for a period it would be unlawful for such a person to acquire directly or indirectly without the consent of the Secretary of State an interest in shares in a company if that company carries on or controls any enterprise to which the reference relates – new section 75(4A) of the 1973 Act.

For these purposes the circumstances in which a person acquires an interest in shares include the following:

(1) he enters into a contract to acquire the shares whether or not for cash,
(2) not being a registered holder he acquires a right to exercise or to control the exercise of any right conferred by the holding of the shares, or
(3) he acquires a right to call for delivery of the shares to himself or to his order or to acquire an interest in the shares or assumes an obligation to acquire such an interest – new section 75(4F) of the 1973 Act.

Such circumstances do not include any acquisition of an interest in pursuance of an obligation assumed before the announcement by the Secretary of State of the merger reference – new section 75(4F) of the 1973 Act. The circumstances do include cases in which the person acquires a right or assumes an obligation, the exercise or fulfillment of which would give him a right to exercise or control the exercise of a right conferred by holding the shares. They do not, however, include circumstances where he is appointed as proxy to vote at a specified meeting of a company or class of a company's members – new section 75(4G) of the 1973 Act.

The period during which this restriction applies begins with the announcement by the Secretary of State of the making of the merger reference and ends:

(1) when the reference is laid aside,
(2) where the time allowed to the MMC for making a report on the reference expires without a report having been made,
(3) at the end of the day on which the report is laid before Parliament where the MMC's report does not conclude that the proposed merger would have certain effects which would be adverse to the public interest, or
(4) if the MMC's report includes such conclusions, at the end of a period of 40 days beginning with the day on which it is so laid – new section 75(4B) of the 1973 Act.

For these purposes if a report is laid before each House of Parliament on different days, it is the earlier date which counts – new section 75(4B) of the 1973 Act.

If he consents to any share dealings the Secretary of State may make his consent general or special, he may revoke his consent and he should ensure that it is published unless he considers publication to be unnecessary – new section 75 (4C) of the 1973 Act.

The enforcement provisions of section 93 of the 1973 Act apply to any contravention of these restrictions – new section 75(4D) of the 1973 Act.

11.5 Obtaining control by stages

The Companies Act 1989 introduces a new section (66A) into the Fair Trading Act 1973 to enable a merger reference to the MMC to be made even where control of a company is obtained in stages – section 150.

The new section applies to any transaction:

(1) which enables a person or group of persons directly or indirectly:
   – to control or to influence materially the policy of any person carrying on a particular enterprise,
   – to do so to a greater degree, or
(2) which is a step (direct or indirect) towards enabling that person or group of persons to do so,
(3) whereby that person or group of persons acquires a controlling interest in the enterprise – new section 66A(2) of the 1973 Act.

Where an enterprise is brought under the control of a person or group of persons by a series of such transactions (i.e. two or more) the Secretary of State or the MMC may regard those transactions as if they occurred simultaneously on the date of the latest transaction – new section 66A(1) of the 1973 Act. In doing this, if a controlling interest has been acquired (i.e. a transaction described in new section 66A(2)(b) has taken place) no later transaction is to be taken into account – new section 66A(3) of the 1973 Act. At the same time, if the series of transactions extends over a period of more than two years, only those transactions which occur within a period of two years may be taken into account – new section 66A(4) of the 1973 Act.

The normal provisions of the Fair Trading Act 1973 apply for deciding when an enterprise is brought under the control of a person or group of persons – new section 66A(5) of the 1973 Act.

11.6 False or misleading information

The Companies Act 1989 introduces a new section (93B) into the Fair Trading Act 1973 concerning the provision of false or misleading information – section

151. A person commits an offence if he knowingly or recklessly furnishes information to the Secretary of State, the Director General or the MMC (in connection with their functions under the 1973 Act and the Competition Act 1980) which is false or misleading in a material respect – new section 93B(1) of the 1973 Act. A person would also be guilty of an offence if he knowingly or recklessly provided such deficient information to another person knowing that it would then be furnished to the Secretary of State, Director General or the MMC in similar situations – new section 95B(2) of the 1973 Act.

11.7   Fees

The Secretary of State is empowered to make regulations requiring the payment to him or the Director General of fees in respect of their functions under the merger control provisions of the Fair Trading Act 1973 – section 110.

11.8   Commencement

Sections 147 to 150 of the 1989 Act (together with the relevant parts of Schedule 20 and section 153) have effect from the date of Royal Assent, i.e. 16 November 1989 – section 215(1)(b). The remainder of these provisions are expected to be brought into effect in April 1990.

Chapter 12

Financial markets and insolvency

12.1 Introduction

A number of amendments to the Financial Services Act 1986 have been introduced to deal with concerns about the effect of insolvency law upon the operation of financial markets. The principal concern is that if the normal provisions of insolvency law operate in respect of certain market obligations of people involved in investment business, there would be a risk to the integrity of those markets as a result of uncertainty about their reliability. These new provisions deal with a number of areas, in particular: the insolvency, winding up or default of a person who is party to certain market transactions, the effectiveness of charges given to secure obligations in connection with such transactions, and rights in relation to property provided as cover for margin in relation to such transactions.

12.2 Recognised investment exchanges and clearing houses

The 1989 Act defines a category of 'market contracts' to which the new provisions apply. In relation to a recognised investment exchange, a market contract is a contract entered into by a member or designated non-member of the exchange which is subject to the rules of the exchange. Market contracts also include a contract subject to the rules of the exchange entered into by the exchange itself for the purpose of provision of clearing services. A person in respect of whom action may be taken under the default rules of the exchange but who is not himself a member of the exchange is a designated non-member for these purposes – section 155(2).

As far as recognised clearing houses are concerned, any contract subject to the rules of the clearing house and entered into by the clearing house for the purposes of or in connection with the provision of clearing services for a recognised investment exchange is a market contract – section 155(3).

The effect of the new provisions is to introduce additional requirements which must be satisfied both by investment exchanges and by clearing houses if they are to be recognised – section 156. In effect these additional requirements oblige such bodies to have default rules which, in the event of a member of the exchange appearing to be unable to meet his obligations in respect of certain market contracts, enables action to be taken in respect of unsettled market contracts to which he is a party – Schedule 21.

In the case of investment exchanges, the default rules must provide for the discharge of all rights and liabilities between those who are party as principal to unsettled market contracts to which the defaulter is party as principal. The rules must also provide for the determination of the amount to be paid by one party to the other. The sums to be payable in respect of different contracts between the same parties are to be aggregated or set off to produce a net sum. This amount is to be certified by or on behalf of the exchange of the net sum payable or, if appropriate, of the fact that no sum is payable – Schedule 21.

In the case of clearing houses, the rules must provide for the discharge of all rights and liabilities of the defaulter under or in respect of unsettled market contracts, and for the determination of the sum of money to be paid by or to the defaulter. The sums payable by or to the defaulter for different contracts are to be aggregated and set off to produce a net sum. If that sum is payable by the defaulter to the clearing house it is to be set off against any property provided by or on behalf of the defaulter as cover for margin so as to produce a further net sum. If the amount is payable by the clearing house to the defaulter, it is to be aggregated with any property provided by or on behalf of the defaulter as cover for margin or the proceeds of realisation of such property. Finally, the rules are to provide for the certification by or on behalf of the clearing house of the sum finally payable – Schedule 21.

Having provided for the introduction of default rules the 1989 Act then deals with the application of the general law of insolvency in relation to market contracts and action taken by recognised investment exchanges or recognised clearing houses in respect of such contracts.

Effectively, market contracts, the default rules of recognised investment exchanges or recognised clearing houses and the rules of such bodies concerning the settlement of market contracts not dealt with under their default rules, are not to be regarded as invalid at law simply on the grounds of inconsistency with insolvency law – section 159(1). Further, the powers of office holders and of the court under the Insolvency Act 1986 are not to be exercised in a way which prevents or interferes with the settlement of a market contract falling outside the default rules of a recognised investment exchange or clearing house or any action taken under the default rules of such a body – section 159(2). Further, any person in control of any assets of a defaulter or in control of documents relating to a defaulter is obliged to give a recognised investment exchange or clearing house the assistance it requires for proceedings under its default rules. Such a person need not provide information or documents which he may refuse to provide on grounds of legal professional privilege in proceedings in the High Court. Any original documents provided under these provisions are to be returned forthwith after the completion of the default proceedings – section 160.

On the completion of proceedings under its default rules, a recognised investment exchange or clearing house is to report to the Secretary of State. For each creditor or debtor, the report must mention the sum certified by the body concerned to be payable from or to the defaulter. A copy of every such report is to be provided to the defaulter himself and to any relevant office holder acting in relation to him or his estate. Notice of the receipt of these reports is to be published by the Secretary of State to bring the reports to the attention of creditors and debtors of the defaulter – section 162.

12.3 Other exchanges and clearing houses

The Secretary of State is given power to make regulations applying all these provisions to contracts involved with an overseas investment exchange or clearing house which is approved by him. He may not approve an overseas investment exchange or clearing house unless he is satisfied that the rules and practices of the body, together with the law of the country in which the body's head office is situated, provide adequate procedures for dealing with the default of persons party to contracts connected with the body – section 170.

Similarly, these provisions may also be extended to cover contracts of any specified description in relation to which settlement arrangements are provided by people included on a list maintained by the Bank of England – section 171.

12.4   Market charges

For these purposes, a 'market charge' is a charge whether fixed or floating which is granted:

(1) in favour of a recognised investment exchange for the purpose of securing debts or liabilities arising in connection with the settlement of market contracts,
(2) in favour of a recognised clearing house for the purpose of securing debts or liabilities arising in connection with their ensuring the performance of market contracts,
(3) in favour of a person who agrees to make payments as a result of the transfer of specified securities made through the medium of a computer-based system established by the Bank of England and The Stock Exchange for the purpose of securing debts or liabilities of the transferee arising in connection with the transfer – section 173(1).

In effect, the 1989 Act provides that market charges are to be effective notwithstanding the general provisions of insolvency law. The particular operation of these provisions is to be dealt with in regulations to be made in due course by the Secretary of State – section 174.

12.5   Market property

Finally, provisions are made in respect of the application by recognised investment exchanges and clearing houses of property (other than land) held by them as margin in relation to a market contract. In effect, the 1989 Act provides that, to the extent that it is necessary to enable the property to be applied in accordance with the rules of the exchange or clearing house, it may be applied notwithstanding any prior equitable interest or right, or any right or remedy arising from the breach of fiduciary duty, unless the exchange or clearing house have notice of the interest right or breach of duty at the time the property was provided as margin. No right or remedy arising subsequently could lead to the property being provided as margin being enforced to prevent or interfere with the application of the property by the exchange or clearing house in accordance with its rules – section 177.

A number of detailed provisions are made to clarify the effect of this general provision. For example, where property subject to an unpaid vendor's lien becomes subject to a market charge, the market charge is to have priority over the lien unless the chargee had actual notice of the lien at the time the property became subject to the charge – section 179.

Power is given to the Secretary of State to make regulations concerning the extent and detailed application of these particular provisions – section 181.

12.6   Commencement

It is expected that these provisions will be implemented by July 1990.

Chapter 13

Financial Services Act

13.1 Introduction

The regime of investment business regulation which was introduced by the Financial Services Act 1986 has been much criticised. In principle, the system was designed to produce a series of sensitive regulations which in each case would be appropriate to those risks which needed to be controlled. The Securities and Investments Board (SIB) would develop its rule book to cover all situations whilst the self-regulating organisations (SROs) and recognised professional bodies (RPBs) by whom most investment businesses would be directly regulated would develop their own rule books taking account of the circumstances of their members' businesses but 'equivalent to' the SIB's rules. In practice, the SIB code of rules became legalistic and detailed, and the term 'equivalent to' has been interpreted to require that the rule books of SROs and RPBs should cover the ground covered by the SIB rules and largely in the same language. As a result, the rule books have been complicated, difficult to understand and costly to apply for smaller investment businesses.

During the past year, the SIB has been examining with the Government, SROs, RPBs and other interested parties how to improve the regime of regulation and to make it more cost-effective. This work has focused particularly on the system of rules. As a result, a consensus emerged that means should be found of giving greater flexibility to the SROs and RPBs in the setting of detailed rules while still seeking to ensure the maintenance of a high level of investor protection.

The essence of the new approach to the maintenance of investor protection is one of simplification in place of the present complexity in the regulatory rule books taken as a whole. Under the changes to the Financial Services Act 1986 introduced in the Companies Act 1989, the SIB is empowered to lay down principles of conduct which would apply to all those carrying out investment business and to designate rules which are then to apply to all member firms of SROs as well as to firms authorised by the SIB itself. Once these principles and designated rules have established a firm central core for the system of rules, SROs will be allowed greater scope as to any more detailed requirements needed to reflect the particular characteristics of the sectors of the industry they regulate.

The result of this new approach to rule books will be a three tier approach. At the highest level of generality, there will be a set of principles setting out the main elements of the conduct and financial standing expected of all firms. Secondly, there will be a set of rules made by the SIB in consultation with the SROs which will be common to all SROs and which will serve as an enforceable backbone for the regulatory system and as a framework for its more detailed aspects. Finally, there will be detailed support which might take the form of rules, codes of practice or any other means chosen by the relevant regulator and which therefore might differ as between SROs.

13.2 Statements of principle

Section 192 of the 1989 Act inserts two new sections, 47A and 47B, in the Financial Services Act 1986.

By these sections, the Secretary of State is empowered to issue statements of principle dealing with the conduct and financial standing expected of persons authorised to carry on investment business. The conduct expected by these statements of principle may include compliance with a code or standard issued by another person but may permit the person who publishes the code or standard to exercise his discretion with the code. Failure to comply with a statement of principle under section 47A will be a ground for the taking of disciplinary action or the use of the power of intervention conferred by the Financial Services Act. Of itself, however, failure to comply with a statement of principle will not give investors or anyone else affected any right of action, nor will it affect the validity of any transaction – new section 47A(1)–(3).

The powers of intervention conferred by the Financial Services Act enable:

(1) the business of a person authorised to conduct investment business to be restricted,
(2) the way in which an authorised person deals with assets to be restricted,
(3) an authorised person to be obliged to transfer his assets and investors' assets to a trustee, and
(4) an authorised person to be obliged to maintain assets of a prescribed value to ensure that he can meet his investment business liabilities in the United Kingdom – sections 64–71 of the Financial Services Act 1986.

Statements of principle are not expected to apply immutably to every authorised person irrespective of his business. On application, SROs, RPBs and the SIB are empowered to modify statements of principle issued under new section 47A to adapt them to the particular circumstances of a person carrying on investment business or to any particular kind of business carried on by him. In addition, the regulatory authorities may dispense such a person from compliance with any statement of principle either generally or in relation to any particular kind of business carried on by him. However these powers may not be used unless the relevant regulatory authority believes that compliance with the statement of principle in question would be unduly burdensome for the applicant and that the exercise of discretion would not create an undue risk for investors. The powers conferred in new section 47B can be exercised either unconditionally or subject to conditions.

The new sections confer the new powers on the Secretary of State. In practice, the Secretary of State has delegated his powers under the Financial Services Act 1986 to the SIB. The SIB has already published a draft of the statements of principle which it would expect to issue. These were published in a discussion paper in August 1989. The ten proposed principles are as follows:

'*Integrity*: A firm should observe high standards of integrity and fair dealing in the conduct of its investment business.
Skill, care and diligence: A firm should act with due skill, care and diligence in the conduct of its investment business.

Observance of standards: A firm should, in the conduct of its investment business, comply with applicable provisions of any code or set of standards published by its regulator, by the Bank of England or the Take-over Panel, or by any authority recognised by law in the United Kingdom (or where the firm carries on activities affecting any other country, in that country) as responsible in the public interest for the supervision or regulation of financial activities.

Information about customers: A firm should seek from its customers, wherever it is appropriate to do so, any information about their circumstances and investment objectives which it might reasonably expect to be relevant in enabling it to fulfil its responsibilities to them.

Information for customers: A firm should avoid misleading or deceptive representations or practices and should take reasonable steps to ensure, wherever it is appropriate to do so for the purposes of enabling customers to take informed investment decisions, that their customers are properly informed about deals envisaged, their implications, and any other relevant facts.

Fairness to customers: A firm should not, in the course of its investment business, treat a customer's interests as subordinate to its own, or take unfair advantage of a customer who has placed reliance on or trust in the firm.

Conflicts of interest: A firm should be vigilant to identify potential conflicts of interest, and, where it cannot avoid conflict, should nevertheless take all reasonable steps, by way of disclosure, internal rules of confidentiality or otherwise, to ensure fair treatment to all of its customers.

Customer assets: Where, in connection with or for the purposes of investment business, a firm has control of or is otherwise responsible for assets belonging to a customer, it should arrange proper protection for them, by way of segregation or identification of those assets or otherwise.

Financial resources: A firm should ensure that it maintains adequate financial resources to meet its investment business commitments and to withstand the risks to which its business is subject.

Internal organisation: A firm should organise and control its internal affairs in a responsible manner and where the firm employs staff or is responsible for the conduct of investment business by others, should have adequate arrangements to ensure that they are suitable, adequately trained and properly supervised and that it has well-defined procedures to facilitate compliance with the regulatory system.'

13.3 Rights to bring action

Section 62 of the Financial Services Act 1986 provides that a contravention of the rules and regulations issued under Chapter V of Part I of that Act is actionable at the suit of a person who suffers loss as a result of the contravention. This applies equally to the contravention by an authorised person of the rules of an SRO or RPB in respect of investment business to which he is subject.

The 1989 Act (section 193) introduces a new section 62A narrowing this right of action. Only in respect of actions by private investors will rights of action remain unrestricted. For this purpose, the term 'private investor' is to be defined in regulations to be issued in due course by the Secretary of State. Any person other than a private investor will only be able to bring an action in circumstances which will in due course be specified in regulations to be made by the Secretary of State – new section 62A.

Similar provisions are made in respect of friendly societies – section 193(3) introducing new paragraph 22A in Schedule 11 to the Financial Services Act 1986.

13.4 Designated rules

Section 194 of the 1989 Act introduces two new sections, 63A and 63B, in the Financial Services Act 1986 which provide for the second new tier of regulation: designated rules.

The Financial Services Act 1986 already empowers the Secretary of State to prescribe conduct of business rules, financial resources rules and clients' money regulations. The new sections empower the Secretary of State when making such rules and regulations to designate certain provisions which are to apply in the way he specifies to members of SROs in respect of investment business which is subject to the SROs' rules. Any member of an SRO who contravenes a rule applying to him by virtue of these new sections will be treated as having contravened the rules of the SRO itself. The Secretary of State may provide that, to a certain specified extent, the designated rules may not be modified or waived in relation to a member of an SRO – new section 63A.

However, an SRO is generally to have the power on the application of an authorised person to modify designated rules or regulations to adapt them to the circumstances of the particular kind of business carried on by the applicant. These powers may only be used if the SRO concerned is persuaded that compliance with the rule would be unduly burdensome for the applicant taking into account the benefit which compliance would confer upon investors and that the exercise of the discretion would not result in an undue risk for investors. An SRO can exercise these powers of adaptation or waiver conditionally or subject to conditions – new section 63B.

Again, the power to designate rules and regulations is conferred upon the Secretary of State although in practice the power will be exercised by the SIB. The discussion document published by the SIB in August 1989 also included a draft of designated rules which may be specified under the new provisions. The draft designated rules are organised by reference to the draft statements of principle. For example, the first statement of principle dealing with integrity leads to a series of rules dealing with independence, inducements, overcharging, churning, timely allocation or transfer and insider dealing.

13.5 Codes of practice

Section 195 of the 1989 Act introduces a new section, 63C, into the Financial Services Act 1986 dealing with the new third tier of regulation: codes of practice.

This new section empowers the Secretary of State to issue codes of practice dealing with any of the matters covered by statements of principle issued under new section 47A or by rules or regulations made under Chapter V of Part I of the Financial Services Act 1986. These codes of practice may be used in determining whether a person has failed to comply with a statement of principle. A failure to comply with the provisions of a code of practice may be relied on as tending to establish failure to comply with a statement of principle and conversely compliance with the provisions of the code of practice may be relied on as tending to negative any failure to comply with a statement of principle. Of itself, however, a contravention of a code of practice in respect of a matter dealt with by rules or regulations will not give rise to a liability or invalidate any transaction. However, in deciding whether a person's conduct amounts to contravention of a rule or regulation, contravention of the provisions of a code of practice or compliance with them may be relied on as tending to establish liability or to negative liability – new section 63C.

13.6 Other regulatory authorities

Section 196 of the 1989 Act introduces new sections 128A, 128B and 128C into the Financial Services Act 1986 dealing with the question of relations with other regulatory authorities.

New section 128A amends the list of matters which should be considered when deciding whether a particular organisation satisfies the conditions for recognition either as an SRO or as an RPB. In future, when determining whether the rules and practices of an organisation are adequate and meet the prescribed conditions (set out in Schedules 2 and 3 to the Financial Services Act 1986) account is to be taken of the effect of any other controls to which the organisation's members are subject – new section 128A. The purpose of the new provision is to encourage cross-correlation of rules and thus to deal with the problem of undue complexity which resulted from the existing rule books of SROs and RPBs being largely the result of bilateral discussions between the individual organisations and the SIB.

New section 128B applies to any person whose principal place of business lies outside the United Kingdom or whose principal business is other than investment business. Such a person may be subject to the requirements of regulatory authorities in countries outside the United Kingdom or alternatively of regulatory authorities dealing with his principal business – new section 128B(1).

New section 128B provides that the Secretary of State may be satisfied with respect to any matter covered by the Financial Services Act 1986 if such an authority tells him that it is satisfied in respect of that matter and if the Secretary of State himself is satisfied as to the nature and scope of the supervision exercised by the authority concerned. Further, in deciding whether to use his powers in relation to such a person, the Secretary of State may take into account whether the regulatory authority concerned has exercised or intends to exercise its powers in relation to that person – new section 128B(2), (8).

New section 128C empowers the Secretary of State to exercise disciplinary powers or powers of intervention at the request of or to assist an overseas regulatory authority. This power extends to any authority in a country outside the United Kingdom which exercises functions corresponding to functions under the Financial Services Act 1986, the Insurance Companies Act 1982 or the Companies Act 1985 or to certain other functions – new section 128C(1)–(3).

In deciding whether to exercise these powers, the Secretary of State may take into account whether corresponding assistance would be given by the overseas authority concerned, whether the case concerns a breach of a law or other require-ment which has no close parallel in the United Kingdom or involves the assertion of a jurisdiction not recognised by the United Kingdom, the seriousness of the case, its importance to persons in the United Kingdom and whether it is appropriate in the public interest to give the assistance which is requested. Such assistance need not be given if the overseas authority does not undertake to contribute a satisfactory sum towards the cost of the assistance – new section 128C(4)–(6).

13.7 Offers of unlisted securities

Section 198 of the 1989 Act introduces a new section, 160A, into the Financial Services Act 1986 which gives the Secretary of State broader powers to exempt from the requirements of that Act certain advertisements issued in connection with offers of unlisted securities – section 198.

Similar provisions are made in respect of offers of securities by private companies and old public companies – section 199.

13.8   International obligations

Section 201 of the 1989 Act replaces the old section 192 of the Financial Services Act 1986 which dealt with international obligations. The main effect of the new section is to make it clear that orders can be issued to anybody within the investment business regulatory system to comply with European Community or other international obligations of the United Kingdom – new section 192.

13.9   Recognition

To reflect the changes made by the 1989 Act in the structure of the rules within the investment business regulatory system, a number of changes are made to the requirements for recognition of SROs.

The first change removes the 'equivalence' test. Originally, the Financial Services Act 1986 required that an SRO's rules governing the carrying on of investment business by its members must afford investors protection at least equivalent to that afforded by the rules and regulations of the SIB. This is replaced by an adequacy test. An SRO's rules and regulations must now be such as to afford an adequate level of protection for investors. In determining whether the level of protection afforded is adequate, attention must be paid to the nature of the investment business carried on by the SRO's members, the kinds of investors involved and the effectiveness of the organisation's arrangements for enforcing compliance – section 203(1).

A similar change is made in respect of the recognition of professional bodies – section 203(2).

The new adequacy test will be different from the old equivalence test in three ways. Firstly, the new test will remove the old requirement to balance the effect of the rule book of the SRO or RPB against that of the SIB's own rules and regulations. Secondly, it will bring into the reckoning not merely the SRO's or RPB's own rules but also the statements of principle and any core rules and codes of practice applying to the SRO's members. Thirdly, the new rule will count not only investor protection delivered by the contents of the rule book itself but also the nature of the investment business carried on by members of the organisation, the kinds of investors involved and the effectiveness of arrangements for enforcing compliance. In other words, it is not only the form of the rules but the vigour with which they are enforced which is to be assessed. The SIB has said that in operating the new 'adequacy' test, it will have two major concerns. Firstly, it will need to be satisfied in respect of any question as to the applicability of or derogation from the core, designated rules. Secondly it will need to be satisfied that the organisation's rules are satisfactorily consistent with other recognised bodies. It is hoped that the new test will provide a greater degree of flexibility than has been possible in the past while continuing to ensure high standards of investor protection.

The second change in the arrangements for recognition concerns costs of compliance. The SIB, SROs and RPBs will be expected to have satisfactory arrangements for taking account, in framing its rules, of the cost of compliance to those to whom the rules will apply. A similar change is made in connection with the recognition of professional bodies – section 204. In the past, there has been no power for account to be taken of the costs of compliance with the regulatory system's rules and of any other controls to which investment businesses were subject.

13.10 Commencement

Section 202 which deals with the circumstances in which certain offers of debentures are not to be treated as offers to the public came into effect on Royal Assent, ie 16 November 1989 – section 215(1)(c). Implementation of other sections amending the Financial Services Act will depend on progress of the review of the SIB's rule book.

Chapter 14

Miscellaneous amendments

14.1 Introduction

Any Government bill provides an opportunity to its sponsoring department to propose provisions which because of their relative insignificance would not justify separate legislation. Inevitably, the result is an Act of Parliament which apart from its main provisions makes a considerable number of amendments to the law. Some of these amendments are more substantial. All of these are reviewed in this chapter.

14.2 Registrar of Companies

Although the functions of the Registrar of Companies are an essential foundation for the Government's oversight of companies in the United Kingdom, the registry which he runs has for many years been beset by the problems of a Victorian system of administration designed for an age when there were many fewer companies and when files were maintained on paper and not electronically. In recent years sterling efforts have been made to correct this situation and these efforts are to be further encouraged by amendments made by the Companies Act 1989.

Firstly, section 125 of the 1989 Act replaces old sections 706 and 707 of the 1985 Act which dealt with the delivery of documents to the Registrar. In future, new section 706 will require that each document which is submitted to the Registrar in legible form must state prominently the registered number of the company to which it relates – new section 706(2)(a). In addition, the Registrar is given the power to specify by regulations any other requirements in respect of such documents and in particular will be able to impose requirements to ensure that the document can be copied – new section 706(2)(a),(b). When the Registrar gives notice to a company that a document submitted to him has not complied with the regulations which he has issued, the original document will be deemed not to have been delivered to the Registrar and cannot be used by the company as evidence that it has complied with the requirements of the 1985 Act for the filing of documents – new section 706(3), (4).

New section 707 empowers the Registrar of Companies to accept the delivery of documents in any non-legible form either prescribed in regulations or approved by the Registrar – new section 707(2). Any such regulations or approval by the Registrar must however indicate how any document which is generally required to be signed or sealed is to be authenticated – new section 707(3). To be acceptable, any document being delivered in non-legible form must generally comply with the requirements of the Registrar and in particular his requirements specified for the purpose of enabling him to read and copy the document – new section 707(4). New section 707 also empowers the Secretary of State to make regulations with respect to the use of instantaneous forms of communication – new section 707(7). This presumably opens the way for the Registrar to allow companies to file documents by telefax.

Secondly, section 126 of the 1989 Act introduces new provisions in respect of the keeping of company records by the Registrar. Essentially, he may record and keep the information contained in the documents delivered to him in any form that he thinks fit provided that it is possible to inspect the information and produce a copy of it in legible form – new section 707A(1). This should permit the Registrar to preserve information in computerised database form rather than as reproductions of original documents filed by companies. He must however keep the originals of documents delivered to him in legible form for ten years, after which they may be destroyed – new section 707A(2). The old provisions of the Companies Act 1985 (section 712) in respect of the records of companies which have been dissolved remain in place. After the lapse of two years from the date of dissolution, the Registrar may direct that any records which he has relating to the company may be removed to the Public Records Office – new section 707A(3).

The new power by which the Registrar may keep records in any form he thinks fit and may accept delivery of documents in non-legible form requires changes in the provisions regarding the inspection of records kept by him. Accordingly, old sections 709 and 710 are replaced by new sections 709, 710 and 710A – section 126(2). Under the old provisions, any person might inspect copies of documents filed with the Registrar. Under the new provisions, the right of inspection applies to any of the records held by the Registrar for the purposes of the Companies Acts. An enquirer may also require a copy of any information contained in the Registrar's records or a certified copy of or extract from those records - new section 709(1). An enquirer only has a right to inspect original documents where the record kept by the Registrar is illegible or unavailable – new section 709(2). For the purpose of legal proceedings, a copy of or extract from the record kept by the Registrar which has been certified by him in writing to be an accurate record of the contents of the document is to be regarded as of equal validity with the original document – new section 709(3).

Where the Companies Acts require the Registrar to supply a document, the Registrar may, if he thinks fit, meet that requirement by providing the information in any non-legible form prescribed by him. Where the document is to be signed or sealed by the Registrar, some other appropriate means of authentication must be prescribed – new section 710(A). Assuming that the Registrar converts his records to the format of a computerised database, these provisions would permit the Registrar to satisfy his statutory obligation in the context of an on-line access service for subscribers.

Lastly, the rules concerning companies' registered numbers are amended. In particular, old section 705 is replaced by a new section 705 - Schedule 19 paragraph 14. This new section continues to provide that the Registrar must allocate to every company a number (the company's registered number) – new section 705(1). These numbers may be in such form consisting of sequences of figures or letters as the Registrar may determine – new section 705(2). However, new section 705 explicitly empowers the Registrar to adopt a new form of registered number and thus to make such changes to existing registered numbers as he believes to be necessary – new section 705(3). Any change in the registered number has effect from the date on which the company is notified of the change. However, within a period of three years, the requirement for the company's registered number to be shown on business letters and order forms may be satisfied by the use of either the old number or the new – new section 705(4). The Registrar has said that these provisions will be used to introduce a check digit into registered numbers.

14.3 Partnership companies

Section 128 of the 1989 Act introduces a new section, 8A, in the 1985 Act enabling the Secretary of State by regulation to prescribe a Table G setting out the articles of association appropriate for a partnership company. A partnership company is a company limited by shares whose shares are intended to be held to a substantial extent by or on behalf of its employees. Whilst doubtless useful in reducing the costs of establishing an employee share ownership plan (ESOP), the provision is nonetheless a disappointment. From time to time, it has been suggested that small businesses could be assisted by the introduction of a simplified form of company: sometimes called a partnership company. Section 128 has nothing to do with these ideas.

14.4 Membership of holding company

Section 23 of the 1985 Act provides that, subject to certain exemptions, a company could not be a member of its own holding company and that any allotment or transfer of shares in a company to its subsidiary or a nominee for its subsidiary would be void. This legislation was first introduced into company law in the Companies Act 1947 to prevent companies from trafficking in their own shares by indirect means. The prohibitions in section 73 do not apply where the subsidiary (or its nominee) is concerned as personal representative or trustee unless the holding company or its subsidiary is beneficially interested in the trust except by way of security issued in the ordinary way of business which includes the lending of money. A subsidiary which was a member of its holding company at the commencement of the 1948 Act may continue to be a member, but with no power to vote at the meetings of the shareholders or of any class thereof of the holding company.

Section 23 contained a notable gap. It does not provide what is to happen if a company on becoming the subsidiary of a holding company after the commencement of the 1948 Act already holds shares in that company. The section does not oblige the subsidiary to sell the shares which it owns in its holding company nor is the continued holding of those shares declared to be unlawful or made subject to criminal sanctions.

The effect of section 129 of the 1989 Act is to replace old section 23 with a new section 23. The new section continues the old prohibition but creates a new exemption from the prohibition and deals with the lacuna relating to companies which become subsidiaries.

The new exemption concerns market makers. Where a subsidiary is concerned in the shares of its holding company only as a market maker, the prohibition does not apply. For these purposes, a person is a market maker if at all normal times he holds himself out as willing to buy and sell securities at specified prices and in compliance with the rules of a recognised investment exchange by which he is recognised as a market maker – new section 23(3).

As for a company which becomes a subsidiary at a time when it already holds shares in its new holding company, new section 23 provides that it may continue to be a member of the holding company. However, for so long as the prohibition would otherwise apply, the new subsidiary company will have no right to vote in respect of those shares at meetings of the holding company or of any class of its members – new section 23(4),(5). If the holding company subsequently proposes to make an allotment to its shareholders (and within them to its subsidiary) of fully paid shares by way of capitalisation of its reserves, the allotment may be made but the shares may not be voted in general meetings of the company or of any class of its members – new section 23(6).

14.5 Company seal

Section 36 of the 1985 Act provides that, in effect, a company may contract in the same form as an individual. Where, according to English law, a contract has to be under seal, the company's common seal has to be affixed. Where an individual is required to contract in writing, the company by its agents may make a contract in writing signed by a person acting under its authority. Where an individual is capable of acting orally, the company, acting by its duly authorised agent, may also do so.

The consequent obligation on a company to have a common seal is effectively removed by section 130 of the 1989 Act which replaces old section 36 by new sections 36, 36A, 36B and 36C.

New section 36 provides that under the law of England and Wales a contract may be made by a company by writing under its common seal or on behalf of a company by any person acting under its authority. Any formalities required by law in the case of a contract made by an individual also apply to a contract made by or on behalf of the company unless there is a clear contrary intention – new section 36.

It remains the case that a document may be executed by a company by the affixing of its common seal – new section 36A(2). However, companies need not have common seals – new section 36A(3). Documents signed by a director and the secretary of a company or by two directors and expressed to be executed by the company have the same effect as if they were executed under the common seal of the company – new section 36A(4). If a document executed by a company makes it clear on its face that it is intended by the people making it to be a deed, that document has effect on delivery as a deed – new section 36A(5). Further, in favour of a purchaser in good faith for valuable consideration, a document is to be treated as having been duly executed by a company if it is signed by a director and the secretary or two directors of the company and it makes it clear on its face that it is intended to be a deed – new section 36A(6).

New section 36B makes amendments in respect of Scottish law which are intended to have a similar effect to those made for the law in England and Wales.

14.6 Members' rights to damages

Section 131 of the 1989 Act is intended to abolish the rule in the case of *Houldsworth v City of Glasgow Bank and Liquidators* (1880) 5 App Cas 317. In February 1877, Houldsworth bought £4,000 of stock in the defendant bank which was an unlimited company incorporated under the 1862 Act. Thereafter,

Houldsworth was registered as a member and received dividends. In October 1878, the bank failed and was put into liquidation. Houldsworth alleged that he had been induced to take the stock by fraud and had as a result lost £29,000 in calls and incurred a potential liability of £200,000 in future calls and he claimed damages in respect of these sums. The House of Lords held that he could not claim damages while he remained a member. Effectively, a subscriber of shares in the company could not claim damages for a misrepresentation or breach of warranty against the company unless his contract of allotment was first rescinded.

There has been doubt about the extent of this rule and in particular about whether a shareholder could rescind his contract of allotment once his name had been added to the Register of Members. The Financial Services Act 1986 amended the rule so that it should not apply to misstatements in listing particulars or prospectuses. But there remained the possibility that the rule would be applied in other circumstances. Section 131 of the 1989 Act introduces a new section, 111A, in the 1985 Act which provides that a person is not to be debarred from obtaining damages or other compensation from a company simply because he holds or has held shares in the company or any right to apply or to subscribe for shares or to be included in the company's register in respect of shares.

14.7 Employees' share scheme

Section 151 of the 1985 Act generally prohibits the provision of financial assistance by a company directly or indirectly related to the acquisition by any person of shares in the company. Section 153 of that Act lists a number of transactions which are not prohibited by section 151. Included in this list is a transaction by which a company provides money for the acquisition of fully paid shares in the company or in its holding company in accordance with an employees' share scheme – section 153(4)(b) of the 1985 Act.

The subsection is revised to make three changes. Firstly, the exemption applies not simply to the provision of money but now to the provision of financial assistance. Secondly, the exemption applies not simply to the acquisition of fully paid shares but now to any assistance for the purposes of an employees' share scheme. Thirdly, a requirement that the assistance should be given in good faith is inserted – section 132.

14.8 Redeemable shares

Section 159 of the 1985 Act enables companies to issue redeemable shares subject to various conditions which are set out in section 160. In particular, section 160(3) provides that shares are to be redeemed on such terms and in such manner as is provided for in companies' articles of association.

This provision is repealed by section 133 of the 1989 Act which introduces a new section 159A into the 1985 Act. This provides that redeemable shares may not be issued unless the company satisfies a number of conditions relating to the redemption of those shares. These conditions require the specification in the company's articles of association of certain matters relating to the redemption (i.e. the dates of redemption or the way in which those dates are to be fixed, any other circumstances in which the shares are to be redeemed, the amounts payable on redemption and any other terms and conditions of redemption) – new section 159A.

14.9 Disclosure of interests in shares

Part VI of the 1985 Act makes a number of provisions with regard to the disclosure to a public company of interests in its shares. For these purposes, interests are notifiable if they exceed 5% of the aggregate nominal value of a company's share capital and the period for notification is five days after a person becomes aware that a notifiable interest existed.

These limits are revised so that an interest is notifiable if it exceeds 3% rather than 5% and it must be notified in two days rather than five – section 134(2), (3).

In addition the Secretary of State is given powers to amend these limits and various definitions (e.g. the definition of relevant share capital) by regulations – new section 210A.

14.10 Registered office

Section 136 of the 1989 Act substitutes a new section 287, for old section 287.

The reason for changing the existing provisions is to remove any uncertainty about the point at which a change of registered office takes effect. Three possible interpretations of the old provisions had been suggested. Firstly, it was suggested that a change of registered office took effect when a company decided that the registered office was to change. Secondly, it was suggested that the date on which the change takes effect is that when the notice of the change is received at Companies House. Thirdly, it was suggested that the effective date of the change is the date on which the new address of the registered office is entered on the Register of Companies.

New section 287 makes it plain that every company must at all times have a registered office – new section 287(1). A change in the registered office is to take effect on registration by the Registrar of Companies (i.e. when the due notice delivered to the Registrar is entered on the Register) – new section 287(4).

This rule matters because of the basic principle that a document may be properly served on a company by sending it to the registered office. A company is required to keep various registers at its registered office and failure to do so is a criminal offence. In choosing the date of registration as the effective date for a change of registered office the intention is to ensure that there could not at any point be a secret registered office which is known only to the company itself.

Choosing the registration date however could create difficulties for companies themselves since without a specific enquiry companies may not know the precise date on which the change in registered office is registered. Thus, new section 287 protects a company from committing a criminal offence when it moves to the new registered office within 14 days of giving notice of the change – new section 287(5). Further protection is given where a company unavoidably ceases to perform its required duties at its registered office in circumstances in which it was not practicable to give prior notice to the Registrar of a change in situation (e.g. if the premises are destroyed by fire). This protection applies provided that the company resumes performance of its duties at other premises as soon as possible and gives notice accordingly to the Registrar of a change in the situation of its registered office within 14 days – new section 287(6). Until the end of a period of 14 days beginning with the date on which a change of registered office is registered by the Registrar, any person may validly serve any document on the company at its previous registered office – new section 287(4).

14.11 Insurance for officers and auditors

Section 310 of the 1985 Act prevents companies from exempting their officers from or indemnifying them against any liability which would attach to them in respect of any negligence, default, breach of duty or breach of trust of which they may be guilty in relation to the company. It has been argued that this provision invalidates indemnity insurance taken out by officers and paid for by their companies.

The 1989 Act introduces a new subsection – section 310(3)(a) – making it clear that section 310 does not prevent a company from purchasing and maintaining for any officer or auditor insurance against any such liability – section 137(1).

Section 137 also requires that where such insurance is purchased or maintained for officers of the company, its directors' report must state that fact – section 137(2).

14.12 Directors' transactions

Section 138 of the 1989 Act increases various limits in the 1985 Act applying to financial transactions between companies and their directors. In particular, the following limits are increased as follows:

(1) The maximum limit for the exemption by which companies may make short term quasi-loans to directors is increased from £1,000 to £5,000 – section 138(a).
(2) The maximum limit permitting companies to make small loans to directors is increased from £2,500 to £5,000 – section 138(b).
(3) The maximum limit for permissible loans or quasi-loans by money-lending companies to directors is increased from £50,000 to £100,000 – section 138(c).

Although these increases in the limits are welcome, the 1989 Act represents another missed opportunity to remove the uncertainty over the effect of the existing legislation on the legality and disclosure of transactions with directors and other officers.

14.13 Annual returns

Each company is required to deliver to the Registrar an annual return providing current confirmation of basic constitutional information concerning the company. Although the requirement for an annual return may be a sensible feature of a system for oversight of companies, the existing system has proved impossible to monitor effectively so for many companies the Registrar's records are incomplete and the existing rules on the content of returns are archaic. Section 139 introduces new sections 363, 364, 364A in the 1985 Act changing the existing requirements.

In future, each company will have to submit an annual return made up to its 'return date'. This date is to be either the anniversary of the company's incorporation or the anniversary of the company's last return if that was made up to a different date – new section 363(1). Previously the date of the return was linked to the holding of the company's annual general meeting and therefore was a moveable feast. The new rule introduces a note of certainty and can more easily be monitored by the Registrar of Companies.

Each annual return must be made up in the prescribed form, containing the information required by the Companies Acts, and must be signed by a director or secretary of the company. The completed return must be delivered to the Registrar within 28 days of the date to which the return must be made up – new section 363(2).

The annual return must show the following required information:

(1) the address of the registered office,
(2) the type of company and its principal business activities,
(3) the name and address of the company secretary,
(4) the name and address of every director,
(5) for each individual director, his nationality, date of birth and business occupation together with prescribed particulars of other directorships and former names as shown in the company's register of directors,
(6) for any corporate director, particulars of other directorships which would be required to be contained in the register of directors for an individual,
(7) the place at which the register of members is kept if it is not the company's registered office,
(8) if any register of debenture holders is held elsewhere than at the registered office, the address at the place at which it is kept,
(9) if appropriate, notice that the company has elected to dispense with the laying of accounts and reports before the company in general meeting or with the holding of annual general meetings – new section 364(1).

Power is given to introduce schemes specifying the company's type and the way in which information concerning the company's principal business activities must be shown in the annual return – new section 364(2), (3).

Detailed information is also to be provided in the annual return concerning the company's issued share capital and the identity of its shareholders – new section 364A.

In June 1989, Companies House published a consultative document entitled 'A new approach to the annual return' seeking views on the way in which the annual return system should operate once the provisions of the Companies Act 1989 have been implemented. In particular, the consultative document proposed that the annual return should be a 'shuttle' document. The basic concept behind the 'shuttle' form is that where Companies House holds information about a company, the company should be invited to confirm or amend this rather than being expected to complete a blank form each year.

Companies House already holds details of each company's name, number and registered office on a computerised database. It is planned also to set up a computerised register of company secretaries and directors. This will be a major undertaking and it is intended to use the first issue of the shuttle document to 'capture' the information required.

14.14 Dissolution of companies

Section 651 of the 1985 Act provides that when a company has been dissolved, the court may at any time within two years make an order declaring that the dissolution of the company is void. The company is then re-registered. The limitations of this provision were recently exposed in *Bradley v Eagle Star Insurance Co Ltd* [1989] 1 AC 957, [1989] 1 All ER 961, HL.

Mrs Bradley had worked at a Bolton cotton mill, Dart Mill, for several periods between 1930 and 1970. She claimed that she had inhaled large quantities of cotton dust at work which caused her to suffer from byssinosis, a respiratory disease, which she had contracted through her employer's negligence. Mrs Bradley brought a claim against Dart Mill's insurers, Eagle Star Insurance, because the company which operated Dart Mill had been dissolved ten years before. The Third Party (Rights against Insurers) Act 1930 provides that where a company has been wound up or become bankrupt, third parties can assume its rights to seek indemnity from its insurers for injuries caused to them. In her claim against Eagle Star, Mrs Bradley sought to assume Dart Mill's rights.

However, in Mrs Bradley's case, the House of Lords found that a company has no right to sue for an indemnity from its insurer until the existence and amount of its liability to a third party had been established by action, arbitration or agreement. Accordingly, although Mrs Bradley assumed the company's rights, she was unable to sue the insurers until she had established the existence and amount of the company's liability. This could only be achieved by bringing an action against the company. In Mrs Bradley's case, this was impossible because the company had been dissolved in 1976 and section 651 of the 1985 Act only permitted that dissolution to be declared void within a period of two years from the date of the dissolution. As a result, in the finding of the House of Lords, the insurance company avoided liability.

Section 141 of the 1989 Act revises section 651 of the 1985 Act to ameliorate the position. The general limit of two years for applications to the court to declare void a dissolution of a company is maintained – new section 651(4). However, this limit will not apply to applications for court orders where the purpose is to bring proceedings against the company concerned for damages in respect of personal injuries or under the Fatal Accidents Act 1976. For this purpose personal injuries include any disease and any impairment of a person's physical or mental condition. The court will not make an order if the court believes that the proceedings would fail because they are out of time – new subsections 651(5)–(7).

An application to the court may be made under these provisions in relation to a company dissolved before their commencement even if the normal time limit (two years) had already expired. There is a maximum limit however. No application may be made in relation to a company dissolved more than twenty years before the commencement of these provisions – section 141(4).

14.15 Doctrine of deemed notice

Section 132 of the 1989 Act inserts a new section, 711A, in the 1985 Act. This section deals with the doctrine of deemed notice and introduces changes which are necessary as a consequence of the abolition of the doctrine of ultra vires.

At common law, a third party dealing with a company is deemed to have constructive notice of the contents of the company's public documents. Although there may be some doubt as to what constitutes a public document for this purpose, it is clear that a company's articles and memorandum of association fall into this category. Thus, if a company's articles or memorandum restrict the authority of its directors or its agents, a third party dealing with the company would be deemed to have constructive notice of any such limitation.

New section 711A provides that a person is not to be taken to have notice of any matter merely because it has been disclosed in a document which is kept by the

Registrar of Companies (and thus available for inspection) or which is made available by the company for inspection – new section 711A(1). For this purpose, a 'document' includes any material containing information – new section 711A(3). These provisions do not affect the question whether a person is affected by notice of any matter by reason of a failure to make any enquiries as he ought reasonably to have made, nor do they affect the provisions of section 3(7) of the Land Charges Act 1972 under which the registration of certain land charges is deemed to constitute actual notice for all purposes connected with the land concerned – new section 711A(2),(4).

14.16   Rights of inspection

The effect of new section 723A of the 1985 Act (inserted by section 143 of the 1989 Act) is to give the Secretary of State power to make regulations concerning the obligations of a company to make available for inspection any register, index or document or to provide copies – new section 723A(1). Regulations may make provision as to the time, duration or manner or inspection including the circumstances and extent to which the copying of information is permitted in the course of inspection – new section 723A(2). They may also define what may be required of the company with respect to the nature, extent and manner of extracting and presenting any information for the purpose of inspection – new section 723A(3). Where a fee may be charged, the regulations may make provisions with respect to the amount of the fee and the basis of its calculation – new section 723A(4).

In effect these matters are in future to be dealt with in secondary rather than primary legislation.

14.17   Transactions involving directors

Section 320 of the 1985 Act provides that companies may not enter into substantial property transactions involving directors unless the arrangement is first approved by resolution of the company in general meeting. Section 321 of that Act provides a number of exceptions from this general provision.

The 1989 Act introduces a new exception: transactions on a recognised investment exchange effected by a director or a person connected with him through the agency of a person who in the context of that transaction acts as an independent broker. For these purposes, where the transaction is effected on behalf of the director, an independent broker is a person who independently of the director selects the person with whom the transaction is to be effected. Where the transaction is undertaken on behalf of the person connected with a director, an independent broker is a person who independently of that person and of the director selects the person with whom the transaction is to be effected – Schedule 19 paragraph 8.

14.18   Extraordinary general meeting

Section 368 of the 1985 Act provides that in certain cases members may requisition a company to convene an extraordinary general meeting. By an oversight, section 368 does not provide the maximum period from the date of the notice convening the meeting to the date on which the meeting is to be held. It is therefore technically possible for directors to comply with the requisition by convening a meeting for a date a long time into the future.

The 1989 Act provides that directors shall be deemed not to have duly convened the meeting if it is convened for a date more than 28 days after the date of the notice convening the meeting – Schedule 19 paragraph 9.

14.19 Unfair prejudice

Sections 459 and 460 of the 1985 Act prescribe circumstances in which members of a company and the Secretary of State respectively may apply to the court for an order giving relief where it appears that any actual or proposed act or omission of the company may be unfairly prejudicial to the interests of some part of the members. The 1989 Act extends the prescribed circumstances to cases in which the interests of the members generally may be unfairly prejudiced – Schedule 19 paragraph 11.

14.20 Offences by partnerships

The 1989 Act amends section 734 of the 1985 Act which deals with criminal proceedings against unincorporated bodies. It provides that where it can be proved that an offence committed by a partnership was committed with the consent or connivance of, or as the result of neglect on the part of a partner, he as well as the partnership will be guilty of the offence and can be proceeded against and punished accordingly. The 1989 Act further provides that where an offence is committed by a unincorporated body other than a partnership and it is shown that the offence was committed with the consent or connivance of, or as a result of the neglect of any officer of the body or a member of its governing body, that person as well as the body is guilty of the offence and may be proceeded against and punished accordingly – Schedule 19 paragraph 18.

14.21 Transfer of securities

Power is given to the Secretary of State to issue regulations to enable title to securities to be endowed and transferred without a record in writing subject to various safeguards – section 207. This clears the way for new arrangements dispensing with share certificates.

14.22 Commencement

It is expected that most of these provisions will be implemented during 1990. The introduction of Table G for partnership companies is likely to be delayed until the early part of 1991 as is the commencement of arrangements for the transfer of securities without written record.

The Companies Act 1989

(1989 c 40)

ARRANGEMENT OF SECTIONS

PART I

COMPANY ACCOUNTS

Introduction

PART II

ELIGIBILITY FOR APPOINTMENT AS COMPANY AUDITOR

Introduction

PART III

INVESTIGATIONS AND POWERS TO OBTAIN INFORMATION

Amendments of the Companies Act 1985

PART IV

REGISTRATION OF COMPANY CHARGES

Introduction

PART V

OTHER AMENDMENTS OF COMPANY LAW

A company's capacity and related matters

121

PART VI

MERGERS AND RELATED MATTERS

PART VII

FINANCIAL MARKETS AND INSOLVENCY

Introduction

An Act to amend the law relating to company accounts; to make new provision with respect to the persons eligible for appointment as company auditors; to amend the Companies Act 1985 and certain other enactments with respect to investigations and powers to obtain information and to confer new powers exercisable to assist overseas regulatory authorities; to make new provision with respect to the registration of company charges and otherwise to amend the law relating to companies; to amend the Fair Trading Act 1973; to enable provision to be made for the payment of fees in connection with the exercise by the Secretary of State, the Director General of Fair Trading and the Monopolies and Mergers Commission of their functions under Part V of that Act; to make provision for safeguarding the operation of certain financial markets; to amend the Financial Services Act 1986; to enable provision to be made for the recording and transfer of title to securities without a written instrument; to amend the Company Directors Disqualification Act 1986, the Company Securities (Insider Dealing) Act 1985, the Policyholders Protection Act 1975 and the law relating to building societies; and for connected purposes

[16 November 1989]

PART I
COMPANY ACCOUNTS

Introduction

1 Introduction

The provisions of this Part amend Part VII of the Companies Act 1985 (accounts and audit) by—

(a) inserting new provisions in place of sections 221 to 262 of that Act, and

(b) amending or replacing Schedules 4 to 10 to that Act and inserting new Schedules.

Provisions applying to companies generally

2 Accounting records

The following sections are inserted in Part VII of the Companies Act 1985 at the beginning of Chapter I (provisions applying to companies generally)—

'*Accounting records*

221 Duty to keep accounting records

(1) Every company shall keep accounting records which are sufficient to show and explain the company's transactions and are such as to—

(a) disclose with reasonable accuracy, at any time, the financial position of the company at that time, and

(b) enable the directors to ensure that any balance sheet and profit and loss account prepared under this Part complies with the requirements of this Act.

(2) The accounting records shall in particular contain—

(a) entries from day to day of all sums of money received and expended by the company, and the matters in respect of which the receipt and expenditure takes place, and

(b) a record of the assets and liabilities of the company.

(3) If the company's business involves dealing in goods, the accounting records shall contain—

(a) statements of stock held by the company at the end of each financial year of the company,

(b) all statements of stocktakings from which any such statement of stock as is mentioned in paragraph (a) has been or is to be prepared, and

(c) except in the case of goods sold by way of ordinary retail trade, statements of all goods sold and purchased, showing the goods and the buyers and sellers in sufficient detail to enable all these to be identified.

(4) A parent company which has a subsidiary undertaking in relation to which the above requirements do not apply shall take reasonable steps to secure that the undertaking keeps such accounting records as to enable the directors of the parent company to ensure that any balance sheet and profit and loss account prepared under this Part complies with the requirements of this Act.

(5) If a company fails to comply with any provision of this section, every officer of the company who is in default is guilty of an offence unless he shows that he acted honestly and that in the circumstances in which the company's business was carried on the default was excusable.

(6) A person guilty of an offence under this section is liable to imprisonment or a fine, or both.

222 Where and for how long records to be kept

(1) A company's accounting records shall be kept at its registered office or such other place as the directors think fit, and shall at all times be open to inspection by the company's officers.

(2) If accounting records are kept at a place outside Great Britain, accounts and returns with respect to the business dealt with in the accounting records so kept shall be sent to, and kept at, a place in Great Britain, and shall at all times be open to such inspection.

(3) The accounts and returns to be sent to Great Britain shall be such as to—

(*a*) disclose with reasonable accuracy the financial position of the business in question at intervals of not more than six months, and

(*b*) enable the directors to ensure that the company's balance sheet and profit and loss account comply with the requirements of this Act.

(4) If a company fails to comply with any provision of subsections (1) to (3), every officer of the company who is in default is guilty of an offence, and liable to imprisonment or a fine or both, unless he shows that he acted honestly and that in the circumstances in which the company's business was carried on the default was excusable.

(5) Accounting records which a company is required by section 221 to keep shall be preserved by it—

(*a*) in the case of a private company, for three years from the date on which they are made, and

(*b*) in the case of a public company, for six years from the date on which they are made.

This is subject to any provision contained in rules made under section 411 of the Insolvency Act 1986 (company insolvency rules).

(6) An officer of a company is guilty of an offence, and liable to imprisonment or a fine or both, if he fails to take all reasonable steps for securing compliance by the company with subsection (5) or intentionally causes any default by the company under that subsection.'.

3 A company's financial year and accounting reference periods

The following sections are inserted in Part VII of the Companies Act 1985—

'*A company's financial year and accounting reference periods*

223 A company's financial year

(1) A company's 'financial year' is determined as follows.

(2) Its first financial year begins with the first day of its first accounting reference

period and ends with the last day of that period or such other date, not more than seven days before or after the end of that period, as the directors may determine.

(3) Subsequent financial years begin with the day immediately following the end of the company's previous financial year and end with the last day of its next accounting reference period or such other date, not more than seven days before or after the end of that period, as the directors may determine.

(4) In relation to an undertaking which is not a company, references in this Act to its financial year are to any period in respect of which a profit and loss account of the undertaking is required to be made up (by its constitution or by the law under which it is established), whether that period is a year or not.

(5) The directors of a parent company shall secure that, except where in their opinion there are good reasons against it, the financial year of each of its subsidiary undertakings coincides with the company's own financial year.

224 Accounting reference periods and accounting reference date

(1) A company's accounting reference periods are determined according to its accounting reference date.

(2) A company may, at any time before the end of the period of nine months beginning with the date of its incorporation, by notice in the prescribed form given to the registrar specify its accounting reference date, that is, the date on which its accounting reference period ends in each calendar year.

(3) Failing such notice, a company's accounting reference date is—

(a) in the case of a company incorporated before the commencement of section 3 of the Companies Act 1989, 31st March;

(b) in the case of a company incorporated after the commencement of that section, the last day of the month in which the anniversary of its incorporation falls.

(4) A company's first accounting reference period is the period of more than six months, but not more than 18 months, beginning with the date of its incorporation and ending with its accounting reference date.

(5) Its subsequent accounting reference periods are successive periods of twelve months beginning immediately after the end of the previous accounting reference period and ending with its accounting reference date.

(6) This section has effect subject to the provisions of section 225 relating to the alteration of accounting reference dates and the consequences of such alteration.

225 Alteration of accounting reference date

(1) A company may by notice in the prescribed form given to the registrar specify a new accounting reference date having effect in relation to the company's current accounting reference period and subsequent periods.

(2) A company may by notice in the prescribed form given to the registrar specify a new accounting reference date having effect in relation to the company's previous accounting reference period and subsequent periods if—

(a) the company is a subsidiary undertaking or parent undertaking of another company and the new accounting reference date coincides with the accounting reference date of that other company, or

(b) an administration order under Part II of the Insolvency Act 1986 is in force.

A company's 'previous accounting reference period' means that immediately preceding its current accounting reference period.

(3) The notice shall state whether the current or previous accounting reference period—

(a) is to be shortened, so as to come to an end on the first occasion on which the new accounting reference date falls or fell after the beginning of the period, or (*b*) is to be extended, so as to come to an end on the second occasion on which that date falls or fell after the beginning of the period.

(4) A notice under subsection (1) stating that the current accounting reference period is to be extended is ineffective, except as mentioned below, if given less than five years after the end of an earlier accounting reference period of the company which was extended by virtue of this section.

This subsection does not apply—

(*a*) to a notice given by a company which is a subsidiary undertaking or parent undertaking of another company and the new accounting reference date coincides with that of the other company, or

(*b*) where an administration order is in force under Part II of the Insolvency Act 1986,

or where the Secretary of State directs that it should not apply, which he may do with respect to a notice which has been given or which may be given.

(5) A notice under subsection (2)(*a*) may not be given if the period allowed for laying and delivering accounts and reports in relation to the previous accounting reference period has already expired.

(6) An accounting reference period may not in any case, unless an administration order is in force under Part II of the Insolvency Act 1986, be extended so as to exceed 18 months and a notice under this section is ineffective if the current or previous accounting reference period as extended in accordance with the notice would exceed that limit.'.

4 Individual company accounts

(1) The following section is inserted in Part VII of the Companies Act 1985—

'*Annual accounts*

226 Duty to prepare individual company accounts

(1) The directors of every company shall prepare for each financial year of the company—

(*a*) a balance sheet as at the last day of the year, and
(*b*) a profit and loss account.

Those accounts are referred to in this Part as the company's 'individual accounts'.

(2) The balance sheet shall give a true and fair view of the state of affairs of the company as at the end of the financial year; and the profit and loss account shall give a true and fair view of the profit or loss of the company for the financial year.

(3) A company's individual accounts shall comply with the provisions of Schedule 4 as to the form and content of the balance sheet and profit and loss account and additional information to be provided by way of notes to the accounts.

(4) Where compliance with the provisions of that Schedule, and the other provisions of this Act as to the matters to be included in a company's individual accounts or in notes to those accounts, would not be sufficient to give a true and fair view, the necessary additional information shall be given in the accounts or in a note to them.

(5) If in special circumstances compliance with any of those provisions is inconsistent with the requirement to give a true and fair view, the directors shall depart from that provision to the extent necessary to give a true and fair view.

Particulars of any such departure, the reasons for it and its effect shall be given in a note to the accounts.'.

(2) Schedule 4 to the Companies Act 1985 (form and content of company accounts) is amended in accordance with Schedule 1 to this Act.

5 Group accounts

(1) The following section is inserted in Part VII of the Companies Act 1985—

'227 Duty to prepare group accounts

(1) If at the end of a financial year a company is a parent company the directors shall, as well as preparing individual accounts for the year, prepare group accounts.

(2) Group accounts shall be consolidated accounts comprising—

(a) a consolidated balance sheet dealing with the state of affairs of the parent company and its subsidiary undertakings, and

(b) a consolidated profit or loss account dealing with the profit and loss of the parent company and its subsidiary undertakings.

(3) The accounts shall give a true and fair view of the state of affairs as at the end of the financial year, and the profit or loss for the financial year, of the undertakings included in the consolidation as a whole, so far as concerns members of the company.

(4) A company's group accounts shall comply with the provisions of Schedule 4A as to the form and content of the consolidated balance sheet and consolidated profit and loss account and additional information to be provided by way of notes to the accounts.

(5) Where compliance with the provisions of that Schedule, and the other provisions of this Act, as to the matters to be included in a company's group accounts or in notes to those accounts, would not be sufficient to give a true and fair view, the necessary additional information shall be given in the accounts or in a note to them.

(6) If in special circumstances compliance with any of those provisions is inconsistent with the requirement to give a true and fair view, the directors shall depart from that provision to the extent necessary to give a true and fair view.

Particulars of any such departure, the reasons for it and its effect shall be given in a note to the accounts.'.

(2) Schedule 2 to this Act (form and content of group accounts) is inserted after Schedule 4 to the Companies Act 1985, as Schedule 4A.

(3) The following sections are inserted in Part VII of the Companies Act 1985—

'228 Exemption for parent companies included in accounts of larger group

(1) A company is exempt from the requirement to prepare group accounts if it is itself a subsidiary undertaking and its immediate parent undertaking is established under the law of a member State of the European Economic Community, in the following cases—

(a) where the company is a wholly-owned subsidiary of that parent undertaking;

(b) where that parent undertaking holds more than 50 per cent of the shares in the company and notice requesting the preparation of group accounts has not been served on the company by shareholders holding in aggregate—
   (i) more than half of the remaining shares in the company, or
   (ii) 5 per cent of the total shares in the company.

Such notice must be served not later than six months after the end of the financial year before that to which it relates.

(2) Exemption is conditional upon compliance with all of the following conditions—

(a) that the company is included in consolidated accounts for a larger group drawn up to the same date, or to an earlier date in the same financial year, by a parent undertaking established under the law of a member State of the European Economic Community;

(b) that those accounts are drawn up and audited, and that parent undertaking's annual report is drawn up, according to that law, in accordance with the provisions of the Seventh Directive (83/349/EEC);

(c) that the company discloses in its individual accounts that it is exempt from the obligation to prepare and deliver group accounts;

    (*d*) that the company states in its individual accounts the name of the parent undertaking which draws up the group accounts referred to above and—
>   (i) if it is incorporated outside Great Britain, the country in which it is incorporated,
>   (ii) if it is incorporated in Great Britain, whether it is registered in England and Wales or in Scotland, and
>   (iii) if it is unincorporated, the address of its principal place of business;

    (*e*) that the company delivers to the registrar, within the period allowed for delivering its individual accounts, copies of those group accounts and of the parent undertaking's annual report, together with the auditors' report on them; and

    (*f*) that if any document comprised in accounts and reports delivered in accordance with paragraph (*e*) is in a language other than English, there is annexed to the copy of that document delivered a translation of it into English, certified in the prescribed manner to be a correct translation.

(3) The exemption does not apply to a company any of whose securities are listed on a stock exchange in any member State of the European Economic Community.

(4) Shares held by directors of a company for the purpose of complying with any share qualification requirement shall be disregarded in determining for the purposes of subsection (1)(*a*) whether the company is a wholly-owned subsidiary.

(5) For the purposes of subsection (1)(*b*) shares held by a wholly-owned subsidiary of the parent undertaking, or held on behalf of the parent undertaking or a wholly-owned subsidiary, shall be attributed to the parent undertaking.

(6) In subsection (3) 'securities' includes—

(*a*) shares and stock,

(*b*) debentures, including debenture stock, loan stock, bonds, certificates of deposit and other instruments creating or acknowledging indebtedness,

(*c*) warrants or other instruments entitling the holder to subscribe for securities falling within paragraph (*a*) or (*b*), and

(*d*) certificates or other instruments which confer—
>   (i) property rights in respect of a security falling within paragraph (*a*), (*b*) or (*c*),
>   (ii) any right to acquire, dispose of, underwrite or convert a security, being a right to which the holder would be entitled if he held any such security to which the certificate or other instrument relates, or
>   (iii) a contractual right (other than an option) to acquire any such security otherwise than by subscription.

229 Subsidiary undertakings included in the consolidation

(1) Subject to the exceptions authorised or required by this section, all the subsidiary undertakings of the parent company shall be included in the consolidation.

(2) A subsidiary undertaking may be excluded from consolidation if its inclusion is not material for the purpose of giving a true and fair view; but two or more undertakings may be excluded only if they are not material taken together.

(3) In addition, a subsidiary undertaking may be excluded from consolidation where—

(*a*) severe long-term restrictions substantially hinder the exercise of the rights of the parent company over the assets or management of that undertaking, or

(*b*) the information necessary for the preparation of group accounts cannot be obtained without disproportionate expense or undue delay, or

(*c*) the interest of the parent company is held exclusively with a view to subsequent resale and the undertaking has not previously been included in consolidated group accounts prepared by the parent company.

The reference in paragraph (*a*) to the rights of the parent company and the reference in paragraph (*c*) to the interest of the parent company are, respectively, to rights and interests held by or attributed to the company for the purposes of section 258 (definition of 'parent undertaking') in the absence of which it would not be the parent company.

(4) Where the activities of one or more subsidiary undertakings are so different from those of other undertakings to be included in the consolidation that their inclusion would be incompatible with the obligation to give a true and fair view, those undertakings shall be excluded from consolidation.

This subsection does not apply merely because some of the undertakings are industrial, some commercial and some provide services, or because they carry on industrial or commercial activities involving different products or provide different services.

(5) Where all the subsidiary undertakings of a parent company fall within the above exclusions, no group accounts are required.'.

(4) The following section is inserted in Part VII of the Companies Act 1985—

'230 Treatment of individual profit and loss account where group accounts prepared

(1) The following provisions apply with respect to the individual profit and loss account of a parent company where—

(*a*) the company is required to prepare and does prepare group accounts in accordance with this Act, and

(*b*) the notes to the company's individual balance sheet show the company's profit or loss for the financial year determined in accordance with this Act.

(2) The profit and loss account need not contain the information specified in paragraphs 52 to 57 of Schedule 4 (information supplementing the profit and loss account).

(3) The profit and loss account must be approved in accordance with section 233(1) (approval by board of directors) but may be omitted from the company's annual accounts for the purposes of the other provisions below in this Chapter.

(4) The exemption conferred by this section is conditional upon its being disclosed in the company's annual accounts that the exemption applies.'.

6 Additional disclosure required in notes to accounts

(1) The following section is inserted in Part VII of the Companies Act 1985—

'231 Disclosure required in notes to accounts: related undertakings

(1) The information specified in Schedule 5 shall be given in notes to a company's annual accounts.

(2) Where the company is not required to prepare group accounts, the information specified in Part I of that Schedule shall be given; and where the company is required to prepare group accounts, the information specified in Part II of that Schedule shall be given.

(3) The information required by Schedule 5 need not be disclosed with respect to an undertaking which—

(*a*) is established under the law of a country outside the United Kingdom, or

(*b*) carries on business outside the United Kingdom,

if in the opinion of the directors of the company the disclosure would be seriously prejudicial to the business of that undertaking, or to the business of the company or any of its subsidiary undertakings, and the Secretary of State agrees that the information need not be disclosed.

This subsection does not apply in relation to the information required under paragraph 5(2), 6 or 20 of that Schedule.

(4) Where advantage is taken of subsection (3), that fact shall be stated in a note to the company's annual accounts.

(5) If the directors of the company are of the opinion that the number of undertakings in respect of which the company is required to disclose information under any provision of Schedule 5 to this Act is such that compliance with that provision would result in information of excessive length being given, the information need only be given in respect of—

    (*a*) the undertakings whose results or financial position, in the opinion of the directors, principally affected the figures shown in the company's annual accounts, and

    (*b*) undertakings excluded from consolidation under section 229(3) or (4).

This subsection does not apply in relation to the information required under paragraph 10 or 29 of that Schedule.

(6) If advantage is taken of subsection (5)—

    (*a*) there shall be included in the notes to the company's annual accounts a statement that the information is given only with respect to such undertakings as are mentioned in that subsection, and

    (*b*) the full information (both that which is disclosed in the notes to the accounts and that which is not) shall be annexed to the company's next annual return.

For this purpose the 'next annual return' means that next delivered to the registrar after the accounts in question have been approved under section 233.

(7) If a company fails to comply with subsection (6)(*b*), the company and every officer of it who is in default is liable to a fine and, for continued contravention, to a daily default fine.'.

(2) Schedule 3 to this Act (disclosure of information: related undertakings) is substituted for Schedule 5 to the Companies Act 1985.

(3) The following section is inserted in Part VII of the Companies Act 1985—

'232 Disclosure required in notes to accounts: emoluments and other benefits of directors and others

(1) The information specified in Schedule 6 shall be given in notes to a company's annual accounts.

(2) In that Schedule—

Part I relates to the emoluments of directors (including emoluments waived), pensions of directors and past directors, compensation for loss of office to directors and past directors and sums paid to third parties in respect of directors' services,

Part II relates to loans, quasi-loans and other dealings in favour of directors and connected persons, and

Part III relates to transactions, arrangements and agreements made by the company or a subsidiary undertaking for officers of the company other than directors.

(3) It is the duty of any director of a company, and any person who is or has at any time in the preceding five years been an officer of the company, to give notice to the company of such matters relating to himself as may be necessary for the purposes of Part I of Schedule 6.

(4) A person who makes default in complying with subsection (3) commits an offence and is liable to a fine.'.

(4) Schedule 6 to the Companies Act 1985 is amended in accordance with Schedule 4 to this Act.

7 Approval and signing of accounts

The following section is inserted in Part VII of the Companies Act 1985—

'Approval and signing of accounts

233 Approval and signing of accounts

(1) A company's annual accounts shall be approved by the board of directors and signed on behalf of the board by a director of the company.

(2) The signature shall be on the company's balance sheet.

(3) Every copy of the balance sheet which is laid before the company in general meeting, or which is otherwise circulated, published or issued, shall state the name of the person who signed the balance sheet on behalf of the board.

(4) The copy of the company's balance sheet which is delivered to the registrar shall be signed on behalf of the board by a director of the company.

(5) If annual accounts are approved which do not comply with the requirements of this Act, every director of the company who is party to their approval and who knows that they do not comply or is reckless as to whether they comply is guilty of an offence and liable to a fine.

For this purpose every director of the company at the time the accounts are approved shall be taken to be a party to their approval unless he shows that he took all reasonable steps to prevent their being approved.

(6) If a copy of the balance sheet—

(a) is laid before the company, or otherwise circulated, published or issued, without the balance sheet having been signed as required by this section or without the required statement of the signatory's name being included, or

(b) is delivered to the registrar without being signed as required by this section,

the company and every officer of it who is in default is guilty of an offence and liable to a fine.'.

8 Directors' report

(1) The following sections are inserted in Part VII of the Companies Act 1985—

'Directors' report

234 Duty to prepare directors' report

(1) The directors of a company shall for each financial year prepare a report—

(a) containing a fair review of the development of the business of the company and its subsidiary undertakings during the financial year and of their position at the end of it, and

(b) stating the amount (if any) which they recommend should be paid as dividend and the amount (if any) which they propose to carry to reserves.

(2) The report shall state the names of the persons who, at any time during the financial year, were directors of the company, and the principal activities of the company and its subsidiary undertakings in the course of the year and any significant change in those activities in the year.

(3) The report shall also comply with Schedule 7 as regards the disclosure of the matters mentioned there.

(4) In Schedule 7—

Part I relates to matters of a general nature, including changes in asset values, directors' shareholdings and other interests and contributions for political and charitable purposes,

Part II relates to the acquisition by a company of its own shares or a charge on them,

Part III relates to the employment, training and advancement of disabled persons,

Part IV relates to the health, safety and welfare at work of the company's employees, and

Part V relates to the involvement of employees in the affairs, policy and performance of the company.

(5) In the case of any failure to comply with the provisions of this Part as to the preparation of a directors' report and the contents of the report, every person who was a director of the company immediately before the end of the period for laying and delivering accounts and reports for the financial year in question is guilty of an offence and liable to a fine.

(6) In proceedings against a person for an offence under this section it is a defence for him to prove that he took all reasonable steps for securing compliance with the requirements in question.

234A Approval and signing of directors' report

(1) The directors' report shall be approved by the board of directors and signed on behalf of the board by a director or the secretary of the company.

(2) Every copy of the directors' report which is laid before the company in general meeting, or which is otherwise circulated, published or issued, shall state the name of the person who signed it on behalf of the board.

(3) The copy of the directors' report which is delivered to the registrar shall be signed on behalf of the board by a director or the secretary of the company.

(4) If a copy of the directors' report—

(a) is laid before the company, or otherwise circulated, published or issued, without the report having been signed as required by this section or without the required statement of the signatory's name being included, or

(b) is delivered to the registrar without being signed as required by this section,

the company and every officer of it who is in default is guilty of an offence and liable to a fine.'.

(2) Schedule 7 to the Companies Act 1985 (matters to be included in directors' report) is amended in accordance with Schedule 5 to this Act.

9 Auditors' report

The following sections are inserted in Part VII of the Companies Act 1985—

'Auditors' report

235 Auditors' report

(1) A company's auditors shall make a report to the company's members on all annual accounts of the company of which copies are to be laid before the company in general meeting during their tenure of office.

(2) The auditors' report shall state whether in the auditors' opinion the annual accounts have been properly prepared in accordance with this Act, and in particular whether a true and fair view is given—

(a) in the case of an individual balance sheet, of the state of affairs of the company as at the end of the financial year,

(b) in the case of an individual profit and loss account, of the profit or loss of the company for the financial year,

(c) in the case of group accounts, of the state of affairs as at the end of the financial year, and the profit or loss for the financial year, of the undertakings included in the consolidation as a whole, so far as concerns members of the company.

(3) The auditors shall consider whether the information given in the directors' report for the financial year for which the annual accounts are prepared is consistent with those accounts; and if they are of opinion that it is not they shall state that fact in their report.

236 Signature of auditors' report

(1) The auditors' report shall state the names of the auditors and be signed by them.

(2) Every copy of the auditors' report which is laid before the company in general meeting, or which is otherwise circulated, published or issued, shall state the names of the auditors.

(3) The copy of the auditors' report which is delivered to the registrar shall state the names of the auditors and be signed by them.

(4) If a copy of the auditors' report—

(*a*) is laid before the company, or otherwise circulated, published or issued, without the required statement of the auditors' names, or

(*b*) is delivered to the registrar without the required statement of the auditors' names or without being signed as required by this section,

the company and every officer of it who is in default is guilty of an offence and liable to a fine.

(5) References in this section to signature by the auditors are, where the office of auditor is held by a body corporate or partnership, to signature in the name of the body corporate or partnership by a person authorised to sign on its behalf.

237 Duties of auditors

(1) A company's auditors shall, in preparing their report, carry out such investigations as will enable them to form an opinion as to—

(*a*) whether proper accounting records have been kept by the company and proper returns adequate for their audit have been received from branches not visited by them, and

(*b*) whether the company's individual accounts are in agreement with the accounting records and returns.

(2) If the auditors are of opinion that proper accounting records have not been kept, or that proper returns adequate for their audit have not been received from branches not visited by them, or if the company's individual accounts are not in agreement with the accounting records and returns, the auditors shall state that fact in their report.

(3) If the auditors fail to obtain all the information and explanations which, to the best of their knowledge and belief, are necessary for the purposes of their audit, they shall state that fact in their report.

(4) If the requirements of Schedule 6 (disclosure of information: emoluments and other benefits of directors and others) are not complied with in the annual accounts, the auditors shall include in their report, so far as they are reasonably able to do so, a statement giving the required particulars.'.

10 Publication of accounts and reports

The following sections are inserted in Part VII of the Companies Act 1985—

'*Publication of accounts and reports*

238 Persons entitled to receive copies of accounts and reports

(1) A copy of the company's annual accounts, together with a copy of the directors' report for that financial year and of the auditors' report on those accounts, shall be sent to—

(*a*) every member of the company,

(*b*) every holder of the company's debentures, and

(*c*) every person who is entitled to receive notice of general meetings,

not less than 21 days before the date of the meeting at which copies of those documents are to be laid in accordance with section 241.

(2) Copies need not be sent—

(*a*) to a person who is not entitled to receive notices of general meetings and of whose address the company is unaware, or (*b*) to more than one of the joint holders of shares or debentures none of whom is entitled to receive such notices, or

(*c*) in the case of joint holders of shares or debentures some of whom are, and some not, entitled to receive such notices, to those who are not so entitled.

(3) In the case of a company not having a share capital, copies need not be sent to anyone who is not entitled to receive notices of general meetings of the company.

(4) If copies are sent less than 21 days before the date of the meeting, they shall, notwithstanding that fact, be deemed to have been duly sent if it is so agreed by all the members entitled to attend and vote at the meeting.

(5) If default is made in complying with this section, the company and every officer of it who is in default is guilty of an offence and liable to a fine.

(6) Where copies are sent out under this section over a period of days, references elsewhere in this Act to the day on which copies are sent out shall be construed as references to the last day of that period.

239 Right to demand copies of accounts and reports

(1) Any member of a company and any holder of a company's debentures is entitled to be furnished, on demand and without charge, with a copy of the company's last annual accounts and directors' report and a copy of the auditors' report on those accounts.

(2) The entitlement under this section is to a single copy of those documents, but that is in addition to any copy to which a person may be entitled under section 238.

(3) If a demand under this section is not complied with within seven days, the company and every officer of it who is in default is guilty of an offence and liable to a fine and, for continued contravention, to a daily default fine.

(4) If in proceedings for such an offence the issue arises whether a person had already been furnished with a copy of the relevant document under this section, it is for the defendant to prove that he had.

240 Requirements in connection with publication of accounts

(1) If a company publishes any of its statutory accounts, they must be accompanied by the relevant auditors' report under section 235.

(2) A company which is required to prepare group accounts for a financial year shall not publish its statutory individual accounts for that year without also publishing with them its statutory group accounts.

(3) If a company publishes non-statutory accounts, it shall publish with them a statement indicating—

(*a*) that they are not the company's statutory accounts,

(*b*) whether statutory accounts dealing with any financial year with which the non-statutory accounts purport to deal have been delivered to the registrar,

(*c*) whether the company's auditors have made a report under section 235 on the statutory accounts for any such financial year, and

(*d*) whether any report so made was qualified or contained a statement under section 237(2) or (3) (accounting records or returns inadequate, accounts not agreeing with records and returns or failure to obtain necessary information and explanations);

and it shall not publish with the non-statutory accounts any auditors' report under section 235.

(4) For the purposes of this section a company shall be regarded as publishing a document if it publishes, issues or circulates it or otherwise makes it available for public inspection in a manner calculated to invite members of the public generally, or any class of members of the public, to read it.

(5) References in this section to a company's statutory accounts are to its individual or group accounts for a financial year as required to be delivered to the registrar under section 242; and references to the publication by a company of 'non-statutory accounts' are to the publication of—

  (a) any balance sheet or profit and loss account relating to, or purporting to deal with, a financial year of the company, or

  (b) an account in any form purporting to be a balance sheet or profit and loss account for the group consisting of the company and its subsidiary undertakings relating to, or purporting to deal with, a financial year of the company,

otherwise than as part of the company's statutory accounts.

(6) A company which contravenes any provision of this section, and any officer of it who is in default, is guilty of an offence and liable to a fine.'.

11 Laying and delivering of accounts and reports

The following sections are inserted in Part VII of the Companies Act 1985—

'Laying and delivering of accounts and reports

241 Accounts and reports to be laid before company in general meeting

(1) The directors of a company shall in respect of each financial year lay before the company in general meeting copies of the company's annual accounts, the directors' report and the auditors' report on those accounts.

(2) If the requirements of subsection (1) are not complied with before the end of the period allowed for laying and delivering accounts and reports, every person who immediately before the end of that period was a director of the company is guilty of an offence and liable to a fine and, for continued contravention, to a daily default fine.

(3) It is a defence for a person charged with such an offence to prove that he took all reasonable steps for securing that those requirements would be complied with before the end of that period.

(4) It is not a defence to prove that the documents in question were not in fact prepared as required by this Part.

242 Accounts and reports to be delivered to the registrar

(1) The directors of a company shall in respect of each financial year deliver to the registrar a copy of the company's annual accounts together with a copy of the directors' report for that year and a copy of the auditors' report on those accounts.

If any document comprised in those accounts or reports is in a language other than English, the directors shall annex to the copy of that document delivered a translation of it into English, certified in the prescribed manner to be a correct translation.

(2) If the requirements of subsection (1) are not complied with before the end of the period allowed for laying and delivering accounts and reports, every person who immediately before the end of that period was a director of the company is guilty of an offence and liable to a fine and, for continued contravention, to a daily default fine.

(3) Further, if the directors of the company fail to make good the default within 14 days after the service of a notice on them requiring compliance, the court may on the application of any member or creditor of the company or of the registrar, make an order directing the directors (or any of them) to make good the default within such time as may be specified in the order.

The court's order may provide that all costs of and incidental to the application shall be borne by the directors.

(4) It is a defence for a person charged with an offence under this section to prove that he took all reasonable steps for securing that the requirements of subsection (1) would be complied with before the end of the period allowed for laying and delivering accounts and reports.

(5) It is not a defence in any proceedings under this section to prove that the documents in question were not in fact prepared as required by this Part.

242A Civil penalty for failure to deliver accounts

(1) Where the requirements of section 242(1) are not complied with before the end of the period allowed for laying and delivering accounts and reports, the company is liable to a civil penalty.

This is in addition to any liability of the directors under section 242.

(2) The amount of the penalty is determined by reference to the length of the period between the end of the period allowed for laying and delivering accounts and reports and the day on which the requirements are complied with, and whether the company is a public or private company, as follows—

Length of period	Public company	Private company
Not more than 3 months	£500	£100
More than 3 months but not more than 6 months	£1,000	£250
More than 6 months but not more than 12 months	£2,000	£500
More than 12 months	£5,000	£1,000

(3) The penalty may be recovered by the registrar and shall be paid by him into the Consolidated Fund.

(4) It is not a defence in proceedings under this section to prove that the documents in question were not in fact prepared as required by this Part.

243 Accounts of subsidiary undertakings to be appended in certain cases

(1) The following provisions apply where at the end of the financial year a parent company has as a subsidiary undertaking—

(a) a body corporate incorporated outside Great Britain which does not have an established place of business in Great Britain, or

(b) an unincorporated undertaking,

which is excluded from consolidation in accordance with section 229(4) (undertaking with activities different from the undertakings included in the consolidation).

(2) There shall be appended to the copy of the company's annual accounts delivered to the registrar in accordance with section 242 a copy of the undertaking's latest individual accounts and, if it is a parent undertaking, its latest group accounts.

If the accounts appended are required by law to be audited, a copy of the auditors' report shall also be appended.

(3) The accounts must be for a period ending not more than twelve months before the end of the financial year for which the parent company's accounts are made up.

(4) If any document required to be appended is in a language other than English, the directors shall annex to the copy of that document delivered a translation of it into English, certified in the prescribed manner to be a correct translation.

(5) The above requirements are subject to the following qualifications—

(a) an undertaking is not required to prepare for the purposes of this section accounts which would not otherwise be prepared, and if no accounts satisfying the above requirements are prepared none need be appended;

(b) a document need not be appended if it would not otherwise be required to be published, or made available for public inspection, anywhere in the world, but in that case the reason for not appending it shall be stated in a note to the company's accounts;

(c) where an undertaking and all its subsidiary undertakings are excluded from consolidation in accordance with section 229(4), the accounts of such of the subsidiary undertakings of that undertaking as are included in its consolidated group accounts need not be appended.

(6) Subsections (2) to (4) of section 242 (penalties, &c in case of default) apply in relation to the requirements of this section as they apply in relation to the requirements of subsection (1) of that section.

244 Period allowed for laying and delivering accounts and reports

(1) The period allowed for laying and delivering accounts and reports is—

(*a*) for a private company, 10 months after the end of the relevant accounting reference period, and

(*b*) for a public company, 7 months after the end of that period.

This is subject to the following provisions of this section.

(2) If the relevant accounting reference period is the company's first and is a period of more than 12 months, the period allowed is—

(*a*) 10 months or 7 months, as the case may be, from the first anniversary of the incorporation of the company, or

(*b*) 3 months from the end of the accounting reference period,

whichever last expires.

(3) Where a company carries on business, or has interests, outside the United Kingdom, the Channel Islands and the Isle of Man, the directors may, in respect of any financial year, give to the registrar before the end of the period allowed by subsection (1) or (2) a notice in the prescribed form—

(*a*) stating that the company so carries on business or has such interests, and

(*b*) claiming a 3 month extension of the period allowed for laying and delivering accounts and reports;

and upon such a notice being given the period is extended accordingly.

(4) If the relevant accounting period is treated as shortened by virtue of a notice given by the company under section 225 (alteration of accounting reference date), the period allowed for laying and delivering accounts is that applicable in accordance with the above provisions or 3 months from the date of the notice under that section, whichever last expires.

(5) If for any special reason the Secretary of State thinks fit he may, on an application made before the expiry of the period otherwise allowed, by notice in writing to a company extend that period by such further period as may be specified in the notice.

(6) In this section 'the relevant accounting reference period' means the accounting reference period by reference to which the financial year for the accounts in question was determined.'.

12 Remedies for failure to comply with accounting requirements

The following sections are inserted in Part VII of the Companies Act 1985—

'Revision of defective accounts and reports

245 Voluntary revision of annual accounts or directors' report

(1) If it appears to the directors of a company that any annual accounts of the company, or any directors' report, did not comply with the requirements of this Act, they may prepare revised accounts or a revised report.

(2) Where copies of the previous accounts or report have been laid before the company in general meeting or delivered to the registrar, the revisions shall be confined to—

(*a*) the correction of those respects in which the previous accounts or report did not comply with the requirements of this Act, and

(*b*) the making of any necessary consequential alterations.

(3) The Secretary of State may make provision by regulations as to the application of the provisions of this Act in relation to revised annual accounts or a revised directors' report.

(4) The regulations may, in particular—

(*a*) make different provision according to whether the previous accounts or report are replaced or are supplemented by a document indicating the corrections to be made;

(*b*) make provision with respect to the functions of the company's auditors in relation to the revised accounts or report;

(*c*) require the directors to take such steps as may be specified in the regulations where the previous accounts or report have been—

(i) sent out to members and others under section 238(1),
(ii) laid before the company in general meeting, or
(iii) delivered to the registrar,

or where a summary financial statement based on the previous accounts or report has been sent to members under section 251;

(*d*) apply the provisions of this Act (including those creating criminal offences) subject to such additions, exceptions and modifications as are specified in the regulations.

(5) Regulations under this section shall be made by statutory instrument which shall be subject to annulment in pursuance of a resolution of either House of Parliament.

245A Secretary of State's notice in respect of annual accounts

(1) Where copies of a company's annual accounts have been sent out under section 238, or a copy of a company's annual accounts has been laid before the company in general meeting or delivered to the registrar, and it appears to the Secretary of State that there is, or may be, a question whether the accounts comply with the requirements of this Act, he may give notice to the directors of the company indicating the respects in which it appears to him that such a question arises, or may arise.

(2) The notice shall specify a period of not less than one month for the directors to give him an explanation of the accounts or prepare revised accounts.

(3) If at the end of the specified period, or such longer period as he may allow, it appears to the Secretary of State that no satisfactory explanation of the accounts has been given and that the accounts have not been revised so as to comply with the requirements of this Act, he may if he thinks fit apply to the court.

(4) The provisions of this section apply equally to revised annual accounts, in which case the references to revised accounts shall be read as references to further revised accounts.

245B Application to court in respect of defective accounts

(1) An application may be made to the court—

(*a*) by the Secretary of State, after having complied with section 245A, or
(*b*) by a person authorised by the Secretary of State for the purposes of this section,

for a declaration or declarator that the annual accounts of a company do not comply with the requirements of this Act and for an order requiring the directors of the company to prepare revised accounts.

(2) Notice of the application, together with a general statement of the matters at issue in the proceedings, shall be given by the applicant to the registrar for registration.

(3) If the court orders the preparation of revised accounts, it may give directions with respect to—

(*a*) the auditing of the accounts,
(*b*) the revision of any directors' report or summary financial statement, and

    (*c*) the taking of steps by the directors to bring the making of the order to the notice of persons likely to rely on the previous accounts,

and such other matters as the court thinks fit.

(4) If the court finds that the accounts did not comply with the requirements of this Act it may order that all or part of—

    (*a*) the costs (or in Scotland expenses) of and incidental to the application, and

    (*b*) any reasonable expenses incurred by the company in connection with or in consequence of the preparation of revised accounts,

shall be borne by such of the directors as were party to the approval of the defective accounts.

For this purpose every director of the company at the time the accounts were approved shall be taken to have been a party to their approval unless he shows that he took all reasonable steps to prevent their being approved.

(5) Where the court makes an order under subsection (4) it shall have regard to whether the directors party to the approval of the defective accounts knew or ought to have known that the accounts did not comply with the requirements of this Act, and it may exclude one or more directors from the order or order the payment of different amounts by different directors.

(6) On the conclusion of proceedings on an application under this section, the applicant shall give to the registrar for registration an office copy of the court order or, as the case may be, notice that the application has failed or been withdrawn.

(7) The provisions of this section apply equally to revised annual accounts, in which case the references to revised accounts shall be read as references to further revised accounts.

245C Other persons authorised to apply to court

(1) The Secretary of State may authorise for the purposes of section 245B any person appearing to him—

    (*a*) to have an interest in, and to have satisfactory procedures directed to securing, compliance by companies with the accounting requirements of this Act,

    (*b*) to have satisfactory procedures for receiving and investigating complaints about the annual accounts of companies, and

    (*c*) otherwise to be a fit and proper person to be authorised.

(2) A person may be authorised generally or in respect of particular classes of case, and different persons may be authorised in respect of different classes of case.

(3) The Secretary of State may refuse to authorise a person if he considers that his authorisation is unnecessary having regard to the fact that there are one or more other persons who have been or are likely to be authorised.

(4) Authorisation shall be by order made by statutory instrument which shall be subject to annulment in pursuance of a resolution of either House of Parliament.

(5) Where authorisation is revoked, the revoking order may make such provision as the Secretary of State thinks fit with respect to pending proceedings.

(6) Neither a person authorised under this section, nor any officer, servant or member of the governing body of such a person, shall be liable in damages for anything done or purporting to be done for the purposes of or in connection with—

    (*a*) the taking of steps to discover whether there are grounds for an application to the court,

    (*b*) the determination whether or not to make such an application, or

    (*c*) the publication of its reasons for any such decision,

unless the act or omission is shown to have been in bad faith.'.

13 Small and medium-sized companies and groups

(1) The following sections are inserted in Part VII of the Companies Act 1985, as the beginning of a Chapter II—

'CHAPTER II

EXEMPTIONS, EXCEPTIONS AND SPECIAL PROVISIONS

Small and medium-sized companies and groups

246 Exemptions for small and medium-sized companies

(1) A company which qualifies as a small or medium-sized company in relation to a financial year—

    (*a*) is exempt from the requirements of paragraph 36A of Schedule 4 (disclosure with respect to compliance with accounting standards), and

    (*b*) is entitled to the exemptions provided by Schedule 8 with respect to the delivery to the registrar under section 242 of individual accounts and other documents for that financial year.

(2) In that Schedule—

Part I relates to small companies,

Part II relates to medium-sized companies, and

Part III contains supplementary provisions.

(3) A company is not entitled to the exemptions mentioned in subsection (1) if it is, or was at any time within the financial year to which the accounts relate—

    (*a*) a public company,

    (*b*) a banking or insurance company, or

    (*c*) an authorised person under the Financial Services Act 1986,

or if it is or was at any time during that year a member of an ineligible group.

(4) A group is ineligible if any of its members is—

    (*a*) a public company or a body corporate which (not being a company) has power under its constitution to offer its shares or debentures to the public and may lawfully exercise that power,

    (*b*) an authorised institution under the Banking Act 1987,

    (*c*) an insurance company to which Part II of the Insurance Companies Act 1982 applies, or

    (*d*) an authorised person under the Financial Services Act 1986.

(5) A parent company shall not be treated as qualifying as a small company in relation to a financial year unless the group headed by it qualifies as a small group, and shall not be treated as qualifying as a medium-sized company in relation to a financial year unless that group qualifies as a medium-sized group (see section 249).

247 Qualification of company as small or medium-sized

(1) A company qualifies as small or medium-sized in relation to a financial year if the qualifying conditions are met—

    (*a*) in the case of the company's first financial year, in that year, and

    (*b*) in the case of any subsequent financial year, in that year and the preceding year.

(2) A company shall be treated as qualifying as small or medium-sized in relation to a financial year—

    (*a*) if it so qualified in relation to the previous financial year under subsection (1); or

    (*b*) if it was treated as so qualifying in relation to the previous year by virtue of paragraph (*a*) and the qualifying conditions are met in the year in question.

(3) The qualifying conditions are met by a company in a year in which it satisfies two or more of the following requirements—

Small company

1. Turnover   Not more than £2 million
2. Balance sheet total   Not more than £975,000
3. Number of employees   Not more than 50

Medium-sized company

1. Turnover   Not more than £8 million
2. Balance sheet total   Not more than £3.9 million
3. Number of employees   Not more than 250.

(4) For a period which is a company's financial year but not in fact a year the maximum figures for turnover shall be proportionately adjusted.

(5) The balance sheet total means—

(a) where in the company's accounts Format 1 of the balance sheet formats set out in Part I of Schedule 4 is adopted, the aggregate of the amounts shown in the balance sheet under the headings corresponding to items A to D in that Format, and

(b) where Format 2 is adopted, the aggregate of the amounts shown under the general heading 'Assets'.

(6) The number of employees means the average number of persons employed by the company in the year (determined on a weekly basis).

That number shall be determined by applying the method of calculation prescribed by paragraph 56(2) and (3) of Schedule 4 for determining the corresponding number required to be stated in a note to the company's accounts.'.

(2) Schedule 6 to this Act is substituted for Schedule 8 to the Companies Act 1985.

(3) The following sections are inserted in Part VII of the Companies Act 1985—

'248 Exemption for small and medium-sized groups

(1) A parent company need not prepare group accounts for a financial year in relation to which the group headed by that company qualifies as a small or medium-sized group and is not an ineligible group.

(2) A group is ineligible if any of its members is—

(a) a public company or body corporate which (not being a company) has power under its constitution to offer its shares or debentures to the public and may lawfully exercise that power,

(b) an authorised institution under the Banking Act 1987,

(c) an insurance company to which Part II of the Insurance Companies Act 1982 applies, or

(d) an authorised person under the Financial Services Act 1986.

(3) If the directors of a company propose to take advantage of the exemption conferred by this section, it is the auditors' duty to provide them with a report stating whether in their opinion the company is entitled to the exemption.

(4) The exemption does not apply unless—

(a) the auditors' report states that in their opinion the company is so entitled, and

(b) that report is attached to the individual accounts of the company.

249 Qualification of group as small or medium-sized

(1) A group qualifies as small or medium-sized in relation to a financial year if the qualifying conditions are met—

(a) in the case of the parent company's first financial year, in that year, and

(b) in the case of any subsequent financial year, in that year and the preceding year.

(2) A group shall be treated as qualifying as small or medium-sized in relation to a financial year—

(a) if it so qualified in relation to the previous financial year under subsection (1); or (*b*) if it was treated as so qualifying in relation to the previous year by virtue of paragraph (*a*) and the qualifying conditions are met in the year in question.

(3) The qualifying conditions are met by a group in a year in which it satisfies two or more of the following requirements—

Small group

1. Aggregate turnover	Not more than £2 million net (or £2.4 million gross)
2. Aggregate balance sheet total	Not more than £1 million net (or £1.2 million gross)
3. Aggregate number of employees	Not more than 50

Medium-sized group

1. Aggregate turnover	Not more than £8 million net (or £9.6 million gross)
2. Aggregate balance sheet total	Not more than £3.9 million net (or £4.7 million gross)
3. Aggregate number of employees	Not more than 250.

(4) The aggregate figures shall be ascertained by aggregating the relevant figures determined in accordance with section 247 for each member of the group.

In relation to the aggregate figures for turnover and balance sheet total, 'net' means with the set-offs and other adjustments required by Schedule 4A in the case of group accounts and 'gross' means without those set-offs and other adjustments; and a company may satisfy the relevant requirements on the basis of either the net or the gross figure.

(5) The figures for each subsidiary undertaking shall be those included in its accounts for the relevant financial year, that is—

    (*a*) if its financial year ends with that of the parent company, that financial year, and

    (*b*) if not, its financial year ending last before the end of the financial year of the parent company.

(6) If those figures cannot be obtained without disproportionate expense or undue delay, the latest available figures shall be taken.'.

14 Dormant companies

The following section is inserted in Part VII of the Companies Act 1985—

'Dormant companies

250 Resolution not to appoint auditors

(1) A company may by special resolution make itself exempt from the provisions of this Part relating to the audit of accounts in the following cases—

    (*a*) if the company has been dormant from the time of its formation, by a special resolution passed before the first general meeting of the company at which annual accounts are laid;

    (*b*) if the company has been dormant since the end of the previous financial year and—

        (i) is entitled in respect of its individual accounts for that year to the exemptions conferred by section 246 on a small company, or would be so entitled but for being a member of an ineligible group, and

        (ii) is not required to prepare group accounts for that year,

    by a special resolution passed at a general meeting of the company at which the annual accounts for that year are laid.

(2) A company may not pass such a resolution if it is—

    (*a*) a public company,

    (*b*) a banking or insurance company, or

    (*c*) an authorised person under the Financial Services Act 1986.

(3) A company is 'dormant' during a period in which no significant accounting transaction occurs, that is, no transaction which is required by section 221 to be entered in the company's accounting records; and a company ceases to be dormant on the occurrence of such a transaction.

For this purpose there shall be disregarded any transaction arising from the taking of shares in the company by a subscriber to the memorandum in pursuance of an undertaking of his in the memorandum.

(4) Where a company is, at the end of a financial year, exempt by virtue of this section from the provisions of this Part relating to the audit of accounts—

(*a*) sections 238 and 239 (right to receive or demand copies of accounts and reports) have effect with the omission of references to the auditors' report;

(*b*) no copies of an auditors' report need be laid before the company in general meeting;

(*c*) no copy of an auditors' report need be delivered to the registrar, and if none is delivered, the copy of the balance sheet so delivered shall contain a statement by the directors, in a position immediately above the signature required by section 233(4), that the company was dormant throughout the financial year; and

(*d*) the company shall be treated as entitled in respect of its individual accounts for that year to the exemptions conferred by section 246 on a small company notwithstanding that it is a member of an ineligible group.

(5) Where a company which is exempt by virtue of this section from the provisions of this Part relating to the audit of accounts—

(*a*) ceases to be dormant, or

(*b*) would no longer qualify (for any other reason) to make itself exempt by passing a resolution under this section,

it shall thereupon cease to be so exempt.'.

15 Public listed companies: provision of summary financial statement

The following section is inserted in Part VII of the Companies Act 1985—

'Listed public companies

251 Provision of summary financial statement to shareholders

(1) A public company whose shares, or any class of whose shares, are listed need not, in such cases as may be specified by regulations made by the Secretary of State, and provided any conditions so specified are complied with, send copies of the documents referred to in section 238(1) to members of the company, but may instead send them a summary financial statement.

In this subsection 'listed' means admitted to the Official List of The International Stock Exchange of the United Kingdom and the Republic of Ireland Limited.

(2) Copies of the documents referred to in section 238(1) shall, however, be sent to any member of the company who wishes to receive them; and the Secretary of State may by regulations make provision as to the manner in which it is to be ascertained whether a member of the company wishes to receive them.

(3) The summary financial statement shall be derived from the company's annual accounts and the directors' report and shall be in such form and contain such information as may be specified by regulations made by the Secretary of State.

(4) Every summary financial statement shall—

(*a*) state that it is only a summary of information in the company's annual accounts and the directors' report;

(*b*) contain a statement by the company's auditors of their opinion as to whether the summary financial statement is consistent with those accounts and that report and complies with the requirements of this section and regulations made under it;

145

    (*c*) state whether the auditors' report on the annual accounts was unqualified or qualified, and if it was qualified set out the report in full together with any further material needed to understand the qualification;

    (*d*) state whether the auditors' report on the annual accounts contained a statement under—

        (i) section 237(2) (accounting records or returns inadequate or accounts not agreeing with records and returns), or

        (ii) section 237(3) (failure to obtain necessary information and explanations), and if so, set out the statement in full.

(5) Regulations under this section shall be made by statutory instrument which shall be subject to annulment in pursuance of a resolution of either House of Parliament.

(6) If default is made in complying with this section or regulations made under it, the company and every officer of it who is in default is guilty of an offence and liable to a fine.

(7) Section 240 (requirements in connection with publication of accounts) does not apply in relation to the provision to members of a company of a summary financial statement in accordance with this section.'.

16 Private companies: election to dispense with laying of accounts and reports before general meeting

The following sections are inserted in Part VII of the Companies Act 1985—

'Private companies

252 Election to dispense with laying of accounts and reports before general meeting

(1) A private company may elect (by elective resolution in accordance with section 379A) to dispense with the laying of accounts and reports before the company in general meeting.

(2) An election has effect in relation to the accounts and reports in respect of the financial year in which the election is made and subsequent financial years.

(3) Whilst an election is in force, the references in the following provisions of this Act to the laying of accounts before the company in general meeting shall be read as references to the sending of copies of the accounts to members and others under section 238(1)—

    (*a*) section 235(1) (accounts on which auditors are to report),

    (*b*) section 270(3) and (4) (accounts by reference to which distributions are justified), and

    (*c*) section 320(2) (accounts relevant for determining company's net assets for purposes of ascertaining whether approval required for certain transactions);

and the requirement in section 271(4) that the auditors' statement under that provision be laid before the company in general meeting shall be read as a requirement that it be sent to members and others along with the copies of the accounts sent to them under section 238(1).

(4) If an election under this section ceases to have effect, section 241 applies in relation to the accounts and reports in respect of the financial year in which the election ceases to have effect and subsequent financial years.

253 Right of shareholder to require laying of accounts

(1) Where an election under section 252 is in force, the copies of the accounts and reports sent out in accordance with section 238(1)—

    (*a*) shall be sent not less than 28 days before the end of the period allowed for laying and delivering accounts and reports, and

    (*b*) shall be accompanied, in the case of a member of the company, by a notice informing him of his right to require the laying of the accounts and reports before a general meeting;

and section 238(5) (penalty for default) applies in relation to the above requirements as to the requirements contained in that section.

(2) Before the end of the period of 28 days beginning with the day on which the accounts and reports are sent out in accordance with section 238(1), any member or auditor of the company may by notice in writing deposited at the registered office of the company require that a general meeting be held for the purpose of laying the accounts and reports before the company.

(3) If the directors do not within 21 days from the date of the deposit of such a notice proceed duly to convene a meeting, the person who deposited the notice may do so himself.

(4) A meeting so convened shall not be held more than three months from that date and shall be convened in the same manner, as nearly as possible, as that in which meetings are to be convened by directors.

(5) Where the directors do not duly convene a meeting, any reasonable expenses incurred by reason of that failure by the person who deposited the notice shall be made good to him by the company, and shall be recouped by the company out of any fees, or other remuneration in respect of their services, due or to become due to such of the directors as were in default.

(6) The directors shall be deemed not to have duly convened a meeting if they convene a meeting for a date more than 28 days after the date of the notice convening it.'.

17 Unlimited companies: exemption from requirement to deliver accounts and reports

The following section is inserted in Part VII of the Companies Act 1985—

'Unlimited companies

254 Exemption from requirement to deliver accounts and reports

(1) The directors of an unlimited company are not required to deliver accounts and reports to the registrar in respect of a financial year if the following conditions are met.

(2) The conditions are that at no time during the relevant accounting reference period—

(a) has the company been, to its knowledge, a subsidiary undertaking of an undertaking which was then limited, or

(b) have there been, to its knowledge, exercisable by or on behalf of two or more undertakings which were then limited rights which if exercisable by one of them would have made the company a subsidiary undertaking of it, or

(c) has the company been a parent company of an undertaking which was then limited.

The references above to an undertaking being limited at a particular time are to an undertaking (under whatever law established) the liability of whose members is at that time limited.

(3) The exemption conferred by this section does not apply if at any time during the relevant accounting period the company carried on business as the promoter of a trading stamp scheme within the Trading Stamps Act 1964.

(4) Where a company is exempt by virtue of this section from the obligation to deliver accounts, section 240 (requirements in connection with publication of accounts) has effect with the following modifications—

(a) in subsection (3)(b) for the words from 'whether statutory accounts' to 'have been delivered to the registrar' substitute 'that the company is exempt from the requirement to deliver statutory accounts', and

(b) in subsection (5) for 'as required to be delivered to the registrar under section 242' substitute 'as prepared in accordance with this Part and approved by the board of directors'.'.

147

18 Banking and insurance companies and groups: special provisions

(1) The following sections are inserted in Part VII of the Companies Act 1985—

'Banking and insurance companies and groups

255 Special provisions for banking and insurance companies

(1) A banking or insurance company may prepare its individual accounts in accordance with Part I of Schedule 9 rather than Schedule 4.

(2) Accounts so prepared shall contain a statement that they are prepared in accordance with the special provisions of this Part relating to banking companies or insurance companies, as the case may be.

(3) In relation to the preparation of individual accounts in accordance with the special provisions of this Part relating to banking or insurance companies, the references to the provisions of Schedule 4 in section 226(4) and (5) (relationship between specific requirements and duty to give true and fair view) shall be read as references to the provisions of Part I of Schedule 9.

(4) The Secretary of State may, on the application or with the consent of the directors of a company which prepares individual accounts in accordance with the special provisions of this Part relating to banking or insurance companies, modify in relation to the company any of the requirements of this Part for the purpose of adapting them to the circumstances of the company.

This does not affect the duty to give a true and fair view.

255A Special provisions for banking and insurance groups

(1) The parent company of a banking or insurance group may prepare group accounts in accordance with the provisions of this Part as modified by Part II of Schedule 9.

(2) Accounts so prepared shall contain a statement that they are prepared in accordance with the special provisions of this Part relating to banking groups or insurance groups, as the case may be.

(3) References in this Part to a banking group are to a group where—

(*a*) the parent company is a banking company, or
(*b*) at least one of the undertakings in the group is an authorised institution under the Banking Act 1987 and the predominant activities of the group are such as to make it inappropriate to prepare group accounts in accordance with the formats in Part I of Schedule 4.

(4) References in this Part to an insurance group are to a group where—

(*a*) the parent company is an insurance company, or
(*b*) the predominant activity of the group is insurance business and activities which are a direct extension of or ancillary to insurance business.

(5) In relation to the preparation of group accounts in accordance with the special provisions of this Part relating to banking or insurance groups, the references to the provisions of Schedule 4A in section 227(5) and (6) (relationship between specific requirements and duty to give true and fair view) shall be read as references to those provisions as modified by Part II of Schedule 9.

(6) The Secretary of State may, on the application or with the consent of the directors of a company which prepares group accounts in accordance with the special provisions of this Part relating to banking or insurance groups, modify in relation to the company any of the requirements of this Part for the purpose of adapting them to the circumstances of the company.

255B Modification of disclosure requirements in relation to banking company or group

(1) In relation to a company which prepares accounts in accordance with the special

provisions of this Part relating to banking companies or groups, the provisions of Schedule 5 (additional disclosure: related undertakings) have effect subject to Part III of Schedule 9.

(2) In relation to a banking company, or the parent company of a banking company, the provisions of Schedule 6 (disclosure: emoluments and other benefits of directors and others) have effect subject to Part IV of Schedule 9.

255C Directors' report where accounts prepared in accordance with special provisions

(1) The following provisions apply in relation to the directors' report of a company for a financial year in respect of which it prepares accounts in accordance with the special provisions of this Part relating to banking or insurance companies or groups.

(2) The information required to be given by paragraph 6, 8 or 13 of Part I of Schedule 9 (which is allowed to be given in a statement or report annexed to the accounts), may be given in the directors' report instead.

Information so given shall be treated for the purposes of audit as forming part of the accounts.

(3) The reference in section 234(1)(*b*) to the amount proposed to be carried to reserves shall be construed as a reference to the amount proposed to be carried to reserves within the meaning of Part I of Schedule 9.

(4) If the company takes advantage, in relation to its individual or group accounts, of the exemptions conferred by paragraph 27 or 28 of Part I of Schedule 9, paragraph 1 of Schedule 7 (disclosure of asset values) does not apply.

(5) The directors' report shall, in addition to complying with Schedule 7, also comply with Schedule 10 (which specifies additional matters to be disclosed).'.

(2) The following section is inserted in Part VII of the Companies Act 1985—

'255D Power to apply provisions to banking partnerships

(1) The Secretary of State may by regulations apply to banking partnerships, subject to such exceptions, adaptations and modifications as he considers appropriate, the provisions of this Part applying to banking companies.

(2) A 'banking partnership' means a partnership which is an authorised institution under the Banking Act 1987.

(3) Regulations under this section shall be made by statutory instrument.

(4) No regulations under this section shall be made unless a draft of the instrument containing the regulations has been laid before Parliament and approved by a resolution of each House.'.

(3) Schedule 9 to the Companies Act 1985 (form and content of special category accounts) is amended in accordance with Schedule 7 to this Act.

(4) In that Schedule—

Part I contains amendments relating to the form and content of accounts of banking and insurance companies and groups,

Part II contains provisions with respect to the group accounts of banking and insurance groups,

Part III contains provisions adapting the requirements of Schedule 5 to the Companies Act 1985 (additional disclosure: related undertakings), and

Part IV contains provisions relating to the requirements of Schedule 6 to that Act (additional disclosure: emoluments and other benefits of directors and others).

(5) Schedule 8 to this Act (directors' report where accounts prepared in accordance with special provisions for banking and insurance companies and groups) is substituted for Schedule 10 to the Companies Act 1985.

19 Accounting standards

The following section is inserted in Part VII of the Companies Act 1985, as the beginning of a Chapter III—

'CHAPTER III

SUPPLEMENTARY PROVISIONS

Accounting standards

256 Accounting standards

(1) In this Part 'accounting standards' means statements of standard accounting practice issued by such body or bodies as may be prescribed by regulations.

(2) References in this Part to accounting standards applicable to a company's annual accounts are to such standards as are, in accordance with their terms, relevant to the company's circumstances and to the accounts.

(3) The Secretary of State may make grants to or for the purposes of bodies concerned with—

(*a*) issuing accounting standards,

(*b*) overseeing and directing the issuing of such standards, or

(*c*) investigating departures from such standards or from the accounting requirements of this Act and taking steps to secure compliance with them.

(4) Regulations under this section may contain such transitional and other supplementary and incidental provisions as appear to the Secretary of State to be appropriate.'.

20 Power to alter accounting requirements

The following section is inserted in Part VII of the Companies Act 1985—

'Power to alter accounting requirements

257 Power of Secretary of State to alter accounting requirements

(1) The Secretary of State may by regulations made by statutory instrument modify the provisions of this Part.

(2) Regulations which—

(*a*) add to the classes of documents required to be prepared, laid before the company in general meeting or delivered to the registrar,

(*b*) restrict the classes of company which have the benefit of any exemption, exception or special provision,

(*c*) require additional matter to be included in a document of any class, or

(*d*) otherwise render the requirements of this Part more onerous,

shall not be made unless a draft of the instrument containing the regulations has been laid before Parliament and approved by a resolution of each House.

(3) Otherwise, a statutory instrument containing regulations under this section shall be subject to annulment in pursuance of a resolution of either House of Parliament.

(4) Regulations under this section may—

(*a*) make different provision for different cases or classes of case,

(*b*) repeal and re-enact provisions with modifications of form or arrangement, whether or not they are modified in substance,

(*c*) make consequential amendments or repeals in other provisions of this Act, or in other enactments, and

(*d*) contain such transitional and other incidental and supplementary provisions as the Secretary of State thinks fit.

(5) Any modification by regulations under this section of section 258 or Schedule

10A (parent and subsidiary undertakings) does not apply for the purposes of enactments outside the Companies Acts unless the regulations so provide.'.

21 Parent and subsidiary undertakings

(1) The following section is inserted in Part VII of the Companies Act 1985—

'Parent and subsidiary undertakings

258 Parent and subsidiary undertakings

(1) The expressions 'parent undertaking' and 'subsidiary undertaking' in this Part shall be construed as follows; and a 'parent company' means a parent undertaking which is a company.

(2) An undertaking is a parent undertaking in relation to another undertaking, a subsidiary undertaking, if—

(*a*) it holds a majority of the voting rights in the undertaking, or

(*b*) it is a member of the undertaking and has the right to appoint or remove a majority of its board of directors, or

(*c*) it has the right to exercise a dominant influence over the undertaking—
  (i) by virtue of provisions contained in the undertaking's memorandum or articles, or
  (ii) by virtue of a control contract, or

(*d*) it is a member of the undertaking and controls alone, pursuant to an agreement with other shareholders or members, a majority of the voting rights in the undertaking.

(3) For the purposes of subsection (2) an undertaking shall be treated as a member of another undertaking—

(*a*) if any of its subsidiary undertakings is a member of that undertaking, or

(*b*) if any shares in that other undertaking are held by a person acting on behalf of the undertaking or any of its subsidiary undertakings.

(4) An undertaking is also a parent undertaking in relation to another undertaking, a subsidiary undertaking, if it has a participating interest in the undertaking and—

(*a*) it actually exercises a dominant influence over it, or

(*b*) it and the subsidiary undertaking are managed on a unified basis.

(5) A parent undertaking shall be treated as the parent undertaking of undertakings in relation to which any of its subsidiary undertakings are, or are to be treated as, parent undertakings; and references to its subsidiary undertakings shall be construed accordingly.

(6) Schedule 10A contains provisions explaining expressions used in this section and otherwise supplementing this section.'.

(2) Schedule 9 to this Act (parent and subsidiary undertakings: supplementary provisions) is inserted after Schedule 10 to the Companies Act 1985, as Schedule 10A.

22 Other interpretation provisions

The following sections are inserted in Part VII of the Companies Act 1985—

'Other interpretation provisions

259 Meaning of 'undertaking' and related expressions

(1) In this Part 'undertaking' means—

(*a*) a body corporate or partnership, or

(*b*) an unincorporated association carrying on a trade or business, with or without a view to profit.

(2) In this Part references to shares—

(*a*) in relation to an undertaking with a share capital, are to allotted shares;

(*b*) in relation to an undertaking with capital but no share capital, are to rights to share in the capital of the undertaking; and

(*c*) in relation to an undertaking without capital, are to interests—

    (i) conferring any right to share in the profits or liability to contribute to the losses of the undertaking, or

    (ii) giving rise to an obligation to contribute to the debts or expenses of the undertaking in the event of a winding up.

(3) Other expressions appropriate to companies shall be construed, in relation to an undertaking which is not a company, as references to the corresponding persons, officers, documents or organs, as the case may be, appropriate to undertakings of that description.

This is subject to provision in any specific context providing for the translation of such expressions.

(4) References in this Part to 'fellow subsidiary undertakings' are to undertakings which are subsidiary undertakings of the same parent undertaking but are not parent undertakings or subsidiary undertakings of each other.

(5) In this Part 'group undertaking', in relation to an undertaking, means an undertaking which is—

(*a*) a parent undertaking or subsidiary undertaking of that undertaking, or

(*b*) a subsidiary undertaking of any parent undertaking of that undertaking.

260 Participating interests

(1) In this Part a 'participating interest' means an interest held by an undertaking in the shares of another undertaking which it holds on a long-term basis for the purpose of securing a contribution to its activities by the exercise of control or influence arising from or related to that interest.

(2) A holding of 20 per cent or more of the shares of an undertaking shall be presumed to be a participating interest unless the contrary is shown.

(3) The reference in subsection (1) to an interest in shares includes—

(*a*) an interest which is convertible into an interest in shares, and

(*b*) an option to acquire shares or any such interest;

and an interest or option falls within paragraph (*a*) or (*b*) notwithstanding that the shares to which it relates are, until the conversion or the exercise of the option, unissued.

(4) For the purposes of this section an interest held on behalf of an undertaking shall be treated as held by it.

(5) For the purposes of this section as it applies in relation to the expression 'participating interest' in section 258(4) (definition of 'subsidiary undertaking')—

(*a*) there shall be attributed to an undertaking any interests held by any of its subsidiary undertakings, and

(*b*) the references in subsection (1) to the purpose and activities of an undertaking include the purposes and activities of any of its subsidiary undertakings and of the group as a whole.

(6) In the balance sheet and profit and loss formats set out in Part I of Schedule 4, 'participating interest' does not include an interest in a group undertaking.

(7) For the purposes of this section as it applies in relation to the expression 'participating interest'—

(*a*) in those formats as they apply in relation to group accounts, and

(*b*) in paragraph 20 of Schedule 4A (group accounts: undertakings to be accounted for as associated undertakings),

the references in subsections (1) to (4) to the interest held by, and the purposes and activities of, the undertaking concerned shall be construed as references to the interest held by, and the purposes and activities of, the group (within the meaning of paragraph 1 of that Schedule).

261 Notes to the accounts

(1) Information required by this Part to be given in notes to a company's annual accounts may be contained in the accounts or in a separate document annexed to the accounts.

(2) References in this Part to a company's annual accounts, or to a balance sheet or profit and loss account, include notes to the accounts giving information which is required by any provision of this Act, and required or allowed by any such provision to be given in a note to company accounts.

262 Minor definitions

(1) In this Part—
'annual accounts' means—

(*a*) the individual accounts required by section 226, and
(*b*) any group accounts required by section 227,
(but see also section 230 (treatment of individual profit and loss account where group accounts prepared));

'annual report', in relation to a company, means the directors' report required by section 234;

'balance sheet date' means the date as at which the balance sheet was made up;

'capitalisation', in relation to work or costs, means treating that work or those costs as a fixed asset;

'credit institution' means an undertaking carrying on a deposit-taking business within the meaning of the Banking Act 1987;

'fixed assets' means assets of a company which are intended for use on a continuing basis in the company's activities, and 'current assets' means assets not intended for such use;

'group' means a parent undertaking and its subsidiary undertakings;

'included in the consolidation', in relation to group accounts, or 'included in consolidated group accounts', means that the undertaking is included in the accounts by the method of full (and not proportional) consolidation, and references to an undertaking excluded from consolidation shall be construed accordingly;

'purchase price', in relation to an asset of a company or any raw materials or consumables used in the production of such an asset, includes any consideration (whether in cash or otherwise) given by the company in respect of that asset or those materials or consumables, as the case may be;

'qualified', in relation to an auditors' report, means that the report does not state the auditors' unqualified opinion that the accounts have been properly prepared in accordance with this Act or, in the case of an undertaking not required to prepare accounts in accordance with this Act, under any corresponding legislation under which it is required to prepare accounts;

'true and fair view' refers—

(*a*) in the case of individual accounts, to the requirement of section 226(2), and
(*b*) in the case of group accounts, to the requirement of section 227(3);

'turnover', in relation to a company, means the amounts derived from the provision of goods and services falling within the company's ordinary activities, after deduction of—

(i) trade discounts,
(ii) value added tax, and
(iii) any other taxes based on the amounts so derived.

(2) In the case of an undertaking not trading for profit, any reference in this Part to a

profit and loss account is to an income and expenditure account; and references to profit and loss and, in relation to group accounts, to a consolidated profit and loss account shall be construed accordingly.

(3) References in this Part to 'realised profits' and 'realised losses', in relation to a company's accounts, are to such profits or losses of the company as fall to be treated as realised in accordance with principles generally accepted, at the time when the accounts are prepared, with respect to the determination for accounting purposes of realised profits or losses.

This is without prejudice to—

(*a*) the construction of any other expression (where appropriate) by reference to accepted accounting principles or practice, or

(*b*) any specific provision for the treatment of profits or losses of any description as realised.

262A Index of defined expressions

The following Table shows the provisions of this Part defining or otherwise explaining expressions used in this Part (other than expressions used only in the same section or paragraph)—

accounting reference date and accounting reference period	section 224
accounting standards and applicable accounting standards	section 256
annual accounts	
(generally)	section 262(1)
(includes notes to the accounts)	section 261(2)
annual report	section 262(1)
associated undertaking (in Schedule 4A)	paragraph 20 of that Schedule
balance sheet (includes notes)	section 261(2)
balance sheet date	section 262(1)
banking group	section 255A(3)
capitalisation (in relation to work or costs)	section 262(1)
credit institution	section 262(1)
current assets	section 262(1)
fellow subsidiary undertaking	section 259(4)
financial year	section 223
fixed assets	section 262(1)
group	section 262(1)
group undertaking	section 259(5)
historical cost accounting rules (in Schedule 4)	paragraph 29 of that Schedule
included in the consolidation and related expressions	section 262(1)
individual accounts	section 262(1)
insurance group	section 255A(4)
land of freehold tenure and land of leasehold tenure (in relation to Scotland)	
—in Schedule 4	paragraph 93 of that Schedule
—in Schedule 9	paragraph 36 of that Schedule
lease, long lease and short lease	
—in Schedule 4	paragraph 83 of that Schedule
—in Schedule 9	paragraph 34 of that Schedule

listed investment	
—in Schedule 4	paragraph 84 of that Schedule
—in Schedule 9	paragraph 33 of that Schedule
notes to the accounts	section 261(1)
parent undertaking (and parent company)	section 258 and Schedule 10A
participating interest	section 260
pension costs (in Schedule 4)	paragraph 94(2) and (3) of that Schedule
period allowed for laying and delivering accounts and reports	section 244
profit and loss account	
(includes notes)	section 261(2)
(in relation to a company not trading for profit)	section 262(2)
provision	
—in Schedule 4	paragraphs 88 and 89 of that Schedule
—in Schedule 9	paragraph 32 of that Schedule
purchase price	section 262(1)
qualified	section 262(1)
realised losses and realised profits	section 262(3)
reserve (in Schedule 9)	paragraph 32 of that Schedule
shares	section 259(2)
social security costs (in Schedule 4)	paragraph 94(1) and (3) of that Schedule
special provisions for banking and insurance companies and groups	sections 255 and 255A
subsidiary undertaking	section 258 and Schedule 10A
true and fair view	section 262(1)
turnover	section 262(1)
undertaking and related expressions	section 259(1) to (3)'.

Consequential amendments

23 Consequential amendments

The enactments specified in Schedule 10 have effect with the amendments specified there, which are consequential on the amendments made by the preceding provisions of this Part.

PART II

ELIGIBILITY FOR APPOINTMENT AS COMPANY AUDITOR

Introduction

24 Introduction

(1) The main purposes of this Part are to secure that only persons who are properly supervised and appropriately qualified are appointed company auditors, and that audits by persons so appointed are carried out properly and with integrity and with a proper degree of independence.

(2) A 'company auditor' means a person appointed as auditor under Chapter V of Part XI of the Companies Act 1985; and the expressions 'company audit' and 'company audit work' shall be construed accordingly.

Eligibility for appointment

25 Eligibility for appointment

(1) A person is eligible for appointment as a company auditor only if he—

(*a*) is a member of a recognised supervisory body, and

(*b*) is eligible for the appointment under the rules of that body.

(2) An individual or a firm may be appointed a company auditor.

(3) In the cases to which section 34 applies (individuals retaining only 1967 Act authorisation) a person's eligibility for appointment as a company auditor is restricted as mentioned in that section.

26 Effect of appointment of partnership

(1) The following provisions apply to the appointment as company auditor of a partnership constituted under the law of England and Wales or Northern Ireland, or under the law of any other country or territory in which a partnership is not a legal person.

(2) The appointment is (unless a contrary intention appears) an appointment of the partnership as such and not of the partners.

(3) Where the partnership ceases, the appointment shall be treated as extending to—

(*a*) any partnership which succeeds to the practice of that partnership and is eligible for the appointment, and

(*b*) any person who succeeds to that practice having previously carried it on in partnership and is eligible for the appointment.

(4) For this purpose a partnership shall be regarded as succeeding to the practice of another partnership only if the members of the successor partnership are substantially the same as those of the former partnership; and a partnership or other person shall be regarded as succeeding to the practice of a partnership only if it or he succeeds to the whole or substantially the whole of the business of the former partnership.

(5) Where the partnership ceases and no person succeeds to the appointment under subsection (3), the appointment may with the consent of the company be treated as extending to a partnership or other person eligible for the appointment who succeeds to the business of the former partnership or to such part of it as is agreed by the company shall be treated as comprising the appointment.

27 Ineligibility on ground of lack of independence

(1) A person is ineligible for appointment as company auditor of a company if he is—

(*a*) an officer or employee of the company, or

(*b*) a partner or employee of such a person, or a partnership of which such a person is a partner,

or if he is ineligible by virtue of paragraph (*a*) or (*b*) for appointment as company auditor of any associated undertaking of the company.

For this purpose an auditor of a company shall not be regarded as an officer or employee of the company.

(2) A person is also ineligible for appointment as company auditor of a company if there exists between him or any associate of his and the company or any associated undertaking a connection of any such description as may be specified by regulations made by the Secretary of State.

The regulations may make different provisions for different cases.

(3) In this section 'associated undertaking', in relation to a company, means—

(*a*) a parent undertaking or subsidiary undertaking of the company, or

(*b*) a subsidiary undertaking of any parent undertaking of the company.

(4) Regulations under this section shall be made by statutory instrument which shall be subject to annulment in pursuance of a resolution of either House of Parliament.

28 Effect of ineligibility

(1) No person shall act as a company auditor if he is ineligible for appointment to the office.

(2) If during his term of office a company auditor becomes ineligible for appointment to the office, he shall thereupon vacate office and shall forthwith give notice in writing to the company concerned that he has vacated it by reason of ineligibility.

(3) A person who acts as company auditor in contravention of subsection (1), or fails to give notice of vacating his office as required by subsection (2), is guilty of an offence and liable—

(*a*) on conviction on indictment, to a fine, and
(*b*) on summary conviction, to a fine not exceeding the statutory maximum.

(4) In the case of continued contravention he is liable on a second or subsequent summary conviction (instead of the fine mentioned in subsection (3)(*b*)) to a fine not exceeding one-tenth of the statutory maximum in respect of each day on which the contravention is continued.

(5) In proceedings against a person for an offence under this section it is a defence for him to show that he did not know and had no reason to believe that he was, or had become, ineligible for appointment.

29 Power of Secretary of State to require second audit

(1) Where a person appointed company auditor was, for any part of the period during which the audit was conducted, ineligible for appointment to that office, the Secretary of State may direct the company concerned to retain a person eligible for appointment as auditor of the company—

(*a*) to audit the relevant accounts again, or
(*b*) to review the first audit and to report (giving his reasons) whether a second audit is needed;

and the company shall comply with such a direction within 21 days of its being given.

(2) If a second audit is recommended the company shall forthwith take such steps as are necessary to comply with the recommendation.

(3) Where a direction is given under this section, the Secretary of State shall send a copy of the direction to the registrar of companies; and the company shall within 21 days of receiving any report under subsection (1)(*b*) send a copy of it to the registrar of companies.

The provisions of the Companies Act 1985 relating to the delivery of documents to the registrar apply for the purposes of this subsection.

(4) Any statutory or other provisions applying in relation to the first audit shall apply, so far as practicable, in relation to a second audit under this section.

(5) If a company fails to comply with the requirements of this section, it is guilty of an offence and liable on summary conviction to a fine not exceeding the statutory maximum; and in the case of continued contravention it is liable on a second or subsequent summary conviction (instead of the fine mentioned above) to a fine not exceeding one-tenth of the statutory maximum in respect of each day on which the contravention is continued.

(6) A direction under this section is, on the application of the Secretary of State, enforceable by injunction or, in Scotland, by an order under section 45 of the Court of Session Act 1988.

(7) If a person accepts an appointment, or continues to act, as company auditor at a time when he knows he is ineligible, the company concerned may recover from him any costs incurred by it in complying with the requirements of this section.

Recognition of supervisory bodies and professional qualifications

30 Supervisory bodies

(1) In this Part a 'supervisory body' means a body established in the United Kingdom

(whether a body corporate or an unincorporated association) which maintains and enforces rules as to—

(a) the eligibility of persons to seek appointment as company auditors, and

(b) the conduct of company audit work,

which are binding on persons seeking appointment or acting as company auditors either because they are members of that body or because they are otherwise subject to its control.

(2) In this Part references to the members of a supervisory body are to the persons who, whether or not members of the body, are subject to its rules in seeking appointment or acting as company auditors.

(3) In this Part references to the rules of a supervisory body are to the rules (whether or not laid down by the body itself) which the body has power to enforce and which are relevant for the purposes of this Part.

This includes rules relating to the admission and expulsion of members of the body, so far as relevant for the purposes of this Part.

(4) In this Part references to guidance issued by a supervisory body are to guidance issued or any recommendation made by it to all or any class of its members or persons seeking to become members which would, if it were a rule, fall within subsection (3).

(5) The provisions of Parts I and II of Schedule 11 have effect with respect to the recognition of supervisory bodies for the purposes of this Part.

31 Meaning of 'appropriate qualification'

(1) A person holds an appropriate qualification for the purposes of this Part if—

(a) he was, by virtue of membership of a body recognised for the purposes of section 389(1)(a) of the Companies Act 1985, qualified for appointment as auditor of a company under that section immediately before 1st January 1990 and immediately before the commencement of section 25 above,

(b) he holds a recognised professional qualification obtained in the United Kingdom, or

(c) he holds an approved overseas qualification and satisfies any additional educational requirements applicable in accordance with section 33(4).

(2) A person who immediately before 1st January 1990 and immediately before the commencement of section 25 above, was qualified for appointment as auditor of a company under section 389 of the Companies Act 1985 otherwise than by virtue of membership of a body recognised for the purposes of section 389(1)(a)—

(a) shall be treated as holding an appropriate qualification for twelve months from the day on which section 25 comes into force, and

(b) shall continue to be so treated if within that period he notifies the Secretary of State that he wishes to retain the benefit of his qualification.

The notice shall be in writing and shall contain such information as the Secretary of State may require.

(3) If a person fails to give such notice within the time allowed he may apply to the Secretary of State, giving such information as would have been required in connection with a notice, and the Secretary of State may, if he is satisfied—

(a) that there was good reason why the applicant did not give notice in time, and

(b) that the applicant genuinely intends to practise as an auditor in Great Britain,

direct that he shall be treated as holding an appropriate qualification for the purposes of this Part.

(4) A person who—

(a) began before 1st January 1990 a course of study or practical training leading to a professional qualification in accountancy offered by a body established in the United Kingdom, and

(b) obtained that qualification on or after that date and before 1st January 1996, shall be treated as holding an appropriate qualification if the qualification is approved by the Secretary of State for the purposes of this subsection.

(5) Approval shall not be given unless the Secretary of State is satisfied that the body concerned has or, as the case may be, had at the relevant time adequate arrangements to ensure that the qualification is, or was, awarded only to persons educated and trained to a standard equivalent to that required in the case of a recognised professional qualification.

(6) A person shall not be regarded as holding an appropriate qualification for the purposes of this Part except in the above cases.

32 Qualifying bodies and recognised professional qualifications

(1) In this Part a 'qualifying body' means a body established in the United Kingdom (whether a body corporate or an unincorporated association) which offers a professional qualification in accountancy.

(2) In this Part references to the rules of a qualifying body are to the rules (whether or not laid down by the body itself) which the body has power to enforce and which are relevant for the purposes of this Part.

This includes rules relating to—

(a) admission to or expulsion from a course of study leading to a qualification,
(b) the award or deprivation of a qualification, or
(c) the approval of a person for the purposes of giving practical training or the withdrawal of such approval,

so far as relevant for the purposes of this Part.

(3) In this Part references to guidance issued by any such body are to any guidance which the body issues, or any recommendation it makes to all or any class of persons holding or seeking to hold a qualification, or approved or seeking to be approved by the body for the purpose of giving practical training, which would, if it were a rule, fall within subsection (2).

(4) The provisions of Parts I and II of Schedule 12 have effect with respect to the recognition for the purposes of this Part of a professional qualification offered by a qualifying body.

33 Approval of overseas qualifications

(1) The Secretary of State may declare that persons who—

(a) are qualified to audit accounts under the law of a specified country or territory outside the United Kingdom, or
(b) hold a specified professional qualification in accountancy recognised under the law of a country or territory outside the United Kingdom,

shall be regarded for the purposes of this Part as holding an approved overseas qualification.

(2) A qualification shall not be so approved by the Secretary of State unless he is satisfied that it affords an assurance of professional competence equivalent to that afforded by a recognised professional qualification.

(3) In exercising the power conferred by subsection (1) the Secretary of State may have regard to the extent to which persons—

(a) eligible under this Part for appointment as a company auditor, or
(b) holding a professional qualification recognised under this Part,

are recognised by the law of the country or territory in question as qualified to audit accounts there.

(4) The Secretary of State may direct that a person holding an approved overseas qualification shall not be treated as holding an appropriate qualification for the purposes of this Part unless he holds such additional educational qualifications as the Secretary of State

159

may specify for the purpose of ensuring that such persons have an adequate knowledge of the law and practice in the United Kingdom relevant to the audit of accounts.

(5) Different directions may be given in relation to different qualifications.

(6) The Secretary of State may if he thinks fit, having regard to the considerations mentioned in subsections (2) and (3), withdraw his approval of an overseas qualification in relation to persons becoming qualified as mentioned in subsection (1)(*a*), or obtaining such a qualification as is mentioned in subsection (1)(*b*), after such date as he may specify.

34 Eligibility of individuals retaining only 1967 Act authorisation

(1) A person whose only appropriate qualification is that he retains an authorisation granted by the Board of Trade or the Secretary of State under section 13(1) of the Companies Act 1967 is eligible only for appointment as auditor of an unquoted company.

(2) A company is 'unquoted' if, at the time of the person's appointment, no shares or debentures of the company, or of a parent undertaking of which it is a subsidiary undertaking, have been quoted on a stock exchange (in Great Britain or elsewhere) or offered (whether in Great Britain or elsewhere) to the public for subscription or purchase.

(3) This section does not authorise the appointment of such a person as auditor of a company that carries on business as the promoter of a trading stamp scheme within the meaning of the Trading Stamps Act 1964.

(4) References to a person eligible for appointment as company auditor under section 25 in enactments relating to eligibility for appointment as auditor of a body other than a company do not include a person to whom this section applies.

Duties of recognised bodies

35 The register of auditors

(1) The Secretary of State shall make regulations requiring the keeping of a register of—

(*a*) the individuals and firms eligible for appointment as company auditor, and

(*b*) the individuals holding an appropriate qualification who are responsible for company audit work on behalf of such firms.

(2) The regulations shall provide that each person's entry in the register shall give—

(*a*) his name and address, and

(*b*) in the case of a person eligible as mentioned in subsection (1)(*a*), the name of the relevant supervisory body,

together with such other information as may be specified by the regulations.

(3) The regulations may impose such obligations as the Secretary of State thinks fit—

(*a*) on recognised supervisory bodies,

(*b*) on persons eligible for appointment as company auditor, and

(*c*) on any person with whom arrangements are made by one or more recognised supervisory bodies with respect to the keeping of the register.

(4) The regulations may include provision—

(*a*) requiring the register to be open to inspection at such times and places as may be specified in the regulations or determined in accordance with them,

(*b*) enabling a person to require a certified copy of an entry in the register, and

(*c*) authorising the charging of fees for inspection, or the provision of copies, of such reasonable amount as may be specified in the regulations or determined in accordance with them;

and may contain such other supplementary and incidental provisions as the Secretary of State thinks fit.

(5) Regulations under this section shall be made by statutory instrument which shall be subject to annulment in pursuance of a resolution of either House of Parliament.

(6) The obligations imposed by regulations under this section on such persons as are mentioned in subsection (3)(*a*) or (*c*) are enforceable on the application of the Secretary of State by injunction or, in Scotland, by order under section 45 of the Court of Session Act 1988.

36 Information about firms to be available to public

(1) The Secretary of State shall make regulations requiring recognised supervisory bodies to keep and make available to the public the following information with respect to the firms eligible under their rules for appointment as a company auditor—

    (*a*) in relation to a body corporate, the name and address of each person who is a director of the body or holds any shares in it,

    (*b*) in relation to a partnership, the name and address of each partner,

and such other information as may be specified in the regulations.

(2) The regulations may impose such obligations as the Secretary of State thinks fit—

    (*a*) on recognised supervisory bodies,

    (*b*) on persons eligible for appointment as company auditor, and

    (*c*) on any person with whom arrangements are made by one or more recognised supervisory bodies with respect to the keeping of the information.

(3) The regulations may include provision—

    (*a*) requiring that the information be open to inspection at such times and places as may be specified in the regulations or determined in accordance with them,

    (*b*) enabling a person to require a certified copy of the information or any part of it, and

    (*c*) authorising the charging of fees for inspection, or the provision of copies, of such reasonable amount as may be specified in the regulations or determined in accordance with them;

and may contain such other supplementary and incidental provisions as the Secretary of State thinks fit.

(4) The regulations may make different provision in relation to different descriptions of information and may contain such other supplementary and incidental provisions as the Secretary of State thinks fit.

(5) Regulations under this section shall be made by statutory instrument which shall be subject to annulment in pursuance of a resolution of either House of Parliament.

(6) The obligations imposed by regulations under this section on such persons as are mentioned in subsection (2)(*a*) or (*c*) are enforceable on the application of the Secretary of State by injunction or, in Scotland, by an order under section 45 of the Court of Session Act 1988.

37 Matters to be notified to the Secretary of State

(1) The Secretary of State may require a recognised supervisory or qualifying body—

    (*a*) to notify him forthwith of the occurrence of such events as he may specify in writing and to give him such information in respect of those events as is so specified;

    (*b*) to give him, at such times or in respect of such periods as he may specify in writing, such information as is so specified.

(2) The notices and information required to be given shall be such as the Secretary of State may reasonably require for the exercise of his functions under this Part.

(3) The Secretary of State may require information given under this section to be given in a specified form or verified in a specified manner.

(4) Any notice or information required to be given under this section shall be given in writing unless the Secretary of State specifies or approves some other manner.

38 Power to call for information

(1) The Secretary of State may by notice in writing require a recognised supervisory or

qualifying body to give him such information as he may reasonably require for the exercise of his functions under this Part.

(2) The Secretary of State may require that any information which he requires under this section shall be given within such reasonable time and verified in such manner as he may specify.

39 Compliance orders

(1) If at any time it appears to the Secretary of State—

(a) in the case of a recognised supervisory body, that any requirement of Schedule 11 is not satisfied,

(b) in the case of a recognised professional qualification, that any requirement of Schedule 12 is not satisfied, or

(c) that a recognised supervisory or qualifying body has failed to comply with an obligation to which it is subject by virtue of this Part,

he may, instead of revoking the relevant recognition order, make an application to the court under this section.

(2) If on such application the court decides that the subsection or requirement in question is not satisfied or, as the case may be, that the body has failed to comply with the obligation in question it may order the supervisory or qualifying body in question to take such steps as the court directs for securing that the subsection or requirement is satisfied or that the obligation is complied with.

(3) The jurisdiction conferred by this section is exercisable by the High Court and the Court of Session.

40 Directions to comply with international obligations

(1) If it appears to the Secretary of State—

(a) that any action proposed to be taken by a recognised supervisory or qualifying body, or a body established by order under section 46, would be incompatible with Community obligations or any other international obligations of the United Kingdom, or

(b) that any action which that body has power to take is required for the purpose of implementing any such obligations,

he may direct the body not to take or, as the case may be, to take the action in question.

(2) A direction may include such supplementary or incidental requirements as the Secretary of State thinks necessary or expedient.

(3) A direction under this section is enforceable on the application of the Secretary of State by injunction or, in Scotland, by an order under section 45 of the Court of Session Act 1988.

Offences

41 False and misleading statements

(1) A person commits an offence if—

(a) for the purposes of or in connection with any application under this Part, or

(b) in purported compliance with any requirement imposed on him by or under this Part,

he furnishes information which he knows to be false or misleading in a material particular or recklessly furnishes information which is false or misleading in a material particular.

(2) It is an offence for a person whose name does not appear on the register of auditors kept under regulations under section 35 to describe himself as a registered auditor or so to hold himself out as to indicate, or be reasonably understood to indicate, that he is a registered auditor.

(3) It is an offence for a body which is not a recognised supervisory or qualifying body to describe itself as so recognised or so to describe itself or hold itself out as to indicate, or be reasonably understood to indicate, that it is so recognised.

(4) A person guilty of an offence under subsection (1) is liable—

(*a*) on conviction on indictment, to imprisonment for a term not exceeding two years or to a fine or both;

(*b*) on summary conviction, to imprisonment for a term not exceeding six months or to a fine not exceeding the statutory maximum or both.

(5) A person guilty of an offence under subsection (2) or (3) is liable on summary conviction to imprisonment for a term not exceeding six months or to a fine not exceeding level 5 on the standard scale or both.

Where a contravention of subsection (2) or (3) involves a public display of the offending description, the maximum fine that may be imposed is (in place of that mentioned above) an amount equal to level 5 on the standard scale multiplied by the number of days for which the display has continued.

(6) It is a defence for a person charged with an offence under subsection (2) or (3) to show that he took all reasonable precautions and exercised all due diligence to avoid the commission of the offence.

42 Offences by bodies corporate, partnerships and unincorporated associations

(1) Where an offence under this Part committed by a body corporate is proved to have been committed with the consent or connivance of, or to be attributable to any neglect on the part of, a director, manager, secretary or other similar officer of the body, or a person purporting to act in any such capacity, he as well as the body corporate is guilty of the offence and liable to be proceeded against and punished accordingly.

(2) Where the affairs of a body corporate are managed by its members, subsection (1) applies in relation to the acts and defaults of a member in connection with his functions of management as to a director of a body corporate.

(3) Where an offence under this Part committed by a partnership is proved to have been committed with the consent or connivance of, or to be attributable to any neglect on the part of, a partner, he as well as the partnership is guilty of the offence and liable to be proceeded against and punished accordingly.

(4) Where an offence under this Part committed by an unincorporated association (other than a partnership) is proved to have been committed with the consent or connivance of, or to be attributable to any neglect on the part of, any officer of the association or any member of its governing body, he as well as the association is guilty of the offence and liable to be proceeded against and punished accordingly.

43 Time limits for prosecution of offences

(1) An information relating to an offence under this Part which is triable by a magistrates' court in England and Wales may be so tried on an information laid at any time within twelve months after the date on which evidence sufficient in the opinion of the Director of Public Prosecutions or the Secretary of State to justify the proceedings comes to his knowledge.

(2) Proceedings in Scotland for an offence under this Part may be commenced at any time within twelve months after the date on which evidence sufficient in the Lord Advocate's opinion to justify the proceedings came to his knowledge or, where such evidence was reported to him by the Secretary of State, within twelve months after the date on which it came to the knowledge of the latter.

For the purposes of this subsection proceedings shall be deemed to be commenced on the date on which a warrant to apprehend or to cite the accused is granted, if the warrant is executed without undue delay.

(3) Subsection (1) does not authorise the trial of an information laid, and subsection (2) does not authorise the commencement of proceedings, more than three years after the commission of the offence.

(4) For the purposes of this section a certificate of the Director of Public Prosecutions, the Lord Advocate or the Secretary of State as to the date on which such evidence as is referred to above came to his knowledge is conclusive evidence.

(5) Nothing in this section affects proceedings within the time limits prescribed by section 127(1) of the Magistrates' Courts Act 1980 or section 331 of the Criminal Procedure (Scotland) Act 1975 (the usual time limits for criminal proceedings).

44 Jurisdiction and procedure in respect of offences

(1) Summary proceedings for an offence under this Part may, without prejudice to any jurisdiction exercisable apart from this section, be taken against a body corporate or unincorporated association at any place at which it has a place of business and against an individual at any place where he is for the time being.

(2) Proceedings for an offence alleged to have been committed under this Part by an unincorporated association shall be brought in the name of the association (and not in that of any of its members), and for the purposes of any such proceedings any rules of court relating to the service of documents apply as in relation to a body corporate.

(3) Section 33 of the Criminal Justice Act 1925 and Schedule 3 to the Magistrates' Courts Act 1980 (procedure on charge of offence against a corporation) apply in a case in which an unincorporated association is charged in England and Wales with an offence under this Part as they apply in the case of a corporation.

(4) In relation to proceedings on indictment in Scotland for an offence alleged to have been committed under this Part by an unincorporated association, section 74 of the Criminal Procedure (Scotland) Act 1975 (proceedings on indictment against bodies corporate) applies as if the association were a body corporate.

(5) A fine imposed on an unincorporated association on its conviction of such an offence shall be paid out of the funds of the association.

Supplementary provisions

45 Fees

(1) An applicant for a recognition order under this Part shall pay such fee in respect of his application as may be prescribed; and no application shall be regarded as duly made unless this subsection is complied with.

(2) Every recognised supervisory or qualifying body shall pay such periodical fees to the Secretary of State as may be prescribed.

(3) In this section 'prescribed' means prescribed by regulations made by the Secretary of State, which may make different provision for different cases or classes of case.

(4) Regulations under this section shall be made by statutory instrument which shall be subject to annulment in pursuance of a resolution of either House of Parliament.

(5) Fees received by the Secretary of State by virtue of this Part shall be paid into the Consolidated Fund.

46 Delegation of functions of Secretary of State

(1) The Secretary of State may by order (a 'delegation order') establish a body corporate to exercise his functions under this Part.

(2) A delegation order has the effect of transferring to the body established by it, subject to such exceptions and reservations as may be specified in the order, all the functions of the Secretary of State under this Part except—

(*a*) such functions under Part I of Schedule 14 (prevention of restrictive practices) as are excepted by regulations under section 47, and (*b*) his functions in relation to the body itself;

and the order may also confer on the body such other functions supplementary or incidental to those transferred as appear to the Secretary of State to be appropriate.

(3) Any transfer of the functions under the following provisions shall be subject to the reservation that they remain exercisable concurrently by the Secretary of State—

(*a*) section 38 (power to call for information), and

(*b*) section 40 (directions to comply with international obligations);

and any transfer of the function of refusing to approve an overseas qualification, or withdrawing such approval, on the grounds referred to in section 33(3) (lack of reciprocity) shall be subject to the reservation that the function is exercisable only with the consent of the Secretary of State.

(4) A delegation order may be amended or, if it appears to the Secretary of State that it is no longer in the public interest that the order should remain in force, revoked by a further order under this section.

(5) Where functions are transferred or resumed, the Secretary of State may by order confer or, as the case may be, take away such other functions supplementary or incidental to those transferred or resumed as appear to him to be appropriate.

(6) The provisions of Schedule 13 have effect with respect to the status, constitution and proceedings of a body established by a delegation order, the exercise by it of certain functions transferred to it and other supplementary matters.

(7) An order under this section shall be made by statutory instrument.

(8) An order which has the effect of transferring or resuming any functions shall not be made unless a draft of it has been laid before and approved by resolution of each House of Parliament; and any other description of order shall be subject to annulment in pursuance of a resolution of either House of Parliament.

47 Restrictive practices

(1) The provisions of Schedule 14 have effect with respect to certain matters relating to restrictive practices and competition law.

(2) The Secretary of State may make provision by regulations as to the discharge of the functions under paragraphs 1 to 7 of that Schedule when a delegation order is in force.

(3) The regulations may—

(*a*) except any function from the effect of the delegation order,

(*b*) modify any of the provisions mentioned in subsection (2), and

(*c*) impose such duties on the body established by the delegation order, the Secretary of State and Director General of Fair Trading as appear to the Secretary of State to be appropriate.

(4) The regulations shall contain such provision as appears to the Secretary of State to be necessary or expedient for reserving to him the decision—

(*a*) to refuse recognition on the ground mentioned in paragraph 1(3) of that Schedule, or

(*b*) to exercise the powers conferred by paragraph 6 of that Schedule.

(5) For that purpose the regulations may—

(*a*) prohibit the body from granting a recognition order without the leave of the Secretary of State, and

(*b*) empower the Secretary of State to direct the body to exercise its powers in such manner as may be specified in the direction.

(6) Regulations under this section shall be made by statutory instrument which shall be subject to annulment in pursuance of a resolution of either House of Parliament.

48 Exemption from liability for damages

(1) Neither a recognised supervisory body, nor any of its officers or employees or

members of its governing body, shall be liable in damages for anything done or omitted in the discharge or purported discharge of functions to which this subsection applies, unless the act or omission is shown to have been in bad faith.

(2) Subsection (1) applies to the functions of the body so far as relating to, or to matters arising out of—

(*a*) such rules, practices, powers and arrangements of the body to which the requirements of Part II of Schedule 11 apply, or

(*b*) the obligations with which paragraph 16 of that Schedule requires the body to comply,

(*c*) any guidance issued by the body, or

(*d*) the obligations to which the body is subject by virtue of this Part.

(3) Neither a body established by a delegation order, nor any of its members, officers or employees, shall be liable in damages for anything done or omitted in the discharge or purported discharge of the functions exercisable by virtue of an order under section 46, unless the act or omission is shown to have been in bad faith.

49 Service of notices

(1) This section has effect in relation to any notice, direction or other document required or authorised by or under this Part to be given to or served on any person other than the Secretary of State.

(2) Any such document may be given to or served on the person in question—

(*a*) by delivering it to him,

(*b*) by leaving it at his proper address, or

(*c*) by sending it by post to him at that address.

(3) Any such document may—

(*a*) in the case of a body corporate, be given to or served on the secretary or clerk of that body;

(*b*) in the case of a partnership, be given to or served on any partner;

(*c*) in the case of an unincorporated association other than a partnership, be given to or served on any member of the governing body of the association.

(4) For the purposes of this section and section 7 of the Interpretation Act 1978 (service of documents by post) in its application to this section, the proper address of any person is his last known address (whether of his residence or of a place where he carries on business or is employed) and also—

(*a*) in the case of a person who is eligible under the rules of a recognised supervisory body for appointment as company auditor and who does not have a place of business in the United Kingdom, the address of that body;

(*b*) in the case of a body corporate, its secretary or its clerk, the address of its registered or principal office in the United Kingdom;

(*c*) in the case of an unincorporated association (other than a partnership) or a member of its governing body, its principal office in the United Kingdom.

50 Power to make consequential amendments

(1) The Secretary of State may by regulations make such amendments of enactments as appear to him to be necessary or expedient in consequence of the provisions of this Part having effect in place of section 389 of the Companies Act 1985.

(2) That power extends to making such amendments as appear to the Secretary of State necessary or expedient of—

(*a*) enactments referring by name to the bodies of accountants recognised for the purposes of section 389(1)(*a*) of the Companies Act 1985, and

(*b*) enactments making with respect to other statutory auditors provision as to the matters dealt with in relation to company auditors by section 389 of the Companies Act 1985.

(3) The provision which may be made with respect to other statutory auditors includes provision as to—

(a) eligibility for the appointment,

(b) the effect of appointing a partnership which is not a legal person and the manner of exercise of the auditor's rights in such a case, and

(c) ineligibility on the ground of lack of independence or any other ground.

(4) The regulations may contain such supplementary, incidental and transitional provision as appears to the Secretary of State to be necessary or expedient.

(5) The Secretary of State shall not make regulations under this section with respect to any statutory auditors without the consent of—

(a) the Minister responsible for their appointment or responsible for the body or person by, or in relation to whom, they are appointed, or

(b) if there is no such Minister, the person by whom they are appointed.

(6) In this section a 'statutory auditor' means a person appointed auditor in pursuance of any enactment authorising or requiring the appointment of an auditor or auditors.

(7) Regulations under this section shall be made by statutory instrument which shall be subject to annulment in pursuance of a resolution of either House of Parliament.

51 Power to make provision in consequence of changes affecting accountancy bodies

(1) The Secretary of State may by regulations make such amendments of enactments as appear to him to be necessary or expedient in consequence of any change of name, merger or transfer of engagements affecting—

(a) a recognised supervisory or qualifying body under this Part, or

(b) a body of accountants referred to in, or approved, authorised or otherwise recognised for the purposes of, any other enactment.

(2) Regulations under this section shall be made by statutory instrument which shall be subject to annulment in pursuance of a resolution of either House of Parliament.

52 Meaning of 'associate'

(1) In this Part 'associate', in relation to a person, shall be construed as follows.

(2) In relation to an individual 'associate' means—

(a) that individual's spouse or minor child or step-child,

(b) any body corporate of which that individual is a director, and

(c) any employee or partner of that individual.

(3) In relation to a body corporate 'associate' means—

(a) any body corporate of which that body is a director,

(b) any body corporate in the same group as that body, and

(c) any employee or partner of that body or of any body corporate in the same group.

(4) In relation to a Scottish firm, or a partnership constituted under the law of any other country or territory in which a partnership is a legal person, 'associate' means—

(a) any body corporate of which the firm is a director,

(b) any employee of or partner in the firm, and

(c) any person who is an associate of a partner in the firm.

(5) In relation to a partnership constituted under the law of England and Wales or Northern Ireland, or the law of any other country or territory in which a partnership is not a legal person, 'associate' means any person who is an associate of any of the partners.

53 Minor definitions

(1) In this Part—
'address' means—

(a) in relation to an individual, his usual residential or business address, and (*b*) in relation to a firm, its registered or principal office in Great Britain;

'company' means any company or other body to which section 384 of the Companies Act 1985 (duty to appoint auditors) applies;

'director', in relation to a body corporate, includes any person occupying in relation to it the position of a director (by whatever name called) and any person in accordance with whose directions or instructions (not being advice given in a professional capacity) the directors of the body are accustomed to act;

'enactment' includes an enactment contained in subordinate legislation within the meaning of the Interpretation Act 1978;

'firm' means a body corporate or a partnership;

'group', in relation to a body corporate, means the body corporate, any other body corporate which is its holding company or subsidiary and any other body corporate which is a subsidiary of that holding company; and

'holding company' and 'subsidiary' have the meaning given by section 736 of the Companies Act 1985;

'parent undertaking' and 'subsidiary undertaking' have the same meaning as in Part VII of the Companies Act 1985.

(2) For the purposes of this Part a body shall be regarded as 'established in the United Kingdom' if and only if—

(*a*) it is incorporated or formed under the law of the United Kingdom or a part of the United Kingdom, or

(*b*) its central management and control is exercised in the United Kingdom;

and any reference to a qualification 'obtained in the United Kingdom' is to a qualification obtained from such a body.

54 Index of defined expressions

The following Table shows provisions defining or otherwise explaining expressions used in this Part (other than provisions defining or explaining an expression used only in the same section)—

address	section 53(1)
appropriate qualification	section 31
associate	section 52
company	section 53(1)
company auditor, company audit and company audit work	section 24(2)
delegation order	section 46
director (of a body corporate)	section 53(1)
Director (in Schedule 14)	paragraph 1(1) of that Schedule
enactment	section 53(1)
established in the United Kingdom	section 53(2)
firm	section 53(1)
group (in relation to a body corporate)	section 53(1)
guidance	
—of a qualifying body	section 32(3)
—of a supervisory body	section 30(4)
holding company	section 53(1)
member (of a supervisory body)	section 30(2)
obtained in the United Kingdom	section 53(2)
parent undertaking	section 53(1)
purposes of this Part	section 24(1)
qualifying body	sectión 32(1)
recognised	
—in relation to a professional qualification	section 32(4) and Schedule 12

—in relation to a qualifying body	paragraph 2(1) of Schedule 12
—in relation to a supervisory body	section 30(5) and Schedule 11
rules	
—of a qualifying body	section 32(2)
—of a supervisory body	section 30(3)
subsidiary and subsidiary undertaking	section 53(1)
supervisory body	section 30(1)

PART III

INVESTIGATIONS AND POWERS TO OBTAIN INFORMATION

Amendments of the Companies Act 1985

55 Investigations by inspectors not leading to published report

In section 432 of the Companies Act 1985 (appointment of inspectors by Secretary of State), after subsection (2) (investigation of circumstances suggesting misconduct) insert—

'(2A) Inspectors may be appointed under subsection (2) on terms that any report they may make is not for publication; and in such a case, the provisions of section 437(3) (availability and publication of inspectors' reports) do not apply.'.

56 Production of documents and evidence to inspectors

(1) Section 434 of the Companies Act 1985 (production of documents and evidence to inspectors) is amended as follows.

(2) In subsection (1) (duty of officers to assist inspectors), for 'books and documents' substitute 'documents'.

(3) For subsection (2) (power to require production of documents, attendance or other assistance) substitute—

'(2) If the inspectors consider that an officer or agent of the company or other body corporate, or any other person, is or may be in possession of information relating to a matter which they believe to be relevant to the investigation, they may require him—

(*a*) to produce to them any documents in his custody or power relating to that matter,

(*b*) to attend before them, and

(*c*) otherwise to give them all assistance in connection with the investigation which he is reasonably able to give;

and it is that person's duty to comply with the requirement.'.

(4) For subsection (3) (power to examine on oath) substitute—

'(3) An inspector may for the purposes of the investigation examine any person on oath, and may administer an oath accordingly.'.

(5) After subsection (5) insert—

'(6) In this section 'documents' includes information recorded in any form; and, in relation to information recorded otherwise than in legible form, the power to require its production includes power to require the production of a copy of the information in legible form.'.

(6) In section 436 of the Companies Act 1985 (obstruction of inspectors treated as contempt of court), for subsections (1) and (2) substitute—

'(1) If any person—

(*a*) fails to comply with section 434(1)(*a*) or (*c*),

(*b*) refuses to comply with a requirement under section 434(1)(*b*) or (2), or

169

(c) refuses to answer any question put to him by the inspectors for the purposes of the investigation,

the inspectors may certify that fact in writing to the court.'.

57 Duty of inspectors to report

In section 437 of the Companies Act 1985 (inspectors' reports), after subsection (1A) insert—

'(1B) If it appears to the Secretary of State that matters have come to light in the course of the inspectors' investigation which suggest that a criminal offence has been committed, and those matters have been referred to the appropriate prosecuting authority, he may direct the inspectors to take no further steps in the investigation or to take only such further steps as are specified in the direction.

(1C) Where an investigation is the subject of a direction under subsection (1B), the inspectors shall make a final report to the Secretary of State only where—

(a) they were appointed under section 432(1) (appointment in pursuance of an order of the court), or

(b) the Secretary of State directs them to do so.'.

58 Power to bring civil proceedings on the company's behalf

In section 438 of the Companies Act 1985 (power to bring civil proceedings on the company's behalf), for the opening words of subsection (1) down to 'it appears to the Secretary of State' substitute 'If from any report made or information obtained under this Part it appears to the Secretary of State'.

59 Expenses of investigating a company's affairs

(1) Section 439 of the Companies Act 1985 (expenses of investigating a company's affairs) is amended as follows.

(2) For subsection (1) substitute—

'(1) The expenses of an investigation under any of the powers conferred by this Part shall be defrayed in the first instance by the Secretary of State, but he may recover those expenses from the persons liable in accordance with this section.

There shall be treated as expenses of the investigation, in particular, such reasonable sums as the Secretary of State may determine in respect of general staff costs and overheads.'.

(3) In subsection (4) for 'the inspectors' report' substitute 'an inspectors' report'.

(4) For subsection (5) substitute—

'(5) Where inspectors were appointed—

(a) under section 431, or

(b) on an application under section 442(3),

the applicant or applicants for the investigation is or are liable to such extent (if any) as the Secretary of State may direct.'.

60 Power of Secretary of State to present winding-up petition

(1) Section 440 of the Companies Act 1985 (power of Secretary of State to present winding-up petition) is repealed; but the following amendments have the effect of re-enacting that provision, with modifications.

(2) In section 124(4) of the Insolvency Act 1986 (application by Secretary of State for company to be wound up by the court), for paragraph (b) substitute—

'(b) in a case falling within section 124A below.'.

(3) After that section insert—

'124A Petition for winding up on grounds of public interest

(1) Where it appears to the Secretary of State from—

(*a*) any report made or information obtained under Part XIV of the Companies Act 1985 (company investigations, &c),

(*b*) any report made under section 94 or 177 of the Financial Services Act 1986 or any information obtained under section 105 of that Act,

(*c*) any information obtained under section 2 of the Criminal Justice Act 1987 or section 52 of the Criminal Justice (Scotland) Act 1987 (fraud investigations), or

(*d*) any information obtained under section 83 of the Companies Act 1989 (powers exercisable for purpose of assisting overseas regulatory authorities),

that it is expedient in the public interest that a company should be wound up, he may present a petition for it to be wound up if the court thinks it just and equitable for it to be so.

(2) This section does not apply if the company is already being wound up by the court.'.

61 Inspectors' reports as evidence

In section 441 of the Companies Act 1985 (inspectors' reports to be evidence), in subsection (1) for 'sections 431 or 432' substitute 'this Part'.

62 Investigation of company ownership

In section 442 of the Companies Act 1985 (power to investigate company ownership), for subsection (3) (investigation on application by members of company) substitute—

'(3) If an application for investigation under this section with respect to particular shares or debentures of a company is made to the Secretary of State by members of the company, and the number of applicants or the amount of shares held by them is not less than that required for an application for the appointment of inspectors under section 431(2)(*a*) or (*b*), then, subject to the following provisions, the Secretary of State shall appoint inspectors to conduct the investigation applied for.

(3A) The Secretary of State shall not appoint inspectors if he is satisfied that the application is vexatious; and where inspectors are appointed their terms of appointment shall exclude any matter in so far as the Secretary of State is satisfied that it is unreasonable for it to be investigated.

(3B) The Secretary of State may, before appointing inspectors, require the applicant or applicants to give security, to an amount not exceeding £5,000, or such other sum as he may by order specify, for payment of the costs of the investigation.

An order under this subsection shall be made by statutory instrument which shall be subject to annulment in pursuance of a resolution of either House of Parliament.

(3C) If on an application under subsection (3) it appears to the Secretary of State that the powers conferred by section 444 are sufficient for the purposes of investigating the matters which inspectors would be appointed to investigate, he may instead conduct the investigation under that section.'.

63 Secretary of State's power to require production of documents

(1) Section 447 of the Companies Act 1985 (power of Secretary of State to require production of documents) is amended as follows.

(2) Omit subsection (1) (bodies in relation to which powers exercisable), and—

(*a*) in subsections (2) and (3) for 'any such body' substitute 'a company',

(*b*) in subsections (4) and (5) for 'any body' and 'a body' substitute 'a company', and

(*c*) in subsections (5) and (6) for 'the body' substitute 'the company'.

(3) For 'books or papers', wherever occurring, substitute 'documents'.

(4) In subsection (3) (power to authorise officer to require production of documents) after 'an officer of his' insert 'or any other competent person', after 'the officer' in the first place where it occurs insert 'or other person' and for 'the officer' in the second place where it occurs substitute 'he (the officer or other person)'.

(5) In subsection (4) (power to require production of documents in possession of third party) after 'an officer of his' and after 'the officer' (twice) insert 'or other person'.

(6) In subsection (6), for the second sentence substitute—

'Sections 732 (restriction on prosecutions), 733 (liability of individuals for corporate default) and 734 (criminal proceedings against unincorporated bodies) apply to this offence.'.

(7) After subsection (8) insert—

'(9) In this section 'documents' includes information recorded in any form; and, in relation to information recorded otherwise than in legible form, the power to require its production includes power to require the production of a copy of it in legible form.'.

(8) In Schedule 24 to the Companies Act 1985 (punishment of offences), in the entry relating to section 447(6), for 'books and papers' substitute 'documents'.

64 Entry and search of premises

(1) For section 448 of the Companies Act 1985 (entry and search of premises) substitute—

'448 Entry and search of premises

(1) A justice of the peace may issue a warrant under this section if satisfied on information on oath given by or on behalf of the Secretary of State, or by a person appointed or authorised to exercise powers under this Part, that there are reasonable grounds for believing that there are on any premises documents whose production has been required under this Part and which have not been produced in compliance with the requirement.

(2) A justice of the peace may also issue a warrant under this section if satisfied on information on oath given by or on behalf of the Secretary of State, or by a person appointed or authorised to exercise powers under this Part—

(a) that there are reasonable grounds for believing that an offence has been committed for which the penalty on conviction on indictment is imprisonment for a term of not less than two years and that there are on any premises documents relating to whether the offence has been committed,

(b) that the Secretary of State, or the person so appointed or authorised, has power to require the production of the documents under this Part, and

(c) that there are reasonable grounds for believing that if production was so required the documents would not be produced but would be removed from the premises, hidden, tampered with or destroyed.

(3) A warrant under this section shall authorise a constable, together with any other person named in it and any other constables—

(a) to enter the premises specified in the information, using such force as is reasonably necessary for the purpose;

(b) to search the premises and take possession of any documents appearing to be such documents as are mentioned in subsection (1) or (2), as the case may be, or to take, in relation to any such documents, any other steps which may appear to be necessary for preserving them or preventing interference with them;

(c) to take copies of any such documents; and

(d) to require any person named in the warrant to provide an explanation of them or to state where they may be found.

(4) If in the case of a warrant under subsection (2) the justice of the peace is satisfied on information on oath that there are reasonable grounds for believing that there are

also on the premises other documents relevant to the investigation, the warrant shall also authorise the actions mentioned in subsection (3) to be taken in relation to such documents.

(5) A warrant under this section shall continue in force until the end of the period of one month beginning with the day on which it is issued.

(6) Any documents of which possession is taken under this section may be retained—

(*a*) for a period of three months; or

(*b*) if within that period proceedings to which the documents are relevant are commenced against any person for any criminal offence, until the conclusion of those proceedings.

(7) Any person who intentionally obstructs the exercise of any rights conferred by a warrant issued under this section or fails without reasonable excuse to comply with any requirement imposed in accordance with subsection (3)(*d*) is guilty of an offence and liable to a fine.

Sections 732 (restriction on prosecutions), 733 (liability of individuals for corporate default) and 734 (criminal proceedings against unincorporated bodies) apply to this offence.

(8) For the purposes of sections 449 and 451A (provision for security of information) documents obtained under this section shall be treated as if they had been obtained under the provision of this Part under which their production was or, as the case may be, could have been required.

(9) In the application of this section to Scotland for the references to a justice of the peace substitute references to a justice of the peace or a sheriff, and for the references to information on oath substitute references to evidence on oath.

(10) In this section 'document' includes information recorded in any form.'.

(2) In Schedule 24 to the Companies Act 1985 (punishment of offences), in the entry relating to section 448(5)—

(*a*) in the first column for '448(5)' substitute '448(7), and

(*b*) for the entry in the second column substitute—

'Obstructing the exercise of any rights conferred by a warrant or failing to comply with a requirement imposed under subsection (3)(*d*).'.

65 Provision for security of information obtained

(1) Section 449 of the Companies Act 1985 (provision for security of information obtained) is amended as follows.

(2) In subsection (1) (purposes for which disclosure permitted)—

(*a*) in the opening words for 'body' (twice) substitute 'company';

(*b*) for paragraph (*c*) substitute—

'(*c*) for the purposes of enabling or assisting any inspector appointed under this Part, or under section 94 or 177 of the Financial Services Act 1986, to discharge his functions;';

(*c*) after that paragraph insert—

'(*cc*) for the purpose of enabling or assisting any person authorised to exercise powers under section 44 of the Insurance Companies Act 1982, section 447 of this Act, section 106 of the Financial Services Act 1986 or section 84 of the Companies Act 1989 to discharge his functions;';

(*d*) in paragraph (*d*) for 'or the Financial Services Act 1986' substitute ', the Financial Services Act 1986 or Part II, III or VII of the Companies Act 1989,';

(*e*) omit paragraph (*e*);

(*f*) in paragraph (*h*) for '(*n*) or (*p*)' substitute 'or (*n*)';

(g) after that paragraph insert—

'(hh) for the purpose of enabling or assisting a body established by order under section 46 of the Companies Act 1989 to discharge its functions under Part II of that Act, or of enabling or assisting a recognised supervisory or qualifying body within the meaning of that Part to discharge its functions as such;';

(h) after paragraph (l) insert—

'(ll) with a view to the institution of, or otherwise for the purposes of, any disciplinary proceedings relating to the discharge by a public servant of his duties;';

(i) for paragraph (m) substitute—

'(m) for the purpose of enabling or assisting an overseas regulatory authority to exercise its regulatory functions.'.

(3) For subsection (1A) substitute—

'(1A) In subsection (1)—

(a) in paragraph (ll) 'public servant' means an officer or servant of the Crown or of any public or other authority for the time being designated for the purposes of that paragraph by the Secretary of State by order made by statutory instrument; and

(b) in paragraph (m) 'overseas regulatory authority' and 'regulatory functions' have the same meaning as in section 82 of the Companies Act 1989.'.

(4) In subsection (1B) (disclosure to designated public authorities) for 'designated for the purposes of this section' substitute 'designated for the purposes of this subsection'.

(5) In subsection (2), for the second sentence substitute—

'Sections 732 (restriction on prosecutions), 733 (liability of individuals for corporate default) and 734 (criminal proceedings against unincorporated bodies) apply to this offence.'.

(6) For subsection (3) substitute—

'(3) For the purposes of this section each of the following is a competent authority—

(a) the Secretary of State,

(b) an inspector appointed under this Part or under section 94 or 177 of the Financial Services Act 1986,

(c) any person authorised to exercise powers under section 44 of the Insurance Companies Act 1982, section 447 of this Act, section 106 of the Financial Services Act 1986 or section 84 of the Companies Act 1989,

(d) the Department of Economic Development in Northern Ireland,

(e) the Treasury,

(f) the Bank of England,

(g) the Lord Advocate,

(h) the Director of Public Prosecutions, and the Director of Public Prosecutions for Northern Ireland,

(i) any designated agency or transferee body within the meaning of the Financial Services Act 1986, and any body administering a scheme under section 54 of or paragraph 18 of Schedule 11 to that Act (schemes for compensation of investors),

(j) the Chief Registrar of friendly societies and the Registrar of Friendly Societies for Northern Ireland,

(k) the Industrial Assurance Commissioner and the Industrial Assurance Commissioner for Northern Ireland,

(l) any constable,

(m) any procurator fiscal.

(3A) Any information which may by virtue of this section be disclosed to a competent authority may be disclosed to any officer or servant of the authority.'.

(7) In subsection (4) (orders) for 'subsection (1B)' substitute 'subsection (1A)(*a*) or (1B)'.

66 Punishment for destroying, mutilating, &c company documents

(1) Section 450 of the Companies Act 1985 (punishment for destroying, mutilating, &c company documents) is amended as follows.

(2) In subsection (1) for the opening words down to 'insurance company' substitute 'An officer of a company, or of an insurance company', for 'body's' substitute 'company's' and for 'the body' substitute 'the company'.

(3) For subsection (4) substitute—

'(4) Sections 732 (restriction on prosecutions), 733 (liability of individuals for corporate default) and 734 (criminal proceedings against unincorporated bodies) apply to an offence under this section.'.

(4) After that subsection insert—

'(5) In this section 'document' includes information recorded in any form.'.

67 Punishment for furnishing false information

In section 451 of the Companies Act 1985 (punishment for furnishing false information), for the second sentence substitute—

'Sections 732 (restriction on prosecutions), 733 (liability of individuals for corporate default) and 734 (criminal proceedings against unincorporated bodies) apply to this offence.'.

68 Disclosure of information by Secretary of State or inspector

For section 451A of the Companies Act 1985 (disclosure of information by the Secretary of State) substitute—

'451A Disclosure of information by Secretary of State or inspector

(1) This section applies to information obtained under sections 434 to 446.

(2) The Secretary of State may, if he thinks fit—

(*a*) disclose any information to which this section applies to any person to whom, or for any purpose for which, disclosure is permitted under section 449, or

(*b*) authorise or require an inspector appointed under this Part to disclose such information to any such person or for any such purpose.

(3) Information to which this section applies may also be disclosed by an inspector appointed under this Part to—

(*a*) another inspector appointed under this Part or an inspector appointed under section 94 or 177 of the Financial Services Act 1986, or

(*b*) a person authorised to exercise powers under section 44 of the Insurance Companies Act 1982, section 447 of this Act, section 106 of the Financial Services Act 1986 or section 84 of the Companies Act 1989.

(4) Any information which may by virtue of subsection (3) be disclosed to any person may be disclosed to any officer or servant of that person.

(5) The Secretary of State may, if he thinks fit, disclose any information obtained under section 444 to—

(*a*) the company whose ownership was the subject of the investigation,

(*b*) any member of the company,

(*c*) any person whose conduct was investigated in the course of the investigation,

(*d*) the auditors of the company, or

(*e*) any person whose financial interests appear to the Secretary of State to be affected by matters covered by the investigation.'.

69 Protection of banking information

(1) Section 452 of the Companies Act 1985 (privileged information) is amended as follows.

(2) In subsection (1), omit paragraph (*b*) (disclosure by bankers of information to their customers).

(3) After that subsection insert—

'(1A) Nothing in section 434, 443 or 446 requires a person (except as mentioned in subsection (1B) below) to disclose information or produce documents in respect of which he owes an obligation of confidence by virtue of carrying on the business of banking unless—

(*a*) the person to whom the obligation of confidence is owed is the company or other body corporate under investigation,

(*b*) the person to whom the obligation of confidence is owed consents to the disclosure or production, or

(*c*) the making of the requirement is authorised by the Secretary of State.

(1B) Subsection (1A) does not apply where the person owing the obligation of confidence is the company or other body corporate under investigation under section 431, 432 or 433.'.

(4) In subsection (3) after 'officer of his' insert 'or other person'.

70 Investigation of oversea companies

In section 453 of the Companies Act 1985 (investigation of oversea companies), for subsection (1) substitute—

'(1) The provisions of this Part apply to bodies corporate incorporated outside Great Britain which are carrying on business in Great Britain, or have at any time carried on business there, as they apply to companies under this Act; but subject to the following exceptions, adaptations and modifications.

(1A) The following provisions do not apply to such bodies—

(*a*) section 431 (investigation on application of company or its members),

(*b*) section 438 (power to bring civil proceedings on the company's behalf),

(*c*) sections 442 to 445 (investigation of company ownership and power to obtain information as to those interested in shares, &c), and

(*d*) section 446 (investigation of share dealings).

(1B) The other provisions of this Part apply to such bodies subject to such adaptations and modifications as may be specified by regulations made by the Secretary of State.'.

71 Investigation of unregistered companies

In Schedule 22 to the Companies Act 1985 (provisions applying to unregistered companies), for the entry relating to Part XIV substitute—

'Part XIV Investigation of companies and their affairs; —'.
(except section requisition of documents.
446)

Amendments of the Financial Services Act 1986

72 Investigations into collective investment schemes

(1) Section 94 of the Financial Services Act 1986 (investigations into collective investment schemes) is amended as follows.

(2) For subsection (7) (privilege on grounds of banker's duty of confidentiality) substitute—

'(7) Nothing in this section requires a person (except as mentioned in subsection

(7A) below) to disclose any information or produce any document in respect of which he owes an obligation of confidence by virtue of carrying on the business of banking unless—

(a) the person to whom the obligation of confidence is owed consents to the disclosure or production, or

(b) the making of the requirement was authorised by the Secretary of State.

(7A) Subsection (7) does not apply where the person owing the obligation of confidence or the person to whom it is owed is—

(a) the manager, operator or trustee of the scheme under investigation, or

(b) a manager, operator or trustee whose own affairs are under investigation.'.

(3) After subsection (8) (duty of inspectors to report) insert—

'(8A) If it appears to the Secretary of State that matters have come to light in the course of the inspectors' investigation which suggest that a criminal offence has been committed, and those matters have been referred to the appropriate prosecuting authority, he may direct the inspectors to take no further steps in the investigation or to take only such further steps as are specified in the direction.

(8B) Where an investigation is the subject of a direction under subsection (8A), the inspectors shall make a final report to the Secretary of State only where the Secretary of State directs them to do so.'.

(4) After subsection (9) add—

'(10) A person who is convicted on a prosecution instituted as a result of an investigation under this section may in the same proceedings be ordered to pay the expenses of the investigation to such extent as may be specified in the order.

There shall be treated as expenses of the investigation, in particular, such reasonable sums as the Secretary of State may determine in respect of general staff costs and overheads.'.

73 Investigations into affairs of persons carrying on investment business

(1) Section 105 of the Financial Services Act 1986 (investigation into affairs of person carrying on investment business) is amended as follows.

(2) Omit subsection (7) (privilege on grounds of banker's duty of confidentiality).

(3) In subsection (9) (interpretation), in the definition of 'documents', for 'references to its production include references to producing' substitute 'the power to require its production includes power to require the production of'.

(4) After subsection (10) add—

'(11) A person who is convicted on a prosecution instituted as a result of an investigation under this section may in the same proceedings be ordered to pay the expenses of the investigation to such extent as may be specified in the order.

There shall be treated as expenses of the investigation, in particular, such reasonable sums as the Secretary of State may determine in respect of general staff costs and overheads.'.

(5) In section 106 of the Financial Services Act 1986 (exercise of investigation powers by officer, &c), after subsection (2) insert—

'(2A) A person shall not by virtue of an authority under this section be required to disclose any information or produce any documents in respect of which he owes an obligation of confidence by virtue of carrying on the business of banking unless—

(a) he is the person under investigation or a related company,

(b) the person to whom the obligation of confidence is owed is the person under investigation or a related company,

(c) the person to whom the obligation of confidence is owed consents to the disclosure or production, or (*d*) the imposing on him of a requirement with respect to such information or documents has been specifically authorised by the Secretary of State.

In this subsection 'documents', 'person under investigation' and 'related company' have the same meaning as in section 105.'.

74 Investigations into insider dealing

(1) Section 177 of the Financial Services Act 1986 (investigations into insider dealing) is amended as follows.

(2) After subsection (2) (power to limit period or scope of investigation) insert—

'(2A) At any time during the investigation the Secretary of State may vary the appointment by limiting or extending the period during which the inspector is to continue his investigation or by confining the investigation to particular matters.'.

(3) After subsection (5) (duty of inspectors to report) insert—

'(5A) If the Secretary of State thinks fit, he may direct the inspector to take no further steps in the investigation or to take only such further steps as are specified in the direction; and where an investigation is the subject of such a direction, the inspectors shall make a final report to the Secretary of State only where the Secretary of State directs them to do so.'.

(4) For subsection (8) (privilege on grounds of banker's duty of confidentiality) substitute—

'(8) A person shall not under this section be required to disclose any information or produce any document in respect of which he owes an obligation of confidence by virtue of carrying on the business of banking unless—

(*a*) the person to whom the obligation of confidence is owed consents to the disclosure or production, or

(*b*) the making of the requirement was authorised by the Secretary of State.'.

(5) In subsection (10) (definition of 'documents') for 'references to its production include references to producing' substitute 'the power to require its production includes power to require the prodution of'.

(6) After subsection (10) add—

'(11) A person who is convicted on a prosecution instituted as a result of an investigation under this section may in the same proceedings be ordered to pay the expenses of the investigation to such extent as may be specified in the order.

There shall be treated as expenses of the investigation, in particular, such reasonable sums as the Secretary of State may determine in respect of general staff costs and overheads.'.

75 Restrictions on disclosure of information

(1) In section 179(3) of the Financial Services Act 1986 (persons who are 'primary recipients' for purposes of provisions restricting disclosure of information)—

(*a*) omit the word 'and' preceding paragraph (i);

(*b*) in that paragraph, after 'any such person' insert 'as is mentioned in paragraphs (*a*) to (*h*) above';

(*c*) after that paragraph insert—

'(*j*) any constable or other person named in a warrant issued under this Act.'.

(2) Section 180 of the Financial Services Act 1986 (exceptions from restrictions on disclosure) is amended as follows.

(3) In subsection (1) (purposes for which disclosure permitted)—

(*a*) in paragraph (*c*), after 'insolvency' insert 'or by Part II, III or VII of the Companies Act 1989';

(*b*) for paragraph (*e*) substitute—

'(e) for the purpose—

    (i) of enabling or assisting a designated agency to discharge its functions under this Act or Part VII of the Companies Act 1989,

    (ii) of enabling or assisting a transferee body or the competent authority to discharge its functions under this Act, or

    (iii) of enabling or assisting the body administrating a scheme under section 54 above to discharge its functions under the scheme;';

(c) after paragraph (h) insert—

'(hh) for the purpose of enabling or assisting a body established by order under section 46 of the Companies Act 1989 to discharge its functions under Part II of that Act, or of enabling or assisting a recognised supervisory or qualifying body within the meaning of that Part to discharge its functions as such;';

(d) after paragraph (o) insert—

'(oo) with a view to the institution of, or otherwise for the purposes of, any disciplinary proceedings relating to the discharge by a public servant of his duties;';

(e) in paragraph (p), after 'under' insert 'section 44 of the Insurance Companies Act 1982, section 447 of the Companies Act 1985,' and after 'above' insert 'or section 84 of the Companies Act 1989';

(f) after paragraph (q) insert—

'(qq) for the purpose of enabling or assisting an overseas regulatory authority to exercise its regulatory functions;'.

(4) After that subsection insert—

'(1A) In subsection (1)—

    (a) in paragraph (oo) 'public servant' means an officer or servant of the Crown or of any public or other authority for the time being designated for the purposes of that paragraph by order of the Secretary of State; and

    (b) in paragraph (qq) 'overseas regulatory authority' and 'regulatory functions' have the same meaning as in section 82 of the Companies Act 1989.'.

(5) In subsection (3) (disclosure to designated public authorities) for 'designated for the purposes of this section' substitute 'designated for the purposes of this subsection'.

(6) Omit subsection (6) (disclosure to certain overseas authorities).

(7) In subsection (9) (orders) for 'subsection (3) or (8)' substitute 'subsection (1A)(a), (3) or (8)'.

76 Entry and search of premises

(1) Section 199 of the Financial Services Act 1986 (powers of entry) is amended as follows.

(2) For subsections (1) and (2) substitute—

'(1) A justice of the peace may issue a warrant under this section if satisfied on information on oath given by or on behalf of the Secretary of State that there are reasonable grounds for believing that an offence has been committed—

    (a) under section 4, 47, 57, 130, 133 or 171(2) or (3) above, or

    (b) section 1, 2, 4 or 5 of the Company Securities (Insider Dealing) Act 1985,

and that there are on any premises documents relevant to the question whether that offence has been committed.

(2) A justice of the peace may also issue a warrant under this section if satisfied on information on oath given by or on behalf of the Secretary of State, or by a person appointed or authorised to exercise powers under section 94, 106 or 177 above, that there are reasonable grounds for believing that there are on any premises documents

whose production has been required under section 94, 105 or 177 above and which have not been produced in compliance with the requirement.'.

(3) In subsection (3)(*b*) for 'subsection (1)(*a*) or (*b*)' substitute 'subsection (1)'.

(4) In subsection (5) (period for which documents may be retained), for paragraph (*b*) substitute—

'(*b*) if within that period proceedings to which the documents are relevant are commenced against any person for any criminal offence, until the conclusion of those proceedings.'.

(5) In subsection (6) (offences) after 'Any person who' insert 'intentionally'.

(6) In subsection (7) for 'subsection (1)(*a*) above' substitute 'subsection (1) above'.

(7) For subsection (8) substitute—

'(8) In the application of this section to Scotland for the references to a justice of the peace substitute references to a justice of the peace or a sheriff, and for the references to information on oath substitute references to evidence on oath.'.

(8) In subsection (9) (definition of 'documents'), omit the words from 'and, in relation' to the end.

Amendments of other enactments

77 Amendments of the Insurance Companies Act 1982

(1) Part II of the Insurance Companies Act 1982 is amended as follows.

(2) In section 44 (power to obtain information and require production of documents), for 'books or papers' (wherever occurring) substitute 'documents', and for subsection (6) substitute—

'(6) In this section 'document' includes information recorded in any form; and, in relation to information recorded otherwise than in legible form, the power to require its production includes power to require the production of a copy of the information in legible form.'.

(3) After that section insert—

'44A Entry and search of premises

(1) A justice of the peace may issue a warrant under this section if satisfied on information on oath given by or on behalf of the Secretary of State, or by a person authorised to exercise powers under section 44 above, that there are reasonable grounds for believing that there are on any premises documents whose production has been required under section 44(2) to (4) above and which have not been produced in compliance with the requirement.

(2) A justice of the peace may also issue a warrant under this section if satisfied on information on oath given by or on behalf of the Secretary of State, or by a person authorised to exercise powers under section 44 above—

(*a*) that there are reasonable grounds for believing that an offence has been committed for which the penalty on conviction on indictment is imprisonment for a term of not less than two years and that there are on any premises documents relating to whether the offence has been committed,

(*b*) that the Secretary of State or, as the case may be, the authorised person has power to require the production of the documents under section 44(2) to (4) above, and

(*c*) that there are reasonable grounds for believing that if production was so required the documents would not be produced but would be removed from the premises, hidden, tampered with or destroyed.

(3) A warrant under this section shall authorise a constable, together with any other person named in it and any other constables—

(*a*) to enter the premises specified in the information, using such force as is reasonably necessary for the purpose;

(*b*) to search the premises and take possession of any documents appearing to be such documents as are mentioned in subsection (1) or (2), as the case may be, or to take, in relation to any such documents, any other steps which may appear to be necessary for preserving them or preventing interference with them;

(*c*) to take copies of any such documents; and

(*d*) to require any person named in the warrant to provide an explanation of them or to state where they may be found.

(4) If in the case of a warrant under subsection (2) the justice of the peace is satisfied on information on oath that there are reasonable grounds for believing that there are also on the premises other documents relevant to the investigation, the warrant shall also authorise the actions mentioned in subsection (3) to be taken in relation to such documents.

(5) A warrant under this section shall continue in force until the end of the period of one month beginning with the day on which it is issued.

(6) Any documents of which possession is taken under this section may be retained—

(*a*) for a period of three months; or

(*b*) if within that period proceedings to which the documents are relevant are commenced against any person for any criminal offence, until the conclusion of those proceedings.

(7) In the application of this section to Scotland for the references to a justice of the peace substitute references to a justice of the peace or a sheriff, and for the references to information on oath substitute references to evidence on oath.

(8) In this section 'document' includes information recorded in any form.'.

(4) In section 47A(1) (restriction on disclosure of information), after 'section 44(2) to (4)' insert 'or 44A'.

(5) In section 71 (offences and penalties), after subsection (2) insert—

'(2A) A person who intentionally obstructs the exercise of any rights conferred by a warrant issued under section 44A above or fails without reasonable excuse to comply with any requirement imposed in accordance with subsection (3)(*d*) of that section is guilty of an offence and liable—

(*a*) on conviction on indictment, to a fine, and

(*b*) on summary conviction, to a fine not exceeding the statutory maximum.'.

(6) In section 71(6) (defence to failure to comply with requirement to produce books or papers) for 'books or papers' substitute 'documents'.

78 Amendment of the Insolvency Act 1986

In section 218(5) of the Insolvency Act 1986 (investigation by Secretary of State on report by liquidator), for paragraph (*a*) substitute—

'(*a*) shall thereupon investigate the matter reported to him and such other matters relating to the affairs of the company as appear to him to require investigation, and'.

79 Amendment of the Company Directors Disqualification Act 1986

In section 8 of the Company Directors Disqualification Act 1986 (disqualification after investigation of company), after 'section 52 of the Criminal Justice (Scotland) Act 1987' insert 'or section 83 of the Companies Act 1989'.

80 Amendment of the Building Societies Act 1986

In section 53 of the Building Societies Act 1986 (confidentiality of information obtained by the Building Societies Commission), in subsection (7)(*b*) (functions of Secretary of State for purposes of which disclosure may be made) after sub-paragraph (ii) insert—

', or
  (iii) Part II, III or VII of the Companies Act 1989;'.

81 Amendments of the Banking Act 1987

(1) In section 84(1) of the Banking Act 1987 (disclosure of information obtained under that Act), the Table showing the authorities to which, and functions for the purposes of which, disclosure may be made is amended as follows.

(2) In the entry relating to the Secretary of State, in column 2, for 'or the Financial Services Act 1986' substitute ', the Financial Services Act 1986 or Part II, III or VII of the Companies Act 1989'.

(3) For the entry relating to inspectors appointed by the Secretary of State substitute—

'An inspector appointed under Part XIV of the Companies Act 1985 or section 94 or 177 of the Financial Services Act 1986.	Functions under that Part or that section.'.

(4) For the entry beginning 'A person authorised by the Secretary of State' substitute—

'A person authorised to exercise powers under section 44 of the Insurance Companies Act 1982, section 447 of the Companies Act 1985, section 106 of the Financial Services Act 1986 or section 84 of the Companies Act 1989.	Functions under that section.'.

(5) For the entry relating to a designated agency or transferee body or the competent authority (within the meaning of the Financial Services Act 1986) substitute—

'A designated agency (within the meaning of the Financial Services Act 1986).	Functions under the Financial Services Act 1986 or Part VII of the Companies Act 1989.
A transferee body or the competent authority (within the meaning of the Financial Services Act 1986).	Functions under the Financial Services Act 1986.'.

Powers exercisable to assist overseas regulatory authorities

82 Request for assistance by overseas regulatory authority

(1) The powers conferred by section 83 are exercisable by the Secretary of State for the purpose of assisting an overseas regulatory authority which has requested his assistance in connection with inquiries being carried out by it or on its behalf.

(2) An 'overseas regulatory authority' means an authority which in a country or territory outside the United Kingdom exercises—

(*a*) any function corresponding to—
    (i) a function under the Financial Services Act 1986 of a designated agency, transferee body or competent authority (within the meaning of that Act),
    (ii) a function of the Secretary of State under the Insurance Companies Act 1982, the Companies Act 1985 or the Financial Services Act 1986, or
    (iii) a function of the Bank of England under the Banking Act 1987, or
(*b*) any function in connection with the investigation of, or the enforcement of rules (whether or not having the force of law) relating to, conduct of the kind prohibited by the Company Securities (Insider Dealing) Act 1985, or
(*c*) any function prescribed for the purposes of this subsection by order of the Secretary of State, being a function which in the opinion of the Secretary of State relates to companies or financial services.

An order under paragraph (*c*) shall be made by statutory instrument which shall be subject to annulment in pursuance of a resolution of either House of Parliament.

(3) The Secretary of State shall not exercise the powers conferred by section 83 unless he is satisfied that the assistance requested by the overseas regulatory authority is for the purposes of its regulatory functions.

An authority's 'regulatory functions' means any functions falling within subsection (2) and any other functions relating to companies or financial services.

(4) In deciding whether to exercise those powers the Secretary of State may take into account, in particular—

(a) whether corresponding assistance would be given in that country or territory to an authority exercising regulatory functions in the United Kingdom;

(b) whether the inquiries relate to the possible breach of a law, or other requirement, which has no close parallel in the United Kingdom or involves the assertion of a jurisdiction not recognised by the United Kingdom;

(c) the seriousness of the matter to which the inquiries relate, the importance to the inquiries of the information sought in the United Kingdom and whether the assistance could be obtained by other means;

(d) whether it is otherwise appropriate in the public interest to give the assistance sought.

(5) Before deciding whether to exercise those powers in a case where the overseas regulatory authority is a banking supervisor, the Secretary of State shall consult the Bank of England.

A 'banking supervisor' means an overseas regulatory authority with respect to which the Bank of England has notified the Secretary of State, for the purposes of this subsection, that it exercises functions corresponding to those of the Bank under the Banking Act 1987.

(6) The Secretary of State may decline to exercise those powers unless the overseas regulatory authority undertakes to make such contribution towards the costs of their exercise as the Secretary of State considers appropriate.

(7) References in this section to financial services include, in particular, investment business, insurance and banking.

83 Power to require information, documents or other assistance.

(1) The following powers may be exercised in accordance with section 82, if the Secretary of State considers there is good reason for their exercise.

(2) The Secretary of State may require any person—

(a) to attend before him at a specified time and place and answer questions or otherwise furnish information with respect to any matter relevant to the inquiries,

(b) to produce at a specified time and place any specified documents which appear to the Secretary of State to relate to any matter relevant to the inquiries, and

(c) otherwise to give him such assistance in connection with the inquiries as he is reasonably able to give.

(3) The Secretary of State may examine a person on oath and may administer an oath accordingly.

(4) Where documents are produced the Secretary of State may take copies or extracts from them.

(5) A person shall not under this section be required to disclose information or produce a document which he would be entitled to refuse to disclose or produce on grounds of legal professional privilege in proceedings in the High Court or on grounds of confidentiality as between client and professional legal adviser in proceedings in the Court of Session, except that a lawyer may be required to furnish the name and address of his client.

(6) A statement by a person in compliance with a requirement imposed under this section may be used in evidence against him.

(7) Where a person claims a lien on a document, its production under this section is without prejudice to his lien.

(8) In this section 'documents' includes information recorded in any form; and, in relation to information recorded otherwise than in legible form, the power to require its production includes power to require the production of a copy of it in legible form.

84 Exercise of powers by officer, &c

(1) The Secretary of State may authorise an officer of his or any other competent person to exercise on his behalf all or any of the powers conferred by section 83.

(2) No such authority shall be granted except for the purpose of investigating—

(*a*) the affairs, or any aspects of the affairs, of a person specified in the authority, or

(*b*) a subject-matter so specified,

being a person who, or subject-matter which, is the subject of the inquiries being carried out by or on behalf of the overseas regulatory authority.

(3) No person shall be bound to comply with a requirement imposed by a person exercising powers by virtue of an authority granted under this section unless he has, if required, produced evidence of his authority.

(4) A person shall not by virtue of an authority under this section be required to disclose any information or produce any documents in respect of which he owes an obligation of confidence by virtue of carrying on the business of banking unless—

(*a*) the imposing on him of a requirement with respect to such information or documents has been specifically authorised by the Secretary of State, or

(*b*) the person to whom the obligation of confidence is owed consents to the disclosure or production.

In this subsection 'documents' has the same meaning as in section 83.

(5) Where the Secretary of State authorises a person other than one of his officers to exercise any powers by virtue of this section, that person shall make a report to the Secretary of State in such manner as he may require on the exercise of those powers and the results of exercising them.

85 Penalty for failure to comply with requirement, &c

(1) A person who without reasonable excuse fails to comply with a requirement imposed on him under section 83 commits an offence and is liable on summary conviction to imprisonment for a term not exceeding six months or to a fine not exceeding level 5 on the standard scale, or both.

(2) A person who in purported compliance with any such requirement furnishes information which he knows to be false or misleading in a material particular, or recklessly furnishes information which is false or misleading in a material particular, commits an offence and is liable—

(*a*) on conviction on indictment, to imprisonment for a term not exceeding two years or to a fine, or both;

(*b*) on summary conviction, to imprisonment for a term not exceeding six months or to a fine not exceeding the statutory maximum, or both.

86 Restrictions on disclosure of information

(1) This section applies to information relating to the business or other affairs of a person which—

(*a*) is supplied by an overseas regulatory authority in connection with a request for assistance, or

(*b*) is obtained by virtue of the powers conferred by section 83, whether or not any requirement to supply it is made under that section.

(2) Except as permitted by section 87 below, such information shall not be disclosed for any purpose—

(*a*) by the primary recipient, or

(*b*) by any person obtaining the information directly or indirectly from him,

without the consent of the person from whom the primary recipient obtained the information and, if different, the person to whom it relates.

(3) The 'primary recipient' means, as the case may be—

(*a*) the Secretary of State,

(*b*) any person authorised under section 84 to exercise powers on his behalf, and

(*c*) any officer or servant of any such person.

(4) Information shall not be treated as information to which this section applies if it has been made available to the public by virtue of being disclosed in any circumstances in which, or for any purpose for which, disclosure is not precluded by this section.

(5) A person who contravenes this section commits an offence and is liable—

(*a*) on conviction on indictment, to imprisonment for a term not exceeding two years or to a fine, or both;

(*b*) on summary conviction, to imprisonment for a term not exceeding three months or to a fine not exceeding the statutory maximum, or both.

87 Exceptions from restrictions on disclosure

(1) Information to which section 86 applies may be disclosed—

(*a*) to any person with a view to the institution of, or otherwise for the purposes of, relevant proceedings,

(*b*) for the purpose of enabling or assisting a relevant authority to discharge any relevant function (including functions in relation to proceedings),

(*c*) to the Treasury, if the disclosure is made in the interests of investors or in the public interest,

(*d*) if the information is or has been available to the public from other sources,

(*e*) in a summary or collection of information framed in such a way as not to enable the identity of any person to whom the information relates to be ascertained, or

(*f*) in pursuance of any Community obligation.

(2) The relevant proceedings referred to in subsection (1)(*a*) are—

(*a*) any criminal proceedings,

(*b*) civil proceedings arising under or by virtue of the Financial Services Act 1986 and proceedings before the Financial Services Tribunal, and

(*c*) disciplinary proceedings relating to—

(i) the exercise by a solicitor, auditor, accountant, valuer or actuary of his professional duties, or

(ii) the discharge by a public servant of his duties.

(3) In subsection (2)(*c*)(ii) 'public servant' means an officer or servant of the Crown or of any public or other authority for the time being designated for the purposes of that provision by order of the Secretary of State.

(4) The relevant authorities referred to in subsection (1)(*b*), and the relevant functions in relation to each such authority, are as follows—

Authority	*Functions*
The Secretary of State.	Functions under the enactments relating to companies, insurance companies or insolvency, or under the Financial Services Act 1986 or Part II, this Part or Part VII of this Act.
An inspector appointed under Part XIV of the Companies Act 1985 or section 94 or 177 of the Financial Services Act 1986.	Functions under that Part of that section.

Authority	*Functions*
A person authorised to exercise powers under section 44 of the Insurance Companies Act 1982, section 447 of the Companies Act 1985, section 106 of the Financial Services Act 1986 or section 84 of this Act.	Functions under that section.
An overseas regulatory authority.	Its regulatory functions (within the meaning of section 82 of this Act).
The Department of Economic Development in Northern Ireland or a person appointed or authorised by that Department.	Functions conferred on it or him by the enactments relating to companies or insolvency.
A designated agency within the meaning of the Financial Services Act 1986.	Functions under that Act or Part VII of this Act.
A transferee body or the competent authority within the meaning of the Financial Services Act 1986.	Functions under that Act.
The body administering a scheme under section 54 of the Financial Services Act 1986.	Functions under the scheme.
A recognised self-regulating organisation, recognised professional body, recognised investment exchange, recognised clearing house or recognised self-regulating organisation for friendly societies (within the meaning of the Financial Services Act 1986).	Functions in its capacity as an organisation, body, exchange or clearing house recognised under that Act.
The Chief Registrar of friendly societies, the Registrar of Friendly Societies for Northern Ireland and the Assistant Registrar of Friendly Societies for Scotland.	Functions under the Financial Services Act 1986 or the enactments relating to friendly societies or building societies.
The Bank of England.	Functions under the Banking Act 1987 and any other functions.
The Deposit Protection Board.	Functions under the Banking Act 1987.
A body established by order under section 46 of this Act.	Functions under Part II of this Act.
A recognised supervisory or qualifying body within the meaning of Part II of this Act.	Functions as such a body.
The Industrial Assurance Commissioner and the Industrial Assurance Commissioner for Northern Ireland.	Functions under the enactments relating to industrial assurance.
The Insurance Brokers Registration Council.	Functions under the Insurance Brokers (Registration) Act 1977.
The Official Receiver or, in Northern Ireland, the Official Assignee for company liquidations or for bankruptcy.	Functions under the enactments relating to insolvency.
A recognised professional body (within the meaning of section 391 of the Insolvency Act 1986).	Functions in its capacity as such a body under the Insolvency Act 1986.
The Building Societies Commission.	Functions under the Building Societies Act 1986.

Authority	*Functions*
The Director General of Fair Trading.	Functions under the Financial Services Act 1986.

(5) The Secretary of State may by order amend the Table in subsection (4) so as to—

(*a*) add any public or other authority to the Table and specify the relevant functions of that authority,

(*b*) remove any authority from the Table, or

(*c*) add functions to, or remove functions from, those which are relevant functions in relation to an authority specified in the Table;

and the order may impose conditions subject to which, or otherwise restrict the circumstances in which, disclosure is permitted.

(6) An order under this section shall be made by statutory instrument which shall be subject to annulment in pursuance of a resolution of either House of Parliament.

88 Exercise of powers in relation to Northern Ireland

(1) The following provisions apply where it appears to the Secretary of State that a request for assistance by an overseas regulatory authority may involve the powers conferred by section 83 being exercised in Northern Ireland in relation to matters which are transferred matters within the meaning of the Northern Ireland Constitution Act 1973.

(2) The Secretary of State shall before deciding whether to accede to the request consult the Department of Economic Development in Northern Ireland, and if he decides to accede to the request and it appears to him—

(*a*) that the powers should be exercised in Northern Ireland, and

(*b*) that the purposes for which they should be so exercised relate wholly or primarily to transferred matters,

he shall by instrument in writing authorise the Department to exercise in Northern Ireland his powers under section 83.

(3) The following provisions have effect in relation to the exercise of powers by virtue of such an authority with the substitution for references to the Secretary of State of references to the Department of Economic Development in Northern Ireland—

(*a*) section 84 (exercise of powers by officer, &c),

(*b*) section 449 of the Companies Act 1985, section 53 or 54 of the Building Societies Act 1986, sections 179 and 180 of the Financial Services Act 1986 and sections 86 and 87 above (restrictions on disclosure of information), and

(*c*) section 89 (authority for institution of criminal proceedings);

and references to the Secretary of State in other enactments which proceed by reference to those provisions shall be construed accordingly as being or including references to the Department.

(4) The Secretary of State may after consultation with the Department of Economic Development in Northern Ireland revoke an authority given to the Department under this section.

(5) In that case nothing in the provisions referred to in subsection (3)(*b*) shall apply so as to prevent the Department from giving the Secretary of State any information obtained by virtue of the authority; and (without prejudice to their application in relation to disclosure by the Department) those provisions shall apply to the disclosure of such information by the Secretary of State as if it had been obtained by him in the first place.

(6) Nothing in this section affects the exercise by the Secretary of State of any powers in Northern Ireland—

(*a*) in a case where at the time of acceding to the request it did not appear to him that the circumstances were such as to require him to authorise the Department of Economic Development in Northern Ireland to exercise those powers, or (*b*) after the revocation by him of any such authority;

and no objection shall be taken to anything done by or in relation to the Secretary of State or the Department on the ground that it should have been done by or in relation to the other.

89 Prosecutions

Proceedings for an offence under section 85 or 86 shall not be instituted—

(*a*) in England and Wales, except by or with the consent of the Secretary of State or the Director of Public Prosecutions;

(*b*) in Northern Ireland, except by or with the consent of the Secretary of State or the Director of Public Prosecutions for Northern Ireland.

90 Offences by bodies corporate, partnerships and unincorporated associations

(1) Where an offence under section 85 or 86 committed by a body corporate is proved to have been committed with the consent or connivance of, or to be attributable to any neglect on the part of, a director, manager, secretary or other similar officer of the body, or a person purporting to act in any such capacity, he as well as the body corporate is guilty of the offence and liable to be proceeded against and punished accordingly.

(2) Where the affairs of a body corporate are managed by its members, subsection (1) applies in relation to the acts and defaults of a member in connection with his functions of management as to a director of a body corporate.

(3) Where an offence under section 85 or 86 committed by a partnership is proved to have been committed with the consent or connivance of, or to be attributable to any neglect on the part of, a partner, he as well as the partnership is guilty of the offence and liable to be proceeded against and punished accordingly.

(4) Where an offence under section 85 or 86 committed by an unincorporated association (other than a partnership) is proved to have been committed with the consent or connivance of, or to be attributable to any neglect on the part of, any officer of the association or any member of its governing body, he as well as the association is guilty of the offence and liable to be proceeded against and punished accordingly.

91 Jurisdiction and procedure in respect of offences

(1) Summary proceedings for an offence under section 85 may, without prejudice to any jurisdiction exercisable apart from this section, be taken against a body corporate or unincorporated association at any place at which it has a place of business and against an individual at any place where he is for the time being.

(2) Proceedings for an offence alleged to have been committed under section 85 or 86 by an unincorporated association shall be brought in the name of the association (and not in that of any of its members), and for the purposes of any such proceedings any rules of court relating to the service of documents apply as in relation to a body corporate.

(3) Section 33 of the Criminal Justice Act 1925 and Schedule 3 to the Magistrates' Courts Act 1980 (procedure on charge of offence against a corporation) apply in a case in which an unincorporated association is charged in England and Wales with an offence under section 85 or 86 as they apply in the case of a corporation.

(4) In relation to proceedings on indictment in Scotland for an offence alleged to have been committed under section 85 or 86 by an unincorporated association, section 74 of the Criminal Procedure (Scotland) Act 1975 (proceedings on indictment against bodies corporate) applies as if the association were a body corporate.

(5) Section 18 of the Criminal Justice Act (Northern Ireland) 1945 and Schedule 4 to the Magistrates' Courts (Northern Ireland) Order 1981 (procedure on charge of offence against a corporation) apply in a case in which an unincorporated association is charged in Northern Ireland with an offence under section 85 or 86 as they apply in the case of a corporation.

(6) A fine imposed on an unincorporated association on its conviction of such an offence shall be paid out of the funds of the association.

PART IV

REGISTRATION OF COMPANY CHARGES

Introduction

92 Introduction

The provisions of this Part amend the provisions of the Companies Act 1985 relating to the registration of company charges—

    (*a*) by inserting in Part XII of that Act (in place of sections 395 to 408 and 410 to 423) new provisions with respect to companies registered in Great Britain, and

    (*b*) by inserting as Chapter III of Part XXIII of that Act (in place of sections 409 and 424) new provisions with respect to oversea companies.

Registration in the companies charges register

93 Charges requiring registration

The following sections are inserted in Part XII of the Companies Act 1985—

'*Registration in the company charges register*

395 Introductory provisions

    (1) The purpose of this Part is to secure the registration of charges on a company's property.

    (2) In this Part—

'charge' means any form of security interest (fixed or floating) over property, other than an interest arising by operation of law; and

'property', in the context of what is the subject of a charge, includes future property.

    (3) It is immaterial for the purposes of this Part where the property subject to a charge is situated.

    (4) References in this Part to 'the registrar' are—

    (*a*) in relation to a company registered in England and Wales, to the registrar of companies for England and Wales, and

    (*b*) in relation to a company registered in Scotland, to the registrar of companies for Scotland;

and references to registration, in relation to a charge, are to registration in the register kept by him under this Part.

396 Charges requiring registration

    (1) The charges requiring registration under this Part are—

    (*a*) a charge on land or any interest in land, other than—

        (i) in England and Wales, a charge for rent or any other periodical sum issuing out of the land,

        (ii) in Scotland, a charge for any rent, ground annual or other periodical sum payable in respect of the land;

    (*b*) a charge on goods or any interest in goods, other than a charge under which the chargee is entitled to possession either of the goods or of a document of title to them;

    (*c*) a charge on intangible movable property (in Scotland, incorporeal moveable property) of any of the following descriptions—

        (i) goodwill,

        (ii) intellectual property,

    (iii) book debts (whether book debts of the company or assigned to the company),

    (iv) uncalled share capital of the company or calls made but not paid;

(d) a charge for securing an issue of debentures; or

(e) a floating charge on the whole or part of the company's property.

(2) The descriptions of charge mentioned in subsection (1) shall be construed as follows—

(a) a charge on a debenture forming part of an issue or series shall not be treated as falling within paragraph (a) or (b) by reason of the fact that the debenture is secured by a charge on land or goods (or on an interest in land or goods);

(b) in paragraph (b) 'goods' means any tangible movable property (in Scotland, corporeal moveable property) other than money;

(c) a charge is not excluded from paragraph (b) because the chargee is entitled to take possession in case of default or on the occurrence of some other event;

(d) in paragraph (c)(ii) 'intellectual property' means—

    (i) any patent, trade mark, service mark, registered design, copyright or design right, or

    (ii) any licence under or in respect of any such right;

(e) a debenture which is part of an issue or series shall not be treated as a book debt for the purposes of paragraph (c)(iii);

(f) the deposit by way of security of a negotiable instrument given to secure the payment of book debts shall not be treated for the purposes of paragraph (c)(iii) as a charge on book debts;

(g) a shipowner's lien on subfreights shall not be treated as a charge on book debts for the purposes of paragraph (c)(iii) or as a floating charge for the purposes of paragraph (e).

(3) Whether a charge is one requiring registration under this Part shall be determined—

(a) in the case of a charge created by a company, as at the date the charge is created, and

(b) in the case of a charge over property acquired by a company, as at the date of the acquisition.

(4) The Secretary of State may by regulations amend subsections (1) and (2) so as to add any description of charge to, or remove any description of charge from, the charges requiring registration under this Part.

(5) Regulations under this section shall be made by statutory instrument which shall be subject to annulment in pursuance of a resolution of either House of Parliament.

(6) In the following provisions of this Part references to a charge are, unless the context otherwise requires, to a charge requiring registration under this Part.

Where a charge not otherwise requiring registration relates to property by virtue of which it requires to be registered and to other property, the references are to the charge so far as it relates to property of the former description.'.

94 The companies charges register

The following section is inserted in Part XII of the Companies Act 1985—

'397 The companies charges register

(1) The registrar shall keep for each company a register, in such form as he thinks fit, of charges on property of the company.

(2) The register shall consist of a file containing with respect to each charge the particulars and other information delivered to the registrar under the provisions of this Part.

(3) Any person may require the registrar to provide a certificate stating the date on which any specified particulars of, or other information relating to, a charge were delivered to him.

(4) The certificate shall be signed by the registrar or authenticated by his official seal.

(5) The certificate shall be conclusive evidence that the specified particulars or other information were delivered to the registrar no later than the date stated in the certificate; and it shall be presumed unless the contrary is proved that they were not delivered earlier than that date.'.

95 Delivery of particulars for registration

The following sections are inserted in Part XII of the Companies Act 1985—

'398 Company's duty to deliver particulars of charge for registration

(1) It is the duty of a company which creates a charge, or acquires property subject to a charge—

(a) to deliver the prescribed particulars of the charge, in the prescribed form, to the registrar for registration, and

(b) to do so within 21 days after the date of the charge's creation or, as the case may be, the date of the acquisition;

but particulars of a charge may be delivered for registration by any person interested in the charge.

(2) Where the particulars are delivered for registration by a person other than the company concerned, that person is entitled to recover from the company the amount of any fees paid by him to the registrar in connection with the registration.

(3) If a company fails to comply with subsection (1), then, unless particulars of the charge have been delivered for registration by another person, the company and every officer of it who is in default is liable to a fine.

(4) Where prescribed particulars in the prescribed form are delivered to the registrar for registration, he shall file the particulars in the register and shall note, in such form as he thinks fit, the date on which they were delivered to him.

(5) The registrar shall send to the company and any person appearing from the particulars to be the chargee, and if the particulars were delivered by another person interested in the charge to that person, a copy of the particulars filed by him and of the note made by him as to the date on which they were delivered.

399 Effect of failure to deliver particulars for registration

(1) Where a charge is created by a company and no prescribed particulars in the prescribed form are delivered for registration within the period of 21 days after the date of the charge's creation, the charge is void against—

(a) an administrator or liquidator of the company, and

(b) any person who for value acquires an interest in or right over property subject to the charge,

where the relevant event occurs after the creation of the charge, whether before or after the end of the 21 day period.

This is subject to section 400 (late delivery of particulars).

(2) In this Part 'the relevant event' means—

(a) in relation to the voidness of a charge as against an administrator or liquidator, the beginning of the insolvency proceedings, and

(b) in relation to the voidness of a charge as against a person acquiring an interest in or right over property subject to a charge, the acquisition of that interest or right;

and references to 'a relevant event' shall be construed accordingly.

191

(3) Where a relevant event occurs on the same day as the charge is created, it shall be presumed to have occurred after the charge is created unless the contrary is proved.

400 Late delivery of particulars

(1) Where prescribed particulars of a charge created by a company, in the prescribed form, are delivered for registration more than 21 days after the date of the charge's creation, section 399(1) does not apply in relation to relevant events occurring after the particulars are delivered.

(2) However, where in such a case—

(*a*) the company is at the date of delivery of the particulars unable to pay its debts, or subsequently becomes unable to pay its debts in consequence of the transaction under which the charge is created, and

(*b*) insolvency proceedings begin before the end of the relevant period beginning with the date of delivery of the particulars,

the charge is void as against the administrator or liquidator.

(3) For this purpose—

(*a*) the company is 'unable to pay its debts' in the circumstances specified in section 123 of the Insolvency Act 1986; and

(*b*) the 'relevant period' is—

(i) two years in the case of a floating charge created in favour of a person connected with the company (within the meaning of section 249 of that Act),

(ii) one year in the case of a floating charge created in favour of a person not so connected, and

(iii) six months in any other case.

(4) Where a relevant event occurs on the same day as the particulars are delivered, it shall be presumed to have occurred before the particulars are delivered unless the contrary is proved.'.

96 Delivery of further particulars

The following section is inserted in Part XII of the Companies Act 1985—

'401 Delivery of further particulars

(1) Further particulars of a charge, supplementing or varying the registered particulars, may be delivered to the registrar for registration at any time.

(2) Further particulars must be in the prescribed form signed by or on behalf of both the company and the chargee.

(3) Where further particulars are delivered to the registrar for registration and appear to him to be duly signed, he shall file the particulars in the register and shall note, in such form as he thinks fit, the date on which they were delivered to him.

(4) The registrar shall send to the company and any person appearing from the particulars to be the chargee, and if the particulars were delivered by another person interested in the charge to that other person, a copy of the further particulars filed by him and of the note made by him as to the date on which they were delivered.'.

97 Effect of omissions and errors in registered particulars

The following section is inserted in Part XII of the Companies Act 1985—

'402 Effect of omissions and errors in registered particulars

(1) Where the registered particulars of a charge created by a company are not complete and accurate, the charge is void, as mentioned below, to the extent that rights are not disclosed by the registered particulars which would be disclosed if they were complete and accurate.

(2) The charge is void to that extent, unless the court on the application of the chargee orders otherwise, as against—

(*a*) an administrator or liquidator of the company, and
(*b*) any person who for value acquires an interest in or right over property subject to the charge,

where the relevant event occurs at a time when the particulars are incomplete or inaccurate in a relevant respect.

(3) Where a relevant event occurs on the same day as particulars or further particulars are delivered, it shall be presumed to have occurred before those particulars are delivered unless the contrary is proved.

(4) The court may order that the charge is effective as against an administrator or liquidator of the company if it is satisfied—

(*a*) that the omission or error is not likely to have misled materially to his prejudice any unsecured creditor of the company, or
(*b*) that no person became an unsecured creditor of the company at a time when the registered particulars of the charge were incomplete or inaccurate in a relevant respect.

(5) The court may order that the charge is effective as against a person acquiring an interest in or right over property subject to the charge if it is satisfied that he did not rely, in connection with the acquisition, on registered particulars which were incomplete or inaccurate in a relevant respect.

(6) For the purposes of this section an omission or inaccuracy with respect to the name of the chargee shall not be regarded as a failure to disclose the rights of the chargee.'.

98 Memorandum of charge ceasing to affect company's property

The following section is inserted in Part XII of the Companies Act 1985—

'403 Memorandum of charge ceasing to affect company's property

(1) Where a charge of which particulars have been delivered ceases to affect the company's property, a memorandum to that effect may be delivered to the registrar for registration.

(2) The memorandum must be in the prescribed form signed by or on behalf of both the company and the chargee.

(3) Where a memorandum is delivered to the registrar for registration and appears to him to be duly signed, he shall file it in the register, and shall note, in such form as he thinks fit, the date on which it was delivered to him.

(4) The registrar shall send to the company and any person appearing from the memorandum to be the chargee, and if the memorandum was delivered by another person interested in the charge to that person, a copy of the memorandum filed by him and of the note made by him as to the date on which it was delivered.

(5) If a duly signed memorandum is delivered in a case where the charge in fact continues to affect the company's property, the charge is void as against—

(*a*) an administrator or liquidator of the company, and
(*b*) any person who for value acquires an interest in or right over property subject to the charge,

where the relevant event occurs after the delivery of the memorandum.

(6) Where a relevant event occurs on the same day as the memorandum is delivered, it shall be presumed to have occurred before the memorandum is delivered unless the contrary is proved.'.

99 Further provisions with respect to voidness of charges

The following sections are inserted in Part XII of the Companies Act 1985—

'Further provisions with respect to voidness of charges

404 Exclusion of voidness as against unregistered charges

(1) A charge is not void by virtue of this Part as against a subsequent charge unless some or all of the relevant particulars of that charge are duly delivered for registration—

(a) within 21 days after the date of its creation, or

(b) before complete and accurate relevant particulars of the earlier charge are duly delivered for registration.

(2) Where relevant particulars of the subsequent charge so delivered are incomplete or inaccurate, the earlier charge is void as against that charge only to the extent that rights are disclosed by registered particulars of the subsequent charge duly delivered for registration before the corresponding relevant particulars of the earlier charge.

(3) The relevant particulars of a charge for the purposes of this section are those prescribed particulars relating to rights inconsistent with those conferred by or in relation to the other charge.

405 Restrictions on voidness by virtue of this Part

(1) A charge is not void by virtue of this Part as against a person acquiring an interest in or right over property where the acquisition is expressly subject to the charge.

(2) Nor is a charge void by virtue of this Part in relation to any property by reason of a relevant event occurring after the company which created the charge has disposed of the whole of its interest in that property.

406 Effect of exercise of power of sale

(1) A chargee exercising a power of sale may dispose of property to a purchaser freed from any interest or right arising from the charge having become void to any extent by virtue of this Part—

(a) against an administrator or liquidator of the company, or

(b) against a person acquiring a security interest over property subject to the charge;

and a purchaser is not concerned to see or inquire whether the charge has become so void.

(2) The proceeds of the sale shall be held by the chargee in trust to be applied—

First, in discharge of any sum effectively secured by prior incumbrances to which the sale is not made subject;

Second, in payment of all costs, charges and expenses properly incurred by him in connection with the sale, or any previous attempted sale, of the property;

Third, in discharge of any sum effectively secured by the charge and incumbrances ranking *pari passu* with the charge;

Fourth, in discharge of any sum effectively secured by incumbrances ranking after the charge;

and any residue is payable to the company or to a person authorised to give a receipt for the proceeds of the sale of the property.

(3) For the purposes of subsection (2)—

(a) prior incumbrances include any incumbrance to the extent that the charge is void as against it by virtue of this Part; and

(b) no sum is effectively secured by a charge to the extent that it is void as against an administrator or liquidator of the company.

(4) In this section—

(a) references to things done by a chargee include things done by a receiver appointed by him, whether or not the receiver acts as his agent;

(b) 'power of sale' includes any power to dispose of, or grant an interest out of, property for the purpose of enforcing a charge (but in relation to Scotland does not include the power to grant a lease), and references to 'sale' shall be construed accordingly; and

(*c*) 'purchaser' means a person who in good faith and for valuable consideration acquires an interest in property.

(5) The provisions of this section as to the order of application of the proceeds of sale have effect subject to any other statutory provision (in Scotland, any other statutory provision or rule of law) applicable in any case.

(6) Where a chargee exercising a power of sale purports to dispose of property freed from any such interest or right as is mentioned in subsection (1) to a person other than a purchaser, the above provisions apply, with any necessary modifications, in relation to a disposition to a purchaser by that person or any successor in title of his.

(7) In Scotland, subsections (2) and (7) of section 27 of the Conveyancing and Feudal Reform (Scotland) Act 1970 apply to a chargee unable to obtain a discharge for any payment which he is required to make under subsection (2) above as they apply to a creditor in the circumstances mentioned in those subsections.

407 Effect of voidness on obligation secured

(1) Where a charge becomes void to any extent by virtue of this Part, the whole of the sum secured by the charge is payable forthwith on demand; and this applies notwithstanding that the sum secured by the charge is also the subject of other security.

(2) Where the charge is to secure the repayment of money, the references in subsection (1) to the sum secured include any interest payable.'.

100 Additional information to be registered

The following sections are inserted in Part XII of the Companies Act 1985—

'Additional information to be registered

408 Particulars of taking up of issue of debentures

(1) Where particulars of a charge for securing an issue of debentures have been delivered for registration, it is the duty of the company—

(*a*) to deliver to the registrar for registration particulars in the prescribed form of the date on which any debentures of the issue are taken up, and of the amount taken up, and

(*b*) to do so before the end of the period of 21 days after the date on which they are taken up.

(2) Where particulars in the prescribed form are delivered to the registrar for registration under this section, he shall file them in the register.

(3) If a company fails to comply with subsection (1), the company and every officer of it who is in default is liable to a fine.

409 Notice of appointment of receiver or manager, &c

(1) If a person obtains an order for the appointment of a receiver or manager of a company's property, or appoints such a receiver or manager under powers contained in an instrument, he shall within seven days of the order or of the appointment under those powers, give notice of that fact in the prescribed form to the registrar for registration.

(2) Where a person appointed receiver or manager of a company's property under powers contained in an instrument ceases to act as such receiver or manager, he shall, on so ceasing, give notice of that fact in the prescribed form to the registrar for registration.

(3) Where a notice under this section in the prescribed form is delivered to the registrar for registration, he shall file it in the register.

(4) If a person makes default in complying with the requirements of subsection (1) or (2), he is liable to a fine.

(5) This section does not apply in relation to companies registered in Scotland (for which corresponding provision is made by sections 53, 54 and 62 of the Insolvency Act 1986).

410 Notice of crystallisation of floating charge, &c

(1) The Secretary of State may by regulations require notice in the prescribed form to be given to the registrar of—

(a) the occurrence of such events as may be prescribed affecting the nature of the security under a floating charge of which particulars have been delivered for registration, and

(b) the taking of such action in exercise of powers conferred by a fixed or floating charge of which particulars have been delivered for registration, or conferred in relation to such a charge by an order of the court, as may be prescribed.

(2) The regulations may make provision as to—

(a) the persons by whom notice is required to be, or may be, given, and the period within which notice is required to be given;

(b) the filing in the register of the particulars contained in the notice and the noting of the date on which the notice was given; and

(c) the consequences of failure to give notice.

(3) As regards the consequences of failure to give notice of an event causing a floating charge to crystallise, the regulations may include provision to the effect that the crystallisation—

(a) shall be treated as ineffective until the prescribed particulars are delivered, and

(b) if the prescribed particulars are delivered after the expiry of the prescribed period, shall continue to be ineffective against such persons as may be prescribed,

subject to the exercise of such powers as may be conferred by the regulations on the court.

(4) The regulations may provide that if there is a failure to comply with such of the requirements of the regulations as may be prescribed, such persons as may be prescribed are liable to a fine.

(5) Regulations under this section shall be made by statutory instrument which shall be subject to annulment in pursuance of a resolution of either House of Parliament.

(6) Regulations under this section shall not apply in relation to a floating charge created under the law of Scotland by a company registered in Scotland.'.

Copies of instruments and register to be kept by company

101 Copies of instruments and register to be kept by company

The following sections are inserted in Part XII of the Companies Act 1985—

'Copies of instruments and register to be kept by company

411 Duty to keep copies of instruments and register

(1) Every company shall keep at its registered office a copy of every instrument creating or evidencing a charge over the company's property.

In the case of a series of uniform debentures, a copy of one debenture of the series is sufficient.

(2) Every company shall also keep at its registered office a register of all such charges, containing entries for each charge giving a short description of the property charged, the amount of the charge and (except in the case of securities to bearer) the names of the persons entitled to it.

(3) This section applies to any charge, whether or not particulars are required to be delivered to the registrar for registration.

(4) If a company fails to comply with any requirement of this section, the company and every officer of it who is in default is liable to a fine.

412 Inspection of copies and register

(1) The copies and the register referred to in section 411 shall be open to the inspection of any creditor or member of the company without fee; and to the inspection of any other person on payment of such fee as may be prescribed.

(2) Any person may request the company to provide him with a copy of—

(*a*) any instrument creating or evidencing a charge over the company's property, or

(*b*) any entry in the register of charges kept by the company, on payment of such fee as may be prescribed.

This subsection applies to any charge, whether or not particulars are required to be delivered to the registrar for registration.

(3) The company shall send the copy to him not later than ten days after the day on which the request is received or, if later, on which payment is received.

(4) If inspection of the copies or register is refused, or a copy requested is not sent within the time specified above—

(*a*) the company and every officer of it who is in default is liable to a fine, and

(*b*) the court may by order compel an immediate inspection of the copies or register or, as the case may be, direct that the copy be sent immediately.'.

Supplementary provisions

102 Power to make further provision by regulations

The following section is inserted in Part XII of the Companies Act 1985—

'Supplementary provisions

413 Power to make further provision by regulations

(1) The Secretary of State may by regulations make further provision as to the application of the provisions of this Part in relation to charges of any description specified in the regulations.

Nothing in the following provisions shall be construed as restricting the generality of that power.

(2) The regulations may require that where the charge is contained in or evidenced or varied by a written instrument there shall be delivered to the registrar for registration, instead of particulars or further particulars of the charge, the instrument itself or a certified copy of it together with such particulars as may be prescribed.

(3) The regulations may provide that a memorandum of a charge ceasing to affect property of the company shall not be accepted by the registrar unless supported by such evidence as may be prescribed, and that a memorandum not so supported shall be treated as not having been delivered.

(4) The regulations may also provide that where the instrument creating the charge is delivered to the registrar in support of such a memorandum, the registrar may mark the instrument as cancelled before returning it and shall send copies of the instrument cancelled to such persons as may be prescribed.

(5) The regulations may exclude or modify, in such circumstances and to such extent as may be prescribed, the operation of the provisions of this Part relating to the voidness of a charge.

(6) The regulations may require, in connection with the delivery of particulars, further particulars or a memorandum of the charge's ceasing to affect property of the company, the delivery of such supplementary information as may be prescribed, and may—

    (*a*) apply in relation to such supplementary information any provisions of this Part relating to particulars, further particulars or such a memorandum, and

    (*b*) provide that the particulars, further particulars or memorandum shall be treated as not having been delivered until the required supplementary information is delivered.

(7) Regulations under this section shall be made by statutory instrument which shall be subject to annulment in pursuance of a resolution of either House of Parliament.'.

103 Other supplementary provisions

The following sections are inserted in Part XII of the Companies Act 1985—

'414 Date of creation of charge

(1) References in this Part to the date of creation of a charge by a company shall be construed as follows.

(2) A charge created under the law of England and Wales shall be taken to be created—

    (*a*) in the case of a charge created by an instrument in writing, when the instrument is executed by the company or, if its execution by the company is conditional, upon the conditions being fulfilled, and

    (*b*) in any other case, when an enforceable agreement is entered into by the company conferring a security interest intended to take effect forthwith or upon the company acquiring an interest in property subject to the charge.

(3) A charge created under the law of Scotland shall be taken to be created—

    (*a*) in the case of a floating charge, when the instrument creating the floating charge is executed by the company, and

    (*b*) in any other case, when the right of the person entitled to the benefit of the charge is constituted as a real right.

(4) Where a charge is created in the United Kingdom but comprises property outside the United Kingdom, any further proceedings necessary to make the charge valid or effectual under the law of the country where the property is situated shall be disregarded in ascertaining the date on which the charge is to be taken to be created.

415 Prescribed particulars and related expressions

(1) References in this Part to the prescribed particulars of a charge are to such particulars of, or relating to, the charge as may be prescribed.

(2) The prescribed particulars may, without prejudice to the generality of subsection (1), include—

    (*a*) whether the company has undertaken not to create other charges ranking in priority to or *pari passu* with the charge, and

    (*b*) whether the charge is a market charge within the meaning of Part VII of the Companies Act 1989 or a charge to which the provisions of that Part apply as they apply to a market charge.

(3) References in this Part to the registered particulars of a charge at any time are to such particulars and further particulars of the charge as have at that time been duly delivered for registration.

(4) References in this Part to the registered particulars of a charge being complete and accurate at any time are to their including all the prescribed particulars which would be required to be delivered if the charge were then newly created.

416 Notice of matters disclosed on register

(1) A person taking a charge over a company's property shall be taken to have notice of any matter requiring registration and disclosed on the register at the time the charge is created.

(2) Otherwise, a person shall not be taken to have notice of any matter by reason of its being disclosed on the register or by reason of his having failed to search the register in the course of making such inquiries as ought reasonably to be made.

(3) The above provisions have effect subject to any other statutory provision as to whether a person is to be taken to have notice of any matter disclosed on the register.

417 Power of court to dispense with signature

(1) Where it is proposed to deliver further particulars of a charge, or to deliver a memorandum of a charge ceasing to affect the company's property, and—

(a) the chargee refuses to sign or authorise a person to sign on his behalf, or cannot be found, or
(b) the company refuses to authorise a person to sign on its behalf,

the court may on the application of the company or the chargee, or of any other person having a sufficient interest in the matter, authorise the delivery of the particulars or memorandum without that signature.

(2) The order may be made on such terms as appear to the court to be appropriate.

(3) Where particulars or a memorandum are delivered to the registrar for registration in reliance on an order under this section, they must be accompanied by an office copy of the order.

In such a case the references in sections 401 and 403 to the particulars or memorandum being duly signed are to their being otherwise duly signed.

(4) The registrar shall file the office copy of the court order along with the particulars or memorandum.'.

104 Interpretation, &c

The following sections are inserted in Part XII of the Companies Act 1985—

'418 Regulations

Regulations under any provision of this Part, or prescribing anything for the purposes of any such provision—

(a) may make different provision for different cases, and
(b) may contain such supplementary, incidental and transitional provisions as appear to the Secretary of State to be appropriate.

419 Minor definitions

(1) In this Part—

'chargee' means the person for the time being entitled to exercise the security rights conferred by the charge;
'issue of debentures' means a group of debentures, or an amount of debenture stock, secured by the same charge; and
'series of debentures' means a group of debentures each containing or giving by reference to another instrument a charge to the benefit of which the holders of debentures of the series are entitled *pari passu*.

(2) References in this Part to the creation of a charge include the variation of a charge which is not registrable so as to include property by virtue of which it becomes registrable.

The provisions of section 414 (construction of references to date of creation of charge) apply in such a case with any necessary modifications.

(3) References in this Part to the date of acquisition of property by a company are—

(a) in England and Wales, to the date on which the acquisition is completed, and
(b) in Scotland, to the date on which the transaction is settled.

(4) In the application of this Part to a floating charge created under the law of

Scotland, references to crystallisation shall be construed as references to the attachment of the charge.

(5) References in this Part to the beginning of insolvency proceedings are to—

(*a*) the presentation of a petition on which an administration order or winding-up order is made, or

(*b*) the passing of a resolution for voluntary winding up.

420 Index of defined expressions

The following Table shows the provisions of this Part defining or otherwise explaining expressions used in this Part (other than expressions used only in the same section)—

charge	sections 395(2) and 396(6)
charge requiring registration	section 396
chargee	section 419(1)
complete and accurate (in relation to registered particulars)	section 415(4)
creation of charge	section 419(2)
crystallisation (in relation to Scottish floating charge)	section 419(4)
date of acquisition (of property by a company)	section 419(3)
date of creation of charge	section 414
further particulars	section 401
insolvency proceedings, beginning of	section 419(5)
issue of debentures	section 419(1)
memorandum of charge ceasing to affect company's property	section 403
prescribed particulars	section 415(1) and (2)
property	section 395(2)
registered particulars	section 415(3)
registrar and registration in relation to a charge	section 395(4)
relevant event	section 399(2)
series of debentures	section 419(1).'.

105 Charges on property of oversea company

The provisions set out in Schedule 15 are inserted in Part XXIII of the Companies Act 1985 (oversea companies), as a Chapter III (registration of charges).

106 Application of provisions to unregistered companies

In Schedule 22 to the Companies Act 1985 (provisions applying to unregistered companies), at the appropriate place insert—

'Part XII   Registration   of   company   Subject to section 718(3).'.
            charges;   copies   of
            instruments and register to
            be kept by company.

107 Consequential amendments

The enactments specified in Schedule 16 have effect with the amendments specified there, which are consequential on the amendments made by the preceding provisions of this Part.

PART V

OTHER AMENDMENTS OF COMPANY LAW

A company's capacity and related matters

108 A company's capacity and the power of the directors to bind it

(1) In Chapter III of Part I of the Companies Act 1985 (a company's capacity; formalities of carrying on business), for section 35 substitute—

'35 A company's capacity not limited by its memorandum

(1) The validity of an act done by a company shall not be called into question on the ground of lack of capacity by reason of anything in the company's memorandum.

(2) A member of a company may bring proceedings to restrain the doing of an act which but for subsection (1) would be beyond the company's capacity; but no such proceedings shall lie in respect of an act to be done in fulfilment of a legal obligation arising from a previous act of the company.

(3) It remains the duty of the directors to observe any limitations on their powers flowing from the company's memorandum; and action by the directors which but for subsection (1) would be beyond the company's capacity may only be ratified by the company by special resolution.

A resolution ratifying such action shall not affect any liability incurred by the directors or any other person; relief from any such liability must be agreed to separately by special resolution.

(4) The operation of this section is restricted by section 30B(1) of the Charities Act 1960 and section 112(3) of the Companies Act 1989 in relation to companies which are charities; and section 322A below (invalidity of certain transactions to which directors or their associates are parties) has effect notwithstanding this section.

35A Power of directors to bind the company

(1) In favour of a person dealing with a company in good faith, the power of the board of directors to bind the company, or authorise others to do so, shall be deemed to be free of any limitation under the company's constitution.

(2) For this purpose—

(*a*) a person 'deals with' a company if he is a party to any transaction or other act to which the company is a party;

(*b*) a person shall not be regarded as acting in bad faith by reason only of his knowing that an act is beyond the powers of the directors under the company's constitution; and

(*c*) a person shall be presumed to have acted in good faith unless the contrary is proved.

(3) The references above to limitations on the directors' powers under the company's constitution include limitations deriving—

(*a*) from a resolution of the company in general meeting or a meeting of any class of shareholders, or

(*b*) from any agreement between the members of the company or of any class of shareholders.

(4) Subsection (1) does not affect any right of a member of the company to bring proceedings to restrain the doing of an act which is beyond the powers of the directors; but no such proceedings shall lie in respect of an act to be done in fulfilment of a legal obligation arising from a previous act of the company.

(5) Nor does that subsection affect any liability incurred by the directors, or any other person, by reason of the directors' exceeding their powers.

(6) The operation of this section is restricted by section 30B(1) of the Charities Act 1960 and section 112(3) of the Companies Act 1989 in relation to companies which are charities; and section 322A below (invalidity of certain transactions to which directors or their associates are parties) has effect notwithstanding this section.

35B No duty to enquire as to capacity of company or authority of directors

A party to a transaction with a company is not bound to enquire as to whether it is permitted by the company's memorandum or as to any limitation on the powers of the board of directors to bind the company or authorise others to do so.'.

(2) In Schedule 21 to the Companies Act 1985 (effect of registration of companies not formed under that Act), in paragraph 6 (general application of provisions of Act), after sub-paragraph (5) insert—

'(6) Where by virtue of sub-paragraph (4) or (5) a company does not have power to alter a provision, it does not have power to ratify acts of the directors in contravention of the provision.'.

(3) In Schedule 22 to the Companies Act 1985 (provisions applying to unregistered companies), in the entries relating to Part I, in the first column for 'section 35' substitute 'sections 35 to 35B'.

109 Invalidity of certain transactions involving directors

(1) In Part X of the Companies Act 1985 (enforcement of fair dealing by directors), after section 322 insert—

'322A Invalidity of certain transactions involving directors, etc

(1) This section applies where a company enters into a transaction to which the parties include—

(a) a director of the company or of its holding company, or

(b) a person connected with such a director or a company with whom such a director is associated,

and the board of directors, in connection with the transaction, exceed any limitation on their powers under the company's constitution.

(2) The transaction is voidable at the instance of the company.

(3) Whether or not it is avoided, any such party to the transaction as is mentioned in subsection (1)(a) or (b), and any director of the company who authorised the transaction, is liable—

(a) to account to the company for any gain which he has made directly or indirectly by the transaction, and

(b) to indemnify the company for any loss or damage resulting from the transaction.

(4) Nothing in the above provisions shall be construed as excluding the operation of any other enactment or rule of law by virtue of which the transaction may be called in question or any liability to the company may arise.

(5) The transaction ceases to be voidable if—

(a) restitution of any money or other asset which was the subject-matter of the transaction is no longer possible, or

(b) the company is indemnified for any loss or damage resulting from the transaction, or

(c) rights acquired bona fide for value and without actual notice of the directors' exceeding their powers by a person who is not party to the transaction would be affected by the avoidance, or

(d) the transaction is ratified by the company in general meeting, by ordinary or special resolution or otherwise as the case may require.

(6) A person other than a director of the company is not liable under subsection (3) if he shows that at the time the transaction was entered into he did not know that the directors were exceeding their powers.

(7) This section does not affect the operation of section 35A in relation to any party to the transaction not within subsection (1)(a) or (b).

But where a transaction is voidable by virtue of this section and valid by virtue of that section in favour of such a person, the court may, on the application of that person or of the company, make such order affirming, severing or setting aside the transaction, on such terms, as appear to the court to be just.

(8) In this section 'transaction' includes any act; and the reference in subsection (1) to limitations under the company's constitution includes limitations deriving—

    (*a*) from a resolution of the company in general meeting or a meeting of any class of shareholders, or

    (*b*) from any agreement between the members of the company or of any class of shareholders.'.

(2) In Schedule 22 to the Companies Act 1985 (provisions applying to unregistered companies), in the entries relating to Part X, insert—

'section 322A   Invalidity of certain transactions   Subject to section 718(3).'
                    involving directors, etc

110 Statement of company's objects

(1) In Chapter I of Part I of the Companies Act 1985 (company formation), after section 3 (forms of memorandum) insert—

'3A Statement of company's objects: general commercial company

Where the company's memorandum states that the object of the company is to carry on business as a general commercial company—

    (*a*) the object of the company is to carry on any trade or business whatsoever, and

    (*b*) the company has power to do all such things as are incidental or conducive to the carrying on of any trade or business by it.'.

(2) In the same Chapter, for section 4 (resolution to alter objects) substitute—

'4 Resolution to alter objects

(1) A company may by special resolution alter its memorandum with respect to the statement of the company's objects.

(2) If an application is made under the following section, an alteration does not have effect except in so far as it is confirmed by the court.'.

111 Charitable companies

(1) In the Charities Act 1960, for section 30 (charitable companies) substitute—

'30 Charitable companies: winding up

Where a charity may be wound up by the High Court under the Insolvency Act 1986, a petition for it to be wound up under that Act by any court in England or Wales having jurisdiction may be presented by the Attorney General, as well as by any person authorised by that Act.

30A Charitable companies: alteration of objects clause

(1) Where a charity is a company or other body corporate having power to alter the instruments establishing or regulating it as a body corporate, no exercise of that power which has the effect of the body ceasing to be a charity shall be valid so as to affect the application of—

    (*a*) any property acquired under any disposition or agreement previously made otherwise than for full consideration in money or money's worth, or any property representing property so acquired,

    (*b*) any property representing income which has accrued before the alteration is made, or

    (*c*) the income from any such property as aforesaid.

(2) Where a charity is a company, any alteration by it of the objects clause in its memorandum of association is ineffective without the prior written consent of the Commissioners; and it shall deliver a copy of that consent to the registrar of companies under section 6(1)(*a*) or (*b*) of the Companies Act 1985 along with the printed copy of the memorandum as altered.

(3) Section 6(3) of that Act (offences) applies in relation to a default in complying with subsection (2) as regards the delivery of a copy of the Commissioners' consent.

30B Charitable companies: invalidity of certain transactions

(1) Sections 35 and 35A of the Companies Act 1985 (capacity of company not limited by its memorandum; power of directors to bind company) do not apply to the acts of a company which is a charity except in favour of a person who—

(*a*) gives full consideration in money or money's worth in relation to the act in question, and

(*b*) does not know that the act is not permitted by the company's memorandum or, as the case may be, is beyond the powers of the directors,

or who does not know at the time the act is done that the company is a charity.

(2) However, where such a company purports to transfer or grant an interest in property, the fact that the act was not permitted by the company's memorandum or, as the case may be, that the directors in connection with the act exceeded any limitation on their powers under the company's constitution, does not affect the title of a person who subsequently acquires the property or any interest in it for full consideration without actual notice of any such circumstances affecting the validity of the company's act.

(3) In any proceedings arising out of subsection (1) the burden of proving—

(*a*) that a person knew that an act was not permitted by the company's memorandum or was beyond the powers of the directors, or

(*b*) that a person knew that the company was a charity,

lies on the person making that allegation.

(4) Where a company is a charity, the ratification of an act under section 35(3) of the Companies Act 1985, or the ratification of a transaction to which section 322A of that Act applies (invalidity of certain transactions to which directors or their associates are parties), is ineffective without the prior written consent of the Commissioners.

30C Charitable companies: status to appear on correspondence, etc

(1) Where a company is a charity and its name does not include the word 'charity' or the word 'charitable', the fact that the company is a charity shall be stated in English in legible characters—

(*a*) in all business letters of the company,

(*b*) in all its notices and other official publications,

(*c*) in all bills of exchange, promissory notes, endorsements, cheques and orders for money or goods purporting to be signed by or on behalf of the company,

(*d*) in all conveyances purporting to be executed by the company, and

(*e*) in all its bills of parcels, invoices, receipts and letters of credit.

(2) In subsection (1)(*d*) 'conveyance' means any instrument creating, transferring, varying or extinguishing an interest in land.

(3) Section 349(2) to (4) of the Companies Act 1985 (offences in connection with failure to include required particulars in business letters, &c) apply in relation to a contravention of subsection (1) above.'.

(2) In section 46 of the Charities Act 1960 (definitions), at the appropriate place insert—

' "company" means a company formed and registered under the Companies Act 1985, or to which the provisions of that Act apply as they apply to such a company;'.

112 Charitable companies (Scotland)

(1) In the following provisions (which extend to Scotland only)—

(*a*) 'company' means a company formed and registered under the Companies Act 1985, or to which the provisions of that Act apply as they apply to such a company; and

(b) 'charity' means a body established for charitable purposes only (that expression having the same meaning as in the Income Tax Acts).

(2) Where a charity is a company or other body corporate having power to alter the instruments establishing or regulating it as a body corporate, no exercise of that power which has the effect of the body ceasing to be a charity shall be valid so as to affect the application of—

(a) any property acquired by virtue of any transfer, contract or obligation previously effected otherwise than for full consideration in money or money's worth, or any property representing property so acquired,

(b) any property representing income which has accrued before the alteration is made, or

(c) the income from any such property as aforesaid.

(3) Sections 35 and 35A of the Companies Act 1985 (capacity of company not limited by its memorandum; power of directors to bind company) do not apply to the acts of a company which is a charity except in favour of a person who—

(a) gives full consideration in money or money's worth in relation to the act in question, and

(b) does not know that the act is not permitted by the company's memorandum or, as the case may be, is beyond the powers of the directors,

or who does not know at the time the act is done that the company is a charity.

(4) However, where such a company purports to transfer or grant an interest in property, the fact that the act was not permitted by the company's memorandum or, as the case may be, that the directors in connection with the act exceeded any limitation on their powers under the company's constitution, does not affect the title of a person who subsequently acquires the property or any interest in it for full consideration without actual notice of any such circumstances affecting the validity of the company's act.

(5) In any proceedings arising out of subsection (3) the burden of proving—

(a) that a person knew that an act was not permitted by the company's memorandum or was beyond the powers of the directors, or

(b) that a person knew that the company was a charity,

lies on the person making that allegation.

(6) Where a company is a charity and its name does not include the word 'charity' or the word 'charitable', the fact that the company is a charity shall be stated in English in legible characters—

(a) in all business letters of the company,

(b) in all its notices and other official publications,

(c) in all bills of exchange, promissory notes, endorsements, cheques and orders for money or goods purporting to be signed by or on behalf of the company,

(d) in all conveyances purporting to be executed by the company, and

(e) in all its bills of parcels, invoices, receipts and letters of credit.

(7) In subsection (6)(d) 'conveyance' means any document for the creation, transfer, variation or extinction of an interest in land.

(8) Section 349(2) to (4) of the Companies Act 1985 (offences in connection with failure to include required particulars in business letters, &c) apply in relation to a contravention of subsection (6) above.

De-regulation of private companies

113 Written resolutions of private companies

(1) Chapter IV of Part XI of the Companies Act 1985 (meetings and resolutions) is amended as follows.

(2) After section 381 insert—

'Written resolutions of private companies

381A Written resolutions of private companies

(1) Anything which in the case of a private company may be done—

(*a*) by resolution of the company in general meeting, or

(*b*) by resolution of a meeting of any class of members of the company,

may be done, without a meeting and without any previous notice being required, by resolution in writing signed by or on behalf of all the members of the company who at the date of the resolution would be entitled to attend and vote at such meeting.

(2) The signatures need not be on a single document provided each is on a document which accurately states the terms of the resolution.

(3) The date of the resolution means when the resolution is signed by or on behalf of the last member to sign.

(4) A resolution agreed to in accordance with this section has effect as if passed—

(*a*) by the company in general meeting, or

(*b*) by a meeting of the relevant class of members of the company,

as the case may be; and any reference in any enactment to a meeting at which a resolution is passed or to members voting in favour of a resolution shall be construed accordingly.

(5) Any reference in any enactment to the date of passing of a resolution is, in relation to a resolution agreed to in accordance with this section, a reference to the date of the resolution, unless section 381B(4) applies in which case it shall be construed as a reference to the date from which the resolution has effect.

(6) A resolution may be agreed to in accordance with this section which would otherwise be required to be passed as a special, extraordinary or elective resolution; and any reference in any enactment to a special, extraordinary or elective resolution includes such a resolution.

(7) This section has effect subject to the exceptions specified in Part I of Schedule 15A; and in relation to certain descriptions of resolution under this section the procedural requirements of this Act have effect with the adaptations specified in Part II of that Schedule.

381B Rights of auditors in relation to written resolution

(1) A copy of any written resolution proposed to be agreed to in accordance with section 381A shall be sent to the company's auditors.

(2) If the resolution concerns the auditors as auditors, they may within seven days from the day on which they receive the copy give notice to the company stating their opinion that the resolution should be considered by the company in general meeting or, as the case may be, by a meeting of the relevant class of members of the company.

(3) A written resolution shall not have effect unless—

(*a*) the auditors notify the company that in their opinion the resolution—

   (i) does not concern them as auditors, or

   (ii) does so concern them but need not be considered by the company in general meeting or, as the case may be, by a meeting of the relevant class of members of the company, or

(*b*) the period for giving a notice under subsection (2) expires without any notice having been given in accordance with that subsection.

(4) A written resolution previously agreed to in accordance with section 381A shall not have effect until that notification is given or, as the case may be, that period expires.

381C Written resolutions: supplementary provisions

(1) Sections 381A and 381B have effect notwithstanding any provision of the company's memorandum or articles.

(2) Nothing in those sections affects any enactment or rule of law as to—

(*a*) things done otherwise than by passing a resolution, or

(*b*) cases in which a resolution is treated as having been passed, or a person is precluded from alleging that a resolution has not been duly passed.'.

(3) After section 382 insert—

'382A Recording of written resolutions

(1) Where a written resolution is agreed to in accordance with section 381A which has effect as if agreed by the company in general meeting, the company shall cause a record of the resolution (and of the signatures) to be entered in a book in the same way as minutes of proceedings of a general meeting of the company.

(2) Any such record, if purporting to be signed by a director of the company or by the company secretary, is evidence of the proceedings in agreeing to the resolution; and where a record is made in accordance with this section, then, until the contrary is proved, the requirements of this Act with respect to those proceedings shall be deemed to be complied with.

(3) Section 382(5) (penalties) applies in relation to a failure to comply with subsection (1) above as it applies in relation to a failure to comply with subsection (1) of that section; and section 383 (inspection of minute books) applies in relation to a record made in accordance with this section as it applies in relation to the minutes of a general meeting.'.

114 Written resolutions: supplementary provisions

(1) In the Companies Act 1985 the following Schedule is inserted after Schedule 15—

'SCHEDULE 15A

WRITTEN RESOLUTIONS OF PRIVATE COMPANIES

PART I

EXCEPTIONS

1. Section 381A does not apply to—

(*a*) a resolution under section 303 removing a director before the expiration of his period of office, or

(*b*) a resolution under section 391 removing an auditor before the expiration of his term of office.

PART II

ADAPTATION OF PROCEDURAL REQUIREMENTS

Introductory

2.—(1) In this Part of this Schedule (which adapts certain requirements of this Act in relation to proceedings under section 381A)—

(*a*) a 'written resolution' means a resolution agreed to, or proposed to be agreed to, in accordance with that section, and

(*b*) a 'relevant member' means a member by whom, or on whose behalf, the resolution is required to be signed in accordance with that section.

(2) A written resolution is not effective if any of the requirements of this Part of this Schedule is not complied with.

Section 95 (disapplication of pre-emption rights)

3.—(1) The following adaptations have effect in relation to a written resolution under section 95(2) (disapplication of pre-emption rights), or renewing a resolution under that provision.

207

(2) So much of section 95(5) as requires the circulation of a written statement by the directors with a notice of meeting does not apply, but such a statement must be supplied to each relevant member at or before the time at which the resolution is supplied to him for signature.

(3) Section 95(6) (offences) applies in relation to the inclusion in any such statement of matter which is misleading, false or deceptive in a material particular.

Section 155 (financial assistance for purchase of company's own shares or those of holding company)

4. In relation to a written resolution giving approval under section 155(4) or (5) (financial assistance for purchase of company's own shares or those of holding company), section 157(4)(*a*) (documents to be available at meeting) does not apply, but the documents referred to in that provision must be supplied to each relevant member at or before the time at which the resolution is supplied to him for signature.

Sections 164, 165 and 167 (authority for off-market purchase or contingent purchase contract of company's own shares)

5.—(1) The following adaptations have effect in relation to a written resolution—

(*a*) conferring authority to make an off-market purchase of the company's own shares under section 164(2),

(*b*) conferring authority to vary a contract for an off-market purchase of the company's own shares under section 164(7), or

(*c*) varying, revoking or renewing any such authority under section 164(3).

(2) Section 164(5) (resolution ineffective if passed by exercise of voting rights by member holding shares to which the resolution relates) does not apply; but for the purposes of section 381A(1) a member holding shares to which the resolution relates shall not be regarded as a member who would be entitled to attend and vote.

(3) Section 164(6) (documents to be available at company's registered office and at meeting) does not apply, but the documents referred to in that provision and, where that provision applies by virtue of section 164(7), the further documents referred to in that provision must be supplied to each relevant member at or before the time at which the resolution is supplied to him for signature.

(4) The above adaptations also have effect in relation to a written resolution in relation to which the provisions of section 164(3) to (7) apply by virtue of—

(*a*) section 165(2) (authority for contingent purchase contract), or

(*b*) section 167(2) (approval of release of rights under contract approved under section 164 or 165).

Section 173 (approval for payment out of capital)

6.—(1) The following adaptations have effect in relation to a written resolution giving approval under section 173(2) (redemption or purchase of company's own shares out of capital).

(2) Section 174(2) (resolution ineffective if passed by exercise of voting rights by member holding shares to which the resolution relates) does not apply; but for the purposes of section 381A(1) a member holding shares to which the resolution relates shall not be regarded as a member who would be entitled to attend and vote.

(3) Section 174(4) (documents to be available at meeting) does not apply, but the documents referred to in that provision must be supplied to each relevant member at or before the time at which the resolution is supplied to him for signature.

Section 319 (approval of director's service contract)

7. In relation to a written resolution approving any such term as is mentioned in section 319(1) (director's contract of employment for more than five years), section

319(5) (documents to be available at company's registered office and at meeting) does not apply, but the documents referred to in that provision must be supplied to each relevant member at or before the time at which the resolution is supplied to him for signature.

Section 337 (funding of director's expenditure in performing his duties)

8. In relation to a written resolution giving approval under section 337(3)(*a*) (funding a director's expenditure in performing his duties), the requirement of that provision that certain matters be disclosed at the meeting at which the resolution is passed does not apply, but those matters must be disclosed to each relevant member at or before the time at which the resolution is supplied to him for signature.'.

(2) The Schedule inserted after Schedule 15 to the Companies Act 1985 by the Companies (Mergers and Divisions) Regulations 1987 is renumbered '15B'; and accordingly, in section 427A of that Act (also inserted by those regulations), in subsections (1) and (8) for '15A' substitute '15B'.

115 Election by private company to dispense with certain requirements

(1) In Part IV of the Companies Act 1985 (allotment of shares and debentures), in section 80(1) (authority of company required for certain allotments) after 'this section' insert 'or section 80A'; and after that section insert—

'80A Election by private company as to duration of authority

(1) A private company may elect (by elective resolution in accordance with section 379A) that the provisions of this section shall apply, instead of the provisions of section 80(4) and (5), in relation to the giving or renewal, after the election, of an authority under that section.

(2) The authority must state the maximum amount of relevant securities that may be allotted under it and may be given—

(*a*) for an indefinite period, or

(*b*) for a fixed period, in which case it must state the date on which it will expire.

(3) In either case an authority (including an authority contained in the articles) may be revoked or varied by the company in general meeting.

(4) An authority given for a fixed period may be renewed or further renewed by the company in general meeting.

(5) A resolution renewing an authority—

(*a*) must state, or re-state, the amount of relevant securities which may be allotted under the authority or, as the case may be, the amount remaining to be allotted under it, and

(*b*) must state whether the authority is renewed for an indefinite period or for a fixed period, in which case it must state the date on which the renewed authority will expire.

(6) The references in this section to the maximum amount of relevant securities that may be allotted shall be construed in accordance with section 80(6).

(7) If an election under this section ceases to have effect, an authority then in force which was given for an indefinite period or for a fixed period of more than five years—

(*a*) if given five years or more before the election ceases to have effect, shall expire forthwith, and

(*b*) otherwise, shall have effect as if it had been given for a fixed period of five years.'.

(2) In Chapter IV of Part XI of the Companies Act 1985 (meetings and resolutions), after section 366 (annual general meeting) insert—

'366A Election by private company to dispense with annual general meetings

(1) A private company may elect (by elective resolution in accordance with section 379A) to dispense with the holding of annual general meetings.

(2) An election has effect for the year in which it is made and subsequent years, but does not affect any liability already incurred by reason of default in holding an annual general meeting.

(3) In any year in which an annual general meeting would be required to be held but for the election, and in which no such meeting has been held, any member of the company may, by notice to the company not later than three months before the end of the year, require the holding of an annual general meeting in that year.

(4) If such a notice is given, the provisions of section 366(1) and (4) apply with respect to the calling of the meeting and the consequences of default.

(5) If the election ceases to have effect, the company is not obliged under section 366 to hold an annual general meeting in that year if, when the election ceases to have effect, less than three months of the year remains.

This does not affect any obligation of the company to hold an annual general meeting in that year in pursuance of a notice given under subsection (3).'.

(3) In the same Chapter, in sections 369(4) and 378(3) (majority required to sanction short notice of meeting) insert—

'A private company may elect (by elective resolution in accordance with section 379A) that the above provisions shall have effect in relation to the company as if for the references to 95 per cent there were substituted references to such lesser percentage, but not less than 90 per cent, as may be specified in the resolution or subsequently determined by the company in general meeting.'.

116 Elective resolution of private company

(1) Chapter IV of Part XI of the Companies Act 1985 (meetings and resolutions) is amended as follows.

(2) After section 379 insert—

'379A Elective resolution of private company

(1) An election by a private company for the purposes of—

(*a*) section 80A (election as to duration of authority to allot shares),
(*b*) section 252 (election to dispense with laying of accounts and reports before general meeting),
(*c*) section 366A (election to dispense with holding of annual general meeting),
(*d*) section 369(4) or 378(3) (election as to majority required to authorise short notice of meeting), or
(*e*) section 386 (election to dispense with appointment of auditors annually),

shall be made by resolution of the company in general meeting in accordance with this section.

Such a resolution is referred to in this Act as an 'elective resolution'.

(2) An elective resolution is not effective unless—

(*a*) at least 21 days' notice in writing is given of the meeting, stating that an elective resolution is to be proposed and stating the terms of the resolution, and
(*b*) the resolution is agreed to at the meeting, in person or by proxy, by all the members entitled to attend and vote at the meeting.

(3) The company may revoke an elective resolution by passing an ordinary resolution to that effect.

(4) An elective resolution shall cease to have effect if the company is re-registered as a public company.

(5) An elective resolution may be passed or revoked in accordance with this section, and the provisions referred to in subsection (1) have effect, notwithstanding any contrary provision in the company's articles of association.'.

(3) In section 380 (registration of resolutions), in subsection (4) (resolutions to which the section applies), after paragraph (*b*) insert—

'(*bb*) an elective resolution or a resolution revoking such a resolution;'.

117 Power to make further provision by regulations

(1) The Secretary of State may by regulations make provision enabling private companies to elect, by elective resolution in accordance with section 379A of the Companies Act 1985, to dispense with compliance with such requirements of that Act as may be specified in the regulations, being requirements which appear to the Secretary of State to relate primarily to the internal administration and procedure of companies.

(2) The regulations may add to, amend or repeal provisions of that Act; and may provide for any such provision to have effect, where an election is made, subject to such adaptations and modifications as appear to the Secretary of State to be appropriate.

(3) The regulations may make different provision for different cases and may contain such supplementary, incidental and transitional provisions as appear to the Secretary of State to be appropriate.

(4) Regulations under this section shall be made by statutory instrument.

(5) No regulations under this section shall be made unless a draft of the instrument containing the regulations has been laid before Parliament and approved by a resolution of each House.

Appointment and removal of auditors and related matters

118 Introduction

(1) The following sections amend the provisions of the Companies Act 1985 relating to auditors by inserting new provisions in Chapter V of Part XI of that Act.

(2) The new provisions, together with the amendment made by section 124, replace the present provisions of that Chapter except section 389 (qualification for appointment as auditor) which is replaced by provisions in Part II of this Act.

119 Appointment of auditors

(1) The following sections are inserted in Chapter V of Part XI of the Companies Act 1985 (auditors)—

'*Appointment of auditors*

384 Duty to appoint auditors

(1) Every company shall appoint an auditor or auditors in accordance with this Chapter.

This is subject to section 388A (dormant company exempt from obligation to appoint auditors).

(2) Auditors shall be appointed in accordance with section 385 (appointment at general meeting at which accounts are laid), except in the case of a private company which has elected to dispense with the laying of accounts in which case the appointment shall be made in accordance with section 385A.

(3) References in this Chapter to the end of the time for appointing auditors are to the end of the time within which an appointment must be made under section 385(2) or 385A(2), according to whichever of those sections applies.

(4) Sections 385 and 385A have effect subject to section 386 under which a private company may elect to dispense with the obligation to appoint auditors annually.

385 Appointment at general meeting at which accounts laid

(1) This section applies to every public company and to a private company which has not elected to dispense with the laying of accounts.

(2) The company shall, at each general meeting at which accounts are laid, appoint an auditor or auditors to hold office from the conclusion of that meeting until the conclusion of the next general meeting at which accounts are laid.

(3) The first auditors of the company may be appointed by the directors at any time before the first general meeting of the company at which accounts are laid; and auditors so appointed shall hold office until the conclusion of that meeting.

(4) If the directors fail to exercise their powers under subsection (3), the powers may be exercised by the company in general meeting.

385A Appointment by private company which is not obliged to lay accounts

(1) This section applies to a private company which has elected in accordance with section 252 to dispense with the laying of accounts before the company in general meeting.

(2) Auditors shall be appointed by the company in general meeting before the end of the period of 28 days beginning with the day on which copies of the company's annual accounts for the previous financial year are sent to members under section 238 or, if notice is given under section 253(2) requiring the laying of the accounts before the company in general meeting, the conclusion of that meeting.

Auditors so appointed shall hold office from the end of that period or, as the case may be, the conclusion of that meeting until the end of the time for appointing auditors for the next financial year.

(3) The first auditors of the company may be appointed by the directors at any time before—

(a) the end of the period of 28 days beginning with the day on which copies of the company's first annual accounts are sent to members under section 238, or

(b) if notice is given under section 253(2) requiring the laying of the accounts before the company in general meeting, the beginning of that meeting;

and auditors so appointed shall hold office until the end of that period or, as the case may be, the conclusion of that meeting.

(4) If the directors fail to exercise their powers under subsection (3), the powers may be exercised by the company in general meeting.

(5) Auditors holding office when the election is made shall, unless the company in general meeting determines otherwise, continue to hold office until the end of the time for appointing auditors for the next financial year; and auditors holding office when an election ceases to have effect shall continue to hold office until the conclusion of the next general meeting of the company at which accounts are laid.

386 Election by private company to dispense with annual appointment

(1) A private company may elect (by elective resolution in accordance with section 379A) to dispense with the obligation to appoint auditors annually.

(2) When such an election is in force the company's auditors shall be deemed to be re-appointed for each succeeding financial year on the expiry of the time for appointing auditors for that year, unless—

(a) a resolution has been passed under section 250 by virtue of which the company is exempt from the obligation to appoint auditors, or

(b) a resolution has been passed under section 393 to the effect that their appointment should be brought to an end.

(3) If the election ceases to be in force, the auditors then holding office shall continue to hold office—

(a) where section 385 then applies, until the conclusion of the next general meeting of the company at which accounts are laid;

(*b*) where section 385A then applies, until the end of the time for appointing auditors for the next financial year under that section.

(4) No account shall be taken of any loss of the opportunity of further deemed re-appointment under this section in ascertaining the amount of any compensation or damages payable to an auditor on his ceasing to hold office for any reason.

387 Appointment by Secretary of State in default of appointment by company

(1) If in any case no auditors are appointed, re-appointed or deemed to be re-appointed before the end of the time for appointing auditors, the Secretary of State may appoint a person to fill the vacancy.

(2) In such a case the company shall within one week of the end of the time for appointing auditors give notice to the Secretary of State of his power having become exercisable.

If a company fails to give the notice required by this subsection, the company and every officer of it who is in default is guilty of an offence and liable to a fine and, for continued contravention, to a daily default fine.

388 Filling of casual vacancies

(1) The directors, or the company in general meeting, may fill a casual vacancy in the office of auditor.

(2) While such a vacancy continues, any surviving or continuing auditor or auditors may continue to act.

(3) Special notice is required for a resolution at a general meeting of a company—

(*a*) filling a casual vacancy in the office of auditor, or
(*b*) re-appointing as auditor a retiring auditor who was appointed by the directors to fill a casual vacancy.

(4) On receipt of notice of such an intended resolution the company shall forthwith send a copy of it—

(*a*) to the person proposed to be appointed, and
(*b*) if the casual vacancy was caused by the resignation of an auditor, to the auditor who resigned.

388A Dormant company exempt from obligation to appoint auditors

(1) A company which by virtue of section 250 (dormant companies: exemption from provisions as to audit of accounts) is exempt from the provisions of Part VII relating to the audit of accounts is also exempt from the obligation to appoint auditors.

(2) The following provisions apply if the exemption ceases.

(3) Where section 385 applies (appointment at general meeting at which accounts are laid), the directors may appoint auditors at any time before the next meeting of the company at which accounts are to be laid; and auditors so appointed shall hold office until the conclusion of that meeting.

(4) Where section 385A applies (appointment by private company not obliged to lay accounts), the directors may appoint auditors at any time before—

(*a*) the end of the period of 28 days beginning with the day on which copies of the company's annual accounts are next sent to members under section 238, or
(*b*) if notice is given under section 253(2) requiring the laying of the accounts before the company in general meeting, the beginning of that meeting;

and auditors so appointed shall hold office until the end of that period or, as the case may be, the conclusion of that meeting.

(5) If the directors fail to exercise their powers under subsection (3) or (4), the powers may be exercised by the company in general meeting.'.

(2) In Schedule 24 to the Companies Act 1985 (punishment of offences), at the appropriate place insert—

'387(2)	Company failing to give Secretary of State notice of non-appointment of auditors.	Summary.	One-fifth of the statutory maximum.	One-fiftieth of the statutory maximum.'.

(3) In section 46(2) of the Banking Act 1987 (duty of auditor of authorised institution to give notice to Bank of England of certain matters) for 'appointed under section 384' substitute 'appointed under Chapter V of Part XI'; and in section 46(4) (adaptation of references in relation to Northern Ireland) for 'sections 384,' substitute 'Chapter V of Part XI and sections'.

120 Rights of auditors

(1) The following sections are inserted in Chapter V of Part XI of the Companies Act 1985 (auditors)—

'Rights of auditors

389A Rights to information

(1) The auditors of a company have right of access at all times to the company's books, accounts and vouchers, and are entitled to require from the company's officers such information and explanations as they think necessary for the performance of their duties as auditors.

(2) An officer of a company commits an offence if he knowingly or recklessly makes to the company's auditors a statement (whether written or oral) which—

(*a*) conveys or purports to convey any information or explanations which the auditors require, or are entitled to require, as auditors of the company, and

(*b*) is misleading, false or deceptive in a material particular.

A person guilty of an offence under this subsection is liable to imprisonment or a fine, or both.

(3) A subsidiary undertaking which is a body corporate incorporated in Great Britain, and the auditors of such an undertaking, shall give to the auditors of any parent company of the undertaking such information and explanations as they may reasonably require for the purposes of their duties as auditors of that company.

If a subsidiary undertaking fails to comply with this subsection, the undertaking and every officer of it who is in default is guilty of an offence and liable to a fine; and if an auditor fails without reasonable excuse to comply with this subsection he is guilty of an offence and liable to a fine.

(4) A parent company having a subsidiary undertaking which is not a body corporate incorporated in Great Britain shall, if required by its auditors to do so, take all such steps as are reasonably open to it to obtain from the subsidiary undertaking such information and explanations as they may reasonably require for the purposes of their duties as auditors of that company.

If a parent company fails to comply with this subsection, the company and every officer of it who is in default is guilty of an offence and liable to a fine.

(5) Section 734 (criminal proceedings against unincorporated bodies) applies to an offence under subsection (3).

390 Right to attend company meetings &c

(1) A company's auditors are entitled—

(*a*) to receive all notices of, and other communications relating to, any general meeting which a member of the company is entitled to receive;

(*b*) to attend any general meeting of the company; and

(*c*) to be heard at any general meeting which they attend on any part of the business of the meeting which concerns them as auditors.

(2) In relation to a written resolution proposed to be agreed to by a private company in accordance with section 381A, the company's auditors are entitled—

(*a*) to receive all such communications relating to the resolution as, by virtue of any provision of Schedule 15A, are required to be supplied to a member of the company,

(*b*) to give notice in accordance with section 381B of their opinion that the resolution concerns them as auditors and should be considered by the company in general meeting or, as the case may be, by a meeting of the relevant class of members of the company,

(*c*) to attend any such meeting, and

(*d*) to be heard at any such meeting which they attend on any part of the business of the meeting which concerns them as auditors.

(3) The right to attend or be heard at a meeting is exercisable in the case of a body corporate or partnership by an individual authorised by it in writing to act as its representative at the meeting.'.

(2) In section 734 of the Companies Act 1985 (criminal proceedings against unincorporated bodies), in subsection (1) (offences in relation to which the provisions apply), after 'under' insert 'section 389A(3) or'.

(3) In Schedule 24 to the Companies Act 1985 (punishment of offences) at the appropriate place insert—

'389A(2)	Officer of company making false, misleading or deceptive statement to auditors.	1. On indictment. 2. Summary.	2 years or a fine; or both. 6 months or the statutory maximum; or both.
389A(3)	Subsidiary undertaking or its auditor failing to give information to auditors of parent company.	Summary.	One-fifth of the statutory maximum.
389A(4)	Parent company failing to obtain from subsidiary undertaking information for purposes of audit.	Summary.	One-fifth of the statutory maximum.'.

(4) In Schedule 4 to the Iron and Steel Act 1982 (constitution and proceedings of publicly-owned companies that are private companies), in paragraph 3(6) (entitlement of auditors to attend and be heard at general meetings, &c) for '387(1)' substitute '390(1)'.

121 Remuneration of auditors

The following sections are inserted in Chapter V of Part XI of the Companies Act 1985 (auditors)—

'Remuneration of auditors

390A Remuneration of auditors

(1) The remuneration of auditors appointed by the company in general meeting shall be fixed by the company in general meeting or in such manner as the company in general meeting may determine.

(2) The remuneration of auditors appointed by the directors or the Secretary of State shall be fixed by the directors or the Secretary of State, as the case may be.

(3) There shall be stated in a note to the company's annual accounts the amount of the remuneration of the company's auditors in their capacity as such.

(4) For the purposes of this section 'remuneration' includes sums paid in respect of expenses.

(5) This section applies in relation to benefits in kind as to payments in cash, and in relation to any such benefit references to its amount are to its estimated money value. The nature of any such benefit shall also be disclosed.

390B Remuneration of auditors or their associates for non-audit work

(1) The Secretary of State may make provision by regulations for securing the disclosure of the amount of any remuneration received or receivable by a company's auditors or their associates in respect of services other than those of auditors in their capacity as such.

(2) The regulations may—

(*a*) provide that 'remuneration' includes sums paid in respect of expenses,

(*b*) apply in relation to benefits in kind as to payments in cash, and in relation to any such benefit require disclosure of its nature and its estimated money value,

(*c*) define 'associate' in relation to an auditor,

(*d*) require the disclosure of remuneration in respect of services rendered to associated undertakings of the company, and

(*e*) define 'associated undertaking' for that purpose.

(3) The regulations may require the auditors to disclose the relevant information in their report or require the relevant information to be disclosed in a note to the company's accounts and require the auditors to supply the directors of the company with such information as is necessary to enable that disclosure to be made.

(4) The regulations may make different provision for different cases.

(5) Regulations under this section shall be made by statutory instrument which shall be subject to annulment in pursuance of a resolution of either House of Parliament.'.

122 Removal, resignation, &c of auditors

(1) The following sections are inserted in Chapter V of Part XI of the Companies Act 1985 (auditors)—

'*Removal, resignation, &c of auditors*

391 Removal of auditors

(1) A company may by ordinary resolution at any time remove an auditor from office, notwithstanding anything in any agreement between it and him.

(2) Where a resolution removing an auditor is passed at a general meeting of a company, the company shall within 14 days give notice of that fact in the prescribed form to the registrar.

If a company fails to give the notice required by this subsection, the company and every officer of it who is in default is guilty of an offence and liable to a fine and, for continued contravention, to a daily default fine.

(3) Nothing in this section shall be taken as depriving a person removed under it of compensation or damages payable to him in respect of the termination of his appointment as auditor or of any appointment terminating with that as auditor.

(4) An auditor of a company who has been removed has, notwithstanding his removal, the rights conferred by section 390 in relation to any general meeting of the company—

(*a*) at which his term of office would otherwise have expired, or

(*b*) at which it is proposed to fill the vacancy caused by his removal.

In such a case the references in that section to matters concerning the auditors as auditors shall be construed as references to matters concerning him as a former auditor.

391A Rights of auditors who are removed or not re-appointed

(1) Special notice is required for a resolution at a general meeting of a company—

(*a*) removing an auditor before the expiration of his term of office, or

(*b*) appointing as auditor a person other than a retiring auditor.

(2) On receipt of notice of such an intended resolution the company shall forthwith send a copy of it to the person proposed to be removed or, as the case may be, to the person proposed to be appointed and to the retiring auditor.

(3) The auditor proposed to be removed or (as the case may be) the retiring auditor may make with respect to the intended resolution representations in writing to the company (not exceeding a reasonable length) and request their notification to members of the company.

(4) The company shall (unless the representations are received by it too late for it to do so)—

(*a*) in any notice of the resolution given to members of the company, state the fact of the representations having been made, and

(*b*) send a copy of the representations to every member of the company to whom notice of the meeting is or has been sent.

(5) If a copy of any such representations is not sent out as required because received too late or because of the company's default, the auditor may (without prejudice to his right to be heard orally) require that the representations be read out at the meeting.

(6) Copies of the representations need not be sent out and the representations need not be read at the meeting if, on the application either of the company or of any other person claiming to be aggrieved, the court is satisfied that the rights conferred by this section are being abused to secure needless publicity for defamatory matter; and the court may order the company's costs on the application to be paid in whole or in part by the auditor, notwithstanding that he is not a party to the application.

392 Resignation of auditors

(1) An auditor of a company may resign his office by depositing a notice in writing to that effect at the company's registered office.

The notice is not effective unless it is accompanied by the statement required by section 394.

(2) An effective notice of resignation operates to bring the auditor's term of office to an end as of the date on which the notice is deposited or on such later date as may be specified in it.

(3) The company shall within 14 days of the deposit of a notice of resignation send a copy of the notice to the registrar of companies.

If default is made in complying with this subsection, the company and every officer of it who is in default is guilty of an offence and liable to a fine and, for continued contravention, a daily default fine.

392A Rights of resigning auditors

(1) This section applies where an auditor's notice of resignation is accompanied by a statement of circumstances which he considers should be brought to the attention of members or creditors of the company.

(2) He may deposit with the notice a signed requisition calling on the directors of the company forthwith duly to convene an extraordinary general meeting of the company for the purpose of receiving and considering such explanation of the circumstances connected with his resignation as he may wish to place before the meeting.

(3) He may request the company to circulate to its members—

(*a*) before the meeting convened on his requisition, or

217

(b) before any general meeting at which his term of office would otherwise have expired or at which it is proposed to fill the vacancy caused by his resignation,

a statement in writing (not exceeding a reasonable length) of the circumstances connected with his resignation.

(4) The company shall (unless the statement is received too late for it to comply)—

(a) in any notice of the meeting given to members of the company, state the fact of the statement having been made, and

(b) send a copy of the statement to every member of the company to whom notice of the meeting is or has been sent.

(5) If the directors do not within 21 days from the date of the deposit of a requisition under this section proceed duly to convene a meeting for a day not more than 28 days after the date on which the notice convening the meeting is given, every director who failed to take all reasonable steps to secure that a meeting was convened as mentioned above is guilty of an offence and liable to a fine.

(6) If a copy of the statement mentioned above is not sent out as required because received too late or because of the company's default, the auditor may (without prejudice to his right to be heard orally) require that the statement be read out at the meeting.

(7) Copies of a statement need not be sent out and the statement need not be read out at the meeting if, on the application either of the company or of any other person who claims to be aggrieved, the court is satisfied that the rights conferred by this section are being abused to secure needless publicity for defamatory matter; and the court may order the company's costs on such an application to be paid in whole or in part by the auditor, notwithstanding that he is not a party to the application.

(8) An auditor who has resigned has, notwithstanding his resignation, the rights conferred by section 390 in relation to any such general meeting of the company as is mentioned in subsection (3)(a) or (b).

In such a case the references in that section to matters concerning the auditors as auditors shall be construed as references to matters concerning him as a former auditor.

393 Termination of appointment of auditors not appointed annually

(1) When an election is in force under section 386 (election by private company to dispense with annual appointment), any member of the company may deposit notice in writing at the company's registered office proposing that the appointment of the company's auditors be brought to an end.

No member may deposit more than one such notice in any financial year of the company.

(2) If such a notice is deposited it is the duty of the directors—

(a) to convene a general meeting of the company for a date not more than 28 days after the date on which the notice was given, and

(b) to propose at the meeting a resolution in a form enabling the company to decide whether the appointment of the company's auditors should be brought to an end.

(3) If the decision of the company at the meeting is that the appointment of the auditors should be brought to an end, the auditors shall not be deemed to be re-appointed when next they would be and, if the notice was deposited within the period immediately following the distribution of accounts, any deemed re-appointment for the financial year following that to which those accounts relate which has already occurred shall cease to have effect.

The period immediately following the distribution of accounts means the period beginning with the day on which copies of the company's annual accounts are sent to members of the company under section 238 and ending 14 days after that day.

(4) If the directors do not within 14 days from the date of the deposit of the notice proceed duly to convene a meeting, the member who deposited the notice (or, if there was more than one, any of them) may himself convene the meeting; but any meeting so convened shall not be held after the expiration of three months from that date.

(5) A meeting convened under this section by a member shall be convened in the same manner, as nearly as possible, as that in which meetings are to be convened by directors.

(6) Any reasonable expenses incurred by a member by reason of the failure of the directors duly to convene a meeting shall be made good to him by the company; and any such sums shall be recouped by the company from such of the directors as were in default out of any sums payable, or to become payable, by the company by way of fees or other remuneration in respect of their services.

(7) This section has effect notwithstanding anything in any agreement between the company and its auditors; and no compensation or damages shall be payable by reason of the auditors' appointment being terminated under this section.'.

(2) In Schedule 24 to the Companies Act 1985 (punishment of offences), at the appropriate place insert—

'391(2)	Failing to give notice to registrar of removal of auditor.	Summary.	One-fifth of the statutory maximum.	One-fiftieth of the statutory maximum.
392(3)	Company failing to forward notice of auditor's resignation to registrar.	1. On indictment. 2. Summary.	A fine. The statutory maximum.	One-tenth of the statutory maximum.
392A(5)	Directors failing to convene meeting requisitioned by resigning auditor.	1. On indictment. 2. Summary.	A fine. The statutory maximum.'.	

123 Statement by person ceasing to hold office as auditor

(1) The following section is inserted in Chapter V of Part XI of the Companies Act 1985 (auditors)—

'394 Statement by person ceasing to hold office as auditor

(1) Where an auditor ceases for any reason to hold office, he shall deposit at the company's registered office a statement of any circumstances connected with his ceasing to hold office which he considers should be brought to the attention of the members or creditors of the company or, if he considers that there are no such circumstances, a statement that there are none.

(2) In the case of resignation, the statement shall be deposited along with the notice of resignation; in the case of failure to seek re-appointment, the statement shall be deposited not less than 14 days before the end of the time allowed for next appointing auditors; in any other case, the statement shall be deposited not later than the end of the period of 14 days beginning with the date on which he ceases to hold office.

(3) If the statement is of circumstances which the auditor considers should be brought to the attention of the members or creditors of the company, the company shall within 14 days of the deposit of the statement either—

(*a*) send a copy of it to every person who under section 238 is entitled to be sent copies of the accounts, or

(*b*) apply to the court.

(4) The company shall if it applies to the court notify the auditor of the application.

(5) Unless the auditor receives notice of such an application before the end of the period of 21 days beginning with the day on which he deposited the statement, he shall within a further seven days send a copy of the statement to the registrar.

(6) If the court is satisfied that the auditor is using the statement to secure needless publicity for defamatory matter—

(*a*) it shall direct that copies of the statement need not be sent out, and

(*b*) it may further order the company's costs on the application to be paid in whole or in part by the auditor, notwithstanding that he is not a party to the application;

and the company shall within 14 days of the court's decision send to the persons mentioned in subsection (3)(*a*) a statement setting out the effect of the order.

(7) If the court is not so satisfied, the company shall within 14 days of the court's decision—

(*a*) send copies of the statement to the persons mentioned in subsection (3)(*a*), and

(*b*) notify the auditor of the court's decision;

and the auditor shall within seven days of receiving such notice send a copy of the statement to the registrar.

394A Offences of failing to comply with s 394

(1) If a person ceasing to hold office as auditor fails to comply with section 394 he is guilty of an offence and liable to a fine.

(2) In proceedings for an offence under subsection (1) it is a defence for the person charged to show that he took all reasonable steps and exercised all due diligence to avoid the commission of the offence.

(3) Sections 733 (liability of individuals for corporate default) and 734 (criminal proceedings against unincorporated bodies) apply to an offence under subsection (1).

(4) If a company makes default in complying with section 394, the company and every officer of it who is in default is guilty of an offence and liable to a fine and, for continued contravention, to a daily default fine.'.

(2) In Schedule 24 to the Companies Act 1985 (punishment of offences), at the appropriate place insert—

'394A(1)	Person ceasing to hold office as auditor failing to deposit statement as to circumstances.	1. On indictment. 2. Summary.	A fine. The statutory maximum.	
394A(4)	Company failing to comply with requirements as to statement of person ceasing to hold office as auditor.	1. On indictment. 2. Summary.	A fine. The statutory maximum.	One-tenth of the statutory maximum.'.

(3) In section 733 of the Companies Act 1985 (liability of individuals for corporate default), in subsection (1) (offences in relation to which provisions apply) after '216(3)' insert ', 394A(1)'.

(4) In section 734 of the Companies Act 1985 (criminal proceedings against unincorporated bodies), in subsection (1) (offences in relation to which the provisions apply), after 'under' insert 'section 394A(1) or'.

(5) In Schedule 22 to the Companies Act 1985 (unregistered companies), in the entry for sections 384 to 393, for '393' substitute '394A'.

124 Auditors of trade unions and employers' associations

In section 11 of the Trade Union and Labour Relations Act 1974 (duties of trade unions and employers' associations as to auditors, &c), after subsection (8) insert—

'(9) Where a trade union or employers' association to which this section applies is a company within the meaning of the Companies Act 1985—

(*a*) subsection (3) above, and the provisions of paragraphs 6 to 15 of Schedule 2 to this Act, do not apply, and

(*b*) the rights and powers conferred, and duties imposed, by paragraphs 16 to 21 of that Schedule belong to the auditors of the company appointed under Chapter V of Part XI of that Act.'.

Company records and related matters

125 Delivery of documents to the registrar

(1) For section 706 of the Companies Act 1985 (size, durability, &c of documents delivered to the registrar) substitute—

'706 Delivery to the registrar of documents in legible form

(1) This section applies to the delivery to the registrar under any provision of the Companies Acts of documents in legible form.

(2) The document must—

(*a*) state in a prominent position the registered number of the company to which it relates,

(*b*) satisfy any requirements prescribed by regulations for the purposes of this section, and

(*c*) conform to such requirements as the registrar may specify for the purpose of enabling him to copy the document.

(3) If a document is delivered to the registrar which does not comply with the requirements of this section, he may serve on the person by whom the document was delivered (or, if there are two or more such persons, on any of them) a notice indicating the respect in which the document does not comply.

(4) Where the registrar serves such a notice, then, unless a replacement document—

(*a*) is delivered to him within 14 days after the service of the notice, and

(*b*) complies with the requirements of this section (or section 707) or is not rejected by him for failure to comply with those requirements,

the original document shall be deemed not to have been delivered to him.

But for the purposes of any enactment imposing a penalty for failure to deliver, so far as it imposes a penalty for continued contravention, no account shall be taken of the period between the delivery of the original document and the end of the period of 14 days after service of the registrar's notice.

(5) Regulations made for the purposes of this section may make different provision with respect to different descriptions of document.'.

(2) For section 707 of the Companies Act 1985 (power of registrar to accept information on microfilm, &c) substitute—

'707 Delivery to the registrar of documents otherwise than in legible form

(1) This section applies to the delivery to the registrar under any provision of the Companies Acts of documents otherwise than in legible form.

(2) Any requirement to deliver a document to the registrar, or to deliver a document in the prescribed form, is satisfied by the communication to the registrar of the requisite

information in any non-legible form prescribed for the purposes of this section by regulations or approved by the registrar.

(3) Where the document is required to be signed or sealed, it shall instead be authenticated in such manner as may be prescribed by regulations or approved by the registrar.

(4) The document must—

(*a*) contain in a prominent position the registered number of the company to which it relates,

(*b*) satisfy any requirements prescribed by regulations for the purposes of this section, and

(*c*) be furnished in such manner, and conform to such requirements, as the registrar may specify for the purpose of enabling him to read and copy the document.

(5) If a document is delivered to the registrar which does not comply with the requirements of this section, he may serve on the person by whom the document was delivered (or, if there are two or more such persons, on any of them) a notice indicating the respect in which the document does not comply.

(6) Where the registrar serves such a notice, then, unless a replacement document—

(*a*) is delivered to him within 14 days after the service of the notice, and

(*b*) complies with the requirements of this section (or section 706) or is not rejected by him for failure to comply with those requirements,

the original document shall be deemed not to have been delivered to him.

But for the purposes of any enactment imposing a penalty for failure to deliver, so far as it imposes a penalty for continued contravention, no account shall be taken of the period between the delivery of the original document and the end of the period of 14 days after service of the registrar's notice.

(7) The Secretary of State may by regulations make further provision with respect to the application of this section in relation to instantaneous forms of communication.

(8) Regulations made for the purposes of this section may make different provision with respect to different descriptions of document and different forms of communication, and as respects delivery to the registrar for England and Wales and delivery to the registrar for Scotland.'.

126 Keeping and inspection of company records

(1) In Part XXIV of the Companies Act 1985 (the registrar of companies, his functions and offices), after the sections inserted by section 125 above, insert—

'707A The keeping of company records by the registrar

(1) The information contained in a document delivered to the registrar under the Companies Acts may be recorded and kept by him in any form he thinks fit, provided it is possible to inspect the information and to produce a copy of it in legible form.

This is sufficient compliance with any duty of his to keep, file or register the document.

(2) The originals of documents delivered to the registrar in legible form shall be kept by him for ten years, after which they may be destroyed.

(3) Where a company has been dissolved, the registrar may, at any time after the expiration of two years from the date of the dissolution, direct that any records in his custody relating to the company may be removed to the Public Record Office; and records in respect of which such a direction is given shall be disposed of in accordance with the enactments relating to that Office and the rules made under them.

This subsection does not extend to Scotland.

(4) In subsection (3) 'company' includes a company provisionally or completely registered under the Joint Stock Companies Act 1844.'.

(2) For sections 709 and 710 of the Companies Act 1985 (inspection of documents kept by the registrar) substitute—

'709 Inspection, &c of records kept by the registrar

(1) Any person may inspect any records kept by the registrar for the purposes of the Companies Acts and may require—

(*a*) a copy, in such form as the registrar considers appropriate, of any information contained in those records, or

(*b*) a certified copy of, or extract from, any such record.

(2) The right of inspection extends to the originals of documents delivered to the registrar in legible form only where the record kept by the registrar of the contents of the document is illegible or unavailable.

(3) A copy of or extract from a record kept at any of the offices for the registration of companies in England and Wales or Scotland, certified in writing by the registrar (whose official position it is unnecessary to prove) to be an accurate record of the contents of any document delivered to him under the Companies Acts, is in all legal proceedings admissible in evidence as of equal validity with the original document and as evidence of any fact stated therein of which direct oral evidence would be admissible.

In England and Wales this is subject to compliance with any applicable rules of court under section 5 of the Civil Evidence Act 1968 or section 69(2) of the Police and Criminal Evidence Act 1984 (which relate to evidence from computer records).

(4) Copies of or extracts from records furnished by the registrar may, instead of being certified by him in writing to be an accurate record, be sealed with his official seal.

(5) No process for compelling the production of a record kept by the registrar shall issue from any court except with the leave of the court; and any such process shall bear on it a statement that it is issued with the leave of the court.

710 Certificate of incorporation

Any person may require a certificate of the incorporation of a company, signed by the registrar or authenticated by his official seal.

710A Provision and authentication by registrar of documents in non-legible form

(1) Any requirement of the Companies Acts as to the supply by the registrar of a document may, if the registrar thinks fit, be satisfied by the communication by the registrar of the requisite information in any non-legible form prescribed for the purposes of this section by regulations or approved by him.

(2) Where the document is required to be signed by him or sealed with his official seal, it shall instead be authenticated in such manner as may be prescribed by regulations or approved by the registrar.'.

127 Supplementary provisions as to company records and related matters

(1) In Part XXIV of the Companies Act 1985 (the registrar of companies, his functions and offices), after section 715 insert—

'715A Interpretation

(1) In this Part—
'document' includes information recorded in any form; and
'legible', in the context of documents in legible or non-legible form, means capable of being read with the naked eye.

(2) References in this Part to delivering a document include sending, forwarding, producing or (in the case of a notice) giving it.'.

(2) In section 708(1) of the Companies Act 1985 (fees)—

(*a*) in paragraph (*a*) for the words from 'any notice or other document' to the end substitute 'any document which under those Acts is required to be delivered to him', and

(b) in paragraph (b) omit 'or other material'.

(3) Omit sections 712 and 715 of the Companies Act 1985 (removal and destruction of old records).

(4) In section 713 (1) (enforcement of duty to make returns, &c), for the words from 'file with' to 'or other document' substitute 'deliver a document to the registrar of companies'.

(5) In section 735A(2) of the Companies Act 1985 (provisions applying to Insolvency Act 1986 and Company Directors Disqualification Act 1986 as to the Companies Acts)—

(a) after '707(1),' insert '707A(1),',

(b) after '708(1)(a) and (4),' insert '709(1) and (3),', and

(c) for '710(5)' substitute '710A'.

(6) After section 735A of the Companies Act 1985 insert—

'735B Relationship of this Act to Parts IV and V of the Financial Services Act 1986

In sections 704(5), 706(1), 707(1), 707A(1), 708(1)(a) and (4), 709(1) and (3), 710A and 713(1) references to the Companies Acts include Parts IV and V of the Financial Services Act 1986.'.

(7) In Schedule 22 to the Companies Act 1985 (unregistered companies), in the entry for Part XXIV for 'sections 706, 708 to 710, 712 and 713' substitute 'sections 706 to 710A, 713 and 715A'.

Miscellaneous

128 Form of articles for partnership company

In Chapter I of Part I of the Companies Act 1985 (company formation), after section 8 (Tables A, C, D and E) insert—

'8A Table G

(1) The Secretary of State may by regulations prescribe a Table G containing articles of association appropriate for a partnership company, that is, a company limited by shares whose shares are intended to be held to a substantial extent by or on behalf of its employees.

(2) A company limited by shares may for its articles adopt the whole or any part of that Table.

(3) If in consequence of regulations under this section Table G is altered, the alteration does not affect a company registered before the alteration takes effect, or repeal as respects that company any portion of the Table.

(4) Regulations under this section shall be made by statutory instrument which shall be subject to annulment in pursuance of a resolution of either House of Parliament.'.

129 Membership of holding company

(1) In Chapter I of Part I of the Companies Act 1985 (company formation), for section 23 (membership of holding company) substitute—

'23 Membership of holding company

(1) Except as mentioned in this section, a body corporate cannot be a member of a company which is its holding company and any allotment or transfer of shares in a company to its subsidiary is void.

(2) The prohibition does not apply where the subsidiary is concerned only as personal representative or trustee unless, in the latter case, the holding company or a subsidiary of it is beneficially interested under the trust.

For the purpose of ascertaining whether the holding company or a subsidiary is so interested, there shall be disregarded—

(a) any interest held only by way of security for the purposes of a transaction entered into by the holding company or subsidiary in the ordinary course of a business which includes the lending of money;

(b) any such interest as is mentioned in Part I of Schedule 2.

(3) The prohibition does not apply where the subsidiary is concerned only as a market maker.

For this purpose a person is a market maker if—

(a) he holds himself out at all normal times in compliance with the rules of a recognised investment exchange other than an overseas investment exchange (within the meaning of the Financial Services Act 1986) as willing to buy and sell securities at prices specified by him, and

(b) he is recognised as so doing by that investment exchange.

(4) Where a body corporate became a holder of shares in a company—

(a) before 1st July 1948, or

(b) on or after that date and before the commencement of section 129 of the Companies Act 1989, in circumstances in which this section as it then had effect did not apply,

but at any time after the commencement of that section falls within the prohibition in subsection (1) above in respect of those shares, it may continue to be a member of that company; but for so long as that prohibition would apply, apart from this subsection, it has no right to vote in respect of those shares at meetings of the company or of any class of its members.

(5) Where a body corporate becomes a holder of shares in a company after the commencement of that section in circumstances in which the prohibition in subsection (1) does not apply, but subsequently falls within that prohibition in respect of those shares, it may continue to be a member of that company; but for so long as that prohibition would apply, apart from this subsection, it has no right to vote in respect of those shares at meetings of the company or of any class of its members.

(6) Where a body corporate is permitted to continue as a member of a company by virtue of subsection (4) or (5), an allotment to it of fully paid shares in the company may be validly made by way of capitalisation of reserves of the company; but for so long as the prohibition in subsection (1) would apply, apart from subsection (4) or (5), it has no right to vote in respect of those shares at meetings of the company or of any class of its members.

(7) The provisions of this section apply to a nominee acting on behalf of a subsidiary as to the subsidiary itself.

(8) In relation to a company other than a company limited by shares, the references in this section to shares shall be construed as references to the interest of its members as such, whatever the form of that interest.'.

(2) In Schedule 2 to the Companies Act 1985 (interpretation of references to 'beneficial interest'), in paragraphs 1(1), 3(1) and 4(2) for 'as respects section 23(4)' substitute 'as this paragraph applies for the purposes of section 23(2)'.

130 Company contracts and execution of documents by companies

(1) In Chapter III of Part I of the Companies Act 1985 (a company's capacity; the formalities of carrying on business), for section 36 (form of company contracts) substitute—

'36 Company contracts: England and Wales

Under the law of England and Wales a contract may be made—

(a) by a company, by writing under its common seal, or

(b) on behalf of a company, by any person acting under its authority, express or implied;

and any formalities required by law in the case of a contract made by an individual also apply, unless a contrary intention appears, to a contract made by or on behalf of a company.'.

(2) After that section insert—

'36A Execution of documents: England and Wales

(1) Under the law of England and Wales the following provisions have effect with respect to the execution of documents by a company.

(2) A document is executed by a company by the affixing of its common seal.

(3) A company need not have a common seal, however, and the following subsections apply whether it does or not.

(4) A document signed by a director and the secretary of a company, or by two directors of a company, and expressed (in whatever form of words) to be executed by the company has the same effect as if executed under the common seal of the company.

(5) A document executed by a company which makes it clear on its face that it is intended by the person or persons making it to be a deed has effect, upon delivery, as a deed; and it shall be presumed, unless a contrary intention is proved, to be delivered upon its being so executed.

(6) In favour of a purchaser a document shall be deemed to have been duly executed by a company if it purports to be signed by a director and the secretary of the company, or by two directors of the company, and, where it makes it clear on its face that it is intended by the person or persons making it to be a deed, to have been delivered upon its being executed.

A 'purchaser' means a purchaser in good faith for valuable consideration and includes a lessee, mortgagee or other person who for valuable consideration acquires an interest in property.'.

(3) After the section inserted by subsection (2) insert—

'36B Execution of documents: Scotland

(1) Under the law of Scotland the following provisions have effect with respect to the execution of documents by a company.

(2) A document—

(*a*) is signed by a company if it is signed on its behalf by a director, or by the secretary, of the company or by a person authorised to sign the document on its behalf, and

(*b*) is subscribed by a company if it is subscribed on its behalf by being signed in accordance with the provisions of paragraph (*a*) at the end of the last page.

(3) A document shall be presumed, unless the contrary is shown, to have been subscribed by a company in accordance with subsection (2) if—

(*a*) it bears to have been subscribed on behalf of the company by a director, or by the secretary, of the company or by a person bearing to have been authorised to subscribe the document on its behalf; and

(*b*) it bears—

(i) to have been signed by a person as a witness of the subscription of the director, secretary or other person subscribing on behalf of the company; or

(ii) (if the subscription is not so witnessed) to have been sealed with the common seal of the company.

(4) A presumption under subsection (3) as to subscription of a document does not include a presumption—

(*a*) that a person bearing to subscribe the document as a director or the secretary of the company was such director or secretary; or

(*b*) that a person subscribing the document on behalf of the company bearing to have been authorised to do so was authorised to do so.

(5) Notwithstanding subsection (3)(*b*)(ii), a company need not have a common seal.

(6) Any reference in any enactment (including an enactment contained in a subordinate instrument) to a probative document shall, in relation to a document executed by a company after the commencement of section 130 of the Companies Act 1989, be construed as a reference to a document which is presumed under subsection (3) above to be subscribed by the company.

(7) Subsections (1) to (4) above do not apply where an enactment (including an enactment contained in a subordinate instrument) provides otherwise.'.

(4) After the section inserted by subsection (3) insert—

'36C Pre-incorporation contracts, deeds and obligations

(1) A contract which purports to be made by or on behalf of a company at a time when the company has not been formed has effect, subject to any agreement to the contrary, as one made with the person purporting to act for the company or as agent for it, and he is personally liable on the contract accordingly.

(2) Subsection (1) applies—

(*a*) to the making of a deed under the law of England and Wales, and

(*b*) to the undertaking of an obligation under the law of Scotland,

as it applies to the making of a contract.'.

(5) In Schedule 22 of the Companies Act 1985 (provisions applying to unregistered companies), at the appropriate place insert—

'Section 36	Company contracts.	Subject to section 718(3).
Sections 36A and 36B	Execution of documents.	Subject to section 718(3).
Section 36C	Pre-incorporation contracts, deeds and obligations.	Subject to section 718(3).'.

(6) The Secretary of State may make provision by regulations applying sections 36 to 36C of the Companies Act 1985 (company contracts; execution of documents; pre-incorporation contracts, deeds and obligations) to companies incorporated outside Great Britain, subject to such exceptions, adaptations or modifications as may be specified in the regulations.

Regulations under this subsection shall be made by statutory instrument which shall be subject to annulment in pursuance of a resolution of either House of Parliament.

(7) Schedule 17 contains further minor and consequential amendments relating to company contracts, the execution of documents by companies and related matters.

131 Members' rights to damages, &c

(1) In Part IV of the Companies Act 1985 (allotment of shares and debentures), before section 112 and after the heading '*Other matters arising out of allotment &c*', insert—

'111A Right to damages, &c not affected

A person is not debarred from obtaining damages or other compensation from a company by reason only of his holding or having held shares in the company or any right to apply or subscribe for shares or to be included in the company's register in respect of shares.'.

(2) In section 116 of the Companies Act 1985 (extended operation of certain provisions applying to public companies) for 'and 110 to 115' substitute ', 110, 111 and 112 to 115'.

132 Financial assistance for purposes of employees' share scheme

In Chapter VI of Part V of the Companies Act 1985 (financial assistance by company for purchase of its own shares), in section 153 (transactions not prohibited), for subsection (4)(*b*) (provision of money in accordance with employees' share scheme) substitute—

'(*b*) the provision by a company, in good faith in the interests of the company, of financial assistance for the purposes of an employees' share scheme,'.

133 Issue of redeemable shares

(1) In Part V of the Companies Act 1985 (share capital, its increase, maintenance and reduction), Chapter III (redeemable shares, purchase by a company of its own shares) is amended as follows.

(2) After section 159 (power to issue redeemable shares) insert—

'159A Terms and manner of redemption

(1) Redeemable shares may not be issued unless the following conditions are satisfied as regards the terms and manner of redemption.

(2) The date on or by which, or dates between which, the shares are to be or may be redeemed must be specified in the company's articles or, if the articles so provide, fixed by the directors, and in the latter case the date or dates must be fixed before the shares are issued.

(3) Any other circumstances in which the shares are to be or may be redeemed must be specified in the company's articles.

(4) The amount payable on redemption must be specified in, or determined in accordance with, the company's articles, and in the latter case the articles must not provide for the amount to be determined by reference to any person's discretion or opinion.

(5) Any other terms and conditions of redemption shall be specified in the company's articles.

(6) Nothing in this section shall be construed as requiring a company to provide in its articles for any matter for which provision is made by this Act.'.

(3) In section 160 (financing, &c of redemption)—

(*a*) omit subsection (3) (which is superseded by the new section 159A), and

(*b*) in subsection (4) (cancellation of shares on redemption) for 'redeemed under this section' substitute 'redeemed under this Chapter'.

(4) In section 162 (power of company to purchase own shares), for subsection (2) (application of provisions relating to redeemable shares) substitute—

'(2) Sections 159, 160 and 161 apply to the purchase by a company under this section of its own shares as they apply to the redemption of redeemable shares.'.

134 Disclosure of interests in shares

(1) Part VI of the Companies Act 1985 (disclosure of interests in shares) is amended as follows.

(2) In section 199(2) (notifiable interests), for the words from 'the percentage' to the end substitute '3 per cent of the nominal value of that share capital'.

The order bringing the above amendment into force may make such provision as appears to the Secretary of State appropriate as to the obligations of a person whose interest in a company's shares becomes notifiable by virtue of the amendment coming into force.

(3) In sections 202(1) and (4) and 206(8) (which require notification of certain matters within a specified period) for '5 days' substitute '2 days'.

(4) In section 202 (particulars to be contained in notification), for subsection (3) substitute—

'(3) A notification (other than one stating that a person no longer has a notifiable interest) shall include the following particulars, so far as known to the person making the notification at the date when it is made—

(*a*) the identity of each registered holder of shares to which the notification relates and the number of such shares held by each of them, and (*b*) the number of such shares in which the interest of the person giving the notification is such an interest as is mentioned in section 208(5).'.

(5) After section 210 insert—

'210A Power to make further provision by regulations

(1) The Secretary of State may by regulations amend—

(*a*) the definition of 'relevant share capital' (section 198(2)),

(*b*) the percentage giving rise to a 'notifiable interest' (section 199(2)),

(*c*) the periods within which an obligation of disclosure must be fulfilled or a notice must be given (sections 202(1) and (4) and 206(8)),

(*d*) the provisions as to what is taken to be an interest in shares (section 208) and what interests are to be disregarded (section 209), and

(*e*) the provisions as to company investigations (section 212);

and the regulations may amend, replace or repeal the provisions referred to above and make such other consequential amendments or repeals of provisions of this Part as appear to the Secretary of State to be appropriate.

(2) The regulations may in any case make different provision for different descriptions of company; and regulations under subsection (1)(*b*), (*c*) or (*d*) may make different provision for different descriptions of person, interest or share capital.

(3) The regulations may contain such transitional and other supplementary and incidental provisions as appear to the Secretary of State to be appropriate, and may in particular make provision as to the obligations of a person whose interest in a company's shares becomes or ceases to be notifiable by virtue of the regulations.

(4) Regulations under this section shall be made by statutory instrument.

(5) No regulations shall be made under this section unless a draft of the regulations has been laid before and approved by a resolution of each House of Parliament.'.

(6) Any regulations made under section 209(1)(*j*) which are in force immediately before the repeal of that paragraph by this Act shall have effect as if made under section 210A(1)(*d*) as inserted by subsection (5) above.

135 Orders imposing restrictions on shares

(1) The Secretary of State may by regulations made by statutory instrument make such amendments of the provisions of the Companies Act 1985 relating to orders imposing restrictions on shares as appear to him necessary or expedient—

(*a*) for enabling orders to be made in a form protecting the rights of third parties;

(*b*) with respect to the circumstances in which restrictions may be relaxed or removed;

(*c*) with respect to the making of interim orders by a court.

(2) The provisions referred to in subsection (1) are section 210(5), section 216(1) and (2), section 445 and Part XV of the Companies Act 1985.

(3) The regulations may make different provision for different cases and may contain such transitional and other supplementary and incidental provisions as appear to the Secretary of State to be appropriate.

(4) Regulations under this section shall not be made unless a draft of the regulations has been laid before Parliament and approved by resolution of each House of Parliament.

136 A company's registered office

For section 287 of the Companies Act 1985 (registered office) substitute—

'287 Registered office

(1) A company shall at all times have a registered office to which all communications and notices may be addressed.

(2) On incorporation the situation of the company's registered office is that specified in the statement sent to the registrar under section 10.

(3) The company may change the situation of its registered office from time to time by giving notice in the prescribed form to the registrar.

(4) The change takes effect upon the notice being registered by the registrar, but until the end of the period of 14 days beginning with the date on which it is registered a person may validly serve any document on the company at its previous registered office.

(5) For the purposes of any duty of a company—

  (a) to keep at its registered office, or make available for public inspection there, any register, index or other document, or

  (b) to mention the address of its registered office in any document,

a company which has given notice to the registrar of a change in the situation of its registered office may act on the change as from such date, not more than 14 days after the notice is given, as it may determine.

(6) Where a company unavoidably ceases to perform at its registered office any such duty as is mentioned in subsection (5)(a) in circumstances in which it was not practicable to give prior notice to the registrar of a change in the situation of its registered office, but—

  (a) resumes performance of that duty at other premises as soon as practicable, and

  (b) gives notice accordingly to the registrar of a change in the situation of its registered office within 14 days of doing so,

it shall not be treated as having failed to comply with that duty.

(7) In proceedings for an offence of failing to comply with any such duty as is mentioned in subsection (5), it is for the person charged to show that by reason of the matters referred to in that subsection or subsection (6) no offence was committed.'.

137 Effecting of insurance for officers and auditors of company

(1) In section 310 of the Companies Act 1985 (provisions exempting officers and auditors from liability), for subsection (3) (permitted provisions) substitute—

'(3) This section does not prevent a company—

  (a) from purchasing and maintaining for any such officer or auditor insurance against any such liability, or

  (b) from indemnifying any such officer or auditor against any liability incurred by him—

    (i) in defending any proceedings (whether civil or criminal) in which judgment is given in his favour or he is acquitted, or

    (ii) in connection with any application under section 144(3) or (4) (acquisition of shares by innocent nominee) or section 727 (general power to grant relief in case of honest and reasonable conduct) in which relief is granted to him by the court.'.

(2) In Part I of Schedule 7 to the Companies Act 1985 (general matters to be dealt with in directors' report), after paragraph 5 insert—

'Insurance effected for officers or auditors

5A. Where in the financial year the company has purchased or maintained any such insurance as is mentioned in section 310(3)(a) (insurance of officers or auditors against liabilities in relation to the company), that fact shall be stated in the report.'

138 Increase of limits on certain exemptions

Part X of the Companies Act 1985 (enforcement of fair dealing by directors) is amended as follows—

  (a) in section 332(1)(b) (short-term quasi-loans) for '£1,000' substitute '£5,000';

  (b) in section 334 (loans of small amounts) for '£2,500' substitute '£5,000';

  (c) in section 338(4) and (6) (loans or quasi-loans by money-lending company) for '£50,000' substitute '£100,000'.

139 Annual returns

(1) In Part XI of the Companies Act 1985 (company administration and procedure), for Chapter III (annual return) substitute—

'CHAPTER III

ANNUAL RETURN

363 Duty to deliver annual returns

(1) Every company shall deliver to the registrar successive annual returns each of which is made up to a date not later than the date which is from time to time the company's 'return date', that is—

(*a*) the anniversary of the company's incorporation, or

(*b*) if the company's last return delivered in accordance with this Chapter was made up to a different date, the anniversary of that date.

(2) Each return shall—

(*a*) be in the prescribed form,

(*b*) contain the information required by or under the following provisions of this Chapter, and

(*c*) be signed by a director or the secretary of the company;

and it shall be delivered to the registrar within 28 days after the date to which it is made up.

(3) If a company fails to deliver an annual return in accordance with this Chapter before the end of the period of 28 days after a return date, the company is guilty of an offence and liable to a fine and, in the case of continued contravention, to a daily default fine.

The contravention continues until such time as an annual return made up to that return date and complying with the requirements of subsection (2) (except as to date of delivery) is delivered by the company to the registrar.

(4) Where a company is guilty of an offence under subsection (3), every director or secretary of the company is similarly liable unless he shows that he took all reasonable steps to avoid the commission or continuation of the offence.

(5) The references in this section to a return being delivered 'in accordance with this Chapter' are—

(*a*) in relation to a return made after the commencement of section 139 of the Companies Act 1989, to a return with respect to which all the requirements of subsection (2) are complied with;

(*b*) in relation to a return made before that commencement, to a return with respect to which the formal and substantive requirements of this Chapter as it then had effect were complied with, whether or not the return was delivered in time.

364 Contents of annual return: general

(1) Every annual return shall state the date to which it is made up and shall contain the following information—

(*a*) the address of the company's registered office;

(*b*) the type of company it is and its principal business activities;

(*c*) the name and address of the company secretary;

(*d*) the name and address of every director of the company;

(*e*) in the case of each individual director—

(i) his nationality, date of birth and business occupation, and

(ii) such particulars of other directorships and former names as are required to be contained in the company's register of directors;

(*f*) in the case of any corporate director, such particulars of other directorships as would be required to be contained in that register in the case of an individual;

231

(*g*) if the register of members is not kept at the company's registered office, the address of the place where it is kept;

(*h*) if any register of debenture holders (or a duplicate of any such register or a part of it) is not kept at the company's registered office, the address of the place where it is kept;

(*i*) if the company has elected—

    (i) to dispense under section 252 with the laying of accounts and reports before the company in general meeting, or

    (ii) to dispense under section 366A with the holding of annual general meetings,

    a statement to that effect.

(2) The information as to the company's type shall be given by reference to the classification scheme prescribed for the purposes of this section.

(3) The information as to the company's principal business activities may be given by reference to one or more categories of any prescribed system of classifying business activities.

(4) A person's 'name' and 'address' mean, respectively—

(*a*) in the case of an individual, his Christian name (or other forename) and surname and his usual residential address;

(*b*) in the case of a corporation or Scottish firm, its corporate or firm name and its registered or principal office.

(5) In the case of a peer, or an individual usually known by a title, the title may be stated instead of his Christian name (or other forename) and surname or in addition to either or both of them.

(6) Where all the partners in a firm are joint secretaries, the name and principal office of the firm may be stated instead of the names and addresses of the partners.

364A Contents of annual return: particulars of share capital and shareholders

(1) The annual return of a company having a share capital shall contain the following information with respect to its share capital and members.

(2) The return shall state the total number of issued shares of the company at the date to which the return is made up and the aggregate nominal value of those shares.

(3) The return shall state with respect to each class of shares in the company—

(*a*) the nature of the class, and

(*b*) the total number and aggregate nominal value of issued shares of that class at the date to which the return is made up.

(4) The return shall contain a list of the names and addresses of every person who—

(*a*) is a member of the company on the date to which the return is made up, or

(*b*) has ceased to be a member of the company since the date to which the last return was made up (or, in the case of the first return, since the incorporation of the company);

and if the names are not arranged in alphabetical order the return shall have annexed to it an index sufficient to enable the name of any person in the list to be easily found.

(5) The return shall also state—

(*a*) the number of shares of each class held by each member of the company at the date to which the return is made up, and

(*b*) the number of shares of each class transferred since the date to which the last return was made up (or, in the case of the first return, since the incorporation of the company) by each member or person who has ceased to be a member, and the dates of registration of the transfers.

(6) The return may, if either of the two immediately preceding returns has given the full particulars required by subsections (4) and (5), give only such particulars as relate to

persons ceasing to be or becoming members since the date of the last return and to shares transferred since that date.

(7) Subsections (4) and (5) do not require the inclusion of particulars entered in an overseas branch register if copies of those entries have not been received at the company's registered office by the date to which the return is made up.

Those particulars shall be included in the company's next annual return after they are received.

(8) Where the company has converted any of its shares into stock, the return shall give the corresponding information in relation to that stock, stating the amount of stock instead of the number or nominal value of shares.

365 Supplementary provisions: regulations and interpretation

(1) The Secretary of State may by regulations make further provision as to the information to be given in a company's annual return, which may amend or repeal the provisions of sections 364 and 364A.

(2) Regulations under this section shall be made by statutory instrument which shall be subject to annulment in pursuance of a resolution of either House of Parliament.

(3) For the purposes of this Chapter, except section 363(2)(*c*) (signature of annual return), a shadow director shall be deemed to be a director.'.

(2) Where a company was, immediately before the commencement of this section, in default with respect to the delivery of one or more annual returns, this section does not affect its obligation to make such a return (in accordance with Chapter III of Part XI of the Companies Act 1985 as it then had effect) or any liability arising from failure to do so.

(3) In Schedule 24 to the Companies Act 1985 (punishment of offences) in the entry relating to section 363(7), in the first column for '363(7)' substitute '363(3)'.

(4) In Schedule 1 to the Company Directors Disqualification Act 1986 (matters relevant to determining unfitness of directors), in paragraph 4 (failure of company to comply with certain provisions), for sub-paragraphs (*f*) and (*g*) substitute—

'(*f*) section 363 (duty of company to make annual returns);'.

(5) In section 565(6) of the Income and Corporation Taxes Act 1988 (conditions for exemption from provisions relating to sub-contractors in construction industry: compliance with requirements of Companies Act 1985), in paragraph (*d*) for 'sections 363, 364 and 365' substitute 'sections 363 to 365'.

140 Floating charges (Scotland)

(1) In section 463 of the Companies Act 1985 (effect of floating charge on winding up), in subsection (1) for the words 'On the commencement of the winding up of a company,' there shall be substituted the words 'Where a company goes into liquidation within the meaning of section 247(2) of the Insolvency Act 1986,'.

(2) Section 464 of the Companies Act 1985 (ranking of floating charges) is amended as follows.

(3) In subsection (1)(*b*) at the beginning there shall be inserted the words 'with the consent of the holder of any subsisting floating charge or fixed security which would be adversely affected,'.

(4) After subsection (1) there shall be inserted the following subsection—

'(1A) Where an instrument creating a floating charge contains any such provision as is mentioned in subsection (1)(*a*), that provision shall be effective to confer priority on the floating charge over any fixed security or floating charge created after the date of the instrument.'.

(5) For subsection (3) there shall be substituted—

'(3) The order of ranking of the floating charge with any other subsisting or future floating charges or fixed securities over all or any part of the company's property is determined in accordance with the provisions of subsections (4) and (5) except where it is determined in accordance with any provision such as is mentioned in paragraph (*a*) or (*b*) of subsection (1).'.

(6) In subsection (5) at the end there shall be added the following paragraph—
'; and
(*e*) (in the case of a floating charge to secure a contingent liability other than a liability arising under any further advances made from time to time) the maximum sum to which that contingent liability is capable of amounting whether or not it is contractually limited.'.

(7) In subsection (6) after the words 'subject to' there shall be inserted the words 'Part XII and to'.

(8) In section 466 of the Companies Act 1985 (alteration of floating charges), subsections (4) and (5) and in subsecton (6) the words 'falling under subsection (4) of this section' shall cease to have effect.

141 Application to declare dissolution of company void

(1) Section 651 of the Companies Act 1985 (power of court to declare dissolution of company void) is amended as follows.

(2) In subsection (1) omit the words 'at any time within 2 years of the date of the dissolution'.

(3) After subsection (3) add—

'(4) Subject to the following provisions, an application under this section may not be made after the end of the period of two years from the date of the dissolution of the company.

(5) An application for the purpose of bringing proceedings against the company—

(*a*) for damages in respect of personal injuries (including any sum claimed by virtue of section 1(2)(*c*) of the Law Reform (Miscellaneous Provisions) Act 1934 (funeral expenses)), or

(*b*) for damages under the Fatal Accidents Act 1976 or the Damages (Scotland) Act 1976,

may be made at any time; but no order shall be made on such an application if it appears to the court that the proceedings would fail by virtue of any enactment as to the time within which proceedings must be brought.

(6) Nothing in subsection (5) affects the power of the court on making an order under this section to direct that the period between the dissolution of the company and the making of the order shall not count for the purposes of any such enactment.

(7) In subsection (5)(*a*) 'personal injuries' includes any disease and any impairment of a person's physical or mental condition.'.

(4) An application may be made under section 651(5) of the Companies Act 1985 as inserted by subsection (3) above (proceedings for damages for personal injury, &c) in relation to a company dissolved before the commencement of this section notwithstanding that the time within which the dissolution might formerly have been declared void under that section had expired before commencement.

But no such application shall be made in relation to a company dissolved more than twenty years before the commencement of this section.

(5) Except as provided by subsection (4), the amendments made by this section do not apply in relation to a company which was dissolved more than two years before the commencement of this section.

142 Abolition of doctrine of deemed notice

(1) In Part XXIV of the Companies Act 1985 (the registrar of companies, his functions and offices), after section 711 insert—

'711A Exclusion of deemed notice

(1) A person shall not be taken to have notice of any matter merely because of its being disclosed in any document kept by the registrar of companies (and thus available for inspection) or made available by the company for inspection.

(2) This does not affect the question whether a person is affected by notice of any matter by reason of a failure to make such inquiries as ought reasonably to be made.

(3) In this section 'document' includes any material which contains information.

(4) Nothing in this section affects the operation of—

(*a*) section 416 of this Act (under which a person taking a charge over a company's property is deemed to have notice of matters disclosed on the companies charges register), or

(*b*) section 198 of the Law of Property Act 1925 as it applies by virtue of section 3(7) of the Land Charges Act 1972 (under which the registration of certain land charges under Part XII, or Chapter III of Part XXIII, of this Act is deemed to constitute actual notice for all purposes connected with the land affected).'.

(2) In Schedule 22 to the Companies Act 1985 (unregistered companies), in the entry for Part XXIV at the appropriate place insert—

'Section 711A   Abolition of doctrine of deemed   Subject to section 718(3).'.
notice.

143 Rights of inspection and related matters

(1) In Part XXV of the Companies Act 1985 (miscellaneous and supplementary provisions), after section 723 insert—

'723A Obligations of company as to inspection of registers, &c

(1) The Secretary of State may make provision by regulations as to the obligations of a company which is required by any provision of this Act—

(*a*) to make available for inspection any register, index or document, or

(*b*) to provide copies of any such register, index or document, or part of it;

and a company which fails to comply with the regulations shall be deemed to have refused inspection or, as the case may be, to have failed to provide a copy.

(2) The regulations may make provision as to the time, duration and manner of inspection, including the circumstances in which and extent to which the copying of information is permitted in the course of inspection.

(3) The regulations may define what may be required of the company as regards the nature, extent and manner of extracting or presenting any information for the purposes of inspection or the provision of copies.

(4) Where there is power to charge a fee, the regulations may make provision as to the amount of the fee and the basis of its calculation.

(5) Regulations under this section may make different provision for different classes of case.

(6) Nothing in any provision of this Act or in the regulations shall be construed as preventing a company from affording more extensive facilities than are required by the regulations or, where a fee may be charged, from charging a lesser fee than that prescribed or no fee at all.

(7) Regulations under this section shall be made by statutory instrument which shall be subject to annulment in pursuance of a resolution of either House of Parliament.'.

(2) In section 169(5) of the Companies Act 1985 (contract for purchase by company of its own shares), omit the words from ', during business hours' to 'for inspection)'.

(3) In section 175(6) of the Companies Act 1985 (statutory declaration and auditors' report relating to payment out of capital), in paragraph (*b*) omit the words from 'during business hours' to 'period'.

(4) In section 191 of the Companies Act 1985 (register of debenture holders)—

(*a*) in subsection (1), omit the words from '(but' to 'for inspection)' and for the words from 'a fee of 5 pence' to the end substitute 'such fee as may be prescribed';

(*b*) in subsection (2) for the words from '10 pence' to the end substitute 'such fee as may be prescribed'; and

(*c*) in subsection (3), after 'on payment' insert 'of such fee as may be prescribed' and omit paragraphs (*a*) and (*b*).

(5) In section 219 of the Companies Act 1985 (register of interests in shares, &c)—

(*a*) in subsection (1), omit the words from 'during' to 'for inspection)'; and

(*b*) in subsection (2) for the words from '10 pence' to 'required to be copied' substitute 'such fee as may be prescribed'.

(6) In section 288 of the Companies Act 1985 (register of directors and secretaries), in subsection (3), omit the words from 'during' to 'for inspection)' and for the words from '5 pence' to the end substitute 'such fee as may be prescribed'.

(7) In section 318 of the Companies Act 1985 (directors' service contracts), in subsection (7) omit the words from ', during business hours' to 'for inspection)'.

(8) In section 356 of the Companies Act 1985 (register and index of members' names)—

(*a*) in subsection (1), omit 'during business hours' and for 'the appropriate charge' substitute 'such fee as may be prescribed';

(*b*) omit subsection (2);

(*c*) in subsection (3) for 'the appropriate charge' substitute 'such fee as may be prescribed'; and

(*d*) omit subsection (4).

(9) In section 383 of the Companies Act 1985 (minutes of proceedings of general meetings)—

(*a*) in subsection (1), omit 'during business hours';

(*b*) omit subsection (2); and

(*c*) in subsection (3), after 'entitled' insert 'on payment of such fee as may be prescribed' and omit the words from 'at a charge' to the end.

(10) In Part IV of Schedule 13 to the Companies Act 1985 (register of directors' interests)—

(*a*) in paragraph 25, omit the words from 'during' to 'for inspection)' and for the words from '5 pence' to the end substitute 'such fee as may be prescribed'; and

(*b*) in paragraph 26(1), for the words from '10 pence' to the end substitute 'such fee as may be prescribed'.

(11) In Schedule 22 to the Companies Act 1985 (provisions applying to unregistered companies), in the entry relating to Part XXV at the appropriate place insert—

| 'Section 723A | Rights of inspection and related matters. | To apply only so far as this provision has effect in relation to provisions applying by virtue of the foregoing provisions of this Schedule.'. |

144 'Subsidiary', 'holding company' and 'wholly-owned subsidiary'

(1) In Part XXVI of the Companies Act 1985 (general interpretation provisions), for section 736 substitute—

'736 'Subsidiary', 'holding company' and 'wholly-owned subsidiary'

(1) A company is a 'subsidiary' of another company, its 'holding company', if that other company—

(*a*) holds a majority of the voting rights in it, or

(*b*) is a member of it and has the right to appoint or remove a majority of its board of directors, or

(*c*) is a member of it and controls alone, pursuant to an agreement with other shareholders or members, a majority of the voting rights in it,

or if it is a subsidiary of a company which is itself a subsidiary of that other company.

(2) A company is a 'wholly-owned subsidiary' of another company if it is has no members except that other and that other's wholly-owned subsidiaries or persons acting on behalf of that other or its wholly-owned subsidiaries.

(3) In this section 'company' includes any body corporate.

736A Provisions supplementing s 736

(1) The provisions of this section explain expressions used in section 736 and otherwise supplement that section.

(2) In section 736(1)(*a*) and (*c*) the references to the voting rights in a company are to the rights conferred on shareholders in respect of their shares or, in the case of a company not having a share capital, on members, to vote at general meetings of the company on all, or substantially all, matters.

(3) In section 736(1)(*b*) the reference to the right to appoint or remove a majority of the board of directors is to the right to appoint or remove directors holding a majority of the voting rights at meetings of the board on all, or substantially all, matters; and for the purposes of that provision—

(*a*) a company shall be treated as having the right to appoint to a directorship if—
  (i) a person's appointment to it follows necessarily from his appointment as director of the company, or
  (ii) the directorship is held by the company itself; and

(*b*) a right to appoint or remove which is exercisable only with the consent or concurrence of another person shall be left out of account unless no other person has a right to appoint or, as the case may be, remove in relation to that directorship.

(4) Rights which are exercisable only in certain circumstances shall be taken into account only—

(*a*) when the circumstances have arisen, and for so long as they continue to obtain, or
(*b*) when the circumstances are within the control of the person having the rights;

and rights which are normally exercisable but are temporarily incapable of exercise shall continue to be taken into account.

(5) Rights held by a person in a fiduciary capacity shall be treated as not held by him.

(6) Rights held by a person as nominee for another shall be treated as held by the other; and rights shall be regarded as held as nominee for another if they are exercisable only on his instructions or with his consent or concurrence.

(7) Rights attached to shares held by way of security shall be treated as held by the person providing the security—

(*a*) where apart from the right to exercise them for the purpose of preserving the value of the security, or of realising it, the rights are exercisable only in accordance with his instructions;

(*b*) where the shares are held in connection with the granting of loans as part of normal business activities and apart from the right to exercise them for the purpose of preserving the value of the security, or of realising it, the rights are exercisable only in his interests.

(8) Rights shall be treated as held by a company if they are held by any of its subsidiaries; and nothing in subsection (6) or (7) shall be construed as requiring rights held by a company to be treated as held by any of its subsidiaries.

(9) For the purposes of subsection (7) rights shall be treated as being exercisable in accordance with the instructions or in the interests of a company if they are exercisable in accordance with the instructions of or, as the case may be, in the interests of—

(a) any subsidiary or holding company of that company, or

(b) any subsidiary of a holding company of that company.

(10) The voting rights in a company shall be reduced by any rights held by the company itself.

(11) References in any provision of subsections (5) to (10) to rights held by a person include rights falling to be treated as held by him by virtue of any other provision of those subsections but not rights which by virtue of any such provision are to be treated as not held by him.

(12) In this section "company" includes any body corporate.'.

(2) Any reference in any enactment (including any enactment contained in subordinate legislation within the meaning of the Interpretation Act 1978) to a 'subsidiary' or 'holding company' within the meaning of section 736 of the Companies Act 1985 shall, subject to any express amendment or saving made by or under this Act, be read as referring to a subsidiary or holding company as defined in section 736 as substituted by subsection (1) above.

This applies whether the reference is specific or general, or express or implied.

(3) In Part XXVI of the Companies Act 1985 (general interpretation provisions), after section 736A insert—

'736B Power to amend ss 736 and 736A

(1) The Secretary of State may by regulations amend sections 736 and 736A so as to alter the meaning of the expressions "holding company", "subsidiary" or "wholly-owned subsidiary".

(2) The regulations may make different provision for different cases or classes of case and may contain such incidental and supplementary provisions as the Secretary of State thinks fit.

(3) Regulations under this section shall be made by statutory instrument which shall be subject to annulment in pursuance of a resolution of either House of Parliament.

(4) Any amendment made by regulations under this section does not apply for the purposes of enactments outside the Companies Acts unless the regulations so provide.

(5) So much of section 23(3) of the Interpretation Act 1978 as applies section 17(2)(a) of that Act (effect of repeal and re-enactment) to deeds, instruments and documents other than enactments shall not apply in relation to any repeal and re-enactment effected by regulations made under this section.'.

(4) Schedule 18 contains amendments and savings consequential on the amendments made by this section; and the Secretary of State may by regulations make such further amendments or savings as appear to him to be necessary or expedient.

(5) Regulations under this section shall be made by statutory instrument which shall be subject to annulment in pursuance of a resolution of either House of Parliament.

(6) So much of section 23(3) of the Interpretation Act 1978 as applies section 17(2)(a) of that Act (presumption as to meaning of references to enactments repealed and re-enacted) to deeds or other instruments or documents does not apply in relation to the repeal and re-enactment by this section of section 736 of the Companies Act 1985.

145 Minor amendments

The Companies Act 1985 has effect with the further amendments specified in Schedule 19.

PART VI

MERGERS AND RELATED MATTERS

146 Restriction on references where prior notice given

After section 75 of the Fair Trading Act 1973 there is inserted—

*'Restriction on power to make merger reference where prior notice
has been given*

75A General rule where notice given by acquirer and no reference made within period for considering notice

(1) Notice may be given to the Director by a person authorised by regulations to do so of proposed arrangements which might result in the creation of a merger situation qualifying for investigation.

(2) The notice must be in the prescribed form and state that the existence of the proposal has been made public.

(3) If the period for considering the notice expires without any reference being made to the Commission with respect to the notified arrangements, no reference may be made under this Part of this Act to the Commission with respect to those arrangements or to the creation or possible creation of any merger situation qualifying for investigation which is created in consequence of carrying those arrangements into effect.

(4) Subsection (3) of this section is subject to sections 75B(5) and 75C of this Act.

(5) A notice under subsection (1) of this section is referred to in sections 75B to 75F of this Act as a "merger notice".

75B The role of the Director

(1) The Director shall, when the period for considering any merger notice begins, take such action as he considers appropriate to bring the existence of the proposal, the fact that the merger notice has been given and the date on which the period for considering the notice may expire to the attention of those who in his opinion would be affected if the arrangements were carried into effect.

(2) The period for considering a merger notice is the period of twenty days, determined in accordance with subsection (9) of this section, beginning with the first day after—

(a) the notice has been received by the Director, and

(b) any fee payable to the Director in respect of the notice has been paid.

(3) The Director may, and shall if required to do so by the Secretary of State, by notice to the person who gave the merger notice—

(a) extend the period mentioned in subsection (2) of this section by a further ten days, and

(b) extend that period as extended under paragraph (a) of this subsection by a further fifteen days.

(4) The Director may by notice to the person who gave the merger notice request him to provide the Director within such period as may be specified in the notice with such information as may be so specified.

(5) If the Director gives to the person who gave the merger notice (in this subsection referred to as "the relevant person") a notice stating that the Secretary of State is seeking undertakings under section 75G of this Act, section 75A(3) of this Act does not prevent a reference being made to the Commission unless—

(a) after the Director has given that notice, the relevant person has given a notice to the Director stating that he does not intend to give such undertakings, and

(b) the period of ten days beginning with the first day after the notice under paragraph (a) of this subsection was received by the Director has expired.

(6) A notice by the Director under subsection (3), (4) or (5) of this section must either be given to the person who gave the merger notice before the period for considering the merger notice expires or be sent in a properly addressed and pre-paid letter posted to him at such time that, in the ordinary course of post, it would be delivered to him before that period expires.

(7) The Director may, at any time before the period for considering any merger notice expires, reject the notice if—

(*a*) he suspects that any information given in respect of the notified arrangements, whether in the merger notice or otherwise, by the person who gave the notice or any connected person is in any material respect false or misleading,

(*b*) he suspects that it is not proposed to carry the notified arrangements into effect, or

(*c*) any prescribed information is not given in the merger notice or any information requested by notice under subsection (4) of this section is not provided within the period specified in the notice.

(8) If—

(*a*) under subsection (3)(*b*) of this section the period for considering a merger notice has been extended by a further fifteen days, but

(*b*) the Director has not made any recommendation to the Secretary of State under section 76(*b*) of this Act as to whether or not it would in the Director's opinion be expedient for the Secretary of State to make a reference to the Commission with respect to the notified arrangements,

then, during the last five of those fifteen days, the power of the Secretary of State to make a reference to the Commission with respect to the notified arrangements is not affected by the absence of any such recommendation.

(9) In determining any period for the purposes of subsections (2), (3) and (5) of this section no account shall be taken of—

(*a*) Saturday, Sunday, Good Friday and Christmas Day, and

(*b*) any day which is a bank holiday in England and Wales.

75C Cases where power to refer unaffected

(1) Section 75A(3) of this Act does not prevent any reference being made to the Commission if—

(*a*) before the end of the period for considering the merger notice, it is rejected by the Director under section 75B(7) of this Act,

(*b*) before the end of that period, any of the enterprises to which the notified arrangements relate cease to be distinct from each other,

(*c*) any information (whether prescribed information or not) that—

(i) is, or ought to be, known to the person who gave the merger notice or any connected person, and

(ii) is material to the notified arrangements;

is not disclosed to the Secretary of State or the Director by such time before the end of that period as may be specified in regulations,

(*d*) at any time after the merger notice is given but before the enterprises to which the notified arrangements relate cease to be distinct from each other, any of those enterprises ceases to be distinct from any enterprise other than an enterprise to which those arrangements relate,

(*e*) the six months beginning with the end of the period for considering the merger notice expires without the enterprises to which the notified arrangements relate ceasing to be distinct from each other,

(*f*) the merger notice is withdrawn, or

(*g*) any information given in respect of the notified arrangements, whether in the merger notice or otherwise, by the person who gave the notice or any connected person is in any material respect false or misleading.

(2) Where—

(*a*) two or more transactions which have occurred or, if any arrangements are carried into effect, will occur may be treated for the purposes of a merger reference as having occurred simultaneously on a particular date, and

(*b*) subsection (3) of section 75A of this Act does not prevent such a reference with respect to the last of those transactions,

that subsection does not prevent such a reference with respect to any of those transactions which actually occurred less than six months before—

(i) that date, or

(ii) the actual occurrence of another of those transactions with respect to which such a reference may be made (whether or not by virtue of this subsection).

(3) In determining for the purposes of subsection (2) of this section the time at which any transaction actually occurred, no account shall be taken of any option or other conditional right until the option is exercised or the condition is satisfied.

75D Regulations

(1) The Secretary of State may make regulations for the purposes of sections 75A to 75C of this Act.

(2) The regulations may, in particular—

(*a*) provide for section 75B(2) or (3) or section 75C(1)(*e*) of this Act to apply as if any reference to a period of days or months were a reference to a period specified in the regulations for the purposes of the provision in question,

(*b*) provide for the manner in which any merger notice is authorised or required to be given, rejected or withdrawn, and the time at which any merger notice is to be treated as received or rejected,

(*c*) provide for the manner in which any information requested by the Director or any other material information is authorised or required to be provided or disclosed, and the time at which such information is to be treated as provided or disclosed,

(*d*) provide for the manner in which any notice under section 75B of this Act is authorised or required to be given,

(*e*) provide for the time at which any notice under section 75B(5)(*a*) of this Act is to be treated as received,

(*f*)provide for the address which is to be treated for the purposes of section 75B(6) of this Act and of the regulations as a person's proper address,

(*g*) provide for the time at which any fee is to be treated as paid, and

(*h*) provide that a person is, or is not, to be treated, in such circumstances as may be specified in the regulations, as acting on behalf of a person authorised by regulations to give a merger notice or a person who has given such a notice.

(3) The regulations may make different provision for different cases.

(4) Regulations under this section shall be made by statutory instrument.

75E Interpretation of sections 75A to 75D

In this section and sections 75A to 75D of this Act—

"connected person", in relation to the person who gave a merger notice, means—

(*a*) any person who, for the purposes of section 77 of this Act, is associated with him, or

(*b*) any subsidiary of the person who gave the merger notice or of any person so associated with him,

"merger notice" is to be interpreted in accordance with section 75A(5) of this Act,

"notified arrangements" means the arrangements mentioned in the merger notice or arrangements not differing from them in any material respect,

"prescribed" means prescribed by the Director by notice having effect for the time being and published in the London, Edinburgh and Belfast Gazettes, "regulations" means regulations under section 75D of this Act, and

"subsidiary" has the meaning given by section 75(4K) of this Act,

and references to the enterprises to which the notified arrangements relate are references to those enterprises that would have ceased to be distinct from one another if the arrangements mentioned in the merger notice in question had been carried into effect at the time when the notice was given.

75F Power to amend sections 75B to 75D

(1) The Secretary of State may, for the purpose of determining the effect of giving a merger notice and the steps which may be or are to be taken by any person in connection with such a notice, by regulations made by statutory instrument amend sections 75B to 75D of this Act.

(2) The regulations may make different provision for different cases and may contain such incidental and supplementary provisions as the Secretary of State thinks fit.

(3) No regulations shall be made under this section unless a draft of the regulations has been laid before and approved by resolution of each House of Parliament.'.

147 Undertakings as alternative to merger reference

In Part V of the Fair Trading Act 1973 after the sections inserted by section 146 of this Act there is inserted—

'*Undertakings as alternative to merger reference*

75G Acceptance of undertakings

(1) Where—

(a) the Secretary of State has power to make a merger reference to the Commission under section 64 or 75 of this Act,

(b) the Director has made a recommendation to the Secretary of State under section 76 of this Act that such a reference should be made, and

(c) the Director has (in making that recommendation or subsequently) given advice to the Secretary of State specifying particular effects adverse to the public interest which in his opinion the creation of the merger situation qualifying for investigation may have or might be expected to have,

the Secretary of State may, instead of making a merger reference to the Commission, accept from such of the parties concerned as he considers appropriate undertakings complying with subsections (2) and (3) of this section to take specified action which the Secretary of State considers appropriate to remedy or prevent the effects adverse to the public interest specified in the advice.

(2) The undertakings must provide for one or more of the following—

(a) the division of a business by the sale of any part of the undertaking or assets or otherwise (for which purpose all the activities carried on by way of business by any one person or by any two or more interconnected bodies corporate may be treated as a single business),

(b) the division of a group of interconnected bodies corporate, and

(c) the separation, by the sale of any part of the undertaking or assets concerned or other means, of enterprises which are under common control otherwise than by reason of their being enterprises of interconnected bodies corporate.

(3) The undertakings may also contain provision—

(a) preventing or restricting the doing of things which might prevent or impede the division or separation,

(b) as to the carrying on of any activities or the safeguarding of any assets until the division or separation is effected,

(c) for any matters necessary to effect or take account of the division or separation, and (*d*) for enabling the Secretary of State to ascertain whether the undertakings are being fulfilled.

(4) If the Secretary of State has accepted one or more undertakings under this section, no reference may be made to the Commission with respect to the creation or possible creation of the merger situation qualifying for investigation by reference to which the undertakings were accepted, except in a case falling within subsection (5) of this section.

(5) Subsection (4) of this section does not prevent a reference being made to the Commission if material facts about the arrangements or transactions, or proposed arrangements or transactions, in consequence of which the enterprises concerned ceased or may cease to be distinct enterprises were not—

(*a*) notified to the Secretary of State or the Director, or
(*b*) made public,

before the undertakings were accepted.

(6) In subsection (5) of this section 'made public' has the same meaning as in section 64 of this Act.

75H Publication of undertakings

(1) The Secretary of State shall arrange for—

(*a*) any undertaking accepted by him under section 75G of this Act,
(*b*) the advice given by the Director for the purposes of subsection (1)(*c*) of that section in any case where such an undertaking has been accepted, and
(*c*) any variation or release of such an undertaking,

to be published in such manner as he may consider appropriate.

(2) In giving advice for the purposes of section 75G(1)(*c*) of this Act the Director shall have regard to the need for excluding, so far as practicable, any matter to which subsection (4) of this section applies.

(3) The Secretary of State shall exclude from any such advice as published under this section—

(*a*) any matter to which subsection (4) of this section applies and in relation to which he is satisfied that its publication in the advice would not be in the public interest, and
(*b*) any other matter in relation to which he is satisfied that its publication in the advice would be against the public interest.

(4) This subsection applies to—

(*a*) any matter which relates to the private affairs of an individual, where publication of that matter would or might, in the opinion of the Director or the Secretary of State, as the case may be, seriously and prejudicially affect the interests of that individual, and
(*b*) any matter which relates specifically to the affairs of a particular body of persons, whether corporate or unincorporate, where publication of that matter would or might, in the opinion of the Director or the Secretary of State, as the case may be, seriously and prejudicially affect the interests of that body, unless in his opinion the inclusion of that matter relating specifically to that body is necessary for the purposes of the advice.

(5) For the purposes of the law relating to defamation, absolute privilege shall attach to any advice given by the Director for the purposes of section 75G(1)(*c*) of this Act.

75J Review of undertakings

Where an undertaking has been accepted by the Secretary of State under section 75G of this Act, it shall be the duty of the Director—

(*a*) to keep under review the carrying out of that undertaking, and from time to time consider whether, by reason of any change of circumstances, the undertaking is no longer appropriate and either—

    (i) one or more of the parties to it can be released from it, or

    (ii) it needs to be varied or to be superseded by a new undertaking, and

(*b*) if it appears to him that the undertaking has not been or is not being fulfilled, that any person can be so released or that the undertaking needs to be varied or superseded, to give such advice to the Secretary of State as he may think proper in the circumstances.

75K Order of Secretary of State where undertaking not fulfilled

(1) The provisions of this section shall have effect where it appears to the Secretary of State that an undertaking accepted by him under section 75G of this Act has not been, is not being or will not be fulfilled.

(2) The Secretary of State may by order made by statutory instrument exercise such one or more of the powers specified in paragraphs 9A and 12 to 12C and Part II of Schedule 8 to this Act as he may consider it requisite to exercise for the purpose of remedying or preventing the adverse effects specified in the advice given by the Director for the purposes of section 75G(1)(*c*) of this Act; and those powers may be so exercised to such extent and in such manner as the Secretary of State considers requisite for that purpose.

(3) In determining whether, or to what extent or in what manner, to exercise any of those powers, the Secretary of State shall take into account any advice given by the Director under section 75J(*b*) of this Act.

(4) The provision contained in an order under this section may be different from that contained in the undertaking.

(5) On the making of an order under this section, the undertaking and any other undertaking accepted under section 75G of this Act by reference to the same merger situation qualifying for investigation are released by virtue of this section.'.

148 Enforcement of undertakings

After section 93 of the Fair Trading Act 1973 there is inserted—

'93A Enforcement of undertakings

(1) This section applies where a person (in this section referred to as "the responsible person") has given an undertaking which—

(*a*) has been accepted by the Secretary of State under section 75G of this Act,

(*b*) has been accepted by the appropriate Minister or Ministers under section 88 of this Act after the commencement of this section, or

(*c*) has been accepted by the Director under section 4 or 9 of the Competition Act 1980 after that time.

(2) Any person may bring civil proceedings in respect of any failure, or apprehended failure, of the responsible person to fulfil the undertaking, as if the obligations imposed by the undertaking on the responsible person had been imposed by an order to which section 90 of this Act applies.'.

149 Temporary restrictions on share dealings

(1) In section 75 of the Fair Trading Act 1973 (reference in anticipation of merger), after subsection (4) there is inserted—

'(4A) Where a merger reference is made under this section, it shall be unlawful, except with the consent of the Secretary of State under subsection (4C) of this section—

(*a*) for any person carrying on any enterprise to which the reference relates or having control of any such enterprise or for any subsidiary of his, or

(*b*) for any person associated with him or for any subsidiary of such a person, directly or indirectly to acquire, at any time during the period mentioned in subsection (4B) of this section, an interest in shares in a company if any enterprise to which the reference relates is carried on by or under the control of that company.

(4B) The period referred to in subsection (4A) of this section is the period beginning with the announcement by the Secretary of State of the making of the merger reference concerned and ending—

(a) where the reference is laid aside at any time, at that time,

(b) where the time (including any further period) allowed to the Commission for making a report on the reference expires without their having made such a report, on the expiration of that time,

(c) where a report of the Commission on the reference not including such conclusions as are referred to in section 73(1)(b) of this Act is laid before Parliament, at the end of the day on which the report is so laid,

(d) where a report of the Commission on the reference including such conclusions is laid before Parliament, at the end of the period of forty days beginning with the day on which the report is so laid,

and where such a report is laid before each House on different days, it is to be treated for the purposes of this subsection as laid on the earlier day.

(4C) The consent of the Secretary of State—

(a) may be either general or special,

(b) may be revoked by the Secretary of State, and

(c) shall be published in such way as, in the opinion of the Secretary of State, to give any person entitled to the benefit of it an adequate opportunity of getting to know of it, unless in the Secretary of State's opinion publication is not necessary for that purpose.

(4D) Section 93 of this Act applies to any contravention or apprehended contravention of subsection (4A) of this section as it applies to a contravention or apprehended contravention of an order to which section 90 of this Act applies.

(4E) Subsections (4F) to (4K) of this section apply for the interpretation of subsection (4A).

(4F) The circumstances in which a person acquires an interest in shares include those where—

(a) he enters into a contract to acquire the shares (whether or not for cash),

(b) not being the registered holder, he acquires a right to exercise, or to control the exercise of, any right conferred by the holding of the shares, or

(c) he acquires a right to call for delivery of the shares to himself or to his order or to acquire an interest in the shares or assumes an obligation to acquire such an interest,

but does not include those where he acquires an interest in pursuance of an obligation assumed before the announcement by the Secretary of State of the making of the merger reference concerned.

(4G) The circumstances in which a person acquires a right mentioned in subsection (4F) of this section—

(a) include those where he acquires a right or assumes an obligation the exercise or fulfilment of which would give him that right, but

(b) does not include those where he is appointed as proxy to vote at a specified meeting of a company or of any class of its members or at any adjournment of the meeting or he is appointed by a corporation to act as its representative at any meeting of the company or of any class of its members,

and references to rights and obligations in this subsection and subsection (4F) of this section include conditional rights and conditional obligations.

(4H) Any reference to a person carrying on or having control of any enterprise includes a group of persons carrying on or having control of an enterprise and any member of such a group.

(4J) Sections 65(2) to (4) and 77(1) and (4) to (6) of this Act apply to determine whether any person or group of persons has control of any enterprise and whether persons are associated as they apply for the purposes of section 65 of this Act to determine whether enterprises are brought under common control.

(4K) "Subsidiary" has the meaning given by section 736 of the Companies Act 1985, but that section and section 736A of that Act also apply to determine whether a company is a subsidiary of an individual or of a group of persons as they apply to determine whether it is a subsidiary of a company and references to a subsidiary in subsections (8) and (9) of section 736A as so applied are to be read accordingly.

(4L) In this section—
"company" includes any body corporate, and
"share" means share in the capital of a company, and includes stock.

(4M) Nothing in subsection (4A) of this section makes anything done by a person outside the United Kingdom unlawful unless he is—

(*a*) a British citizen, a British Dependent Territories citizen, a British Overseas citizen or a British National (Overseas),

(*b*) a body corporate incorporated under the law of the United Kingdom or of a part of the United Kingdom, or

(*c*) a person carrying on business in the United Kingdom, either alone or in partnership with one or more other persons.'.

(2) This section does not apply in relation to any merger reference made before the passing of this Act.

150 Obtaining control by stages

(1) After section 66 of the Fair Trading Act 1973 there is inserted—

'66A Obtaining control by stages

(1) Where an enterprise is brought under the control of a person or group of persons in the course of two or more transactions (referred to in this section as a 'series of transactions') falling within subsection (2) of this section, those transactions may, if the Secretary of State or, as the case may be, the Commission thinks fit, be treated for the purposes of a merger reference as having occurred simultaneously on the date on which the latest of them occurred.

(2) The transactions falling within this subsection are—

(*a*) any transaction which—
(i) enables that person or group of persons directly or indirectly to control or materially to influence the policy of any person carrying on the enterprise,
(ii) enables that person or group of persons to do so to a greater degree, or
(iii) is a step (whether direct or indirect) towards enabling that person or group of persons to do so, and

(*b*) any transaction whereby that person or group of persons acquires a controlling interest in the enterprise or, where the enterprise is carried on by a body corporate, in that body corporate.

(3) Where a series of transactions includes a transaction falling within subsection (2)(*b*) of this section, any transaction occurring after the occurrence of that transaction is to be disregarded for the purposes of subsection (1) of this section.

(4) Where the period within which a series of transactions occurs exceeds two years, the transactions that may be treated as mentioned in subsection (1) of this section are any of those transactions that occur within a period of two years.

(5) Sections 65(2) to (4) and 77(1) and (4) to (6) of this Act apply for the purposes of this section to determine whether an enterprise is brought under the control of a person

or group of persons and whether a transaction falls within subsection (2) of this section as they apply for the purposes of section 65 of this Act to determine whether enterprises are brought under common control.

(6) In determining for the purposes of this section the time at which any transaction occurs, no account shall be taken of any option or other conditional right until the option is exercised or the condition is satisfied.'.

(2) This section does not apply in relation to any merger reference made before the passing of this Act.

151 False or misleading information

At the end of Part VIII of the Fair Trading Act 1973 there is inserted—

'93B False or misleading information

(1) If a person furnishes any information—

  (a) to the Secretary of State, the Director or the Commission in connection with any of their functions under Parts IV, V, VI or this Part of this Act or under the Competition Act 1980, or

  (b) to the Commission in connection with the functions of the Commission under the Telecommunications Act 1984 or the Airports Act 1986,

and either he knows the information to be false or misleading in a material particular, or he furnishes the information recklessly and it is false or misleading in a material particular, he is guilty of an offence.

(2) A person who—

  (a) furnishes any information to another which he knows to be false or misleading in a material particular, or

  (b) recklessly furnishes any information to another which is false or misleading in a material particular,

knowing that the information is to be used for the purpose of furnishing information as mentioned in subsection (1)(a) or (b) of this section, is guilty of an offence.

(3) A person guilty of an offence under subsection (1) or (2) of this section is liable—

  (a) on summary conviction, to a fine not exceeding the statutory maximum, and

  (b) on conviction on indictment, to imprisonment for a term not exceeding two years or to a fine or to both.

(4) Section 129(1) of this Act does not apply to an offence under this section.'.

152 Fees

(1) The Secretary of State may by regulations made by statutory instrument require the payment to him or to the Director of such fees as may be prescribed by the regulations in connection with the exercise by the Secretary of State, the Director and the Commission of their functions under Part V of the Fair Trading Act 1973.

(2) The regulations may provide for fees to be payable—

  (a) in respect of—

    (i) an application for the consent of the Secretary of State under section 58(1) of the Fair Trading Act 1973 to the transfer of a newspaper or of newspaper assets, and

    (ii) a notice under section 75A(1) of that Act, and

  (b) on the occurrence of any event specified in the regulations.

(3) The events that may be specified in the regulations by virtue of subsection (2)(b) above include—

  (a) the making by the Secretary of State of a merger reference to the Commission under section 64 or 75 of the Fair Trading Act 1973,

(b) the announcement by the Secretary of State of his decision not to make a merger reference in any case where, at the time the announcement is made, he would under one of those sections have power to make a such a reference.

(4) The regulations may also contain provision—

(a) for ascertaining the persons by whom fees are payable,

(b) specifying whether any fee is payable to the Secretary of State or to the Director,

(c) for the amount of any fee to be calculated by reference to matters which may include—

    (i) in a case involving functions of the Secretary of State under sections 57 to 61 of the Fair Trading Act 1973, the number of newspapers concerned, the number of separate editions (determined in accordance with the regulations) of each newspaper and the average circulation per day of publication (within the meaning of Part V of that Act) of each newspaper, and

    (ii) in any other case, the value (determined in accordance with the regulations) of any assets concerned,

(d) as to the time when any fee is to be paid, and

(e) for the repayment by the Secretary of State or the Director of the whole or part of any fee in specified circumstances.

(5) The regulations may make different provision for different cases.

(6) Subsections (2) to (5) above do not prejudice the generality of subsection (1) above.

(7) In determining the amount of any fees to be prescribed by the regulations, the Secretary of State may take into account all costs incurred by him and by the Director in respect of the exercise by him, by the Commission and by the Director of their respective functions—

(a) under Part V of the Fair Trading Act 1973, and

(b) under Parts I, VII and VIII of that Act in relation to merger references or other matters arising under Part V.

(8) A statutory instrument containing regulations under this section shall be subject to annulment in pursuance of a resolution of either House of Parliament.

(9) Fees paid to the Secretary of State or the Director under this section shall be paid into the Consolidated Fund.

(10) In this section—
'the Commission',
'the Director', and
'merger reference',

have the same meaning as in the Fair Trading Act 1973, and 'newspaper' has the same meaning as in Part V of that Act.

(11) References in this section to Part V of the Fair Trading Act 1973 and to merger references under section 64 or 75 of that Act or under that Part include sections 29 and 30 of the Water Act 1989 and any reference under section 29 of that Act.

153 Other amendments about mergers and related matters

Schedule 20 to this Act has effect.

PART VII

FINANCIAL MARKETS AND INSOLVENCY

Introduction

154 Introduction

This Part has effect for the purposes of safeguarding the operation of certain financial markets by provisions with respect to—

(a) the insolvency, winding up or default of a person party to transactions in the market (sections 155 to 172),

(b) the effectiveness or enforcement of certain charges given to secure obligations in connection with such transactions (sections 173 to 176), and

(c) rights and remedies in relation to certain property provided as cover for margin in relation to such transactions or subject to such a charge (sections 177 to 181).

Recognised investment exchanges and clearing houses

155 Market contracts

(1) This Part applies to the following descriptions of contract connected with a recognised investment exchange or recognised clearing house.

The contracts are referred to in this Part as 'market contracts'.

(2) In relation to a recognised investment exchange, this Part applies to—

(a) contracts entered into by a member or designated non-member of the exchange which are made on or otherwise subject to the rules of the exchange; and

(b) contracts subject to the rules of the exchange entered into by the exchange for the purposes of or in connection with the provision of clearing services.

A 'designated non-member' means a person in respect of whom action may be taken under the default rules of the exchange but who is not a member of the exchange.

(3) In relation to a recognised clearing house, this Part applies to contracts subject to the rules of the clearing house entered into by the clearing house for the purposes of or in connection with the provision of clearing services for a recognised investment exchange.

(4) The Secretary of State may by regulations make further provision as to the contracts to be treated as 'market contracts', for the purposes of this Part, in relation to a recognised investment exchange or recognised clearing house.

(5) The regulations may add to, amend or repeal the provisions of subsections (2) and (3) above.

156 Additional requirements for recognition: default rules, &c

(1) The Financial Services Act 1986 shall have effect as if the requirements set out in Schedule 21 to this Act (the 'additional requirements') were among those specified in that Act for recognition of an investment exchange or clearing house.

(2) In particular, that Act shall have effect—

(a) as if the requirements set out in Part I of that Schedule were among those specified in Schedule 4 to that Act (requirements for recognition of UK investment exchange),

(b) as if the requirements set out in Part II of that Schedule were among those specified in section 39(4) of that Act (requirements for recognition of UK clearing house), and

(c) as if the requirement set out in Part III of that Schedule was among those specified in section 40(2) of that Act (requirements for recognition of overseas investment exchange or clearing house).

(3) The additional requirements do not affect the status of an investment exchange or clearing house recognised before the commencement of this section, but if the Secretary of State is of the opinion that any of those requirements is not met in the case of such a body, he shall within one month of commencement give notice to the body stating his opinion.

(4) Where the Secretary of State gives such a notice, he shall not—

(a) take action to revoke the recognition of such a body on the ground that any of the additional requirements is not met, unless he considers it essential to do so in the interests of investors, or

(b) apply on any such ground for a compliance order under section 12 of the Financial Services Act 1986, until after the end of the period of six months beginning with the date on which the notice was given.

(5) The Secretary of State may extend, or further extend, that period if he considers there is good reason to do so.

157 Change in default rules

(1) A recognised UK investment exchange or recognised UK clearing house shall give the Secretary of State at least 14 days' notice of any proposal to amend, revoke or add to its default rules; and the Secretary of State may within 14 days from receipt of the notice direct the exchange or clearing house not to proceed with the proposal, in whole or in part.

(2) A direction under this section may be varied or revoked.

(3) Any amendment or revocation of, or addition to, the default rules of an exchange or clearing house in breach of a direction under this section is ineffective.

158 Modifications of the law of insolvency

(1) The general law of insolvency has effect in relation to market contracts, and action taken under the rules of a recognised investment exchange or recognised clearing house with respect to such contracts, subject to the provisions of sections 159 to 165.

(2) So far as those provisions relate to insolvency proceedings in respect of a person other than a defaulter, they apply in relation to—

(a) proceedings in respect of a member or designated non-member of a recognised investment exchange or a member of a recognised clearing house, and

(b) proceedings in respect of a party to a market contract begun after a recognised investment exchange or recognised clearing house has taken action under its default rules in relation to a person party to the contract as principal,

but not in relation to any other insolvency proceedings, notwithstanding that rights or liabilities arising from market contracts fall to be dealt with in the proceedings.

(3) The reference in subsection (2)(b) to the beginning of insolvency proceedings is to—

(a) the presentation of a bankruptcy petition or a petition for sequestration of a person's estate, or

(b) the presentation of a petition for an administration order or a winding-up petition or the passing of a resolution for voluntary winding up, or

(c) the appointment of an administrative receiver.

(4) The Secretary of State may make further provision by regulations modifying the law of insolvency in relation to the matters mentioned in subsection (1).

(5) The regulations may add to, amend or repeal the provisions mentioned in subsection (1), and any other provision of this Part as it applies for the purposes of those provisions, or provide that those provisions have effect subject to such additions, exceptions or adaptations as are specified in the regulations.

159 Proceedings of exchange or clearing house take precedence over insolvency procedures

(1) None of the following shall be regarded as to any extent invalid at law on the ground of inconsistency with the law relating to the distribution of the assets of a person on bankruptcy, winding up or sequestration, or in the administration of an insolvent estate—

(a) a market contract,

(b) the default rules of a recognised investment exchange or recognised clearing house,

(c) the rules of a recognised investment exchange or recognised clearing house as to the settlement of market contracts not dealt with under its default rules.

(2) The powers of a relevant office-holder in his capacity as such, and the powers of the court under the Insolvency Act 1986 or the Bankruptcy (Scotland) Act 1985 shall not be exercised in such a way as to prevent or interfere with—

(*a*) the settlement in accordance with the rules of a recognised investment exchange or recognised clearing house of a market contract not dealt with under its default rules, or

(*b*) any action taken under the default rules of such an exchange or clearing house.

This does not prevent a relevant office-holder from afterwards seeking to recover any amount under section 163(4) or 164(4) or prevent the court from afterwards making any such order or decree as is mentioned in section 165(1) or (2) (but subject to subsections (3) and (4) of that section).

(3) Nothing in the following provisions of this Part shall be construed as affecting the generality of the above provisions.

(4) A debt or other liability arising out of a market contract which is the subject of default proceedings may not be proved in a winding up or bankruptcy, or in Scotland claimed in a winding up or sequestration, until the completion of the default proceedings.

A debt or other liability which by virtue of this subsection may not be proved or claimed shall not be taken into account for the purposes of any set-off until the completion of the default proceedings.

(5) For the purposes of subsection (4) the default proceedings shall be taken to be completed in relation to a person when a report is made under section 162 stating the sum (if any) certified to be due to or from him.

160 Duty to give assistance for purposes of default proceedings

(1) It is the duty of—

(*a*) any person who has or had control of any assets of a defaulter, and

(*b*) any person who has or had control of any documents of or relating to a defaulter,

to give a recognised investment exchange or recognised clearing house such assistance as it may reasonably require for the purposes of its default proceedings.

This applies notwithstanding any duty of that person under the enactments relating to insolvency.

(2) A person shall not under this section be required to provide any information or produce any document which he would be entitled to refuse to provide or produce on grounds of legal professional privilege in proceedings in the High Court or on grounds of confidentiality as between client and professional legal adviser in proceedings in the Court of Session.

(3) Where original documents are supplied in pursuance of this section, the exchange or clearing house shall return them forthwith after the completion of the relevant default proceedings, and shall in the meantime allow reasonable access to them to the person by whom they were supplied and to any person who would be entitled to have access to them if they were still in the control of the person by whom they were supplied.

(4) The expenses of a relevant office-holder in giving assistance under this section are recoverable as part of the expenses incurred by him in the discharge of his duties; and he shall not be required under this section to take any action which involves expenses which cannot be so recovered, unless the exchange or clearing house undertakes to meet them.

There shall be treated as expenses of his such reasonable sums as he may determine in respect of time spent in giving the assistance.

(5) The Secretary of State may by regulations make further provision as to the duties of persons to give assistance to a recognised investment exchange or recognised clearing house for the purposes of its default proceedings, and the duties of the exchange or clearing house with respect to information supplied to it.

The regulations may add to, amend or repeal the provisions of subsections (1) to (4) above.

(6) In this section 'document' includes information recorded in any form.

161 Supplementary provisions as to default proceedings

(1) If the court is satisfied on an application by a relevant office-holder that a party to a market contract with a defaulter intends to dissipate or apply his assets so as to prevent the officer-holder recovering such sums as may become due upon the completion of the default proceedings, the court may grant such interlocutory relief (in Scotland, such interim order) as it thinks fit.

(2) A liquidator or trustee of a defaulter or, in Scotland, a permanent trustee on the sequestrated estate of the defaulter shall not—

(*a*) declare or pay any dividend to the creditors, or

(*b*) return any capital to contributories,

unless he has retained what he reasonably considers to be an adequate reserve in respect of any claims arising as a result of the default proceedings of the exchange or clearing house concerned.

(3) The court may on an application by a relevant office-holder make such order as it thinks fit altering or dispensing from compliance with such of the duties of his office as are affected by the fact that default proceedings are pending or could be taken, or have been or could have been taken.

(4) Nothing in sections 10(1)(*c*), 11(3), 126, 128, 130, 185 or 285 of the Insolvency Act 1986 (which restrict the taking of certain legal proceedings and other steps), and nothing in any rule of law in Scotland to the like effect as the said section 285, in the Bankruptcy (Scotland) Act 1985 or in the Debtors (Scotland) Act 1987 as to the effect of sequestration, shall affect any action taken by an exchange or clearing house for the purpose of its default proceedings.

162 Duty to report on completion of default proceedings

(1) A recognised investment exchange or recognised clearing house shall, on the completion of proceedings under its default rules, report to the Secretary of State on its proceedings stating in respect of each creditor or debtor the sum certified by them to be payable from or to the defaulter or, as the case may be, the fact that no sum is payable.

(2) The exchange or clearing house may make a single report or may make reports from time to time as proceedings are completed with respect to the transactions affecting particular persons.

(3) The exchange or clearing house shall supply a copy of every report under this section to the defaulter and to any relevant office-holder acting in relation to him or his estate.

(4) When a report under this section is received by the Secretary of State, he shall publish notice of that fact in such manner as he thinks appropriate for bringing it to the attention of creditors and debtors of the defaulter.

(5) An exchange or clearing house shall make available for inspection by a creditor or debtor of the defaulter so much of any report by it under this section as relates to the sum (if any) certified to be due to or from him or to the method by which that sum was determined.

(6) Any such person may require the exchange or clearing house, on payment of such reasonable fee as the exchange or clearing house may determine, to provide him with a copy of any part of a report which he is entitled to inspect.

163 Net sum payable on completion of default proceedings

(1) The following provisions apply with respect to the net sum certified by a recognised investment exchange or recognised clearing house, upon proceedings under its default rules being duly completed in accordance with this Part, to be payable by or to a defaulter.

(2) If, in England and Wales, a bankruptcy or winding-up order has been made, or a resolution for voluntary winding up has been passed, the debt—

(*a*) is provable in the bankruptcy or winding up or, as the case may be, is payable to the relevant officer-holder, and (*b*) shall be taken into account, where appropriate, under section 323 of the Insolvency Act 1986 (mutual dealings and set-off) or the corresponding provision applicable in the case of winding up,

in the same way as a debt due before the commencement of the bankruptcy, the date on which the body corporate goes into liquidation (within the meaning of section 247 of the Insolvency Act 1986) or, in the case of a partnership, the date of the winding-up order.

(3) If, in Scotland, an award of sequestration or a winding-up order has been made, or a resolution for voluntary winding up has been passed, the debt—

(*a*) may be claimed in the sequestration or winding up or, as the case may be, is payable to the relevant officer-holder, and

(*b*) shall be taken into account for the purposes of any rule of law relating to set-off applicable in sequestration or winding up,

in the same way as a debt due before the date of sequestration (within the meaning of section 73(1) of the Bankruptcy (Scotland) Act 1985) or the commencement of the winding up (within the meaning of section 129 of the Insolvency Act 1986).

(4) However, where (or to the extent that) a sum is taken into account by virtue of subsection (2)(*b*) or (3)(*b*) which arises from a contract entered into at a time when the creditor had notice—

(*a*) that a bankruptcy petition or, in Scotland, a petition for sequestration was pending, or

(*b*) that a meeting of creditors had been summoned under section 98 of the Insolvency Act 1986 or that a winding-up petition was pending,

the value of any profit to him arising from the sum being so taken into account (or being so taken into account to that extent) is recoverable from him by the relevant office-holder unless the court directs otherwise.

(5) Subsection (4) does not apply in relation to a sum arising from a contract effected under the default rules of a recognised investment exchange or recognised clearing house.

(6) Any sum recoverable by virtue of subsection (4) ranks for priority, in the event of the insolvency of the person from whom it is due, immediately before preferential or, in Scotland, preferred debts.

164 Disclaimer of property, rescission of contracts, &c

(1) Sections 178, 186, 315 and 345 of the Insolvency Act 1986 (power to disclaim onerous property and court's power to order rescission of contracts, &c) do not apply in relation to—

(*a*) a market contract, or

(*b*) a contract effected by the exchange or clearing house for the purpose of realising property provided as margin in relation to market contracts.

In the application of this subsection in Scotland, the reference to sections 178, 315 and 345 shall be construed as a reference to any rule of law having the like effect as those sections.

(2) In Scotland, a permanent trustee on the sequestrated estate of a defaulter or a liquidator is bound by any market contract to which that defaulter is a party and by any contract as is mentioned in subsection (1)(*b*) above notwithstanding section 42 of the Bankruptcy (Scotland) Act 1985 or any rule of law to the like effect applying in liquidations.

(3) Sections 127 and 284 of the Insolvency Act 1986 (avoidance of property dispositions effected after commencement of winding up or presentation of bankruptcy petition), and section 32(8) of the Bankruptcy (Scotland) Act 1985 (effect of dealing with debtor relating to estate vested in permanent trustee) do not apply to—

(*a*) a market contract, or any disposition of property in pursuance of such a contract,

(*b*) the provision of margin in relation to market contracts, (*c*) a contract effected by the exchange or clearing house for the purpose of realising property provided as margin in relation to a market contract, or any disposition of property in pursuance of such a contract, or

(*d*) any disposition of property in accordance with the rules of the exchange or clearing house as to the application of property provided as margin.

(4) However, where—

(*a*) a market contract is entered into by a person who has notice that a petition has been presented for the winding up or bankruptcy or sequestration of the estate of the other party to the contract, or

(*b*) margin in relation to a market contract is accepted by a person who has notice that such a petition has been presented in relation to the person by whom or on whose behalf the margin is provided,

the value of any profit to him arising from the contract or, as the case may be, the amount or value of the margin is recoverable from him by the relevant office-holder unless the court directs otherwise.

(5) Subsection (4)(*a*) does not apply where the person entering into the contract is a recognised investment exchange or recognised clearing house acting in accordance with its rules, or where the contract is effected under the default rules of such an exchange or clearing house; but subsection (4)(*b*) applies in relation to the provision of margin in relation to such a contract.

(6) Any sum recoverable by virtue of subsection (4) ranks for priority, in the event of the insolvency of the person from whom it is due, immediately before preferential or, in Scotland, preferred debts.

165 Adjustment of prior transactions

(1) No order shall be made in relation to a transaction to which this section applies under—

(*a*) section 238 or 339 of the Insolvency Act 1986 (transactions at an under-value),
(*b*) section 239 or 340 of that Act (preferences), or
(*c*) section 423 of that Act (transactions defrauding creditors).

(2) As respects Scotland, no decree shall be granted in relation to any such transaction—

(*a*) under section 34 or 36 of the Bankruptcy (Scotland) Act 1985 or section 242 or 243 of the Insolvency Act 1986 (gratuitous alienations and unfair preferences), or
(*b*) at common law on grounds of gratuitous alienations or fraudulent preferences.

(3) This section applies to—

(*a*) a market contract to which a recognised investment exchange or recognised clearing house is a party or which is entered into under its default rules, and
(*b*) a disposition of property in pursuance of such a market contract.

(4) Where margin is provided in relation to a market contract and (by virtue of subsection (3)(*a*) or otherwise) no such order or decree as is mentioned in subsection (1) or (2) has been, or could be, made in relation to that contract, this section applies to—

(*a*) the provision of the margin,
(*b*) any contract effected by the exchange or clearing house in question for the purpose of realising the property provided as margin, and
(*c*) any disposition of property in accordance with the rules of the exchange or clearing house as to the application of property provided as margin.

166 Powers of Secretary of State to give directions

(1) The powers conferred by this section are exercisable in relation to a recognised UK investment exchange or recognised UK clearing house.

(2) Where in any case an exchange or clearing house has not taken action under its default rules—

(a) if it appears to the Secretary of State that it could take action, he may direct it to do so, and

(b) if it appears to the Secretary of State that it is proposing to take or may take action, he may direct it not to do so.

(3) Before giving such a direction the Secretary of State shall consult the exchange or clearing house in question; and he shall not give a direction unless he is satisfied, in the light of that consultation—

(a) in the case of a direction to take action, that failure to take action would involve undue risk to investors or other participants in the market, or

(b) in the case of a direction not to take action, that the taking of action would be premature or otherwise undesirable in the interests of investors or other participants in the market.

(4) A direction shall specify the grounds on which it is given.

(5) A direction not to take action may be expressed to have effect until the giving of a further direction (which may be a direction to take action or simply revoking the earlier direction).

(6) No direction shall be given not to take action if, in relation to the person in question—

(a) a bankruptcy order or an award of sequestration of his estate has been made, or an interim receiver or interim trustee has been appointed, or

(b) a winding up order has been made, a resolution for voluntary winding up has been passed or an administrator, administrative receiver or provisional liquidator has been appointed;

and any previous direction not to take action shall cease to have effect on the making or passing of any such order, award or appointment.

(7) Where an exchange or clearing house has taken or been directed to take action under its default rules, the Secretary of State may direct it to do or not to do such things (being things which it has power to do under its default rules) as are specified in the direction.

The Secretary of State shall not give such a direction unless he is satisfied that it will not impede or frustrate the proper and efficient conduct of the default proceedings.

(8) A direction under this section is enforceable, on the application of the Secretary of State, by injunction or, in Scotland, by an order under section 45 of the Court of Session Act 1988; and where an exchange or clearing house has not complied with a direction, the court may make such order as it thinks fit for restoring the position to what it would have been if the direction had been complied with.

167 Application to determine whether default proceedings to be taken

(1) Where there has been made or passed in relation to a member or designated non-member of a recognised investment exchange or a member of a recognised clearing house—

(a) a bankruptcy order or an award of sequestration of his estate, or an order appointing an interim receiver of his property, or

(b) an administration or winding up order, a resolution for voluntary winding up or an order appointing a provisional liquidator,

and the exchange or clearing house has not taken action under its default rules in consequence of the order, award or resolution or the matters giving rise to it, a relevant office-holder appointed by, or in consequence of or in connection with, the order, award or resolution may apply to the Secretary of State.

(2) The application shall specify the exchange or clearing house concerned and the grounds on which it is made.

(3) On receipt of the application the Secretary of State shall notify the exchange or

clearing house, and unless within three business days after the day on which the notice is received the exchange or clearing house—

(*a*) takes action under its default rules, or

(*b*) notifies the Secretary of State that it proposes to do so forthwith,

then, subject as follows, the provisions of sections 158 to 165 above do not apply in relation to market contracts to which the member or designated non-member in question is a party or to anything done by the exchange or clearing house for the purposes of, or in connection with, the settlement of any such contract.

For this purpose a 'business day' means any day which is not a Saturday or Sunday, Christmas Day, Good Friday or a bank holiday in any part of the United Kingdom under the Banking and Financial Dealings Act 1971.

(4) The provisions of sections 158 to 165 are not disapplied if before the end of the period mentioned in subsection (3) the Secretary of State gives the exchange or clearing house a direction under section 166(2)(*a*) (direction to take action under default rules).

No such direction may be given after the end of that period.

(5) If the exchange or clearing house notifies the Secretary of State that it proposes to take action under its default rules forthwith, it shall do so; and that duty is enforceable, on the application of the Secretary of State, by injunction or, in Scotland, by an order under section 45 of the Court of Session Act 1988.

168 Delegation of functions to designated agency

(1) Section 114 of the Financial Services Act 1986 (power to transfer functions to designated agency) applies to the functions of the Secretary of State under this Part in relation to a UK investment exchange or clearing house, with the exception of his functions with respect to the making of orders and regulations.

(2) If immediately before the commencement of this section—

(*a*) a designated agency is exercising all functions in relation to such bodies which are capable of being transferred under that section, and

(*b*) no draft order is lying before Parliament resuming any of those functions,

the order bringing this section into force shall have effect as a delegation order made under that section transferring to that agency all the functions which may be transferred by virtue of this section.

(3) The Secretary of State may—

(*a*) in the circumstances mentioned in subsection (3), (4) or (5) of section 115 of the Financial Services Act 1986, or

(*b*) if it appears to him that a designated agency is unable or unwilling to discharge all or any of the functions under this Part which have been transferred to it,

make an order under that section resuming all functions under this Part which have been transferred to the agency.

This does not affect his power to make an order under subsection (1) or (2) of that section with respect to such functions.

169 Supplementary provisions

(1) Section 61 of the Financial Services Act 1986 (injunctions and restitution orders) applies in relation to a contravention of any provision of the rules of a recognised investment exchange or recognised clearing house relating to the matters mentioned in Schedule 21 to this Act as it applies in relation to a contravention of any provision of such rules relating to the carrying on of investment business.

(2) The following provisions of the Financial Services Act 1986—

section 12 (compliance orders), as it applies by virtue of section 37(8) or 39(8),

section 37(7)(*b*) (revocation of recognition of UK investment exchange), and

section 39(7)(*b*) (revocation of recognition of UK clearing house), apply in relation to a failure by a recognised investment exchange or recognised clearing house to comply with an obligation under this Part as to a failure to comply with an obligation under that Act.

(3) Where the recognition of an investment exchange or clearing house is revoked under the Financial Services Act 1986, the Secretary of State may, before or after the revocation order, give such directions as he thinks fit with respect to the continued application of the provisions of this Part, with such exceptions, additions and adaptations as may be specified in the direction, in relation to cases where a relevant event of any description specified in the directions occurred before the revocation order takes effect.

(4) The references in sections 119 and 121 of the Financial Services Act 1986 (competition) to what is necessary for the protection of investors shall be construed as including references to what is necessary for the purposes of this Part.

(5) Section 204 of the Financial Services Act 1986 (service of notices) applies in relation to a notice, direction or other document required or authorised by or under this Part to be given to or served on any person other than the Secretary of State.

Other exchanges and clearing houses

170 Certain overseas exchanges and clearing houses

(1) The Secretary of State may by regulations provide that this Part applies in relation to contracts connected with an overseas investment exchange or clearing house which is approved by him in accordance with such procedures as may be specified in the regulations, as satisfying such requirements as may be so specified, as it applies in relation to contracts connected with a recognised investment exchange or clearing house.

(2) The Secretary of State shall not approve an overseas investment exchange or clearing house unless he is satisfied—

(*a*) that the rules and practices of the body, together with the law of the country in which the body's head office is situated, provide adequate procedures for dealing with the default of persons party to contracts connected with the body, and

(*b*) that it is otherwise appropriate to approve the body.

(3) The reference in subsection (2)(*a*) to default is to a person being unable to meet his obligations.

(4) The regulations may apply in relation to the approval of a body under this section such of the provisions of the Financial Services Act 1986 as the Secretary of State considers appropriate.

(5) The Secretary of State may make regulations which, in relation to a body which is so approved—

(*a*) apply such of the provisions of the Financial Services Act 1986 as the Secretary of State considers appropriate, and

(*b*) provide that the provisions of this Part apply with such exceptions, additions and adaptations as appear to the Secretary of State to be necessary or expedient;

and different provision may be made with respect to different bodies or descriptions of body.

(6) Where the regulations apply any provisions of the Financial Services Act 1986, they may provide that those provisions apply with such exceptions, additions and adaptations as appear to the Secretary of State to be necessary or expedient.

171 Certain money market institutions

(1) The Secretary of State may by regulations provide that this Part applies to contracts of any specified description in relation to which settlement arrangements are provided by a person for the time being included in a list maintained by the Bank of England for the purposes of this section, as it applies to contracts connected with a recognised investment exchange or recognised clearing house.

(2) The Secretary of State shall not make any such regulations unless he is satisfied, having regard to the extent to which the contracts in question—

(a) involve, or are likely to involve, investments falling within paragraph 2 of Schedule 5 to the Financial Services Act 1986 (money market investments), or

(b) are otherwise of a kind dealt in by persons supervised by the Bank of England,

that it is appropriate that the arrangements should be subject to the supervision of the Bank of England.

(3) The approval of the Treasury is required for—

(a) the conditions imposed by the Bank of England for admission to the list maintained by it for the purposes of this section, and

(b) the arrangements for a person's admission to and removal from the list;

and any regulations made under this section shall cease to have effect if the approval of the Treasury is withdrawn, but without prejudice to their having effect again if approval is given for fresh conditions or arrangements.

(4) The Bank of England shall publish the list as for the time being in force and provide a certified copy of it at the request of any person wishing to refer to it in legal proceedings.

A certified copy shall be evidence (in Scotland, sufficient evidence) of the contents of the list; and a copy purporting to be certified by or on behalf of the Bank shall be deemed to have been duly certified unless the contrary is shown.

(5) Regulations under this section may, in relation to a person included in the list—

(a) apply, with such exceptions, additions and adaptations as appear to the Secretary of State to be necessary or expedient, such of the provisions of the Financial Services Act 1986 as he considers appropriate, and

(b) provide that the provisions of this Part apply with such exceptions, additions and adaptations as appear to the Secretary of State to be necessary or expedient.

(6) Before making any regulations under this section, the Secretary of State shall consult the Treasury and the Bank of England.

(7) In section 84(1) of the Banking Act 1987 (disclosure of information obtained under that Act), in the Table showing the authorities to which, and functions for the purposes of which, disclosure may be made, at the end add—

'A person included in the list maintained by the Bank for the purposes of section 171 of the Companies Act 1989. Functions under settlement arrangements to which regulations under that section relate.'.

172 Settlement arrangements provided by the Bank of England

(1) The Secretary of State may by regulations provide that this Part applies to contracts of any specified description in relation to which settlement arrangements are provided by the Bank of England, as it applies to contracts connected with a recognised investment exchange or recognised clearing house.

(2) Regulations under this section may provide that the provisions of this Part apply with such exceptions, additions and adaptations as appear to the Secretary of State to be necessary or expedient.

(3) Before making any regulations under this section, the Secretary of State shall consult the Treasury and the Bank of England.

Market charges

173 Market charges

(1) In this Part 'market charge' means a charge whether fixed or floating, granted—

(a) in favour of a recognised investment exchange, for the purpose of securing debts or liabilities arising in connection with the settlement of market contracts,

(b) in favour of a recognised clearing house, for the purpose of securing debts or liabilities arising in connection with their ensuring the performance of market contracts, or

(c) in favour of a person who agrees to make payments as a result of the transfer of specified securities made through the medium of a computer-based system established by the Bank of England and The Stock Exchange, for the purpose of securing debts or liabilities of the transferee arising in connection therewith.

(2) Where a charge is granted partly for purposes specified in subsection (1)(*a*), (*b*) or (*c*) and partly for other purposes, it is a 'market charge' so far as it has effect for the specified purposes.

(3) In subsection (1)(*c*)—

'specified securities' means securities for the time being specified in the list in Schedule 1 to the Stock Transfer Act 1982, and includes any right to such securities; and

'transfer', in relation to any such securities or right, means a transfer of the beneficial interest.

(4) The Secretary of State may by regulations make further provision as to the charges granted in favour of any such person as is mentioned in subsection (1)(*a*), (*b*) or (*c*) which are to be treated as 'market charges' for the purposes of this Part; and the regulations may add to, amend or repeal the provisions of subsections (1) to (3) above.

(5) The regulations may provide that a charge shall or shall not be treated as a market charge if or to the extent that it secures obligations of a specified description, is a charge over property of a specified description or contains provisions of a specified description.

(6) Before making regulations under this section in relation to charges granted in favour of a person within subsection (1)(*c*), the Secretary of State shall consult the Treasury and the Bank of England.

174 Modifications of the law of insolvency

(1) The general law of insolvency has effect in relation to market charges and action taken in enforcing them subject to the provisions of section 175.

(2) The Secretary of State may by regulations make further provision modifying the law of insolvency in relation to the matters mentioned in subsection (1).

(3) The regulations may add to, amend or repeal the provisions mentioned in subsection (1), and any other provision of this Part as it applies for the purposes of those provisions, or provide that those provisions have effect with such exceptions, additions or adaptations as are specified in the regulations.

(4) The regulations may make different provision for cases defined by reference to the nature of the charge, the nature of the property subject to it, the circumstances, nature or extent of the obligations secured by it or any other relevant factor.

(5) Before making regulations under this section in relation to charges granted in favour of a person within section 173(1)(*c*), the Secretary of State shall consult the Treasury and the Bank of England.

175 Administration orders, &c

(1) The following provisions of the Insolvency Act 1986 (which relate to administration orders and administrators) do not apply in relation to a market charge—

(a) sections 10(1)(*b*) and 11(3)(*c*) (restriction on enforcement of security while petition for administration order pending or order in force), and

(b) section 15(1) and (2) (power of administrator to deal with charged property);

and section 11(2) of that Act (receiver to vacate office when so required by administrator) does not apply to a receiver appointed under a market charge.

(2) However, where a market charge falls to be enforced after an administration order has been made or a petition for an administration order has been presented, and there exists another charge over some or all of the same property ranking in priority to or *pari passu*

259

with the market charge, the court may order that there shall be taken after enforcement of the market charge such steps as the court may direct for the purpose of ensuring that the chargee under the other charge is not prejudiced by the enforcement of the market charge.

(3) The following provisions of the Insolvency Act 1986 (which relate to the powers of receivers) do not apply in relation to a market charge—

(*a*) section 43 (power of administrative receiver to dispose of charged property), and

(*b*) section 61 (power of receiver in Scotland to dispose of an interest in property).

(4) Sections 127 and 284 of the Insolvency Act 1986 (avoidance of property dispositions effected after commencement of winding up or presentation of bankruptcy petition), and section 32(8) of the Bankruptcy (Scotland) Act 1985 (effect of dealing with debtor relating to estate vested in permanent trustee), do not apply to a disposition of property as a result of which the property becomes subject to a market charge or any transaction pursuant to which that disposition is made.

(5) However, if a person (other than the chargee under the market charge) who is party to a disposition mentioned in subsection (4) has notice at the time of the disposition that a petition has been presented for the winding up or bankruptcy or sequestration of the estate of the party making the disposition, the value of any profit to him arising from the disposition is recoverable from him by the relevant office-holder unless the court directs otherwise.

(6) Any sum recoverable by virtue of subsection (5) ranks for priority, in the event of the insolvency of the person from whom it is due, immediately before preferential or, in Scotland, preferred debts.

(7) In a case falling within both subsection (4) above (as a disposition of property as a result of which the property becomes subject to a market charge) and section 164(3) (as the provision of margin in relation to a market contract), section 164(4) applies with respect to the recovery of the amount or value of the margin and subsection (5) above does not apply.

176 Power to make provision about certain other charges

(1) The Secretary of State may by regulations provide that the general law of insolvency has effect in relation to charges of such descriptions as may be specified in the regulations, and action taken in enforcing them, subject to such provisions as may be specified in the regulations.

(2) The regulations may specify any description of charge granted in favour of—

(*a*) a body approved under section 170 (certain overseas exchanges and clearing houses),

(*b*) a person included in the list maintained by the Bank of England for the purposes of section 171 (certain money market institutions),

(*c*) the Bank of England,

(*d*) an authorised person within the meaning of the Financial Services Act 1986, or

(*e*) an international securities self-regulating organisation within the meaning of that Act,

for the purpose of securing debts or liabilities arising in connection with or as a result of the settlement of contracts or the transfer of assets, rights or interests on a financial market.

(3) The regulations may specify any description of charge granted for that purpose in favour of any other person in connection with exchange facilities or clearing services provided by a recognised investment exchange or recognised clearing house or by any such body, person, authority or organisation as is mentioned in subsection (2).

(4) Where a charge is granted partly for the purpose specified in subsection (2) and partly for other purposes, the power conferred by this section is exercisable in relation to the charge so far as it has effect for that purpose.

(5) The regulations may—

(*a*) make the same or similar provision in relation to the charges to which they apply as is made by or under sections 174 and 175 in relation to market charges, or (*b*) apply any of those provisions with such exceptions, additions or adaptations as are specified in the regulations.

(6) Before making regulations under this section relating to a description of charges defined by reference to their being granted—

(*a*) in favour of a person included in the list maintained by the Bank of England for the purposes of section 171, or in connection with exchange facilities or clearing services provided by a person included in that list, or

(*b*) in favour of the Bank of England, or in connection with settlement arrangements provided by the Bank,

the Secretary of State shall consult the Treasury and the Bank of England.

(7) Regulations under this section may provide that they apply or do not apply to a charge if or to the extent that it secures obligations of a specified description, is a charge over property of a specified description or contains provisions of a specified description.

Market property
177 Application of margin not affected by certain other interests

(1) The following provisions have effect with respect to the application by a recognised investment exchange or recognised clearing house of property (other than land) held by the exchange or clearing house as margin in relation to a market contract.

(2) So far as necessary to enable the property to be applied in accordance with the rules of the exchange or clearing house, it may be so applied notwithstanding any prior equitable interest or right, or any right or remedy arising from a breach of fiduciary duty, unless the exchange or clearing house had notice of the interest, right or breach of duty at the time the property was provided as margin.

(3) No right or remedy arising subsequently to the property being provided as margin may be enforced so as to prevent or interfere with the application of the property by the exchange or clearing house in accordance with its rules.

(4) Where an exchange or clearing house has power by virtue of the above provisions to apply property notwithstanding an interest, right or remedy, a person to whom the exchange or clearing house disposes of the property in accordance with its rules takes free from that interest, right or remedy.

178 Priority of floating market charge over subsequent charges

(1) The Secretary of State may by regulations provide that a market charge which is a floating charge has priority over a charge subsequently created or arising, including a fixed charge.

(2) The regulations may make different provision for cases defined, as regards the market charge or the subsequent charge, by reference to the description of charge, its terms, the circumstances in which it is created or arises, the nature of the charge, the person in favour of whom it is granted or arises or any other relevant factor.

179 Priority of market charge over unpaid vendor's lien

Where property subject to an unpaid vendor's lien becomes subject to a market charge, the charge has priority over the lien unless the chargee had actual notice of the lien at the time the property became subject to the charge.

180 Proceedings against market property by unsecured creditors

(1) Where property (other than land) is held by a recognised investment exchange or recognised clearing house as margin in relation to market contracts or is subject to a market charge, no execution or other legal process for the enforcement of a judgment or order may be commenced or continued, and no distress may be levied, against the property by a person not seeking to enforce any interest in or security over the property, except with the consent of—

261

(*a*) in the case of property provided as cover for margin, the investment exchange or clearing house in question, or

(*b*) in the case of property subject to a market charge, the person in whose favour the charge was granted.

(2) Where consent is given the proceedings may be commenced or continued notwithstanding any provision of the Insolvency Act 1986 or the Bankruptcy (Scotland) Act 1985.

(3) Where by virtue of this section a person would not be entitled to enforce a judgment or order against any property, any injunction or other remedy granted with a view to facilitating the enforcement of any such judgment or order shall not extend to that property.

(4) In the application of this section to Scotland, the reference to execution being commenced or continued includes a reference to diligence being carried out or continued, and the reference to distress being levied shall be omitted.

181 Power to apply provisions to other cases

(1) The power of the Secretary of State to make provision by regulations under—

(*a*) section 170, 171 or 172 (power to extend provisions relating to market contracts), or
(*b*) section 176 (power to extend provisions relating to market charges),

includes power to apply sections 177 to 180 to any description of property provided as cover for margin in relation to contracts in relation to which the power is exercised or, as the case may be, property subject to charges in relation to which the power is exercised.

(2) The regulations may provide that those sections apply with such exceptions, additions and adaptations as may be specified in the regulations.

Supplementary provisions

182 Powers of court in relation to certain proceedings begun before commencement

(1) The powers conferred by this section are exercisable by the court where insolvency proceedings in respect of—

(*a*) a member of a recognised investment exchange or a recognised clearing house, or
(*b*) a person by whom a market charge has been granted,

are begun on or after 22nd December 1988 and before the commencement of this section. That person is referred to in this section as 'the relevant person'.

(2) For the purposes of this section 'insolvency proceedings' means proceedings under Part II, IV, V or IX of the Insolvency Act 1986 (administration, winding up and bankruptcy) or under the Bankruptcy (Scotland) Act 1985; and references in this section to the beginning of such proceedings are to—

(*a*) the presentation of a petition on which an administration order, winding-up order, bankruptcy order or award of sequestration is made, or
(*b*) the passing of a resolution for voluntary winding up.

(3) This section applies in relation to—

(*a*) in England and Wales, the administration of the insolvent estate of a deceased person, and
(*b*) in Scotland, the administration by a judicial factor appointed under section 11A of the Judicial Factors (Scotland) Act 1889 of the insolvent estate of a deceased person,

as it applies in relation to insolvency proceedings.

In such a case references to the beginning of the proceedings shall be construed as references to the death of the relevant person.

(4) The court may on an application made, within three months after the commencement of this section, by—

(*a*) a recognised investment exchange or recognised clearing house, or (*b*) a person in whose favour a market charge has been granted,

make such order as it thinks fit for achieving, except so far as assets of the relevant person have been distributed before the making of the application, the same result as if the provisions of Schedule 22 had come into force on 22nd December 1988.

(5) The provisions of that Schedule ('the relevant provisions') reproduce the effect of certain provisions of this Part as they appeared in the Bill for this Act as introduced into the House of Lords and published on that date.

(6) The court may in particular—

(*a*) require the relevant person or a relevant office-holder—
  (i) to return property provided as cover for margin or which was subject to a market charge, or to pay to the applicant or any other person the proceeds of realisation of such property, or
  (ii) to pay to the applicant or any other person such amount as the court estimates would have been payable to that person if the relevant provisions had come into force on 22nd December 1988 and market contracts had been settled in accordance with the rules of the recognised investment exchange or recognised clearing house, or a proportion of that amount if the property of the relevant person or relevant office-holder is not sufficient to meet the amount in full;

(*b*) provide that contracts, rules and dispositions shall be treated as not having been void;

(*c*) modify the functions of a relevant office-holder, or the duties of the applicant or any other person, in relation to the insolvency proceedings, or indemnify any such person in respect of acts or omissions which would have been proper if the relevant provisions had been in force;

(*d*) provide that conduct which constituted an offence be treated as not having done so;

(*e*) dismiss proceedings which could not have been brought if the relevant provisions had come into force on 22nd December 1988, and reverse the effect of any order of a court which could not, or would not, have been made if those provisions had come into force on that date.

(7) An order under this section shall not be made against a relevant officer-holder if the effect would be that his remuneration, costs and expenses could not be met.

183 Insolvency proceedings in other jurisdictions

(1) The references to insolvency law in section 426 of the Insolvency Act 1986 (co-operation with courts exercising insolvency jurisdiction in other jurisdictions) include, in relation to a part of the United Kingdom, the provisions made by or under this Part and, in relation to a relevant country or territory within the meaning of that section, so much of the law of that country or territory as corresponds to any provisions made by or under this Part.

(2) A court shall not, in pursuance of that section or any other enactment or rule of law, recognise or give effect to—

(*a*) any order of a court exercising jurisdiction in relation to insolvency law in a country or territory outside the United Kingdom, or

(*b*) any act of a person appointed in such a country or territory to discharge any functions under insolvency law,

in so far as the making of the order or the doing of the act would be prohibited in the case of a court in the United Kingdom or a relevant office-holder by provisions made by or under this Part.

(3) Subsection (2) does not affect the recognition or enforcement of a judgment required to be recognised or enforced under or by virtue of the Civil Jurisdiction and Judgments Act 1982.

184 Indemnity for certain acts, &c

(1) Where a relevant office-holder takes any action in relation to property of a defaulter

which is liable to be dealt with in accordance with the default rules of a recognised investment exchange or recognised clearing house, and believes and has reasonable grounds for believing that he is entitled to take that action, he is not liable to any person in respect of any loss or damage resulting from his action except in so far as the loss or damage is caused by the office-holder's own negligence.

(2) Any failure by a recognised investment exchange or recognised clearing house to comply with its own rules in respect of any matter shall not prevent that matter being treated for the purposes of this Part as done in accordance with those rules so long as the failure does not substantially affect the rights of any person entitled to require compliance with the rules.

(3) No recognised investment exchange or recognised clearing house, nor any officer or servant or member of the governing body of a recognised investment exchange or recognised clearing house, shall be liable in damages for anything done or omitted in the discharge or purported discharge of any functions to which this subsection applies unless the act or omission is shown to have been in bad faith.

(4) The functions to which subsection (3) applies are the functions of the exchange or clearing house so far as relating to, or to matters arising out of—

(*a*) its default rules, or
(*b*) any obligations to which it is subject by virtue of this Part.

(5) No person exercising any functions by virtue of arrangements made pursuant to paragraph 5 or 12 of Schedule 21 (delegation of functions in connection with default procedures), nor any officer or servant of such a person, shall be liable in damages for anything done or omitted in the discharge or purported discharge of those functions unless the act or omission is shown to have been in bad faith.

185 Power to make further provision by regulations

(1) The Secretary of State may by regulations make such further provision as appears to him necessary or expedient for the purposes of this Part.

(2) Provision may, in particular, be made—

(*a*) for integrating the provisions of this Part with the general law of insolvency, and
(*b*) for adapting the provisions of this Part in their application to overseas investment exchanges and clearing houses.

(3) Regulations under this section may add to, amend or repeal any of the provisions of this Part or provide that those provisions have effect subject to such additions, exceptions or adaptations as are specified in the regulations.

186 Supplementary provisions as to regulations

(1) Regulations under this Part may make different provision for different cases and may contain such incidental, transitional and other supplementary provisions as appear to the Secretary of State to be necessary or expedient.

(2) Regulations under this Part shall be made by statutory instrument which shall be subject to annulment in pursuance of a resolution of either House of Parliament.

187 Construction of references to parties to market contracts

(1) Where a person enters into market contracts in more than one capacity, the provisions of this Part apply (subject as follows) as if the contracts entered into in each different capacity were entered into by different persons.

(2) References in this Part to a market contract to which a person is a party include (subject as follows, and unless the context otherwise requires) contracts to which he is party as agent.

(3) The Secretary of State may by regulations—

(*a*) modify or exclude the operation of subsections (1) and (2), and (*b*) make provision as to the circumstances in which a person is to be regarded for the purposes of those provisions as acting in different capacities.

188 Meaning of 'default rules' and related expressions

(1) In this Part 'default rules' means rules of a recognised investment exchange or recognised clearing house which provide for the taking of action in the event of a person appearing to be unable, or likely to become unable, to meet his obligations in respect of one or more market contracts connected with the exchange or clearing house.

(2) References in this Part to a 'defaulter' are to a person in respect of whom action has been taken by a recognised investment exchange or recognised clearing house under its default rules, whether by declaring him to be a defaulter or otherwise; and references in this Part to 'default' shall be construed accordingly.

(3) In this Part 'default proceedings' means proceedings taken by a recognised investment exchange or recognised clearing house under its default rules.

(4) If an exchange or clearing house takes action under its default rules in respect of a person, all subsequent proceedings under its rules for the purposes of or in connection with the settlement of market contracts to which the defaulter is a party shall be treated as done under its default rules.

189 Meaning of 'relevant office-holder'

(1) The following are relevant office-holders for the purposes of this Part—

(*a*) the official receiver,
(*b*) any person acting in relation to a company as its liquidator, provisional liquidator, administrator or administrative receiver,
(*c*) any person acting in relation to an individual (or, in Scotland, any debtor within the meaning of the Bankruptcy (Scotland) Act 1985) as his trustee in bankruptcy or interim receiver of his property or as permanent or interim trustee in the sequestration of his estate,
(*d*) any person acting as administrator of an insolvent estate of a deceased person.

(2) In subsection (1)(*b*) 'company' means any company, society, association, partnership or other body which may be wound up under the Insolvency Act 1986.

190 Minor definitions

(1) In this Part—

'administrative receiver' has the meaning given by section 251 of the Insolvency Act 1986;
'charge' means any form of security, including a mortgage and, in Scotland, a heritable security;
'clearing house' has the same meaning as in the Financial Services Act 1986;
'interim trustee' and 'permanent trustee' have the same meaning as in the Bankruptcy (Scotland) Act 1985;
'investment' and 'investment exchange' have the same meaning as in the Financial Services Act 1986;
'overseas', in relation to an investment exchange or clearing house, means having its head office outside the United Kingdom;
'recognised' means recognised under the Financial Services Act 1986;
'set off', in relation to Scotland, includes compensation;
'The Stock Exchange' means The International Stock Exchange of the United Kingdom and the Republic of Ireland Limited;
'UK', in relation to an investment exchange or clearing house, means having its head office in the United Kingdom.

(2) References in this Part to settlement in relation to a market contract are to the discharge of the rights and liabilities of the parties to the contract, whether by performance, compromise or otherwise.

(3) In this Part the expressions 'margin' and 'cover for margin' have the same meaning.

(4) References in this Part to ensuring the performance of a transaction have the same meaning as in the Financial Services Act 1986.

(5) For the purposes of this Part a person shall be taken to have notice of a matter if he deliberately failed to make enquiries as to that matter in circumstances in which a reasonable and honest person would have done so.

This does not apply for the purposes of a provision requiring 'actual notice'.

(6) References in this Part to the law of insolvency include references to every provision made by or under the Insolvency Act 1986 or the Bankruptcy (Scotland) Act 1985; and in relation to a building society references to insolvency law or to any provision of the Insolvency Act 1986 are to that law or provision as modified by the Building Societies Act 1986.

(7) In relation to Scotland, references in this Part—

(*a*) to sequestration include references to the administration by a judicial factor of the insolvent estate of a deceased person, and

(*b*) to an interim or permanent trustee include references to a judicial factor on the insolvent estate of a deceased person,

unless the context otherwise requires.

191 Index of defined expressions

The following Table shows provisions defining or otherwise explaining expressions used in this Part (other than provisions defining or explaining an expression used only in the same section or paragraph)—

administrative receiver	section 190(1)
charge	section 190(1)
clearing house	section 190(1)
cover for margin	section 190(3)
default rules (and related expressions)	section 188
designated non-member	section 155(2)
ensuring the performance of a transaction	section 190(4)
insolvency law (and similar expressions)	section 190(6)
interim trustee	section 190(1) and (7)(*b*)
investment	section 190(1)
investment exchange	section 190(1)
margin	section 190(3)
market charge	section 173
market contract	section 155
notice	section 190(5)
overseas (in relation to an investment exchange or clearing house)	section 190(1)
party (in relation to a market contract)	section 187
permanent trustee	section 190(1) and (7)(*b*)
recognised	section 190(1)
relevant office-holder	section 189
sequestration	section 190(7)(*a*)
settlement and related expressions (in relation to a market contract)	section 190(2)
set off (in relation to Scotland)	section 190(1)
The Stock Exchange	section 190(1)
trustee, interim or permanent (in relation to Scotland)	section 190(7)(*b*)
UK (in relation to an investment exchange or clearing house)	section 190(1).

PART VIII

AMENDMENTS OF THE FINANCIAL SERVICES ACT 1986

192 Statements of principle

In Chapter V of Part I of the Financial Services Act 1986 (conduct of investment business), after section 47 insert—

'47A Statements of principle

(1) The Secretary of State may issue statements of principle with respect to the conduct and financial standing expected of persons authorised to carry on investment business.

(2) The conduct expected may include compliance with a code or standard issued by another person, as for the time being in force, and may allow for the exercise of discretion by any person pursuant to any such code or standard.

(3) Failure to comply with a statement of principle under this section is a ground for the taking of disciplinary action or the exercise of powers of intervention, but it does not give rise to any right of action by investors or other persons affected or affect the validity of any transaction.

(4) The disciplinary action which may be taken by virtue of subsection (3) is—

(a) the withdrawal or suspension of authorisation under section 28 or the termination or suspension of authorisation under section 33,

(b) the giving of a disqualification direction under section 59,

(c) the making of a public statement under section 60, or

(d) the application by the Secretary of State for an injunction, interdict or other order under section 61(1);

and the reference in that subsection to powers of intervention is to the powers conferred by Chapter VI of this Part.

(5) Where a statement of principle relates to compliance with a code or standard issued by another person, the statement of principle may provide—

(a) that failure to comply with the code or standard shall be a ground for the taking of disciplinary action, or the exercise of powers of intervention, only in such cases and to such extent as may be specified; and

(b) that no such action shall be taken, or any such power exercised, except at the request of the person by whom the code or standard in question was issued.

(6) The Secretary of State shall exercise his powers in such manner as appears to him appropriate to secure compliance with statements of principle under this section.

47B Modification or waiver of statements of principle in particular cases

(1) The relevant regulatory authority may on the application of any person—

(a) modify a statement of principle issued under section 47A so as to adapt it to his circumstances or to any particular kind of business carried on by him, or

(b) dispense him from compliance with any such statement of principle, generally or in relation to any particular kind of business carried on by him.

(2) The powers conferred by this section shall not be exercised unless it appears to the relevant regulatory authority—

(a) that compliance with the statement of principle in question would be unduly burdensome for the applicant having regard to the benefit which compliance would confer on investors, and

(b) that the exercise of those powers will not result in any undue risk to investors.

(3) The powers conferred by this section may be exercised unconditionally or subject to conditions; and section 47A(3) applies in the case of failure to comply with a condition as in the case of failure to comply with a statement of principle.

(4) The relevant regulatory authority for the purposes of this section is—

(*a*) in the case of a member of a recognised self-regulating organisation or professional body, in relation to investment business in the carrying on of which he is subject to the rules of the organisation or body, that organisation or body;

(*b*) in any other case, or in relation to other investment business, the Secretary of State.

(5) The references in paragraph 4(1) of Schedule 2 and paragraph 4(2) of Schedule 3 (requirements for recognition of self-regulating organisations and professional bodies) to monitoring and enforcement of compliance with statements of principle include monitoring and enforcement of compliance with conditions imposed by the organisation or body under this section.'.

193 Restriction of right to bring action for contravention of rules, regulations, &c

(1) In Chapter V of Part I of the Financial Services Act 1986 (conduct of investment business), after section 62 (actions for damages) insert—

'62A Restriction of right of action

(1) No action in respect of a contravention to which section 62 above applies shall lie at the suit of a person other than a private investor, except in such circumstances as may be specified by regulations made by the Secretary of State.

(2) The meaning of the expression 'private investor' for the purposes of subsection (1) shall be defined by regulations made by the Secretary of State.

(3) Regulations under subsection (1) may make different provision with respect to different cases.

(4) The Secretary of State shall, before making any regulations affecting the right to bring an action in respect of a contravention of any rules or regulations made by a person other than himself, consult that person.'.

(2) In section 114(5) of the Financial Services Act 1986 (transfer of functions to designated agency: excluded functions), after paragraph (*d*) insert—

'(*dd*) section 62A;'.

(3) In Schedule 11 to the Financial Services Act 1986 (friendly societies), after paragraph 22 insert—

'22A.—(1) No action in respect of a contravention to which paragraph 22(4) above applies shall lie at the suit of a person other than a private investor, except in such circumstances as may be specified by regulations made by the Registrar.

(2) The meaning of the expression 'private investor' for the purposes of sub-paragraph (1) shall be defined by regulations made by the Registrar.

(3) Regulations under sub-paragraph (1) may make different provision with respect to different cases.

(4) The Registrar shall, before making any regulations affecting the right to bring an action in respect of a contravention of any rules or regulations made by a person other than himself, consult that person.'.

(4) In paragraph 28(5) of Schedule 11 to the Financial Services Act 1986 (transfer of Registrar's functions to transferee body), after 'paragraphs 2 to 25' insert '(except paragraph 22A)'.

194 Application of designated rules and regulations to members of self-regulating organisations

In Chapter V of Part I of the Financial Services Act 1986 (conduct of investment business), after section 63 insert—

'63A Application of designated rules and regulations to members of self-regulating organisations

(1) The Secretary of State may in rules and regulations under—

(*a*) section 48 (conduct of business rules),
(*b*) section 49 (financial resources rules),
(*c*) section 55 (clients' money regulations), or
(*d*) section 56 (regulations as to unsolicited calls),

designate provisions which apply, to such extent as may be specified, to a member of a recognised self-regulating organisation in respect of investment business in the carrying on of which he is subject to the rules of the organisation.

(2) It may be provided that the designated rules or regulations have effect, generally or to such extent as may be specified, subject to the rules of the organisation.

(3) A member of a recognised self-regulating organisation who contravenes a rule or regulation applying to him by virtue of this section shall be treated as having contravened the rules of the organisation.

(4) It may be provided that, to such extent as may be specified, the designated rules or regulations may not be modified or waived (under section 63B below or section 50) in relation to a member of a recognised self-regulating organisation.

Where such provision is made any modification or waiver previously granted shall cease to have effect, subject to any transitional provision or saving contained in the rules or regulations.

(5) Except as mentioned in subsection (1), the rules and regulations referred to in that subsection do not apply to a member of a recognised self-regulating organisation in respect of investment business in the carrying on of which he is subject to the rules of the organisation.

63B Modification or waiver of designated rules and regulations

(1) A recognised self-regulating organisation may on the application of a member of the organisation—

(*a*) modify a rule or regulation designated under section 63A so as to adapt it to his circumstances or to any particular kind of business carried on by him, or
(*b*) dispense him from compliance with any such rule or regulation, generally or in relation to any particular kind of business carried on by him.

(2) The powers conferred by this section shall not be exercised unless it appears to the organisation—

(*a*) that compliance with the rule or regulation in question would be unduly burdensome for the applicant having regard to the benefit which compliance would confer on investors, and
(*b*) that the exercise of those powers will not result in any undue risk to investors.

(3) The powers conferred by this section may be exercised unconditionally or subject to conditions; and section 63A(3) applies in the case of a contravention of a condition as in the case of contravention of a designated rule or regulation.

(4) The reference in paragraph 4(1) of Schedule 2 (requirements for recognition of self-regulating organisations) to monitoring and enforcement of compliance with rules and regulations includes monitoring and enforcement of compliance with conditions imposed by the organisation under this section.'.

195 Codes of practice

In Chapter V of Part I of the Financial Services Act 1986 (conduct of investment business), after the sections inserted by section 194 above, insert—

'**63C Codes of practice**

(1) The Secretary of State may issue codes of practice with respect to any matters dealt with by statements of principle issued under section 47A or by rules or regulations made under any provision of this Chapter.

(2) In determining whether a person has failed to comply with a statement of principle—

(*a*) a failure by him to comply with any relevant provision of a code of practice may be relied on as tending to establish failure to comply with the statement of principle, and

(*b*) compliance by him with the relevant provisions of a code of practice may be relied on as tending to negative any such failure.

(3) A contravention of a code of practice with respect to a matter dealt with by rules or regulations shall not of itself give rise to any liability or invalidate any transaction; but in determining whether a person's conduct amounts to contravention of a rule or regulation—

(*a*) contravention by him of any relevant provision of a code of practice may be relied on as tending to establish liability, and

(*b*) compliance by him with the relevant provisions of a code of practice may be relied on as tending to negative liability.

(4) Where by virtue of section 63A (application of designated rules and regulations to members of self-regulating organisations) rules or regulations—

(*a*) do not apply, to any extent, to a member of a recognised self-regulating organisation, or

(*b*) apply, to any extent, subject to the rules of the organisation,

a code of practice with respect to a matter dealt with by the rules or regulations may contain provision limiting its application to a corresponding extent.'.

196 Relations with other regulatory authorities

In Part I of the Financial Services Act 1986 (regulation of investment business), after section 128 insert—

'CHAPTER XV
RELATIONS WITH OTHER REGULATORY AUTHORITIES

128A Relevance of other controls

In determining—

(*a*) in relation to a self-regulating organisation, whether the requirements of Schedule 2 are met, or

(*b*) in relation to a professional body, whether the requirements of Schedule 3 are met,

the Secretary of State shall take into account the effect of any other controls to which members of the organisation or body are subject.

128B Relevance of information given and action taken by other regulatory authorities

(1) The following provisions apply in the case of—

(*a*) a person whose principal place of business is in a country or territory outside the United Kingdom, or

(*b*) a person whose principal business is other than investment business;

and in relation to such a person 'the relevant regulatory authority' means the appropriate regulatory authority in that country or territory or, as the case may be, in relation to his principal business.

(2) The Secretary of State may regard himself as satisfied with respect to any matter relevant for the purposes of this Part if—

(*a*) the relevant regulatory authority informs him that it is satisfied with respect to that matter, and

(*b*) he is satisfied as to the nature and scope of the supervision exercised by that authority.

(3) In making any decision with respect to the exercise of his powers under this Part

in relation to any such person, the Secretary of State may take into account whether the relevant regulatory authority has exercised, or proposes to exercise, its powers in relation to that person.

(4) The Secretary of State may enter into such arrangements with other regulatory authorities as he thinks fit for the purposes of this section.

(5) Where any functions under this Part have been transferred to a designated agency, nothing in this section shall be construed as affecting the responsibility of the Secretary of State for the discharge of Community obligations or other international obligations of the United Kingdom.

128C Enforcement in support of overseas regulatory authority

(1) The Secretary of State may exercise his disciplinary powers or powers of intervention at the request of, or for the purpose of assisting, an overseas regulatory authority.

(2) The disciplinary powers of the Secretary of State means his powers—

(*a*) to withdraw or suspend authorisation under section 28 or to terminate or suspend authorisation under section 33,

(*b*) to give a disqualification direction under section 59,

(*c*) to make a public statement under section 60, or

(*d*) to apply for an injunction, interdict or other order under section 61(1);

and the reference to his powers of intervention is to the powers conferred by Chapter VI of this Part.

(3) An 'overseas regulatory authority' means an authority in a country or territory outside the United Kingdom which exercises—

(*a*) any function corresponding to—
   (i) a function of the Secretary of State under this Act, the Insurance Companies Act 1982 or the Companies Act 1985,
   (ii) a function under this Act of a designated agency, transferee body or competent authority, or
   (iii) a function of the Bank of England under the Banking Act 1987, or

(*b*) any functions in connection with the investigation of, or the enforcement of rules (whether or not having the force of law) relating to, conduct of the kind prohibited by the Company Securities (Insider Dealing) Act 1985, or

(*c*) any function prescribed for the purposes of this subsection, being a function which in the opinion of the Secretary of State relates to companies or financial services.

(4) In deciding whether to exercise those powers the Secretary of State may taken into account, in particular—

(*a*) whether corresponding assistance would be given in that country or territory to an authority exercising regulatory functions in the United Kingdom;

(*b*) whether the case concerns the breach of a law, or other requirement, which has no close parallel in the United Kingdom or involves the assertion of a jurisdiction not recognised by the United Kingdom;

(*c*) the seriousness of the case and its importance to persons in the United Kingdom;

(*d*) whether it is otherwise appropriate in the public interest to give the assistance sought.

(5) The Secretary of State may decline to exercise those powers unless the overseas regulatory authority undertakes to make such contribution towards the cost of their exercise as the Secretary of State considers appropriate.

(6) The reference in subsection (3)(*c*) to financial services includes, in particular, investment business, insurance and banking.'.

197 Construction of references to incurring civil liability

(1) In section 150(6) of the Financial Services Act 1986 (exclusion of liability in respect of false or misleading listing particulars), at the end insert—

'The reference above to a person incurring liability includes a reference to any other person being entitled as against that person to be granted any civil remedy or to rescind or repudiate any agreement.'.

(2) In section 154(5) of the Financial Services Act 1986 (exclusion of civil liability in respect of advertisements or other information in connection with listing application), at the end insert—

'The reference above to a person incurring civil liability includes a reference to any other person being entitled as against that person to be granted any civil remedy or to rescind or repudiate any agreement.'.

198 Offers of unlisted securities

(1) In Part V of the Financial Services Act 1986 (offers of unlisted securities), after section 160 insert—

'160A Exemptions

(1) The Secretary of State may by order exempt from sections 159 and 160 when issued in such circumstances as may be specified in the order—

    (*a*) advertisements appearing to him to have a private character, whether by reason of a connection between the person issuing them and those to whom they are addressed or otherwise;

    (*b*) advertisements appearing to him to deal with investments only incidentally;

    (*c*) advertisements issued to persons appearing to him to be sufficiently expert to understand any risks involved;

    (*d*) such other classes of advertisements as he thinks fit.

(2) The Secretary of State may by order exempt from sections 159 and 160 an advertisement issued in whatever circumstances which relates to securities appearing to him to be of a kind that can be expected normally to be bought or dealt in only by persons sufficiently expert to understand any risks involved.

(3) An order under subsection (1) or (2) may require a person who by virtue of the order is authorised to issue an advertisement to comply with such requirements as are specified in the order.

(4) An order made by virtue of subsection (1)(*a*), (*b*) or (*c*) or subsection (2) shall be subject to annulment in pursuance of a resolution of either House of Parliament; and no order shall be made by virtue of subsection (1)(*d*) unless a draft of it has been laid before and approved by a resolution of each House of Parliament.'.

(2) The following amendments of the Financial Services Act 1986 are consequential on that above.

(3) In section 159, in subsection (1) omit the words from the beginning to 'section 161 below,' and after subsection (2) insert—

'(3) Subsection (1) above has effect subject to section 160A (exemptions) and section 161 (exceptions).'.

(4) In section 160, in subsection (1) omit the words from the beginning to 'section 161 below,' and for subsections (6) to (9) substitute—

'(6) Subsection (1) above has effect subject to section 160A (exemptions) and section 161 (exceptions).'.

(5) In section 171, in subsection (1)(*b*) and subsection (3) for 'section 160(6) or (7)' substitute 'section 160A'.

199 Offers of securities by private companies and old public companies

In Part V of the Financial Services Act 1986 (offers of unlisted securities), in section 170 (advertisements by private companies and old public companies), for subsections (2) to (4) substitute—

'(2) The Secretary of State may by order exempt from subsection (1) when issued in such circumstances as may be specified in the order—

(*a*) advertisements appearing to him to have a private character, whether by reason of a connection between the person issuing them and those to whom they are addressed or otherwise;

(*b*) advertisements appearing to him to deal with investments only incidentally;

(*c*) advertisements issued to persons appearing to him to be sufficiently expert to understand any risks involved;

(*d*) such other classes of advertisements as he thinks fit.

(3) The Secretary of State may by order exempt from subsection (1) an advertisement issued in whatever circumstances which relates to securities appearing to him to be of a kind that can be expected normally to be bought or dealt in only by persons sufficiently expert to understand any risks involved.

(4) An order under subsection (2) or (3) may require a person who by virtue of the order is authorised to issue an advertisement to comply with such requirements as are specified in the order.

(4A) An order made by virtue of subsection (2)(*a*), (*b*) or (*c*) or subsection (3) shall be subject to annulment in pursuance of a resolution of either House of Parliament; and no order shall be made by virtue of subsection (2)(*d*) unless a draft of it has been laid before and approved by a resolution of each House of Parliament.'.

200 Jurisdiction of High Court and Court of Session

(1) In the Financial Services Act 1986, for section 188 (jurisdiction as respects actions concerning designated agency, &c), substitute—

'188 Jurisdiction of High Court and Court of Session

(1) Proceedings arising out of any act or omission (or proposed act or omission) of—

(*a*) a recognised self-regulating organisation,

(*b*) a designated agency,

(*c*) a transferee body, or

(*d*) the competent authority,

in the discharge or purported discharge of any of its functions under this Act may be brought in the High Court or the Court of Session.

(2) The jurisdiction conferred by subsection (1) is in addition to any other jurisdiction exercisable by those courts.'.

(2) In Schedule 5 to the Civil Jurisdiction and Judgments Act 1982 (proceedings excluded from general provisions as to allocation of jurisdiction within the United Kingdom), for paragraph 10 substitute—

'Financial Services Act 1986

10. Proceedings such as are mentioned in section 188 of the Financial Services Act 1986.'.

201 Directions to secure compliance with international obligations

In the Financial Services Act 1986, for section 192 (international obligations) substitute—

'192 International obligations

(1) If it appears to the Secretary of State—

(*a*) that any action proposed to be taken by an authority or body to which this section applies would be incompatible with Community obligations or any other international obligations of the United Kingdom, or

(*b*) that any action which that authority or body has power to take is required for the purpose of implementing any such obligation,

he may direct the authority or body not to take or, as the case may be, to take the action in question.

(2) The authorities and bodies to which this section applies are the following—

(*a*) a recognised self-regulating organisation,

(*b*) a recognised investment exchange (other than an overseas investment exchange),

(*c*) a recognised clearing house (other than an overseas clearing house),

(*d*) a designated agency,

(*e*) a transferee body,

(*f*) a competent authority.

(3) This section also applies to an approved exchange within the meaning of Part V of this Act in respect of any action which it proposes to take or has power to take in respect of rules applying to a prospectus by virtue of a direction under section 162(3) above.

(4) A direction under this section may include such supplementary or incidental requirements as the Secretary of State thinks necessary or expedient.

(5) Where the function of making or revoking a recognition order in respect of an authority or body to which this section applies is exercisable by a designated agency, any direction in respect of that authority or body shall be a direction requiring the agency to give the authority or body such a direction as is specified in the direction given by the Secretary of State.

(6) A direction under this section is enforceable, on the application of the person who gave it, by injunction or, in Scotland, by an order under section 45 of the Court of Session Act 1988.'.

202 Offers of short-dated debentures

In section 195 of the Financial Services Act 1986 (circumstances in which certain offers of debentures not treated as offers to the public), for 'repaid within less than one year of the date of issue' substitute 'repaid within five years of the date of issue'.

203 Standard of protection for investors

(1) In Schedule 2 to the Financial Services Act 1986 (requirements for recognition of self-regulating organisations), in paragraph 3 (safeguards for investors) for sub-paragraphs (1) and (2) substitute—

'(1) The organisation must have rules governing the carrying on of investment business by its members which, together with the statements of principle, rules, regulations and codes of practice to which its members are subject under Chapter V of Part I of this Act, are such as to afford an adequate level of protection for investors.

(2) In determining in any case whether an adequate level of protection is afforded for investors of any description, regard shall be had to the nature of the investment business carried on by members of the organisation, the kinds of investors involved and the effectiveness of the organisation's arrangements for enforcing compliance.'.

(2) In Schedule 3 to the Financial Services Act 1986 (requirements for recognition of professional bodies), for paragraph 3 (safeguards for investors) substitute—

'3.—(1) The body must have rules regulating the carrying on of investment business by persons certified by it which, together with the statements of principle, rules, regulations and codes of practice to which those persons are subject under Chapter V of Part I of this Act, afford an adequate level of protection for investors.

(2) In determining in any case whether an adequate level of protection is afforded for investors of any description, regard shall be had to the nature of the investment business

carried on by persons certified by the body, the kinds of investors involved and the effectiveness of the body's arrangements for enforcing compliance.'.

(3) The order bringing this section into force may provide that, for a transitional period, a self-regulating organisation or professional body may elect whether to comply with the new requirement having effect by virtue of subsection (1) or (2) above or with the requirement which it replaces.

The Secretary of State may by order specify when the transitional period is to end.

204 Costs of compliance

(1) In Schedule 2 to the Financial Services Act 1986 (requirements for recognition of self-regulating organisations), after paragraph 3 insert—

'Taking account of costs of compliance

3A. The organisation must have satisfactory arrangements for taking account, in framing its rules, of the cost to those to whom the rules would apply of complying with those rules and any other controls to which they are subject.';

and in Schedule 3 to that Act (requirements for recognition of professional body), after paragraph 3 insert—

'Taking account of costs of compliance

3A. The body must have satisfactory arrangements for taking account, in framing its rules, of the cost to those to whom the rules would apply of complying with those rules and any other controls to which they are subject.'.

(2) The additional requirements having effect by virtue of subsection (1) do not affect the status of a self-regulating organisation or professional body recognised before the commencement of that subsection; but if the Secretary of State is of the opinion that any of those requirements is not met in the case of such an organisation or body, he shall within one month of commencement give notice to the organisation or body stating his opinion.

(3) Where the Secretary of State gives such a notice, he shall not—

(*a*) take action to revoke the recognition of such an organisation or body on the ground that any of the additional requirements is not met, unless he considers it essential to do so in the interests of investors, or

(*b*) apply on any such ground for a compliance order under section 12 of the Financial Services Act 1986,

until after the end of the period of six months beginning with the date on which the notice was given.

(4) In Schedule 7 to the Financial Services Act 1986 (qualifications of designated agency), after paragraph 2 insert—

'Taking account of costs of compliance

2A.—(1) The agency must have satisfactory arrangements for taking account, in framing any provisions which it proposes to make in the exercise of its legislative functions, of the cost to those to whom the provisions would apply of complying with those provisions and any other controls to which they are subject.

(2) In this paragraph "legislative functions" means the functions of issuing or making statements of principle, rules, regulations or codes of practice.'.

(5) The additional requirement having effect by virtue of subsection (4) above does not affect the status of a designated agency to which functions have been transferred before the commencement of that subsection; but if the Secretary of State is of the opinion the requirement is not met in the case of such an agency, he shall within one month of commencement give notice to the agency stating his opinion.

(6) Where the Secretary of State gives such a notice he shall not take action under

section 115(2) of the Financial Services Act 1986 to resume any functions exercisable by such an agency on the ground that the additional requirement is not met until after the end of the period of six months beginning with the date on which the notice was given.

(7) References in this section to a recognised self-regulating organisation inlcude a recognised self-regulating organisation for friendly societies and references to a designated agency include a transferee body (within the meaning of that Act).
In relation to such an organisation or body—

(*a*) references to the Secretary of State shall be construed as references to the Registrar (within the meaning of Schedule 11 to the Financial Services Act 1986), and

(*b*) the reference to section 12 of that Act shall be construed as a reference to paragraph 6 of that Schedule.

205 Requirements for recognition of investment exchange

(1) In Schedule 4 to the Financial Services Act 1986 (requirements for recognition of investment exchange), after paragraph 5 insert—

'Supplementary

6.—(1) The provisions of this Schedule relate to an exchange only so far as it provides facilities for the carrying on of investment business; and nothing in this Schedule shall be construed as requiring an exchange to limit dealings on the exchange to dealings in investments.

(2) The references in this Schedule, and elsewhere in this Act, to ensuring the performance of transactions on an exchange are to providing satisfactory procedures (including default procedures) for the settlement of transactions on the exchange.'.

(2) The above amendment shall be deemed always to have had effect.

(3) In section 207(1) of the Financial Services Act 1986 (interpretation), at the appropriate place insert—
'"ensure" and "ensuring", in relation to the performance of transactions on an investment exchange, have the meaning given in paragraph 6 of Schedule 4 to this Act;'.

206 Consequential amendments and delegation of functions on commencement

(1) The Financial Services Act 1986 has effect with the amendments specified in Schedule 23 which are consequential on the amendments made by sections 192, 194, and 195.

(2) If immediately before the commencement of any provision of this Part which amends Part I of the Financial Services Act 1986—

(*a*) a designated agency is exercising by virtue of a delegation order under section 114 of that Act any functions of the Secretary of State under that Part, and

(*b*) no draft order is lying before Parliament resuming any of those functions,

the order bringing that provision into force may make, in relation to any functions conferred on the Secretary of State by the amendment, any such provision as may be made by an order under that section.

(3) If immediately before the commencement of any provision of Schedule 23, which amends Part III of the Financial Services Act 1986—

(*a*) a transferee body (within the meaning of that Act) is exercising by virtue of a transfer order under paragraph 28 of Schedule 11 to that Act any functions of the Registrar under that Part, and

(*b*) no draft order is lying before Parliament resuming any of those functions,

the order bringing that provision into force may make, in relation to any functions conferred on the Registrar by the amendment, any such provision as may be made by an order under that paragraph.

(4) References in the Financial Services Act 1986 to a delegation order made under section 114 of that Act or to a transfer order made under paragraph 28 of Schedule 11 to that Act include an order made containing any such provision as is authorised by subsection (2) or (3).

PART IX

TRANSFER OF SECURITIES

207 Transfer of securities

(1) The Secretary of State may make provision by regulations for enabling title to securities to be evidenced and transferred without a written instrument.

In this section—

(a) 'securities' means shares, stock, debentures, debenture stock, loan stock, bonds, units of a collective investment scheme within the meaning of the Financial Services Act 1986 and other securities of any description;

(b) references to title to securities include any legal or equitable interest in securities; and

(c) references to a transfer of title include a transfer by way of security.

(2) The regulations may make provision—

(a) for procedures for recording and transferring title to securities, and

(b) for the regulation of those procedures and the persons responsible for or involved in their operation.

(3) The regulations shall contain such safeguards as appear to the Secretary of State appropriate for the protection of investors and for ensuring that competition is not restricted, distorted or prevented.

(4) The regulations may for the purpose of enabling or facilitating the operation of the new procedures make provision with respect to the rights and obligations of persons in relation to securities dealt with under the procedures.

But the regulations shall be framed so as to secure that the rights and obligations in relation to securities dealt with under the new procedures correspond, so far as practicable, with those which would arise apart from any regulations under this section.

(5) The regulations may include such supplementary, incidental and transitional provisions as appear to the Secretary of State to be necessary or expedient.

In particular, provision may be made for the purpose of giving effect to—

(a) the transmission of title to securities by operation of law;

(b) any restriction on the transfer of title to securities arising by virtue of the provisions of any enactment or instrument, court order or agreement;

(c) any power conferred by any such provision on a person to deal with securities on behalf of the person entitled.

(6) The regulations may make provision with respect to the persons responsible for the operation of the new procedures—

(a) as to the consequences of their insolvency or incapacity, or

(b) as to the transfer from them to other persons of their functions in relation to the new procedures.

(7) The regulations may for the purposes mentioned above—

(a) modify or exclude any provision of any enactment or instrument, or any rule of law;

(b) apply, with such modifications as may be appropriate, the provisions of any enactment or instrument (including provisions creating criminal offences);

(c) require the payment of fees, or enable persons to require the payment of fees, of such amounts as may be specified in the regulations or determined in accordance with them;

(*d*) empower the Secretary of State to delegate to any person willing and able to discharge them any functions of his under the regulations.

(8) The regulations may make different provision for different cases.

(9) Regulations under this section shall be made by statutory instrument; and no such regulations shall be made unless a draft of the instrument has been laid before and approved by resolution of each House of Parliament.

PART X

MISCELLANEOUS AND GENERAL PROVISIONS

Miscellaneous

208 Summary proceedings in Scotland for offences in connection with disqualification of directors

In section 21 of the Company Directors Disqualification Act 1986 (application of provisions of the Insolvency Act 1986), after subsection (3) add—

'(4) For the purposes of summary proceedings in Scotland, section 431 of that Act applies to summary proceedings for an offence under section 11 or 13 of this Act as it applies to summary proceedings for an offence under Parts I to VII of that Act.'.

209 Prosecutions in connection with insider dealing

In section 8 of the Company Securities (Insider Dealing) Act 1985 (punishment of contraventions), in subsection (2) (institution of proceedings in England and Wales), for 'by the Secretary of State or by, or with the consent of, the Director of Public Prosecutions' substitute 'by, or with the consent of, the Secretary of State or the Director of Public Prosecutions'.

210 Restriction of duty to supply statements of premium income

(1) Schedule 3 to the Policyholders Protection Act 1975 (provisions with respect to levies on authorised insurance companies) is amended as follows.

(2) For paragraph 4 (statements of premium income to be sent to Secretary of State) substitute—

'4.—(1) The Secretary of State may by notice in writing require an authorised insurance company to send him a statement of—

(*a*) any income of the company for the year preceding that in which the notice is received by the company which is income liable to the general business levy, and

(*b*) any income of the company for that year which is income liable to the long term business levy.

(2) An authorised insurance company which receives a notice under this paragraph shall send the statement required by the notice to the Secretary of State within three months of receiving the notice.

(3) Where an authorised insurance company is required under this paragraph to send a statement to the Secretary of State in respect of income of both descriptions mentioned in sub-paragraph (1)(*a*) and (*b*) above it shall send a separate statement in respect of income of each description.'.

(3) In paragraph 5(3) (application of provisions of the Insurance Companies Act 1982 to failure to meet obligation imposed by paragraph 4) for 'the obligation imposed on an insurance company by paragraph 4' substitute 'an obligation imposed on an insurance company under paragraph 4'.

(4) In paragraph 6 (declaration and enforcement of levies) omit sub-paragraph (4) (provision about notices).

(5) After paragraph 7 insert—

'Notices under paragraphs 4 and 6

8. A notice under paragraph 4 or 6 above may be sent by post, and a letter containing such a notice shall be deemed to be properly addressed if it is addressed to the insurance company to which it is sent at its last known place of business in the United Kingdom.'.

211 Building societies: miscellaneous amendments

(1) In section 104 of the Building Societies Act 1986 (power to assimilate law relating to building societies and law relating to companies), in subsection (2) (relevant provisions of that Act), omit the word 'and' before paragraph (*d*) and after that paragraph add—

'; and

(*e*) section 110 (provisions exempting officers and auditors from liability).'.

(2) In Schedule 15 to the Building Societies Act 1986 (application of companies winding-up legislation)—

(*a*) in paragraph 1(*a*) (provisions of Insolvency Act 1986 applied) for 'and XII' substitute, ', XII and XIII';

(*b*) in paragraph 3(2)(*b*) (adaptations: references to be omitted), omit ', a shadow director'.

(3) In the Company Directors Disqualification Act 1986, after section 22 insert—

'22A Application of Act to building societies

(1) This Act applies to building societies as it applies to companies.

(2) References in this Act to a company, or to a director or an officer of a company include, respectively, references to a building society within the meaning of the Building Societies Act 1986 or to a director or officer, within the meaning of that Act, of a building society.

(3) In relation to a building society the definition of 'shadow director' in section 22(5) applies with the substitution of 'building society' for 'company'.

(4) In the application of Schedule 1 to the directors of a building society, references to provisions of the Insolvency Act or the Companies Act include references to the corresponding provisions of the Building Societies Act 1986.'.

General

212 Repeals

The enactments mentioned in Schedule 24 are repealed to the extent specified there.

213 Provisions extending to Northern Ireland

(1) The provisions of this Act extend to Northern Ireland so far as they amend, or provide for the amendment of, an enactment which so extends.

(2) So far as any provision of this Act amends the Companies Act 1985 or the Insolvency Act 1986, its application to companies registered or incorporated in Northern Ireland is subject to section 745(1) of the Companies Act 1985 or section 441(2) of the Insolvency Act 1986, as the case may be.

(3) In Part III (investigations and powers to obtain information), sections 82 to 91, (powers exercisable to assist overseas regulatory authorities) extend to Northern Ireland.

(4) Part VI (mergers and related matters) extends to Northern Ireland.

(5) In Part VII (financial markets and insolvency) the following provisions extend to Northern Ireland—

(*a*) sections 154 and 155 (introductory provisions and definition of 'market contract'),

(*b*) section 156 and Schedule 21 (additional requirements for recognition of investment exchange or clearing house),

(*c*) sections 157, 160, 162, and 166 to 169 (provisions relating to recognised investment exchanges and clearing houses), (*d*) sections 170 to 172 (power to extend provisions to other financial markets),

(*e*) section 184 (indemnity for certain acts), and

(*f*)sections 185 to 191 (supplementary provisions).

(6) Part VIII (amendments of Financial Services Act 1986) extends to Northern Ireland.

(7) Part IX (transfer of securities) extends to Northern Ireland.

Subject to any Order made after the passing of this Act by virtue of section 3(1)(*a*) of the Northern Ireland Constitution Act 1973, the transfer of securities shall not be a transferred matter for the purposes of that Act but shall for the purposes of section 3(2) be treated as specified in Schedule 3 to that Act.

(8) In Part X (miscellaneous and general provisions), this section and sections 214 to 216 (general provisions) extend to Northern Ireland.

(9) Except as mentioned above, the provisions of this Act do not extend to Northern Ireland.

214 Making of corresponding provision for Northern Ireland

(1) An Order in Council under paragraph 1(1)(*b*) of Schedule 1 to the Northern Ireland Act 1974 (legislation for Northern Ireland in the interim period) which contains a statement that it is only made for purposes corresponding to the purposes of provisions of this Act to which this section applies—

(*a*) shall not be subject to paragraph 1(4) and (5) of that Schedule (affirmative resolution of both Houses of Parliament), but

(*b*) shall be subject to annulment in pursuance of a resolution of either House of Parliament.

(2) The provisions of this Act to which this section applies are—

(*a*) Parts I to V, and

(*b*) Part VII, except sections 156, 157, 169 and Schedule 21.

215 Commencement and transitional provisions

(1) The following provisions of this Act come into force on Royal Assent—

(*a*) in Part V (amendments of company law), section 141 (application to declare dissolution of company void);

(*b*) in Part VI (mergers)—

    (i) sections 147 to 150, and

    (ii) paragraphs 2 to 12, 14 to 16, 18 to 20, 22 to 25 of Schedule 20, and section 153 so far as relating to those paragraphs;

(*c*) in Part VIII (amendments of the Financial Services Act 1986), section 202 (offers of short-dated debentures);

(*d*) in Part X (miscellaneous and general provisions), the repeals made by Schedule 24 in sections 71, 74, 88 and 89 of, and Schedule 9 to, the Fair Trading Act 1973, and section 212 so far as relating to those repeals.

(2) The other provisions of this Act come into force on such day as the Secretary of State may appoint by order made by statutory instrument; and different days may be appointed for different provisions and different purposes.

(3) An order bringing into force any provision may contain such transitional provisions and savings as appear to the Secretary of State to be necessary or expedient.

(4) The Secretary of State may also by order under this section amend any enactment which refers to the commencement of a provision brought into force by the order so as to substitute a reference to the actual date on which it comes into force.

216 Short title

This Act may be cited as the Companies Act 1989.

SCHEDULES
SCHEDULE 1

Section 4(2)

FORM AND CONTENT OF COMPANY ACCOUNTS

1. Schedule 4 to the Companies Act 1985 (form and content of company accounts) is amended as follows.

Group undertakings

2.—(1) For 'group companies', wherever occurring, substitute 'group undertakings'.

(2) That expression occurs—

 (*a*) in Balance Sheet Format 1, in Items B.III.1 and 2, C.II.2, C.III.1, E.6 and H.6;
 (*b*) in Balance Sheet Format 2—

   (i) under the heading 'ASSETS', in Items B.III.1 and 2, C.II.2 and C.III.1;
   (ii) under the heading 'LIABILITIES', in Item C.6;

 (*c*) in the Profit and Loss Accounts Formats—

   (i) in Format 1, Item 7;
   (ii) in Format 2, Item 9;
   (iii) in Format 3, Item B.3;
   (iv) in Format 4, Item B.5;

 (*d*) in Notes (15) and (16) to the profit and loss account formats; and
 (*e*) in the second sentence of paragraph 53(2) (exclusion from requirement to state separately certain loans).

Participating interests

3.—(1) For 'shares in related companies', wherever occurring, substitute 'participating interests'.

(2) That expression occurs—

 (*a*) in Balance Sheet Format 1, Item B.III.3;
 (*b*) in Balance Sheet Format 2, under the heading 'ASSETS', in Item B.III.3;
 (*c*) in the Profit and Loss Accounts Formats—

   (i) in Format 1, Item 8;
   (ii) in Format 2, Item 10;
   (iii) in Format 3, Item B.4;
   (iv) in Format 4, item B.6.

4.—(1) For 'related companies', wherever occurring in any other context, substitute 'undertakings in which the company has a participating interest'.

(2) Those contexts are—

 (*a*) in Balance Sheet Format 1, in Items B.III.4, C.II.3, E.7 and H.7;
 (*b*) in Balance Sheet Format 2—

   (i) under the heading 'ASSETS', in Items B.III.4 and C.II.3;
   (ii) under the heading 'LIABILITIES', in Item C.7.

Consistency of accounting policies

5. For paragraph 11 (consistency of accounting policy from one year to the next) substitute—

'11. Accounting policies shall be applied consistently within the same accounts and from one financial year to the next.'.

Revaluation reserve

6. In paragraph 34 (revaluation reserve), for sub-paragraph (3) (circumstances in which reduction of reserve required or permitted) substitute—

'(3) An amount may be transferred from the revaluation reserve—

 (*a*) to the profit and loss account, if the amount was previously charged to that account or represents realised profit, or
 (*b*) on capitalisation;

and the revaluation reserve shall be reduced to the extent that the amounts transferred to it are no longer necessary for the purposes of the valuation method used.

(3A) In sub-paragraph (3)(*b*) 'capitalisation', in relation to an amount standing to the credit of the revaluation reserve, means applying it in wholly or partly paying up unissued shares in the company to be allotted to members of the company as fully or partly paid shares.

(3B) The revaluation reserve shall not be reduced except as mentioned in this paragraph.'.

Compliance with accounting standards

7. After paragraph 36 (disclosure of accounting policies) insert—

'36A. It shall be stated whether the accounts have been prepared in accordance with applicable accounting standards and particulars of any material departure from those standards and the reasons for it shall be given.'.

Provision for taxation

8. For paragraph 47 (provision for taxation) substitute—

'47. The amount of any provision for deferred taxation shall be stated separately from the amount of any provision for other taxation.'.

Loans in connection with assistance for purchase of company's own shares

9. In paragraph 51(2) (disclosure of outstanding loans in connection with certain cases of financial assistance for purchase of company's own shares), after '153(4)(*b*)' insert ', (*bb*)'.

Obligation to show corresponding amounts for previous financial year

10. In paragraph 58(3) (exceptions from obligation to show corresponding amount for previous financial year), for paragraphs (*a*) to (*c*) substitute—

'(*a*) paragraph 13 of Schedule 4A (details of accounting treatment of acquisitions),
(*b*) paragraphs 2, 8(3), 16, 21(1)(*d*), 22(4) and (5), 24(3) and (4) and 27(3) and (4) of Schedule 5 (shareholdings in other undertakings),
(*c*) Parts II and III of Schedule 6 (loans and other dealings in favour of directors and others), and
(*d*) paragraphs 42 and 46 above (fixed assets and reserves and provisions).'.

Special provisions where company is parent company or subsidiary undertaking

11.—(1) For the heading to Part IV (special provisions where the company is a holding or subsidiary company) substitute—

'PART IV

SPECIAL PROVISIONS WHERE COMPANY IS A PARENT COMPANY OR
SUBSIDIARY UNDERTAKING'.

(2) In that Part for paragraph 59 substitute—

'*Dealings with or interests in group undertakings*

59. Where a company is a parent company or a subsidiary undertaking and any item required by Part I of this Schedule to be shown in the company's balance sheet in relation to group undertakings includes—

(*a*) amounts attributable to dealings with or interests in any parent undertaking or fellow subsidiary undertaking, or
(*b*) amounts attributable to dealings with or interests in any subsidiary undertaking of the company,

the aggregate amounts within paragraphs (*a*) and (*b*) respectively shall be shown as separate items, either by way of subdivision of the relevant item in the balance sheet or in a note to the company's accounts.'.

(3) After that paragraph insert—

'*Guarantees and other financial commitments in favour of group undertakings*

59A. Commitments within any of sub-paragraphs (1) to (5) of paragraph 50 (guarantees and other financial commitements) which are undertaken on behalf of or for the benefit of—

(*a*) any parent undertaking or fellow subsidiary undertaking, or
(*b*) any subsidiary undertaking of the company,

shall be stated separately from the other commitments within that sub-paragraph, and commitments within paragraph (*a*) shall also be stated separately from those within paragraph (*b*).'.

SCHEDULE 2

Section 5(2)

[Schedule 4A to the Companies Act 1985]

Form and Content of Group Accounts

General rules

1.—(1) Group accounts shall comply so far as practicable with the provisions of Schedule 4 as if the undertakings included in the consolidation ('the group') were a single company.

(2) In particular, for the purposes of paragraph 59 of that Schedule (dealings with or interests in group undertakings) as it applies to group accounts—

  (a) any subsidiary undertakings of the parent company not included in the consolidation shall be treated as subsidiary undertakings of the group, and

  (b) if the parent company is itself a subsidiary undertaking, the group shall be treated as a subsidiary undertaking of any parent undertaking of that company, and the reference to fellow-subsidiary undertakings shall be construed accordingly.

(3) Where the parent company is treated as an investment company for the purposes of Part V of that Schedule (special provisions for investment companies) the group shall be similarly treated.

2.—(1) The consolidated balance sheet and profit and loss account shall incorporate in full the information contained in the individual accounts of the undertakings included in the consolidation, subject to the adjustments authorised or required by the following provisions of this Schedule and to such other adjustments (if any) as may be appropriate in accordance with generally accepted accounting principles or practice.

(2) If the financial year of a subsidiary undertaking included in the consolidation differs from that of the parent company, the group accounts shall be made up—

  (a) from the accounts of the subsidiary undertaking for its financial year last ending before the end of the parent company's financial year, provided that year ended no more than three months before that of the parent company, or

  (b) from interim accounts prepared by the subsidiary undertaking as at the end of the parent company's financial year.

3.—(1) Where assets and liabilities to be included in the group accounts have been valued or otherwise determined by undertakings according to accounting rules differing from those used for the group accounts, the values or amounts shall be adjusted so as to accord with the rules used for the group accounts.

(2) If it appears to the directors of the parent company that there are special reasons for departing from sub-paragraph (1) they may do so, but particulars of any such departure, the reasons for it and its effect shall be given in a note to the accounts.

(3) The adjustments referred to in this paragraph need not be made if they are not material for the purpose of giving a true and fair view.

4. Any differences of accounting rules as between a parent company's individual accounts for a financial year and its group accounts shall be disclosed in a note to the latter accounts and the reasons for the difference given.

5. Amounts which in the particular context of any provision of this Schedule are not material may be disregarded for the purposes of that provision.

Elimination of group transactions

6.—(1) Debts and claims between undertakings included in the consolidation, and income and expenditure relating to transactions between such undertakings, shall be eliminated in preparing the group accounts.

(2) Where profits and losses resulting from transactions between undertakings included in the consolidation are included in the book value of assets, they shall be eliminated in preparing the group accounts.

(3) The elimination required by sub-paragraph (2) may be effected in proportion to the group's interest in the shares of the undertakings.

(4) Sub-paragraphs (1) and (2) need not be complied with if the amounts concerned are not material for the purpose of giving a true and fair view.

Acquisition and merger accounting

7.—(1) The following provisions apply where an undertaking becomes a subsidiary undertaking of the parent company.

(2) That event is referred to in those provisions as an 'acquisition', and references to the 'undertaking acquired' shall be construed accordingly.

8. An acquisition shall be accounted for by the acquisition method of accounting unless the conditions for accounting for it as a merger are met and the merger method of accounting is adopted.

9.—(1) The acquisition method of accounting is as follows.

(2) The identifiable assets and liabilities of the undertaking acquired shall be included in the consolidated balance sheet at their fair values as at the date of acquisition.

In this paragraph the 'identifiable' assets or liabilities of the undertaking acquired means the assets or liabilities which are capable of being disposed of or discharged separately, without disposing of a business of the undertaking.

(3) The income and expenditure of the undertaking acquired shall be brought into the group accounts only as from the date of the acquisition.

(4) There shall be set off against the acquisition cost of the interest in the shares of the undertaking held by the parent company and its subsidiary undertakings the interest of the parent company and its subsidiary undertakings in the adjusted capital and reserves of the undertaking acquired.

For this purpose—

'the acquisition cost' means the amount of any cash consideration and the fair value of any other consideration, together with such amount (if any) in respect of fees and other expenses of the acquisition as the company may determine, and

'the adjusted capital and reserves' of the undertaking acquired means its capital and reserves at the date of the acquisition after adjusting the identifiable assets and liabilities of the undertaking to fair values as at that date.

(5) The resulting amount if positive shall be treated as goodwill, and if negative as a negative consolidation difference.

10.—(1) The conditions for accounting for an acquisition as a merger are—

(a) that at least 90 per cent of the nominal value of the relevant shares in the undertaking acquired is held by or on behalf of the parent company and its subsidiary undertakings,

(b) that the proportion referred to in paragraph (a) was attained pursuant to an arrangement providing for the issue of equity shares by the parent company or one or more of its subsidiary undertakings,

(c) that the fair value of any consideration other than the issue of equity shares given pursuant to the arrangement by the parent company and its subsidiary undertakings did not exceed 10 per cent of the nominal value of the equity shares issued, and

(d) that adoption of the merger method of accounting accords with generally accepted accounting principles or practice.

(2) The reference in sub-paragraph (1)(a) to the 'relevant shares' in an undertaking acquired is to those carrying unrestricted rights to participate both in distributions and in the assets of the undertaking upon liquidation.

11.—(1) The merger method of accounting is as follows.

(2) The assets and liabilities of the undertaking acquired shall be brought into the group accounts at the figures at which they stand in the undertaking's accounts, subject to any adjustment authorised or required by this Schedule.

(3) The income and expenditure of the undertaking acquired shall be included in the group accounts for the entire financial year, including the period before the acquisition.

(4) The group accounts shall show corresponding amounts relating to the previous financial year as if the undertaking acquired had been included in the consolidation throughout that year.

(5) There shall be set off against the aggregate of—

(a) the appropriate amount in respect of qualifying shares issued by the parent company or its subsidiary undertakings in consideration for the acquisition of shares in the undertaking acquired, and

(b) the fair value of any other consideration for the acquisition of shares in the undertaking acquired, determined as at the date when those shares were acquired, the nominal value of the issued share capital of the undertaking acquired held by the parent company and its subsidiary undertakings.

(6) The resulting amount shall be shown as an adjustment to the consolidated reserves.

(7) In sub-paragraph (5)(*a*) 'qualifying shares' means—

(*a*) shares in relation to which section 131 (merger relief) applies, in respect of which the appropriate amount is the nominal value; or

(*b*) shares in relation to which section 132 (relief in respect of group reconstructions) applies, in respect of which the appropriate amount is the nominal value together with any minimum premium value within the meaning of that section.

12.—(1) Where a group is acquired, paragraphs 9 to 11 apply with the following adaptations.

(2) References to shares of the undertaking acquired shall be construed as references to shares of the parent undertaking of the group.

(3) Other references to the undertaking acquired shall be construed as references to the group; and references to the assets and liabilities, income and expenditure and capital and reserves of the undertaking acquired shall be construed as references to the assets and liabilities, income and expenditure and capital and reserves of the group after making the set-offs and other adjustments required by this Schedule in the case of group accounts.

13.—(1) The following information with respect to acquisitions taking place in the financial year shall be given in a note to the accounts.

(2) There shall be stated—

(*a*) the name of the undertaking acquired or, where a group was acquired, the name of the parent undertaking of that group, and

(*b*) whether the acquisition has been accounted for by the acquisition or the merger method of accounting;

and in relation to an acquisition which significantly affects the figures shown in the group accounts, the following further information shall be given.

(3) The composition and fair value of the consideration for the acquisition given by the parent company and its subsidiary undertakings shall be stated.

(4) The profit or loss of the undertaking or group acquired shall be stated—

(*a*) for the period from the beginning of the financial year of the undertaking or, as the case may be, of the parent undertaking of the group, up to the date of the acquisition, and

(*b*) for the previous financial year of that undertaking or parent undertaking;

and there shall also be stated the date on which the financial year referred to in paragraph (*a*) began.

(5) Where the acquisition method of accounting has been adopted, the book values immediately prior to the acquisition, and the fair values at the date of acquisition, of each class of assets and liabilities of the undertaking or group acquired shall be stated in tabular form, including a statement of the amount of any goodwill or negative consolidation difference arising on the acquisition, together with an explanation of any significant adjustments made.

(6) Where the merger method of accounting has been adopted, an explanation shall be given of any significant adjustments made in relation to the amounts of the assets and liabilities of the undertaking or group acquired, together with a statement of any resulting adjustment to the consolidated reserves (including the re-statement of opening consolidated reserves).

(7) In ascertaining for the purposes of sub-paragraph (4), (5) or (6) the profit or loss of a group, the book values of assets and liabilities of a group or the amount of the assets and liabilities of a group, the set-offs and other adjustments required by this Schedule in the case of group accounts shall be made.

14.—(1) There shall also be stated in a note to the accounts the cumulative amount of goodwill resulting from acquisitions in that and earlier financial years which has been written off.

(2) That figure shall be shown net of any goodwill attributable to subsidiary undertakings or businesses disposed of prior to the balance sheet date.

15. Where during the financial year there has been a disposal of an undertaking or group which significantly affects the figures shown in the group accounts, there shall be stated in a note to the accounts—

(*a*) the name of that undertaking or, as the case may be, of the parent undertaking of that group, and

(*b*) the extent to which the profit or loss shown in the group accounts is attributable to profit or loss of that undertaking or group.

16. The information required by paragraph 13, 14 or 15 above need not be disclosed with respect to an undertaking which —

(a) is established under the law of a country outside the United Kingdom, or

(b) carries on business outside the United Kingdom,

if in the opinion of the directors of the parent company the disclosure would be seriously prejudicial to the business of that undertaking or to the business of the parent company or any of its subsidiary undertakings and the Secretary of State agrees that the information should not be disclosed.

Minority interests

17.—(1) The formats set out in Schedule 4 have effect in relation to group accounts with the following additions.

(2) In the Balance Sheet Formats a further item headed 'Minority interests' shall be added—

(a) in Format 1, either after item J or at the end (after item K), and

(b) in Format 2, under the general heading 'LIABILITIES', between items A and B;

and under that item shall be shown the amount of capital and reserves attributable to shares in subsidiary undertakings included in the consolidation held by or on behalf of persons other than the parent company and its subsidiary undertakings.

(3) In the Profit and Loss Account Formats a further item headed 'Minority interests' shall be added—

(a) in Format 1, between items 14 and 15,

(b) in Format 2, between items 16 and 17,

(c) in Format 3, between items 7 and 8 in both sections A and B, and

(d) in Format 4, between items 9 and 10 in both sections A and B;

and under that item shall be shown the amount of any profit or loss on ordinary activities attributable to shares in subsidiary undertakings included in the consolidation held by or on behalf of persons other than the parent company and its subsidiary undertakings.

(4) In the Profit and Loss Account Formats a further item headed 'Minority interests' shall be added—

(a) in Format 1, between items 18 and 19,

(b) in Format 2, between items 20 and 21,

(c) in Format 3, between items 9 and 10 in section A and between items 8 and 9 in section B, and

(d) in Format 4, between items 11 and 12 in section A and between items 10 and 11 in section B;

and under that item shall be shown the amount of any profit or loss on extraordinary activities attributable to shares in subsidiary undertakings included in the consolidation held by or on behalf of persons other than the parent company and its subsidiary undertakings.

(5) For the purposes of paragraph 3(3) and (4) of Schedule 4 (power to adapt or combine items)—

(a) the additional item required by sub-paragraph (2) above shall be treated as one to which a letter is assigned, and

(b) the additional items required by sub-paragraphs (3) and (4) above shall be treated as ones to which an Arabic number is assigned.

Interests in subsidiary undertakings excluded from consolidation

18. The interest of the group in subsidiary undertakings excluded from consolidation under section 229(4) (undertakings with activities different from those of undertakings included in the consolidation), and the amount of profit or loss attributable to such an interest, shall be shown in the consolidated balance sheet or, as the case may be, in the consolidated profit and loss account by the equity method of accounting (including dealing with any goodwill arising in accordance with paragraphs 17 to 19 and 21 of Schedule 4).

Joint ventures

19.—(1) Where an undertaking included in the consolidation manages another undertaking jointly with one or more undertakings not included in the consolidation, that other undertaking ('the joint venture') may, if it is not—

(a) a body corporate, or

(b) a subsidiary undertaking of the parent company,

be dealt with in the group accounts by the method of proportional consolidation.

(2) The provisions of this Part relating to the preparation of consolidated accounts apply, with any necessary modifications, to proportional consolidation under this paragraph.

Associated undertakings

20.—(1) An 'associated undertaking' means an undertaking in which an undertaking included in the consolidation has a participating interest and over whose operating and financial policy it exercises a significant influence, and which is not—

 (a) a subsidiary undertaking of the parent company, or
 (b) a joint venture dealt with in accordance with paragraph 19.

(2) Where an undertaking holds 20 per cent or more of the voting rights in another undertaking, it shall be presumed to exercise such an influence over it unless the contrary is shown.

(3) The voting rights in an undertaking means the rights conferred on shareholders in respect of their shares or, in the case of an undertaking not having a share capital, on members, to vote at general meetings of the undertaking on all, or substantially all, matters.

(4) The provisions of paragraphs 5 to 11 of Schedule 10A (rights to be taken into account and attribution of rights) apply in determining for the purposes of this paragraph whether an undertaking holds 20 per cent or more of the voting rights in another undertaking.

21.—(1) The formats set out in Schedule 4 have effect in relation to group accounts with the following modifications.

(2) In the Balance Sheet Formats the items headed 'Participating interests', that is—

 (a) in Format 1, item B.III.3, and
 (b) In Format 2, item B.III.3 under the heading 'ASSETS',

shall be replaced by two items, 'Interests in associated undertakings' and 'Other participating interests'.

(3) In the Profit and Loss Account Formats, the items headed 'Income from participating interests', that is—

 (a) in Format 1, item 8,
 (b) in Format 2, item 10,
 (c) in Format 3, item B.4, and
 (d) in Format 4, item B.6,

shall be replaced by two items, 'Income from interests in associated undertakings' and 'Income from other participating interests'.

22.—(1) The interest of an undertaking in an associated undertaking, and the amount of profit or loss attributable to such an interest, shall be shown by the equity method of accounting (including dealing with any goodwill arising in accordance with paragraphs 17 to 19 and 21 of Schedule 4).

(2) Where the associated undertaking is itself a parent undertaking, the net assets and profits or losses to be taken into account are those of the parent and its subsidiary undertakings (after making any consolidation adjustments).

(3) The equity method of accounting need not be applied if the amounts in question are not material for the purpose of giving a true and fair view.

SCHEDULE 3

Section 6(2)

[Schedule 5 to the Companies Act 1985]

Disclosure of Information: Related Undertakings

Part I

Companies not Required to Prepare Group Accounts

Subsidiary undertakings

1.—(1) The following information shall be given where at the end of the financial year the company has subsidiary undertakings.

(2) The name of each subsidiary undertaking shall be stated.

(3) There shall be stated with respect to each subsidiary undertaking—

 (a) if it is incorporated outside Great Britain, the country in which it is incorporated;

(b) if it is incorporated in Great Britain, whether it is registered in England and Wales or in Scotland;

(c) if it is unincorporated, the address of its principal place of business.

(4) The reason why the company is not required to prepare group accounts shall be stated.

(5) If the reason is that all the subsidiary undertakings of the company fall within the exclusions provided for in section 229, it shall be stated with respect to each subsidiary undertaking which of those exclusions applies.

Holdings in subsidiary undertakings

2.—(1) There shall be stated in relation to shares of each class held by the company in a subsidiary undertaking—

(a) the identity of the class, and

(b) the proportion of the nominal value of the shares of that class represented by those shares.

(2) The shares held by or on behalf of the company itself shall be distinguished from those attributed to the company which are held by or on behalf of a subsidiary undertaking.

Financial information about subsidiary undertakings

3.—(1) There shall be disclosed with respect to each subsidiary undertaking—

(a) the aggregate amount of its capital and reserves as at the end of its relevant financial year, and

(b) its profit or loss for that year.

(2) That information need not be given if the company is exempt by virtue of section 228 from the requirement to prepare group accounts (parent company included in accounts of larger group).

(3) That information need not be given if—

(a) the subsidiary undertaking is not required by any provision of this Act to deliver a copy of its balance sheet for its relevant financial year and does not otherwise publish that balance sheet in Great Britain or elsewhere, and

(b) the company's holding is less than 50 per cent of the nominal value of the shares in the undertaking.

(4) Information otherwise required by this paragraph need not be given if it is not material.

(5) For the purposes of this paragraph the 'relevant financial year' of a subsidiary undertaking is—

(a) if its financial year ends with that of the company, that year, and

(b) if not, its financial year ending last before the end of the company's financial year.

Financial years of subsidiary undertakings

4. Where the financial year of one or more subsidiary undertakings did not end with that of the company, there shall be stated in relation to each such undertaking—

(a) the reasons why the company's directors consider that its financial year should not end with that of the company, and

(b) the date on which its last financial year ended (last before the end of the company's financial year).

Instead of the dates required by paragraph (b) being given for each subsidiary undertaking the earliest and latest of those dates may be given.

Further information about subsidiary undertakings

5.—(1) There shall be disclosed—

(a) any qualifications contained in the auditors' reports on the accounts of subsidiary undertakings for financial years ending with or during the financial year of the company, and

(b) any note or saving contained in such accounts to call attention to a matter which, apart from the note or saving, would properly have been referred to in such a qualification,

in so far as the matter which is the subject of the qualification or note is not covered by the company's own accounts and is material from the point of view of its members.

(2) The aggregate amount of the total investment of the company in the shares of subsidiary undertakings shall be stated by way of the equity method of valuation, unless—

(a) the company is exempt from the requirement to prepare group accounts by virtue of section 228 (parent company included in accounts of larger group), and (*b*) the directors state their opinion that the aggregate value of the assets of the company consisting of shares in, or amounts owing (whether on account of a loan or otherwise) from, the company's subsidiary undertakings is not less than the aggregate of the amounts at which those assets are stated or included in the company's balance sheet.

(3) In so far as information required by this paragraph is not obtainable, a statement to that effect shall be given instead.

Shares and debentures of company held by subsidiary undertakings

6.—(1) The number, description and amount of the shares in and debentures of the company held by or on behalf of its subsidiary undertakings shall be disclosed.

(2) Sub-paragraph (1) does not apply in relation to shares or debentures in the case of which the subsidiary undertaking is concerned as personal representative or, subject as follows, as trustee.

(3) The exception for shares or debentures in relation to which the subsidiary undertaking is concerned as trustee does not apply if the company, or any subsidiary undertaking of the company, is beneficially interested under the trust, otherwise than by way of security only for the purposes of a transaction entered into by it in the ordinary course of a business which includes the lending of money.

(4) Schedule 2 to this Act has effect for the interpretation of the reference in sub-paragraph (3) to a beneficial interest under a trust.

Significant holdings in undertakings other than subsidiary undertakings

7.—(1) The information required by paragraphs 8 and 9 shall be given where at the end of the financial year the company has a significant holding in an undertaking which is not a subsidiary undertaking of the company.

(2) A holding is significant for this purpose if—

(*a*) it amounts to 10 per cent or more of the nominal value of any class of shares in the undertaking, or

(*b*) the amount of the holding (as stated or included in the company's accounts) exceeds one-tenth of the amount (as so stated) of the company's assets.

8.—(1) The name of the undertaking shall be stated.

(2) There shall be stated—

(*a*) if the undertaking is incorporated outside Great Britain, the country in which it is incorporated;

(*b*) if it is incorporated in Great Britain, whether it is registered in England and Wales or in Scotland;

(*c*) if it is unincorporated, the address of its principal place of business.

(3) There shall also be stated—

(*a*) the identity of each class of shares in the undertaking held by the company, and

(*b*) the proportion of the nominal value of the shares of that class represented by those shares.

9.—(1) Where the company has a significant holding in an undertaking amounting to 20 per cent or more of the nominal value of the shares in the undertaking, there shall also be stated—

(*a*) the aggregate amount of the capital and reserves of the undertaking as at the end of its relevant financial year, and

(*b*) its profit or loss for that year.

(2) That information need not be given if—

(*a*) the company is exempt by virtue of section 228 from the requirement to prepare group accounts (parent company included in accounts of larger group), and

(*b*) the investment of the company in all undertakings in which it has such a holding as is mentioned in sub-paragraph (1) is shown, in aggregate, in the notes to the accounts by way of the equity method of valuation.

(3) That information need not be given in respect of an undertaking if—

(*a*) the undertaking is not required by any provision of this Act to deliver a copy of its balance sheet for its relevant financial year and does not otherwise publish that balance sheet in Great Britain or elsewhere, and

(*b*) the company's holding is less than 50 per cent of the nominal value of the shares in the undertaking.

(4) Information otherwise required by this paragraph need not be given if it is not material.

(5) For the purposes of this paragraph the 'relevant financial year' of an undertaking is—

    (*a*) if its financial year ends with that of the company, that year, and

    (*b*) if not, its financial year ending last before the end of the company's financial year.

Arrangements attracting merger relief

10.—(1) This paragraph applies to arrangements attracting merger relief, that is, where a company allots shares in consideration for the issue, transfer or cancellation of shares in another body corporate ('the other company') in circumstances such that section 130 of this Act (share premium account) does not, by virtue of section 131(2) (merger relief), apply to the premiums on the shares.

(2) If the company makes such an arrangement during the financial year, the following information shall be given—

    (*a*) the name of the other company,

    (*b*) the number, nominal value and class of shares allotted,

    (*c*) the number, nominal value and class of shares in the other company issued, transferred or cancelled, and

    (*d*) particulars of the accounting treatment adopted in the company's accounts in respect of the issue, transfer or cancellation.

(3) Where the company made such an arrangement during the financial year, or during either of the two preceding financial years, and there is included in the company's profit and loss account—

    (*a*) any profit or loss realised during the financial year by the company on the disposal of—

        (i) any shares in the other company, or

        (ii) any assets which were fixed assets of the other company or any of its subsidiary undertakings at the time of the arrangement, or

    (*b*) any part of any profit or loss realised during the financial year by the company on the disposal of any shares (other than shares in the other company) which was attributable to the fact that there were at the time of the disposal amongst the assets of the company which issued the shares, or any of its subsidiary undertakings, such shares or assets as are described in paragraph (*a*) above,

then, the net amount of that profit or loss or, as the case may be, the part so attributable shall be shown, together with an explanation of the transactions to which the information relates.

(4) For the purposes of this paragraph the time of the arrangement shall be taken to be—

    (*a*) where as a result of the arrangement the other company becomes a subsidiary undertaking of the company, the date on which it does so or, if the arrangement in question becomes binding only on the fulfilment of a condition, the date on which that condition is fulfilled;

    (*b*) if the other company is already a subsidiary undertaking of the company, the date on which the shares are allotted or, if they are allotted on different days, the first day.

Parent undertaking drawing up accounts for larger group

11.—(1) Where the company is a subsidiary undertaking, the following information shall be given with respect to the parent undertaking of—

    (*a*) the largest group of undertakings for which group accounts are drawn up and of which the company is a member, and

    (*b*) the smallest such group of undertakings.

(2) The name of the parent undertaking shall be stated.

(3) There shall be stated—

    (*a*) if the undertaking is incorporated outside Great Britain, the country in which it is incorporated;

    (*b*) if it is incorporated in Great Britain, whether it is registered in England and Wales or in Scotland;

    (*c*) if it is unincorporated, the address of its principal place of business.

(4) If copies of the group accounts referred to in sub-paragraph (1) are available to the public, there shall also be stated the addresses from which copies of the accounts can be obtained.

Identification of ultimate parent company

12.—(1) Where the company is a subsidiary undertaking, the following information shall be given with respect to the company (if any) regarded by the directors as being the company's ultimate parent company.

(2) The name of that company shall be stated.

(3) If known to the directors, there shall be stated—

    (*a*) if that company is incorporated outside Great Britain, the country in which it is incorporated;

    (*b*) if it is incorporated in Great Britain, whether it is registered in England and Wales or in Scotland.

(4) In this paragraph 'company' includes any body corporate.

Constructions of references to shares held by company

13.—(1) References in this Part of this Schedule to shares held by a company shall be construed as follows.

(2) For the purposes of paragraphs 2 to 5 (information about subsidiary undertakings)—

    (*a*) there shall be attributed to the company any shares held by a subsidiary undertaking, or by a person acting on behalf of the company or a subsidiary undertaking; but

    (*b*) there shall be treated as not held by the company any shares held on behalf of a person other than the company or a subsidiary undertaking.

(3) For the purposes of paragraphs 7 to 9 (information about undertakings other than subsidiary undertakings)—

    (*a*) there shall be attributed to the company shares held on its behalf by any person; but

    (*b*) there shall be treated as not held by a company shares held on behalf of a person other than the company.

(4) For the purposes of any of those provisions, shares held by way of security shall be treated as held by the person providing the security—

    (*a*) where apart from the right to exercise them for the purpose of preserving the value of the security, or of realising it, the rights attached to the shares are exercisable only in accordance with his instructions, and

    (*b*) where the shares are held in connection with the granting of loans as part of normal business activities and apart from the right to exercise them for the purpose of preserving the value of the security, or of realising it, the rights attached to the shares are exercisable only in his interests.

PART II

COMPANIES REQUIRED TO PREPARE GROUP ACCOUNTS

Introductory

14. In this Part of this Schedule 'the group' means the group consisting of the parent company and its subsidiary undertakings.

Subsidiary undertakings

15.—(1) The following information shall be given with respect to the undertakings which are subsidiary undertakings of the parent company at the end of the financial year.

(2) The name of each undertaking shall be stated.

(3) There shall be stated—

    (*a*) if the undertaking is incorporated outside Great Britain, the country in which it is incorporated;

    (*b*) if it is incorporated in Great Britain, whether it is registered in England and Wales or in Scotland;

    (*c*) it if is unincorporated, the address of its principal place of business.

(4) It shall also be stated whether the subsidiary undertaking is included in the consolidation and, if it is not, the reasons for excluding it from consolidation shall be given.

(5) It shall be stated with respect to each subsidiary undertaking by virtue of which of the conditions specified in section 258(2) or (4) it is a subsidiary undertaking of its immediate parent undertaking.

That information need not be given if the relevant condition is that specified in subsection (2)(*a*) of that section (holding of a majority of the voting rights) and the immediate parent undertaking holds the same proportion of the shares in the undertaking as it holds voting rights.

Holdings in subsidiary undertakings

16.—(1) The following information shall be given with respect to the shares of a subsidiary undertaking held—

    (*a*) by the parent company, and

(*b*) by the group;

and the information under paragraphs (*a*) and (*b*) shall (if different) be shown separately.

(2) There shall be stated—

    (*a*) the identity of each class of shares held, and

    (*b*) the proportion of the nominal value of the shares of that class represented by those shares.

Financial information about subsidiary undertakings not included in the consolidation

17.—(1) There shall be shown with respect to each subsidiary undertaking not included in the consolidation—

    (*a*) the aggregate amount of its capital and reserves as at the end of its relevant financial year, and

    (*b*) its profit or loss for that year.

(2) That information need not be given if the group's investment in the undertaking is included in the accounts by way of the equity method of valuation or if—

    (*a*) the undertaking is not required by any provision of this Act to deliver a copy of its balance sheet for its relevant financial year and does not otherwise publish that balance sheet in Great Britain or elsewhere, and

    (*b*) the holding of the group is less than 50 per cent of the nominal value of the shares in the undertaking.

(3) Information otherwise required by this paragraph need not be given if it is not material.

(4) For the purposes of this paragraph the 'relevant financial year' of a subsidiary undertaking is—

    (*a*) if its financial year ends with that of the company, that year, and

    (*b*) if not, its financial year ending last before the end of the company's financial year.

Further information about subsidiary undertakings excluded from consolidation

18.—(1) The following information shall be given with respect to subsidiary undertakings excluded from consolidation.

(2) There shall be disclosed—

    (*a*) any qualifications contained in the auditors' reports on the accounts of the undertaking for financial years ending with or during the financial year of the company, and

    (*b*) any note or saving contained in such accounts to call attention to a matter which, apart from the note or saving, would properly have been referred to in such a qualification,

in so far as the matter which is the subject of the qualification or note is not covered by the consolidated accounts and is material from the point of view of the members of the parent company.

(3) In so far as information required by this paragraph is not obtainable, a statement to that effect shall be given instead.

Financial years of subsidiary undertakings

19. Where the financial year of one or more subsidiary undertakings did not end with that of the company, there shall be stated in relation to each such undertaking—

    (*a*) the reasons why the company's directors consider that its financial year should not end with that of the company, and

    (*b*) the date on which its last financial year ended (last before the end of the company's financial year).

Instead of the dates required by paragraph (*b*) being given for each subsidiary undertaking the earliest and latest of those dates may be given.

Shares and debentures of company held by subsidiary undertakings

20.—(1) The number, description and amount of the shares in and debentures of the company held by or on behalf of its subsidiary undertakings shall be disclosed.

(2) Sub-paragraph (1) does not apply in relation to shares or debentures in the case of which the subsidiary undertaking is concerned as personal representative or, subject as follows, as trustee.

(3) The exception for shares or debentures in relation to which the subsidiary undertaking is concerned as trustee does not apply if the company or any of its subsidiary undertakings is beneficially interested under the trust, otherwise than by way of security only for the purposes of a transaction entered into by it in the ordinary course of a business which includes the lending of money.

(4) Schedule 2 to this Act has effect for the interpretation of the reference in sub-paragraph (3) to a beneficial interest under a trust.

Joint ventures

21.—(1) The following information shall be given where an undertaking is dealt with in the consolidated accounts by the method of proportional consolidation in accordance with paragraph 19 of Schedule 4A (joint ventures)—

    (*a*) the name of the undertaking;

    (*b*) the address of the principal place of business of the undertaking;

    (*c*) the factors on which joint management of the undertaking is based; and

    (*d*) the proportion of the capital of the undertaking held by undertakings included in the consolidation.

(2) Where the financial year of the undertaking did not end with that of the company, there shall be stated the date on which a financial year of the undertaking last ended before that date.

Associated undertakings

22.—(1) The following information shall be given where an undertaking included in the consolidation has an interest in an associated undertaking.

(2) The name of the associated undertaking shall be stated.

(3) There shall be stated—

    (*a*) if the undertaking is incorporated outside Great Britain, the country in which it is incorporated;

    (*b*) if it is incorporated in Great Britain, whether it is registered in England and Wales or in Scotland;

    (*c*) if it is unincorporated, the address of its principal place of business.

(4) The following information shall be given with respect to the shares of the undertaking held—

    (*a*) by the parent company, and

    (*b*) by the group;

and the information under paragraphs (*a*) and (*b*) shall be shown separately.

(5) There shall be stated—

    (*a*) the identity of each class of shares held, and

    (*b*) the proportion of the nominal value of the shares of that class represented by those shares.

(6) In this paragraph 'associated undertaking' has the meaning given by paragraph 20 of Schedule 4A; and the information required by this paragraph shall be given notwithstanding that paragraph 22(3) of that Schedule (materiality) applies in relation to the accounts themselves.

Other significant holdings of parent company or group

23.—(1) The information required by paragraphs 24 and 25 shall be given where at the end of the financial year the parent company has a significant holding in an undertaking which is not one of its subsidiary undertakings and does not fall within paragraph 21 (joint ventures) or paragraph 22 (associated undertakings).

(2) A holding is significant for this purpose if—

    (*a*) it amounts to 10 per cent or more of the nominal value of any class of shares in the undertaking, or

    (*b*) the amount of the holding (as stated or included in the company's individual accounts) exceeds one-tenth of the amount of its assets (as so stated).

24.—(1) The name of the undertaking shall be stated.

(2) There shall be stated—

    (*a*) if the undertaking is incorporated outside Great Britain, the country in which it is incorporated;

    (*b*) if it is incorporated in Great Britain, whether it is registered in England and Wales or in Scotland;

    (*c*) if it is unincorporated, the address of its principal place of business.

(3) The following information shall be given with respect to the shares of the undertaking held by the parent company.

(4) There shall be stated—

    (*a*) the identity of each class of shares held, and

293

(*b*) the proportion of the nominal value of the shares of that class represented by those shares.

25.—(1) Where the company has a significant holding in an undertaking amounting to 20 per cent or more of the nominal value of the shares in the undertaking, there shall also be stated—

(*a*) the aggregate amount of the capital and reserves of the undertaking as at the end of its relevant financial year, and

(*b*) its profit or loss for that year.

(2) That information need not be given in respect of an undertaking if—

(*a*) the undertaking is not required by any provision of this Act to deliver a copy of its balance sheet for its relevant financial year and does not otherwise publish that balance sheet in Great Britain or elsewhere, and

(*b*) the company's holding is less than 50 per cent of the nominal value of the shares in the undertaking.

(3) Information otherwise required by this paragraph need not be given if it is not material.

(4) For the purposes of this paragraph the 'relevant financial year' of an undertaking is—

(*a*) if its financial year ends with that of the company, that year, and

(*b*) if not, its financial year ending last before the end of the company's financial year.

26.—(1) The information required by paragraphs 27 and 28 shall be given where at the end of the financial year the group has a significant holding in an undertaking which is not a subsidiary undertaking of the parent company and does not fall within paragraph 21 (joint ventures) or paragraph 22 (associated undertakings).

(2) A holding is significant for this purpose if—

(*a*) it amounts to 10 per cent or more of the nominal value of any class of shares in the undertaking, or

(*b*) the amount of the holding (as stated or included in the group accounts) exceeds one-tenth of the amount of the group's assets (as so stated).

27.—(1) The name of the undertaking shall be stated.

(2) There shall be stated—

(*a*) if the undertaking is incorporated outside Great Britain, the country in which it is incorporated;

(*b*) if it is incorporated in Great Britain, whether it is registered in England and Wales or in Scotland;

(*c*) if it is unincorporated, the address of its principal place of business.

(3) The following information shall be given with respect to the shares of the undertaking held by the group.

(4) There shall be stated—

(*a*) the identity of each class of shares held, and

(*b*) the proportion of the nominal value of the shares of that class represented by those shares.

28.—(1) Where the holding of the group amounts to 20 per cent or more of the nominal value of the shares in the undertaking, there shall also be stated—

(*a*) the aggregate amount of the capital and reserves of the undertaking as at the end of its relevant financial year, and

(*b*) its profit or loss for that year.

(2) That information need not be given if—

(*a*) the undertaking is not required by any provision of this Act to deliver a copy of its balance sheet for its relevant financial year and does not otherwise publish that balance sheet in Great Britain or elsewhere, and

(*b*) the holding of the group is less than 50 per cent of the nominal value of the shares in the undertaking.

(3) Information otherwise required by this paragraph need not be given if it is not material.

(4) For the purposes of this paragraph the 'relevant financial year' of an outside undertaking is—

(*a*) if its financial year ends with that of the parent company, that year, and

(*b*) if not, its financial year ending last before the end of the parent company's financial year.

Arrangements attracting merger relief

29.—(1) This paragraph applies to arrangements attracting merger relief, that is, where a company allots shares in consideration for the issue, transfer or cancellation of shares in another body corporate ('the other company') in circumstances such that section 130 of this Act (share premium account) does not, by virtue of section 131(2) (merger relief), apply to the premiums on the shares.

(2) If the parent company made such an arrangement during the finanical year, the following information shall be given—

(a) the name of the other company,

(b) the number, nominal value and class of shares allotted,

(c) the number, nominal value and class of shares in the other company issued, transferred or cancelled, and

(d) particulars of the accounting treatment adopted in the parent company's individual and group accounts in respect of the issue, transfer or cancellation, and

(e) particulars of the extent to which and manner in which the profit or loss for the financial year shown in the group accounts is affected by any profit or loss of the other company, or any of its subsidiary undertakings, which arose before the time of the arrangement.

(3) Where the parent company made such an arrangement during the financial year, or during either of the two preceding financial years, and there is included in the consolidated profit and loss acount—

(a) any profit or loss realised during the financial year on the disposal of—

(i) any shares in the other company, or

(ii) any assets which were fixed assets of the other company or any of its subsidiary undertakings at the time of the arrangement, or

(b) any part of any profit or loss realised during the financial year on the disposal of any shares (other than shares in the other company) which was attributable to the fact that there were at the time of the disposal amongst the assets of the company which issued the shares, or any of its subsidiary undertakings, such shares or assets as are described in paragraph (a) above,

then, the net amount of that profit or loss or, as the case may be, the part so attributable shall be shown, together with an explanation of the transactions to which the information relates.

(4) For the purposes of this paragraph the time of the arrangement shall be taken to be—

(a) where as a result of the arrangement the other company becomes a subsidiary undertaking of the company in question, the date on which it does so or, if the arrangement in question becomes binding only on the fulfilment of a condition, the date on which that condition is fulfilled;

(b) if the other company is already a subsidiary undertaking of that company, the date on which the shares are allotted or, if they are allotted on different days, the first day.

Parent undertaking drawing up accounts for larger group

30.—(1) Where the parent company is itself a subsidiary undertaking, the following information shall be given with respect to that parent undertaking of the company which heads—

(a) the largest group of undertakings for which group accounts are drawn up and of which that company is a member, and

(b) the smallest such group of undertakings.

(2) The name of the parent undertaking shall be stated.

(3) There shall be stated—

(a) if the undertaking is incorporated outside Great Britain, the country in which it is incorporated;

(b) if it is incorporated in Great Britain, whether it is registered in England and Wales or in Scotland;

(c) if it is unincorporated, the address of its principal place of business.

(4) If copies of the group accounts referred to in sub-paragraph (1) are available to the public, there shall also be stated the addresses from which copies of the accounts can be obtained.

Identification of ultimate parent company

31.—(1) Where the parent company is itself a subsidiary undertaking, the following information shall be given with respect to the company (if any) regarded by the directors as being that company's ultimate parent company.

(2) The name of that company shall be stated.

(3) If known to the directors, there shall be stated—

(a) if that company is incorporated outside Great Britain, the country in which it is incorporated;

(b) if it is incorporated in Great Britain, whether it is registered in England and Wales or in Scotland.

(4) In this paragraph 'company' includes any body corporate.

Construction of references to shares held by parent company or group

32.—(1) References in this Part of this Schedule to shares held by the parent company or the group shall be construed as follows.

(2) For the purposes of paragraphs 16, 22(4) and (5) and 23 to 25 (information about holdings in subsidiary and other undertakings)—

(a) there shall be attributed to the parent company shares held on its behalf by any person; but

(b) there shall be treated as not held by the parent company shares held on behalf of a person other than the company.

(3) References to shares held by the group are to any shares held by or on behalf of the parent company or any of its subsidiary undertakings; but there shall be treated as not held by the group any shares held on behalf of a person other than the parent company or any of its subsidiary undertakings.

(4) Shares held by way of security shall be treated as held by the person providing the security—

(a) where apart from the right to exercise them for the purpose of preserving the value of the security, or of realising it, the rights attached to the shares are exercisable only in accordance with his instructions, and

(b) where the shares are held in connection with the granting of loans as part of normal business activities and apart from the right to exercise them for the purpose of preserving the value of the security, or of realising it, the rights attached to the shares are exercisable only in his interests.

SCHEDULE 4

Section 6(4)

DISCLOSURE OF INFORMATION: EMOLUMENTS AND OTHER BENEFITS OF DIRECTORS AND OTHERS

1. Schedule 6 to the Companies Act 1985 is amended as follows.

2. For the heading substitute—

'DISCLOSURE OF INFORMATION: EMOLUMENTS AND OTHER BENEFITS OF DIRECTORS AND OTHERS'.

3. Insert the following provisions (which reproduce, with amendments, the former Part V of Schedule 5 to that Act) as Part I—

'PART I

CHAIRMAN'S AND DIRECTORS' EMOLUMENTS, PENSIONS AND COMPENSATION FOR LOSS OF OFFICE

Aggregate amount of directors' emoluments

1.—(1) The aggregate amount of directors' emoluments shall be shown.

(2) This means the emoluments paid to or receivable by any person in respect of—

(a) his services as a director of the company, or

(b) his services while director of the company—

(i) as director of any of its subsidiary undertakings, or

(ii) otherwise in connection with the management of the affairs of the company or any of its subsidiary undertakings.

(3) There shall also be shown, separately, the aggregate amount within sub-paragraph (2)(a) and (b)(i) and the aggregate amount within sub-paragraph (2)(b)(ii).

(4) For the purposes of this paragraph the 'emoluments' of a person include—

(a) fees and percentages,

(b) sums paid by way of expenses allowance (so far as those sums are chargeable to United Kingdom income tax),

(c) contributions paid in respect of him under any pension scheme, and

(d) the estimated money value of any other benefits received by him otherwise than in cash,

and emoluments in respect of a person's accepting office as a director shall be treated as emoluments in respect of his services as director.

Details of chairman's and directors' emoluments

2. Where the company is a parent company or a subsidiary undertaking, or where the amount shown in compliance with paragraph 1(1) is £60,000 or more, the information required by paragraphs 3 to 6 shall be given with respect to the emoluments of the chairman and directors, and emoluments waived.

3.—(1) The emoluments of the chairman shall be shown.

(2) The 'chairman' means the person elected by the directors to be chairman of their meetings, and includes a person who, though not so elected, holds an office (however designated) which in accordance with the company's constitution carries with it functions substantially similar to those discharged by a person so elected.

(3) Where there has been more than one chairman during the year, the emoluments of each shall be stated so far as attributable to the period during which he was chairman.

(4) The emoluments of a person need not be shown if his duties as chairman were wholly or mainly discharged outside the United Kingdom.

4.—(1) The following information shall be given with respect to the emoluments of directors.

(2) There shall be shown the number of directors whose emoluments fell within each of the following bands—

not more than £5,000,
more than £5,000 but not more than £10,000,
more than £10,000 but not more than £15,000,
and so on.

(3) If the emoluments of any of the directors exceeded that of the chairman, there shall be shown the greatest amount of emoluments of any director.

(4) Where more than one person has been chairman during the year, the reference in sub-paragraph (3) to the emoluments of the chairman is to the aggregate of the emoluments of each person who has been chairman, so far as attributable to the period during which he was chairman.

(5) The information required by sub-paragraph (2) need not be given in respect of a director who discharged his duties as such wholly or mainly outside the United Kingdom; and any such director shall be left out of account for the purposes of sub-paragraph (3).

5. In paragraphs 3 and 4 'emoluments' has the same meaning as in paragraph 1, except that it does not include contributions paid in respect of a person under a pension scheme.

Emoluments waived

6.—(1) There shall be shown—

  (a) the number of directors who have waived rights to receive emoluments which, but for the waiver, would have fallen to be included in the amount shown under paragraph 1(1), and
  (b) the aggregate amount of those emoluments.

(2) For the purposes of this paragraph it shall be assumed that a sum not receivable in respect of a period would have been paid at the time at which it was due, and if such a sum was payable only on demand, it shall be deemed to have been due at the time of the waiver.

Pensions of directors and past directors

7.—(1) There shall be shown the aggregate amount of directors' or past directors' pensions.

(2) This amount does not include any pension paid or receivable under a pension scheme if the scheme is such that the contributions under it are substantially adequate for the maintenance of the scheme; but, subject to this, it includes any pension paid or receivable in respect of any such services of a director or past director as are mentioned in paragraph 1(2), whether to or by him or, on his nomination or by virtue of dependence on or other connection with him, to or by any other person.

(3) The amount shown shall distinguish between pensions in respect of services as director, whether of the company or any of its subsidiary undertakings, and other pensions.

(4) References to pensions include benefits otherwise than in cash and in relation to so much of a pension as consists of such a benefit references to its amount are to the estimated money value of the benefit.

The nature of any such benefit shall also be disclosed.

Compensation to directors for loss of office

8.—(1) There shall be shown the aggregate amount of any compensation to directors or past directors in respect of loss of office.

(2) This amount includes compensation received or receivable by a director or past director for—

(a) loss of office as director of the company, or

(b) loss, while director of the company or on or in connection with his ceasing to be a director of it, of—

(i) any other office in connection with the management of the company's affairs, or

(ii) any office as director or otherwise in connection with the management of the affairs of any subsidiary undertaking of the company;

and shall distinguish between compensation in respect of the office of director, whether of the company or any of its subsidiary undertakings, and compensation in respect of other offices.

(3) References to compensation include benefits otherwise than in cash; and in relation to such compensation references to its amount are to the estimated money value of the benefit.

The nature of any such compensation shall be disclosed.

(4) References to compensation for loss of office include compensation in consideration for, or in connection with, a person's retirement from office.

Sums paid to third parties in respect of directors' services

9.—(1) There shall be shown the aggregate amount of any consideration paid to or receivable by third parties for making available the services of any person—

(a) as a director of the company, or

(b) while director of the company—

(i) as director of any of its subsidiary undertakings, or

(ii) otherwise in connection with the management of the affairs of the company or any of its subsidiary undertakings.

(2) The reference to consideration includes benefits otherwise than in cash; and in relation to such consideration the reference to its amount is to the estimated money value of the benefit.

The nature of any such consideration shall be disclosed.

(3) The reference to third parties is to persons other than—

(a) the director himself or a person connected with him or body corporate controlled by him, and

(b) the company or any of its subsidiary undertakings.

Supplementary

10.—(1) The following applies with respect to the amounts to be shown under paragraphs 1, 7, 8 and 9.

(2) The amount in each case includes all relevant sums paid by or receivable from—

(a) the company; and

(b) the company's subsidiary undertakings; and

(c) any other person,

except sums to be accounted for to the company or any of its subsidiary undertakings or, by virtue of sections 314 and 315 of this Act (duty of directors to make disclosure on company takeover; consequence of non-compliance), to past or present members of the company or any of its subsidiaries or any class of those members.

(3) The amount to be shown under paragraph 8 shall distinguish between the sums respectively paid by or receivable from the company, the company's subsidiary undertakings and persons other than the company and its subsidiary undertakings.

(4) References to amounts paid to or receivable by a person include amounts paid to or receivable by a person connected with him or a body corporate controlled by him (but not so as to require an amount to be counted twice).

11.—(1) The amounts to be shown for any financial year under paragraphs 1, 7, 8 and 9 are the sums receivable in respect of that year (whenever paid) or, in the case of sums not receivable in respect of a period, the sums paid during that year.

(2) But where—

    (*a*) any sums are not shown in a note to the accounts for the relevant financial year on the ground that the person receiving them is liable to account for them as mentioned in paragraph 10(2), but the liability is thereafter wholly or partly released or is not enforced within a period of 2 years; or

    (*b*) any sums paid by way of expenses allowance are charged to United Kingdom income tax after the end of the relevant financial year,

those sums shall, to the extent to which the liability is released or not enforced or they are charged as mentioned above (as the case may be), be shown in a note to the first accounts in which it is practicable to show them and shall be distinguished from the amounts to be shown apart from this provision.

12. Where it is necessary to do so for the purpose of making any distinction required by the preceding paragraphs in an amount to be shown in compliance with this Part of this Schedule, the directors may apportion any payments between the matters in respect of which these have been paid or are receivable in such manner as they think appropriate.

Interpretation

13.—(1) The following applies for the interpretation of this Part of this Schedule.

(2) A reference to a subsidiary undertaking of the company—

    (*a*) in relation to a person who is or was, while a director of the company, a director also, by virtue of the company's nomination (direct or indirect) of any other undertaking, includes (subject to the following sub-paragraph) that undertaking, whether or not it is or was in fact a subsidiary undertaking of the company, and

    (*b*) for the purposes of paragraphs 1 to 7 (including any provision of this Part of this Schedule referring to paragraph 1) is to an undertaking which is a subsidiary undertaking at the time the services were rendered, and for the purposes of paragraph 8 to a subsidiary undertaking immediately before the loss of office as director.

(3) The following definitions apply—

    (*a*) 'pension' includes any superannuation allowance, superannuation gratuity or similar payment,

    (*b*) 'pension scheme' means a scheme for the provision of pensions in respect of services as director or otherwise which is maintained in whole or in part by means of contributions, and

    (*c*) 'contribution', in relation to a pension scheme, means any payment (including an insurance premium) paid for the purposes of the scheme by or in respect of persons rendering services in respect of which pensions will or may become payable under the scheme except that it does not include any payment in respect of two or more persons if the amount paid in respect of each of them is not ascertainable.

(4) References in this Part of this Schedule to a person being 'connected' with a director, and to a director 'controlling' a body corporate, shall be construed in accordance with section 346.

Supplementary

14. This Part of this Schedule requires information to be given only so far as it is contained in the company's books and papers or the company has the right to obtain it from the persons concerned.'.

4.—(1) For the heading to the present Part I substitute—

'PART II

LOANS, QUASI-LOANS AND OTHER DEALINGS IN FAVOUR OF DIRECTORS'

(2) Paragraphs 1 to 3 and 5 to 14 of that Part shall be renumbered 15 to 27, and internal cross-references in that Part shall be renumbered accordingly.

(3) Paragraph 4 is omitted.

(4) In paragraph 1 (renumbered 15) for 'Group accounts' substitute 'The group accounts of a holding company, or if it is not required to prepare group accounts its individual accounts,'.

(5) For the heading before paragraph 11 (renumbered 24) substitute—

'Excluded transactions'

5. In paragraph 14 (renumbered 27), make the existing provision sub-paragraph (1) and after it insert—

'(2) In this Part of this Schedule 'director' includes a shadow director.'.

299

6.—(1) For the heading to the present Part II subsitute—

'PART III

OTHER TRANSACTIONS, ARRANGEMENTS AND AGREEMENTS'

(2) Paragraphs 15 to 17 of that Part shall be renumbered 28 to 30, and internal cross-references in that Part shall be renumbered accordingly.

(3) In paragraph 16 (renumbered 29), for 'made as mentioned in section 233(1)' substitute 'made by the company or a subsidiary of it for persons who at any time during the financial year were officers of the company (but not directors or shadow directors)'.

7. Omit the present Part III (disclosure required in case of banking companies), the substance of which is reproduced in Part IV of Schedule 7 to this Act.

SCHEDULE 5

Section 8(2)

MATTERS TO BE INCLUDED IN DIRECTORS' REPORT

1. Schedule 7 to the Companies Act 1985 (matters to be included in directors' report) is amended as follows.

Subsidiary undertakings

2.—(1) In paragraph 1(1) (significant changes in fixed assets) for 'subsidiaries' substitute 'subsidiary undertakings'.

(2) In paragraph 6 (general information), for 'subsidiaries' in each place where it occurs (three times) substitute 'subsidiary undertakings'.

Directors' interests

3. For paragraph 2 (directors' interests) substitute—

'2.—(1) The information required by paragraphs 2A and 2B shall be given in the directors' report, or by way of notes to the company's annual accounts, with respect to each person who at the end of the financial year was a director of the company.

(2) In those paragraphs—

    (*a*) 'the register' means the register of directors' interests kept by the company under section 325; and

    (*b*) references to a body corporate being in the same group as the company are to its being a subsidiary or holding company, or another subsidiary of a holding company, of the company.

2A.—(1) It shall be stated with respect to each director whether, according to the register, he was at the end of the financial year interested in shares in or debentures of the company or any other body corporate in the same group.

(2) If he was so interested, there shall be stated the number of shares in and amount of debentures of each body (specifying it) in which, according to the register, he was then interested.

(3) If a director was interested at the end of the financial year in shares in or debentures of the company or any other body corporate in the same group—

    (*a*) it shall also be stated whether, according to the register, he was at the beginning of the financial year (or, if he was not then a director, when he became one) interested in shares in or debentures of the company or any other body corporate in the same group, and

    (*b*) if he was so interested, there shall be stated the number of shares in and amount of debentures of each body (specifying it) in which, according to the register, he was then interested.

(4) In this paragraph references to an interest in shares or debentures have the same meaning as in section 324; and references to the interest of a director include any interest falling to be treated as his for the purposes of that section.

(5) The reference above to the time when a person became a director is, in the case of a person who became a director on more than one occasion, to the time when he first became a director.

2B.—(1) It shall be stated with respect to each director whether, according to the register, any right to subscribe for shares in or debentures of the company or another body corporate in the same group was during the financial year granted to, or exercised by, the director or a member of his immediate family.

(2) If any such right was granted to, or exercised by, any such person during the financial year, there shall be stated the number of shares in and amount of debentures of each body (specifying it) in respect of which, according to the register, the right was granted or exercised.

(3) A director's 'immediate family' means his or her spouse and infant children; and for this purpose 'children' includes step-children, and 'infant', in relation to Scotland, means pupil or minor.

(4) The reference above to a member of the director's immediate family does not include a person who is himself or herself a director of the company.'.

SCHEDULE 6

Section 13(2)

[SCHEDULE 8 TO THE COMPANIES ACT 1985]

EXEMPTIONS FOR SMALL AND MEDIUM-SIZED COMPANIES

PART I

SMALL COMPANIES

Balance sheet

1.—(1) The company may deliver a copy of an abbreviated version of the full balance sheet, showing only those items to which a letter or Roman number is assigned in the balance sheet format adopted under Part I of Schedule 4, but in other respects corresponding to the full balance sheet.

(2) If a copy of an abbreviated balance sheet is delivered, there shall be disclosed in it or in a note to the company's accounts delivered—

(a) the aggregate of the amounts required by note (5) of the notes on the balance sheet formats set out in Part I of Schedule 4 to be shown separately for each item included under debtors (amounts falling due after one year), and

(b) the aggregate of the amounts required by note (13) of those notes to be shown separately for each item included under creditors in Format 2 (amounts falling due within one year or after more than one year).

(3) The provisions of section 233 as to the signing of the copy of the balance sheet delivered to the registrar apply to a copy of an abbreviated balance sheet delivered in accordance with this paragraph.

Profit and loss account

2. A copy of the company's profit and loss account need not be delivered.

Disclosure of information in notes to accounts

3.—(1) Of the information required by Part III of Schedule 4 (information to be given in notes to accounts if not given in the accounts themselves) only the information required by the following provisions need be given—

paragraph 36 (accounting policies),
paragraph 38 (share capital),
paragraph 39 (particulars of allotments),
paragraph 42 (fixed assets), so far as it relates to those items to which a letter or Roman number is assigned in the balance sheet format adopted,
paragraph 48(1) and (4) (particulars of debts),
paragraph 58(1) (basis of conversion of foreign currency amounts into sterling),
paragraph 58(2) (corresponding amounts for previous financial year), so far as it relates to amounts stated in a note to the company's accounts by virtue of a requirement of Schedule 4 or under any other provision of this Act.

(2) Of the information required by Schedule 5 to be given in notes to the accounts, the information required by the following provisions need not be given—

paragraph 4 (financial years of subsidiary undertakings),
paragraph 5 (additional information about subsidiary undertakings),
paragraph 6 (shares and debentures of company held by subsidiary undertakings),
paragraph 10 (arrangements attracting merger relief).

(3) Of the information required by Schedule 6 to be given in notes to the accounts, the information required by Part I (directors' and chairman's emoluments, pensions and compensation for loss of office) need not be given.

Directors' report

4. A copy of the directors' report need not be delivered.

PART II

MEDIUM-SIZED COMPANIES

Profit and loss account

5. The company may deliver a profit and loss account in which the following items listed in the profit and loss account formats set out in Part I of Schedule 4 are combined as one item under the heading 'gross profit or loss'—

Items 1, 2, 3 and 6 in Format 1;
Items 1 to 5 in Format 2;
Items A.1, B.1 and B.2 in Format 3;
Items A.1, A.2 and B.1 to B.4 in Format 4.

Disclosure of information in notes to accounts

6. The information required by paragraph 55 of Schedule 4 (particulars of turnover) need not be given.

PART III

SUPPLEMENTARY PROVISIONS

Statement that advantage taken of exemptions

7.—(1) Where the directors of a company take advantage of the exemptions conferred by Part I or Part II of this Schedule, the company's balance sheet shall contain—

(a) a statement that advantage is taken of the exemptions conferred by Part I or, as the case may be, Part II of this Schedule, and
(b) a statement of the grounds on which, in the directors' opinion, the company is entitled to those exemptions.

(2) The statements shall appear in the balance sheet immediately above the signature required by section 233.

Special auditors' report

8.—(1) If the directors of a company propose to take advantage of the exemptions conferred by Part I or II of this Schedule, it is the auditors' duty to provide them with a report stating whether in their opinion the company is entitled to those exemptions and whether the documents to be proposed to be delivered in accordance with this Schedule are properly prepared.

(2) The accounts delivered shall be accompanied by a special report of the auditors stating that in their opinion—

(a) the company is entitled to the exemptions claimed in the directors' statement, and
(b) the accounts to be delivered are properly prepared in accordance with this Schedule.

(3) In such a case a copy of the auditors' report under section 235 need not be delivered separately, but the full text of it shall be reproduced in the special report; and if the report under section 235 is qualified there shall be included in the special report any further material necessary to understand the qualification.

(4) Section 236 (signature of auditors' report) applies to a special report under this paragraph as it applies to a report under section 235.

Dormant companies

9. Paragraphs 7 and 8 above do not apply where the company is exempt by virtue of section 250 (dormant companies) from the obligation to appoint auditors.

Requirements in connection with publication of accounts

10.—(1) Where advantage is taken of the exemptions conferred by Part I or II of this Schedule, section 240 (requirements in connection with publication of accounts) has effect with the following adaptations.

(2) Accounts delivered in accordance with this Schedule and accounts in the form in which they would be required to be delivered apart from this Schedule are both 'statutory accounts' for the purposes of that section.

(3) References in that section to the auditors' report under section 235 shall be read, in relation to accounts delivered in accordance with this Schedule, as references to the special report under paragraph 8 above.

SCHEDULE 7

Section 18(3) and (4)

SPECIAL PROVISIONS FOR BANKING AND INSURANCE COMPANIES AND GROUPS

Preliminary

Schedule 9 to the Companies Act 1985 is amended in accordance with this Schedule, as follows—

(a) for the heading of the Schedule substitute 'Special Provisions for Banking and Insurance Companies and Groups';
(b) omit the introductory paragraph preceding Part I, together with its heading;
(c) make the present provisions of Parts I to V of the Schedule (as amended by Part I of this Schedule) Part I of the Schedule, and accordingly—

  (i) for the descriptive Part heading before paragraph 2 substitute 'Form and Content of Accounts', and
  (ii) omit the Part headings before paragraphs 19, 27, 31 and 32;

(d) the provisions of Parts II, III and IV of this Schedule have effect as Parts II, III and IV of Schedule 9 to the Companies Act 1985.

PART I

FORM AND CONTENT OF ACCOUNTS

1. In paragraph 10(1)(c) of Schedule 9 to the Companies Act 1985 (disclosure of outstanding loans in connection with certain cases of financial assistance for purchase of company's own shares), after '153(4)(b)' insert ', (bb)'.

2. In paragraph 13 of that Schedule (information supplementing balance sheet), omit sub-paragraph (3) (information as to acquisition of, or creation of lien or charge over, company's own shares).

3. In paragraph 17(5) of that Schedule (statement of turnover: companies exempt from requirement) for 'neither a holding company nor a subsidiary of another body corporate' substitute 'neither a parent company nor a subsidiary undertaking'.

4. After paragraph 18 of that Schedule insert—

'Supplementary provisions

18A.—(1) Accounting policies shall be applied consistently within the same accounts and from one financial year to the next.

(2) If it appears to the directors of a company that there are special reasons for departing from the principle stated in sub-paragraph (1) in preparing the company's accounts in respect of any financial year, they may do so; but particulars of the departure, the reasons for it and its effect shall be given in a note to the accounts.

18B. It shall be stated whether the accounts have been prepared in accordance with applicable accounting standards, and particulars of any material departure from those standards and the reasons for it shall be given.

18C.—(1) In respect of every item shown in the balance sheet or profit and loss account, or stated in a note to the accounts, there shall be shown or stated the corresponding amount for the financial year immediately preceding that to which the accounts relate, subject to sub-paragraph (3).

(2) Where the corresponding amount is not comparable, it shall be adjusted and particulars of the adjustment and the reasons for it shall be given in a note to the accounts.

(3) Sub-paragraph (1) does not apply in relation to an amount shown—

   (*a*) as an amount the source or application of which is required by paragraph 8 above (reserves and provisions),
   (*b*) in pursuance of paragraph 13(10) above (acquisitions and disposals of fixed assets),
   (*c*) by virtue of paragraph 13 of Schedule 4A (details of accounting treatment of acquisitions),
   (*d*) by virtue of paragraph 2, 8(3), 16, 21(1)(*d*), 22(4) or (5), 24(3) or (4) or 27(3) or (4) of Schedule 5 (shareholdings in other undertakings), or
   (*e*) by virtue of Part II or III of Schedule 6 (loans and other dealings in favour of directors and others).'.

5.—(1) Before paragraph 19 of that Schedule insert the heading '*Provisions where company is parent company or subsidiary undertaking*'; and that paragraph is amended as follows.

(2) In sub-paragraph (1) for the words from 'is a holding company' onwards substitute 'is a parent company'.

(3) In sub-paragraph (2)—

   (*a*) for 'subsidiaries' (four times) substitute 'subsidiary undertakings', and
   (*b*) in paragraph (*a*), for 'Part I' substitute 'paragraphs 5, 6, 10, 13 and 14'.

(4) Omit sub-paragraphs (3) to (7).

6. For paragraph 20 of that Schedule substitute—

   '20.—(1) This paragraph applies where the company is a subsidiary undertaking.

   (2) The balance sheet of the company shall show—

      (*a*) the aggregate amount of its indebtedness to undertakings of which it is a subsidiary undertaking or which are fellow subsidiary undertakings, and
      (*b*) the aggregate amount of the indebtedness of all such undertakings to it,

   distinguishing in each case between indebtedness in respect of debentures and otherwise.

   (3) The balance sheet shall also show the aggregate amount of assets consisting of shares in fellow subsidiary undertakings.'.

7. Omit paragraphs 21 to 26 of that Schedule.

8.—(1) Before paragraph 27 of that Schedule insert the heading '*Exceptions for certain companies*'; and that paragraph is amended as follows.

(2) In sub-paragraph (2)—

   (*a*) for 'Part I of this Schedule' substitute 'paragraphs 2 to 18 of this Schedule', and
   (*b*) in paragraph (*b*) for the words from 'paragraphs 15' to the end substitute 'and paragraph 15'.

(3) In sub-paragraph (4), omit 'of the said Part I'.

9. In paragraph 28 of that Schedule, in sub-paragraph (1) (twice) and in sub-paragraph (2) for 'Part I' substitute 'paragraphs 2 to 18'.

10 After that paragraph insert—

   '28A. Where a company is entitled to, and has availed itself of, any of the provisions of paragraph 27 or 28 of this Schedule, section 235(2) only requires the auditors to state whether in their opinion the accounts have been properly prepared in accordance with this Act.'.

11. Omit paragraphs 29 to 31 of that Schedule.

12. Before paragraph 32 of that Schedule insert the heading '*Interpretation*'; and in sub-paragraphs (1) and (2) of that paragraph for 'this Schedule' substitute 'this Part of this Schedule'.

13. In paragraph 36 of that Schedule for 'this Schedule' substitute 'this Part of this Schedule'.

PART II

[PART II OF SCHEDULE 9 TO THE COMPANIES ACT 1985]

ACCOUNTS OF BANKING OR INSURANCE GROUP

Undertakings to be included in consolidation

1. The following descriptions of undertaking shall not be excluded from consolidation under section 229(4) (exclusion or undertakings whose activities are different from those of the undertakings consolidated)—

   (*a*) in the case of a banking group, an undertaking (other than a credit institution) whose activities are a direct extension of or ancillary to banking business;

(*b*) in the case of an insurance group, an undertaking (other than one carrying on insurance business) whose activities are a direct extension of or ancillary to insurance business.

For the purposes of paragraph (*a*) 'banking' means the carrying on of a deposit-taking business within the meaning of the Banking Act 1987.

General application of provisions applicable to individual accounts

2.—(1) In paragraph 1 of Schedule 4A (application to group accounts of provisions applicable to individual accounts), the reference in sub-paragraph (1) to the provisions of Schedule 4 shall be construed as a reference to the provisions of Part I of this Schedule; and accordingly—

(*a*) the reference in sub-paragraph (2) to paragraph 59 of Schedule 4 shall be construed as a reference to paragraphs 19(2) and 20 of Part I of this Schedule; and
(*b*) sub-paragraph (3) shall be omitted.

(2) The general application of the provisions of Part I of this Schedule in place of those of Schedule 4 is subject to the following provisions.

Treatment of goodwill

3.—(1) The rules in paragraph 21 of Schedule 4 relating to the treatment of goodwill, and the rules in paragraphs 17 to 19 of that Schedule (valuation of fixed assets) so far as they relate to goodwill, apply for the purpose of dealing with any goodwill arising on consolidation.

(2) Goodwill shall be shown as a separate item in the balance sheet under an appropriate heading; and this applies notwithstanding anything in paragraph 10(1)(*b*) or (2) of Part I of this Schedule (under which goodwill, patents and trade marks may be stated in the company's individual accounts as a single item).

Minority interests and associated undertakings

4. The information required by paragraphs 17 and 20 to 22 of Schedule 4A (minority interests and associated undertakings) to be shown under separate items in the formats set out in Part I of Schedule 4 shall be shown separately in the balance sheet and profit and loss account under appropriate headings.

Companies entitled to benefit of exemptions

5.—(1) Where a banking or insurance company is entitled to the exemptions conferred by paragraph 27 or 28 of Part I of this Schedule, a group headed by that company is similarly entitled.

(2) Paragraphs 27(4), 28(2) and 28A (accounts not to be taken to be other than true and fair; duty of auditors) apply accordingly where advantage is taken of those exemptions in relation to group accounts.

Information as to undertaking in which shares held as result of financial assistance operation

6.—(1) The following provisions apply where the parent company of a banking group has a subsidiary undertaking which—

(*a*) is a credit institution of which shares are held as a result of a financial assistance operation with a view to its reorganisation or rescue, and
(*b*) is excluded from consolidation under section 229(3)(*c*) (interest held with a view to resale).

(2) Information as to the nature and terms of the operation shall be given in a note to the group accounts and there shall be appended to the copy of the group accounts delivered to the registrar in accordance with section 242 a copy of the undertaking's latest individual accounts and, if it is a parent undertaking, its latest group accounts.

If the accounts appended are required by law to be audited, a copy of the auditors' report shall also be appended.

(3) If any document required to be appended is in a language other than English, the directors shall annex to the copy of that document delivered a translation of it into English, certified in the prescribed manner to be a correct translation.

(4) The above requirements are subject to the following qualifications—

(*a*) an undertaking is not required to prepare for the purposes of this paragraph accounts which would not otherwise be prepared, and if no accounts satisfying the above requirements are prepared none need be appended;
(*b*) the accounts of an undertaking need not be appended if they would not otherwise be required to

be published, or made available for public inspection, anywhere in the world, but in that case the reason for not appending the accounts shall be stated in a note to the consolidated accounts.

(5) Where a copy of an undertaking's accounts is required to be appended to the copy of the group accounts delivered to the registrar, that fact shall be stated in a note to the group accounts.

(6) Subsections (2) to (4) of section 242 (penalties, &c in case of default) apply in relation to the requirements of this paragraph as regards the delivery of documents to the registrar as they apply in relation to the requirements of subsection (1) of that section.

PART III

[PART III OF SCHEDULE 9 TO THE COMPANIES ACT 1985]

Additional Disclosure: Related Undertakings

1. Where accounts are prepared in accordance with the special provisions of this Part relating to banking companies or groups, there shall be disregarded for the purposes of—

   (a) paragraphs 7(2)(a), 23(2)(a) and 26(2)(a) of Schedule 5 (information about significant holdings in undertakings other than subsidiary undertakings: definition of 10 per cent holding), and
   (b) paragraphs 9(1), 25(1) and 28(1) of that Schedule (additional information in case of 20 per cent holding),

any holding of shares not comprised in the equity share capital of the undertaking in question.

PART IV

[PART IV OF SCHEDULE 9 TO THE COMPANIES ACT 1985]

Additional Disclosure: Emoluments and Other Benefits of Directors and Others

1. The provisions of this Part of this Schedule have effect with respect to the application of Schedule 6 (additional disclosure: emoluments and other benefits of directors and others) to a banking company or the holding company of such a company.

Loans, quasi-loans and other dealings

2. Part II of Schedule 6 (loans, quasi-loans and other dealings) does not apply for the purposes of accounts prepared by a banking company, or a company which is the holding company of a banking company, in relation to a transaction or arrangement of a kind mentioned in section 330, or an agreement to enter into such a transaction or arrangement, to which that banking company is a party.

Other transactions, arrangements and agreements

3.—(1) Part III of Schedule 6 (other transactions, arrangements and agreements) applies for the purposes of accounts prepared by a banking company, or a company which is the holding company of a banking company, only in relation to a transaction, arrangement or agreement made by that banking company for—

   (a) a person who was a director of the company preparing the accounts or who was connected with such a director, or
   (b) a person who was a chief exeuctive or manager (within the meaning of the Banking Act 1987) of that company or its holding company.

(2) References in that Part to officers of the company shall be construed accordingly as including references to such persons.

(3) In this paragraph 'director' includes a shadow director.

(4) For the purposes of that Part as it applies by virtue of this paragraph, a company which a person does not control shall not be treated as connected with him.

(5) Section 346 of this Act applies for the purposes of this paragraph as regards the interpretation of references to a person being connected with a director or controlling a company.

SCHEDULE 8

Section 18(5)

[SCHEDULE 10 TO THE COMPANIES ACT 1985]

DIRECTORS' REPORT WHERE ACCOUNTS PREPARED IN ACCORDANCE WITH SPECIAL PROVISIONS FOR BANKING OR INSURANCE COMPANIES OR GROUPS

Recent issues

1.—(1) This paragraph applies where a company prepares individual accounts in accordance with the special provisions of this Part relating to banking or insurance companies.

(2) If in the financial year to which the accounts relate the company has issued any shares or debentures, the directors' report shall state the reason for making the issue, the classes of shares or debentures issued and, as respects each class, the number of shares or amount of debentures issued and the consideration received by the company for the issue.

Turnover and profitability

2.—(1) This paragraph applies where a company prepares group accounts in accordance with the special provisions of this Part relating to banking or insurance groups.

(2) If in the course of the financial year to which the accounts relate the group carried on business of two or more classes (other than banking or discounting or a class prescribed for the purposes of paragraph 17(2) of Part I of Schedule 9) that in the opinion of the directors differ substantially from each other, there shall be contained in the directors' report a statement of—

(a) the proportions in which the turnover for the financial year (so far as stated in the consolidated accounts) is divided amongst those classes (describing them), and

(b) as regards business of each class, the extent or approximate extent (expressed in money terms) to which, in the opinion of the directors, the carrying on of business of that class contributed to or restricted the profit or loss of the group for that year (before taxation).

(3) In sub-paragraph (2) 'the group' means the undertakings included in the consolidation.

(4) For the purposes of this paragraph classes of business which in the opinion of the directors do not differ substantially from each other shall be treated as one class.

Labour force and wages paid

3.—(1) This paragraph applies where a company prepares individual or group accounts in accordance with the special provisions of this Part relating to banking or insurance companies or groups.

(2) There shall be stated in the directors' report—

(a) the average number of persons employed by the company or, if the company prepares group accounts, by the company and its subsidiary undertakings, and

(b) the aggregate amount of the remuneration paid or payable to persons so employed.

(3) The average number of persons employed shall be determined by adding together the number of persons employed (whether throughout the week or not) in each week of the financial year and dividing that total by the number of weeks in the financial year.

(4) The aggregate amount of the remuneration paid or payable means the total amount of remuneration paid or payable in respect of the financial year; and for this purpose remuneration means gross remuneration and includes bonuses, whether payable under contract or not.

(5) The information required by this paragraph need not be given if the average number of persons employed is less than 100.

(6) No account shall be taken for the purposes of this paragraph of persons who worked wholly or mainly outside the United Kingdom.

(7) This paragraph does not apply to a company which is a wholly-owned subsidiary of a company incorporated in Great Britain.

SCHEDULE 9

Section 21(2)

[SCHEDULE 10A TO THE COMPANIES ACT 1985]

PARENT AND SUBSIDIARY UNDERTAKINGS: SUPPLEMENTARY PROVISIONS

Introduction

1. The provisions of this Schedule explain expressions used in section 258 (parent and subsidiary undertakings) and otherwise supplement that section.

Voting rights in an undertaking

2.—(1) In section 258(2)(a) and (d) the references to the voting rights in an undertaking are to the rights conferred on shareholders in respect of their shares or, in the case of an undertaking not having a share capital, on members, to vote at general meetings of the undertaking on all, or substantially all, matters.

(2) In relation to an undertaking which does not have general meetings at which matters are decided by the exercise of voting rights, the references to holding a majority of the voting rights in the

undertaking shall be construed as references to having the right under the constitution of the undertaking to direct the overall policy of the undertaking or to alter the terms of its constitution.

Right to appoint or remove a majority of the directors

3.—(1) In section 258(2)(*b*) the reference to the right to appoint or remove a majority of the board of directors is to the right to appoint or remove directors holding a majority of the voting rights at meetings of the board on all, or substantially all, matters.

(2) An undertaking shall be treated as having the right to appoint to a directorship if—

    (*a*) a person's appointment to it follows necessarily from his appointment as director of the undertaking, or

    (*b*) the directorship is held by the undertaking itself.

(3) A right to appoint or remove which is exercisable only with the consent or concurrence of another person shall be left out of account unless no other person has a right to appoint or, as the case may be, remove in relation to that directorship.

Right to exercise dominant influence

4.—(1) For the purposes of section 258(2)(*c*) an undertaking shall not be regarded as having the right to exercise a dominant influence over another undertaking unless it has a right to give directions with respect to the operating and financial policies of that other undertaking which its directors are obliged to comply with whether or not they are for the benefit of that other undertaking.

(2) A 'control contract' means a contract in writing conferring such a right which—

    (*a*) is of a kind authorised by the memorandum or articles of the undertaking in relation to which the right is exercisable, and

    (*b*) is permitted by the law under which that undertaking is established.

(3) This paragraph shall not be read as affecting the construction of the expression 'actually exercises a dominant influence' in section 258(4)(*a*).

Rights exercisable only in certain circumstances or temporarily incapable of exercise

5.—(1) Rights which are exercisable only in certain circumstances shall be taken into account only—

    (*a*) when the circumstances have arisen, and for so long as they continue to obtain, or

    (*b*) when the circumstances are within the control of the person having the rights.

(2) Rights which are normally exercisable but are temporarily incapable of exercise shall continue to be taken into account.

Rights held by one person on behalf of another

6. Rights held by a person in a fiduciary capacity shall be treated as not held by him.

7.—(1) Rights held by a person as nominee for another shall be treated as held by the other.

(2) Rights shall be regarded as held as nominee for another if they are exercisable only on his instructions or with his consent or concurrence.

Rights attached to shares held by way of security

8. Rights attached to shares held by way of security shall be treated as held by the person providing the security—

    (*a*) where apart from the right to exercise them for the purpose of preserving the value of the security, or of realising it, the rights are exercisable only in accordance with his instructions, and

    (*b*) where the shares are held in connection with the granting of loans as part of normal business activities and apart from the right to exercise them for the purpose of preserving the value of the security, or of realising it, the rights are exercisable only in his interests.

Rights attributed to parent undertaking

9.—(1) Rights shall be treated as held by a parent undertaking if they are held by any of its subsidiary undertakings.

(2) Nothing in paragraph 7 or 8 shall be construed as requiring rights held by a parent undertaking to be treated as held by any of its subsidiary undertakings.

(3) For the purposes of paragraph 8 rights shall be treated as being exercisable in accordance with the

instructions or in the interests of an undertaking if they are exercisable in accordance with the instructions of or, as the case may be, in the interests of any group undertaking.

Disregard of certain rights

10. The voting rights in an undertaking shall be reduced by any rights held by the undertaking itself.

Supplementary

11. References in any provision of paragraphs 6 to 10 to rights held by a person include rights falling to be treated as held by him by virtue of any other provision of those paragraphs but not rights which by virtue of any such provision are to be treated as not held by him.

SCHEDULE 10

Section 23

AMENDMENTS CONSEQUENTIAL ON PART I

PART I

AMENDMENTS OF THE COMPANIES ACT 1985

1. In section 46 (meaning of 'unqualified' auditors' report in section 43(3)), for subsections (2) to (6) substitute—

'(2) If the balance sheet was prepared for a financial year of the company, the reference is to an auditors' report stating without material qualification the auditors' opinion that the balance sheet has been properly prepared in accordance with this Act.

(3) If the balance sheet was not prepared for a financial year of the company, the reference is to an auditors' report stating without material qualification the auditors' opinion that the balance sheet has been properly prepared in accordance with the provisions of this Act which would have applied if it had been so prepared.

For the purposes of an auditors' report under this subsection the provisions of this Act shall be deemed to apply with such modifications as are necessary by reason of the fact that the balance sheet is not prepared for a financial year of the company.

(4) A qualification shall be regarded as material unless the auditors state in their report that the matter giving rise to the qualification is not material for the purpose of determining (by reference to the company's balance sheet) whether at the balance sheet date the amount of the company's net assets was not less than the aggregate of its called up share capital and undistributable reserves.

In this subsection 'net assets' and 'undistributable reserves' have the meaning given by section 264(2) and (3).'.

2. In section 209(5)(*a*)(i) for 'an authorised institution' substitute 'a banking company'.

3. In sections 211(9) and 215(4) for 'paragraph 3 or 10 of Schedule 5' substitute 'section 231(3)'.

4. In section 271(3), for 'section 236' substitute 'section 235'.

5. In section 272(3)—

(*a*) for 'section 228' substitute 'section 226', and
(*b*) for 'section 238' substitute 'section 233'.

6. In sections 272(5) and 273(7) for 'section 241(3)(*b*)' substitute 'the second sentence of section 242(1)'.

7. In section 276(*b*) for '34(4)(*b*)' substitute '34(3)(*a*)'.

8. For section 279 substitute—

'279 Distributions by banking or insurance companies

Where a company's accounts relevant for the purposes of this Part are prepared in accordance with the special provisions of Part VII relating to banking or insurance companies, sections 264 to 275 apply with the modifications shown in Schedule 11.'.

9. In section 289(4) for 'section 252(5)' substitute 'section 250(3)'.

10. In sections 338(4), 339(4), 343(1)(*a*) and 344(2) for 'an authorised institution', wherever occurring, substitute 'a banking company'.

11. In section 343(2) and (4) for 'paragraph 4 of Schedule 6, be required by section 232' substitute 'paragraph 2 of Part IV of Schedule 9, be required'.

12. In section 699(3) for 'section 241(3)' substitute 'section 242(1)'.

13. In Part XXIII (oversea companies), for Chapter II (delivery of accounts) substitute—

'CHAPTER II

DELIVERY OF ACCOUNTS AND REPORTS

700 Preparation of accounts and reports by oversea companies

(1) Every oversea company shall in respect of each financial year of the company prepare the like accounts and directors' report, and cause to be prepared such an auditors' report, as would be required if the company were formed and registered under this Act.

(2) The Secretary of State may by order—

(a) modify the requirements referred to in subsection (1) for the purpose of their application to oversea companies;

(b) exempt an oversea company from those requirements or from such of them as may be specified in the order.

(3) An order may make different provision for different cases or classes of case and may contain such incidental and supplementary provisions as the Secretary of State thinks fit.

(4) An order under this section shall be made by statutory instrument which shall be subject to annulment in pursuance of a resolution of either House of Parliament.

701 Oversea company's financial year and accounting reference periods

(1) Sections 223 to 225 (financial year and accounting reference periods) apply to an oversea company, subject to the following modifications.

(2) For the references to the incorporation of the company substitute references to the company establishing a place of business in Great Britain.

(3) Omit section 225(4) (restriction on frequency with which current accounting reference period may be extended).

702 Delivery to registrar of accounts and reports of oversea company

(1) An oversea company shall in respect of each financial year of the company deliver to the registrar copies of the accounts and reports prepared in accordance with section 700.

If any document comprised in those accounts or reports is in a language other than English, the directors shall annex to the copy delivered a translation of it into English, certified in the prescribed manner to be a correct translation.

(2) In relation to an oversea company the period allowed for delivering accounts and reports is 13 months after the end of the relevant accounting reference period.

This is subject to the following provisions of this section.

(3) If the relevant accounting reference period is the company's first and is a period of more than 12 months, the period allowed is 13 months from the first anniversary of the company's establishing a place of business in Great Britain.

(4) If the relevant accounting period is treated as shortened by virtue of a notice given by the company under section 225 (alteration of accounting reference date), the period allowed is that applicable in accordance with the above provisions or three months from the date of the notice under that section, whichever last expires.

(5) If for any special reason the Secretary of State thinks fit he may, on an application made before the expiry of the period otherwise allowed, by notice in writing to an oversea company extend that period by such further period as may be specified in the notice.

(6) In this section 'the relevant accounting reference period' means the accounting reference period by reference to which the financial year for the accounts in question was determined.

703 Penalty for non-compliance

(1) If the requirements of section 702(1) are not complied with before the end of the period allowed for delivering accounts and reports, or if the accounts and reports delivered do not comply with the requirements of this Act, the company and every person who immediately before the end of that period was a director of the company is guilty of an offence and liable to a fine and, for continued contravention, to a daily default fine.

(2) It is a defence for a person charged with such an offence to prove that he took all reasonable steps for securing that the requirements in question would be complied with.

(3) It is not a defence in relation to a failure to deliver copies to the registrar to prove that the documents in question were not in fact prepared as required by this Act.'.

14. In section 711(1)(*k*) for 'section 241 (annual accounts)' substitute 'section 242(1) (accounts and reports)'.

15. For section 742 (expressions used in connection with accounts) substitute—

'742 Expressions used in connection with accounts

(1) In this Act, unless a contrary intention appears, the following expressions have the same meaning as in Part VII (accounts)—

'annual accounts',
'accounting reference date' and 'accounting reference period',
'balance sheet' and 'balance sheet date',
'current assets',
'financial year', in relation to a company,
'fixed assets',
'parent company' and 'parent undertaking',
'profit and loss account', and
'subsidiary undertaking'.

(2) References in this Act to 'realised profits' and 'realised losses', in relation to a company's accounts, shall be construed in accordance with section 262(3).'.

16. In section 744 (interpretation), omit the definition of 'authorised institution' and at the appropriate place insert—

"banking company' means a company which is authorised under the Banking Act 1987;'.

17. In Schedule 1, in paragraph 2(2)(*a*) for 'section 252(5)' substitute 'section 250(3)'.

18.—(1) Schedule 2 (interpretation of references to 'beneficial interest') is amended as follows.

(2) After the heading at the beginning of the Schedule, and before the cross-heading preceding paragraph 1, insert the following heading—

'PART I

REFERENCES IN SECTIONS 23, 145, 146 AND 148'.

(3) In paragraph 1—

(*a*) in sub-paragraph (1) omit 'paragraph 60(2) of Schedule 4, or paragraph 19(3) of Schedule 9'; and
(*b*) omit sub-paragraph (5).

(4) In paragraph 3—

(*a*) in sub-paragraph (1) omit ', paragraph 60(2) of Schedule 4 or paragraph 19(3) of Schedule 9'; and
(*b*) omit sub-paragraph (3).

(5) In paragraph 4—

(*a*) in sub-paragraph (1) omit '(whether as personal representative or otherwise)', and
(*b*) in sub-paragraph (2) omit ', paragraph 60(2) of Schedule 4 and paragraph 19(3) of Schedule 9';

and at the end add—

'(3) As respects sections 145, 146 and 148, sub-paragraph (1) above applies where a company is a personal representative as it applies where a company is a trustee.'.

(6) In paragraph 5(1) for 'this Schedule' substitute 'this Part of this Schedule'.

(7) After paragraph 5 insert the following—

'PART II

REFERENCES IN SCHEDULE 5

Residual interests under pension and employees' share schemes

6.—(1) Where shares in an undertaking are held on trust for the purposes of a pension scheme or an employees' share scheme, there shall be disregarded any residual interest which has not vested in possession, being an interest of the undertaking or any of its subsidiary undertakings.

(2) In this paragraph a 'residual interest' means a right of the undertaking in question (the 'residual beneficiary') to receive any of the trust property in the event of—

    (*a*) all the liabilities arising under the scheme having been satisfied or provided for, or

    (*b*) the residual beneficiary ceasing to participate in the scheme, or

    (*c*) the trust property at any time exceeding what is necessary for satisfying the liabilities arising or expected to arise under the scheme.

(3) In sub-paragraph (2) references to a right include a right dependent on the exercise of a discretion vested by the scheme in the trustee or any other person; and references to liabilities arising under a scheme include liabilities that have resulted or may result from the exercise of any such discretion.

(4) For the purposes of this paragraph a residual interest vests in possession—

    (*a*) in a case within sub-paragraph (2)(*a*), on the occurrence of the event there mentioned, whether or not the amount of the property receivable pursuant to the right mentioned in that sub-paragraph is then ascertained;

    (*b*) in a case within sub-paragraph (2)(*b*) or (*c*), when the residual beneficiary becomes entitled to require the trustee to transfer to that beneficiary any of the property receivable pursuant to that right.

Employer's charges and other rights of recovery

7.—(1) Where shares in an undertaking are held on trust, there shall be disregarded—

    (*a*) if the trust is for the purposes of a pension scheme, any such rights as are mentioned in sub-paragraph (2) below;

    (*b*) if the trust is for the purposes of an employees' share scheme, any such rights as are mentioned in paragraph (*a*) of that sub-paragraph,

being rights of the undertaking or any of its subsidiary undertakings.

(2) The rights referred to are—

    (*a*) any charge or lien on, or set-off against, any benefit or other right or interest under the scheme for the purpose of enabling the employer or former employer of a member of the scheme to obtain the discharge of a monetary obligation due to him from the member, and

    (*b*) any right to receive from the trustee of the scheme, or as trustee of the scheme to retain, an amount that can be recovered or retained under section 47 of the Social Security Pensions Act 1975 (deduction of premium from refund of pension contributions) or otherwise as reimbursement or partial reimbursement for any state scheme premium paid in connection with the scheme under Part III of that Act.

Trustee's right to expenses, remuneration, indemnity, &c

8. Where an undertaking is a trustee, there shall be disregarded any rights which the undertaking has in its capacity as trustee including, in particular, any right to recover its expenses or be remunerated out of the trust property and any right to be indemnified out of that property for any liability incurred by reason of any act or omission of the undertaking in the performance of its duties as trustee.

Supplementary

9.—(1) The following applies for the interpretation of this Part of this Schedule.

(2) 'Undertaking' and 'shares', in relation to an undertaking, have the same meaning as in Part VII.

(3) This Part of this Schedule applies in relation to debentures as it applies in relation to shares.

(4) 'Pension scheme' means any scheme for the provision of benefits consisting of or including relevant benefits for or in respect of employees or former employees; and 'relevant benefits' means any pension, lump sum, gratuity or other like benefit given or to be given on retirement or on death or in anticipation of retirement or, in connection with past service, after retirement or death.

(5) In sub-paragraph (4) of this paragraph and in paragraph 7(2) 'employee' and 'employer' shall be read as if a director of an undertaking were employed by it.'.

19.—(1) Part II of Schedule 3 (prospectuses: auditors' and accountants' reports to be set out) is amended as follows.

(2) In paragraph 16 (auditors' reports), in sub-paragraph (2) for 'subsidiaries' substitute 'subsidiary undertakings' and for sub-paragraph (3) substitute—

'(3) If the company has subsidiary undertakings, the report shall—

(a) deal separately with the company's profits or losses as provided by sub-paragraph (2), and in addition deal either—

(i) as a whole with the combined profits or losses of its subsidiary undertakings, so far as they concern members of the company, or

(ii) individually with the profits or losses of each of its subsidiary undertakings, so far as they concern members of the company,

or, instead of dealing separately with the company's profits or losses, deal as a whole with the profits or losses of the company and (so far as they concern members of the company) with the combined profits and losses of its subsidiary undertakings; and

(b) deal separately with the company's assets and liabilities as provided by sub-paragraph (2), and in addition deal either—

(i) as a whole with the combined assets and liabilities of its subsidiary undertakings, with or without the company's assets and liabilities, or

(ii) individually with the assets and liabilities of each of its subsidiary undertakings,

indicating, as respects the assets and liabilities of its subsidiary undertakings, the allowance to be made for persons other than members of the company.'.

(3) For paragraph 18 (accountants' reports) substitute—

'18.—(1) The following provisions apply if—

(a) the proceeds of the issue are to be applied directly or indirectly in any manner resulting in the acquisition by the company of shares in any other undertaking, or any part of the proceeds is to be so applied, and

(b) by reason of that acquisition or anything to be done in consequence of or in connection with it, that undertaking will become a subsidiary undertaking of the company.

(2) There shall be set out in the prospectus a report made by accountants upon—

(a) the profits or losses of the other undertaking in respect of each of the five financial years immediately preceding the issue of the prospectus, and

(b) the assets and liabilities of the other undertaking at the last date to which its accounts were made up.

(3) The report shall—

(a) indicate how the profits or losses of the other undertaking would in respect of the shares to be acquired have concerned members of the company and what allowance would have fallen to be made, in relation to assets and liabilities so dealt with, for holders of other shares, if the company had at all material times held the shares to be acquired, and

(b) where the other undertaking is a parent undertaking, deal with the profits or losses and the assets and liabilities of the undertaking and its subsidiary undertakings in the manner provided by paragraph 16(3) above in relation to the company and its subsidiary undertakings.

(4) In this paragraph 'undertaking' and 'shares', in relation to an undertaking, have the same meaning as in Part VII.'.

(4) In paragraph 22 (eligibility of accountants to make reports), for sub-paragraph (2) substitute—

'(2) Such a report shall not be made by an accountant who is an officer or servant, or a partner of or in the employment of an officer or servant, of—

(a) the company or any of its subsidiary undertakings,

(b) a parent undertaking of the company or any subsidiary undertaking of such an undertaking.'.

20. In paragraph 12(b) of Schedule 4, for 'section 238' substitute 'section 233'.

21.—(1) Schedule 11 is amended as follows.

(2) For the heading substitute 'Modifications of Part VIII Where Company's Accounts Prepared in Accordance with Special Provisions for Banking or Insurance Companies'.

(3) In paragraphs 1 and 2(a) for 'Schedule 9' substitute 'Part I of Schedule 9'.

(4) In paragraph 4—

(a) in sub-paragraph (a) for 'Schedule 9' substitute 'Part I of Schedule 9', and

(b) omit sub-paragraphs (b) and (c).

(5) In paragraph 5—

    (*a*) in sub-paragraph (*a*) for 'Part III of Schedule 9' substitute 'paragraph 27 or 28 of Schedule 9', and

    (*b*) omit sub-paragraph (*b*).

(6) In paragraph 6—

    (*a*) in sub-paragraph (*a*), for 'section 228' substitute 'section 226' and for 'section 258 and Schedule 9' substitute 'section 255 and Part I of Schedule 9', and

    (*b*) in sub-paragraph (*b*), for 'Part III of Schedule 9' substitute 'paragraph 27 or 28 of Schedule 9'.

(7) In paragraph 7(*a*) for 'Schedule 9' substitute 'Part I of Schedule 9'.

22.—(1) In Schedule 15A (renumbered 15B) (provisions applicable to mergers and divisions of public companies), paragraph 6 (documents to be made available for inspection) is amended as follows.

(2) In sub-paragraph (1)(*b*) (directors' report on merger or division), after 'directors' report' insert 'referred to in paragraph 4 above'.

(3) For sub-paragraph (1)(*d*) and (*e*) substitute—

    '(*d*) the company's annual accounts, together with the relevant directors' report and auditors' report, for the last three financial years ending on or before the relevant date; and

    (*e*) if the last of those financial years ended more than six months before the relevant date, an accounting statement in the form described in the following provisions.'.

(4) In sub-paragraph (1), after the paragraphs add—

    'In paragraphs (*d*) and (*e*) 'the relevant date' means one month before the first meeting of the company summoned under section 425(1) or for the purposes of paragraph 1.'.

(5) For sub-paragraphs (2) to (5) substitute—

    '(2) The accounting statement shall consist of—

        (*a*) a balance sheet dealing with the state of the affairs of the company as at a date not more than three months before the draft terms were adopted by the directors, and

        (*b*) where the company would be required to prepare group accounts if that date were the last day of a financial year, a consolidated balance sheet dealing with the state of affairs of the company and its subsidiary undertakings as at that date.

    (3) The requirements of this Act as to balance sheets forming part of a company's annual accounts, and the matters to be included in notes thereto, apply to any balance sheet required for the accounting statement, with such modifications as are necessary by reason of its being prepared otherwise than as at the last day of a financial year.

    (4) Any balance sheet required for the accounting statement shall be approved by the board of directors and signed on behalf of the board by a director of the company.

    (5) In relation to a company within the meaning of Article 3 of the Companies (Northern Ireland) Order 1986, the references in this paragraph to the requirements of this Act shall be construed as reference to the corresponding requirements of that Order.'.

23. In Schedule 22 (provisions applying to unregistered companies), in the entry relating to Part VII, in column 1, for 'Schedule 10' substitute 'Schedules 10 and 10A'.

24.—(1) Schedule 24 (punishment of offences) is amended as follows.

(2) The existing entries for provisions in Part VII are amended as follows, and shall be re-ordered according to the new order of the sections in that Part:

Provision of Part VII	Amendment
223(1)	In column 1, for '223(1)' substitute '221 (5) or 222(4)'.
223(2)	In column 1, for '223(2)' subsitute '222(6)'.
	In column 2, for '222(4)' substitute '222(5)'.
231(3)	In column 1, for '231(3)' substitute '231(6)'.
231(4)	In column 1, for '231(4)' substitute '232(4)'.
	In column 2, for 'Schedule 5, Part V' substitute 'Schedule 6, Part I'.
235(7)	In column 1, for '235(7)' substitute '234(5)'.
	In column 2, for 'the section' substitute 'Part VII'.
238(2)	In column 1, for '238(2)' substitute '233(6)'.
240(5)	In column 1, for '240(5)' substitute '238(5)'.
	In column 2, for 'company balance sheet' substitute 'company's annual accounts'.

Provision of Part VII	*Amendment*
243(1)	In column 1, for '243(1)' substitute '241(2) or 242(2)'.
	In column 2, for 'company accounts' substitute 'company's annual accounts, directors' report and auditors' report'.
245(1)	Omit the entry.
245(2)	Omit the entry.
246(2)	In column 1, for '246(2)' substitute '239(3)'.
	In column 2, after 'accounts' insert 'and reports'.
254(6)	In column 1, for '254(6)' substitute '240(6)'.
	In column 2, for the present words substitute 'Failure to comply with requirements in connection with publication of accounts'.
255(5)	Omit the entry.
260(3)	Omit the entry.

(3) At the appropriate places insert the following new entries—

'233(5)	Approving defective accounts.	1. On indictment.	A fine.
		2. Summary.	The statutory maximum.
234A(4)	Laying, circulating or delivering directors' report without required signature.	Summary.	One-fifth of the statutory maximum.
236(4)	Laying, circulating or delivering auditors' report without required signature.	Summary.	One fifth of the statutory maximum.
251(6)	Failure to comply with requirements in relation to summary financial statements.	Summary.	One-fifth of the statutory maximum.'.

(4) In the entry for section 703(1) (failure by oversea company to comply with requirements as to accounts and reports), in column 2 for the words from 's 700' to the end substitute 'requirements as to accounts and reports'.

PART II

AMENDMENTS OF OTHER ENACTMENTS

Betting, Gaming and Lotteries Act 1963 (c 2)

25. In Schedule 2 to the Betting, Gaming and Lotteries Act 1963 (registered pool promoters), in paragraph 24(2) (duties with respect to delivery of accounts and audit) for the words from 'and the following provisions' to 'their report)' substitute 'and sections 235(2) and 237(1) and (3) of the Companies Act 1985 (matters to be stated in auditors' report and responsibility of auditors in preparing their report)'.

Harbours Act 1964 (c 40)

26.—(1) Section 42 of the Harbours Act 1964 (accounts and reports of statutory harbour undertakers) is amended as follows.

(2) For subsection (2) substitute—

'(2) Where a statutory harbour undertaker is a parent undertaking with subsidiary undertakings which carry on harbour activities or any associated activities, then, it shall be the duty of the company also to prepare group accounts relating to the harbour activities and associated activities carried on by it and its subsidiary undertakings.'

(3) In subsection (6) (application of provisions of the Companies Act 1985)—

(*a*) in paragraph (*a*) for 'company accounts' substitute 'individual company accounts';
(*b*) in paragraph (*c*) omit the words 'required to be attached to a company's balance sheet'.

(4) In subsection (9), for the definition of 'holding company' and 'subsidiary' substitute—

"parent undertaking' and 'subsidiary undertaking' have the same meaning as in Part VII of the Companies Act 1985;'.

Coal Industry Act 1971 (c 16)

27.—(1) Section 8 of the Coal Industry Act 1971 (further provisions as to accounts of British Coal Corporation) is amended as follows.

(2) In subsections (1) and (2) for 'subsidiaries' (three times) substitute 'subsidiary undertakings'.

(3) After subsection (2) insert—

'(3) In this section 'subsidiary undertaking' has the same meaning as in Part VII of the Companies Act 1985.'.

Aircraft and Shipbuilding Industries Act 1977 (c 3)

28.—(1) Section 17 of the Aircraft and Shipbuilding Industries Act 1977 (British Shipbuilders: accounts and audit) is amended as follows.

(2) In subsection (1)(c) (duty to prepare consolidated accounts) for 'subsidiaries' substitute 'subsidiary undertakings'.

(3) In subsection (9) (copies of accounts to be sent to the Secretary of State) for 'subsidiaries' substitute 'subsidiary undertakings' and for 'subsidiary' substitute 'subsidiary undertaking'.

(4) After subsection (9) add—

'(10) In this section 'subsidiary undertaking' has the same meaning as in Part VII of the Companies Act 1985.'.

Crown Agents Act 1979 (c 43)

29. In section 22 of the Crown Agents Act 1979 (accounts and audit), in subsection (2) (duty to prepare consolidated accounts) for 'subsidiaries' (three times) substitute 'subsidiary undertakings', and at the end of that subsection add—

'In this subsection 'subsidiary undertaking' has the same meaning as in Part VII of the Companies Act 1985.'.

British Telecommunications Act 1981 (c 38)

30. In section 75 of the British Telecommunications Act 1981 (accounts of the Post Office), in subsection (1)(c)(i) for 'subsidiaries' substitute 'subsidiary undertakings within the meaning of Part VII of the Companies Act 1985'.

Transport Act 1981 (c 56)

31. In section 11(4) of the Transport Act 1981, for 'section 235' substitute 'section 234'.

Iron and Steel Act 1982 (c 25)

32. In section 24(5) of the Iron and Steel Act 1982 (meaning of 'directors' report') for the words from 'which, under section 235' to the end substitute 'which is required to be prepared under section 234 of the Companies Act 1985'.

Oil and Pipelines Act 1985 (c 62)

33. In Schedule 3 to the Oil and Pipelines Act 1985 (Oil and Pipelines Agency: financial and other provisions), in paragraph 9(2) (duty to prepare consolidated accounts) for 'subsidiaries' (three times) substitute 'subsidiary undertakings', and at the end of that sub-paragraph add—

'In this sub-paragraph 'subsidiary undertaking' has the same meaning as in Part VII of the Companies Act 1985.'.

Patents, Designs and Marks Act 1986 (c 39)

34. In Schedule 2 to the Patents, Designs and Marks Act 1986 (service marks), in paragraph 1(2) (provisions in which reference to trade mark includes service mark) for sub-paragraph (ii) substitute—

'(ii) Part I of Schedule 4 and paragraphs 5(2)(d) and 10(1)(b) and (2) of Schedule 9 (form of company balance sheets); and'.

Company Directors Disqualification Act 1986 (c 46)

35.—(1) The Company Directors Disqualification Act 1986 is amended as follows.

(2) In section 3(3)(b) (default orders)—

(a) in sub-paragraph (i) for 'section 244' substitute 'section 242(4)', and
(b) after that sub-paragraph insert—

'(ia) section 245B of that Act (order requiring preparation of revised accounts),'.

(3) In Schedule 1, for paragraph 5 substitute—

'5. The extent of the director's responsibility for any failure by the directors of the company to comply with—

(*a*) section 226 or 227 of the Companies Act (duty to prepare annual accounts), or

(*b*) section 233 of that Act (approval and signature of accounts).'.

Financial Services Act 1986 (c 60)

36.—(1) The Financial Services Act 1986 is amended as follows.

(2) In section 117(4) and (5), for 'section 227' substitute 'section 226'.

(3) In Schedule 1, for paragraph 30 substitute—

'30.—(1) For the purposes of this Schedule a group shall be treated as including any body corporate in which a member of the group holds a qualifying capital interest.

(2) A qualifying capital interest means an interest in relevant shares of the body corporate which the member holds on a long-term basis for the purpose of securing a contribution to its own activities by the exercise of control or influence arising from that interest.

(3) Relevant shares means shares comprised in the equity share capital of the body corporate of a class carrying rights to vote in all circumstances at general meetings of the body.

(4) A holding of 20 per cent or more of the nominal value of the relevant shares of a body corporate shall be presumed to be a qualifying capital interest unless the contrary is shown.

(5) In this paragraph 'equity share capital' has the same meaning as in the Companies Act 1985 and the Companies (Northern Ireland) Order 1986.'.

Banking Act 1987 (c 22)

37.—(1) The Banking Act 1987 is amended as follows.

(2) In section 46(2) (duties of auditor of authorised institution), in paragraph (*c*) for 'section 236' substitute 'section 235(2)' and for 'section 237' substitute 'section 235(3) or section 237'; and in section 46(4) (adaptation of references for Northern Ireland) for '236 and 237' substitute '235(2) and 235(3) and 237'.

(3) After section 105 insert—

'105A Meaning of 'related company'

(1) In this Act a 'related company', in relation to an institution or the holding company of an institution, means a body corporate (other than a subsidiary) in which the institution or holding company holds a qualifying capital interest.

(2) A qualifying capital interest means an interest in relevant shares of the body corporate which the institution or holding company holds on a long-term basis for the purpose of securing a contribution to its own activities by the exercise of control or influence arising from that interest.

(3) Relevant shares means shares comprised in the equity share capital of the body corporate of a class carrying rights to vote in all circumstances at general meetings of the body.

(4) A holding of 20 per cent or more of the nominal value of the relevant shares of a body corporate shall be presumed to be a qualifying capital interest unless the contrary is shown.

(5) In this paragraph 'equity share capital' has the same meaning as in the Companies Act 1985 and the Companies (Northern Ireland) Order 1986.'.

(4) In section 106(1) (interpretation), for the definition of 'related company' substitute—

''related company' has the meaning given by section 105A above;'.

Income and Corporation Taxes Act 1988 (c 1)

38.—(1) The Income and Corporation Taxes Act 1988 is amended as follows.

(2) In section 180 (annual return of registered profit-related pay scheme), in subsection (3) for 'section 242(3)' substitute 'section 244(3)'.

(3) In section 565(6) (conditions for exemption from provisions relating to sub-contractors in construction industry: compliance with requirements of Companies Act 1985), in paragraph (*a*) for 'section 227 and 241' substitute 'sections 226, 241 and 242'.

Darford–Thurrock Crossing Act 1988 (c 20)

39. In section 33 of the Dartford–Thurrock Crossing Act 1988 (duty to lay before Parliament copies of accounts of persons appointed to levy tolls), for subsection (2) substitute—

'(2) In relation to a company 'accounts' in subsection (1) means the company's annual accounts for a financial year, together with the relevant directors' report and the auditors' report on those accounts.

Expressions used in this subsection have the same meaning as in Part VII of the Companies Act 1985.'.

SCHEDULE 11

Section 30(5)

RECOGNITION OF SUPERVISORY BODY

PART I

GRANT AND REVOCATION OF RECOGNITION

Application for recognition of supervisory body

1.—(1) A supervisory body may apply to the Secretary of State for an order declaring it to be a recognised supervisory body for the purposes of this Part of this Act.

(2) Any such application—

 (a) shall be made in such manner as the Secretary of State may direct, and

 (b) shall be accompanied by such information as the Secretary of State may reasonably require for the purpose of determining the application.

(3) At any time after receiving an application and before determining it the Secretary of State may require the applicant to furnish additional information.

(4) The directions and requirements given or imposed under sub-paragraphs (2) and (3) may differ as between different applications.

(5) Any information to be furnished to the Secretary of State under this paragraph shall, if he so requires, be in such form or verified in such manner as he may specify.

(6) Every application shall be accompanied by a copy of the applicant's rules and of any guidance issued by the applicant which is intended to have continuing effect and is issued in writing or other legible form.

Grant and refusal of recognition

2.—(1) The Secretary of State may, on an application duly made in accordance with paragraph 1 and after being furnished with all such information as he may require under that paragraph, make or refuse to make an order (a 'recognition order') declaring the applicant to be a recognised supervisory body for the purposes of this Part of this Act.

(2) The Secretary of State shall not make a recognition order unless it appears to him, from the information furnished by the body and having regard to any other information in his possession, that the requirements of Part II of this Schedule are satisfied as respects that body.

(3) The Secretary of State may refuse to make a recognition order in respect of a body if he considers that its recognition is unnecessary having regard to the existence of one or more other bodies which maintain and enforce rules as to the appointment and conduct of company auditors and which have been or are likely to be recognised.

(4) Where the Secretary of State refuses an application for a recognition order he shall give the applicant a written notice to that effect specifying which requirements in the opinion of the Secretary of State are not satisfied or stating that the application is refused on the ground mentioned in sub-paragraph (3).

(5) A recognition order shall state the date on which it takes effect.

Revocation of recognition

3.—(1) A recognition order may be revoked by a further order made by the Secretary of State if at any time it appears to him—

 (a) that any requirement of Part II of this Schedule is not satisfied in the case of the body to which the recognition order relates ('the recognised body'),

 (b) that the recognised body has failed to comply with any obligation to which it is subject by virtue of this Part of this Act, or (*c*) that the continued recognition of the body is undesirable having regard to the existence of one or more other bodies which have been or are to be recognised.

(2) An order revoking a recognition order shall state the date on which it takes effect and that date shall not be earlier than three months after the day on which the revocation order is made.

(3) Before revoking a recognition order the Secretary of State shall give written notice of his intention to do so to the recognised body, take such steps as he considers reasonably practicable for bringing the notice to the attention of members of the body and publish it in such manner as he thinks appropriate for bringing it to the attention of any other persons who are in his opinion likely to be affected.

(4) A notice under sub-paragraph (3) shall state the reasons for which the Secretary of State proposes to act and give particulars of the rights conferred by sub-paragraph (5).

(5) A body on which a notice is served under sub-paragraph (3), any member of the body and any other person who appears to the Secretary of State to be affected may within three months after the date of service or publication, or within such longer time as the Secretary of State may allow, make written representations to the Secretary of State and, if desired, oral representations to a person appointed for that purpose by the Secretary of State; and the Secretary of State shall have regard to any representations made in accordance with this sub-paragraph in determining whether to revoke the recognition order.

(6) If in any case the Secretary of State considers it essential to do so in the public interest he may revoke a recognition order without regard to the restriction imposed by sub-paragraph (2) and notwithstanding that no notice has been given or published under sub-paragraph (3) or that the time for making representations in pursuance of such a notice has not expired.

(7) An order revoking a recognition order may contain such transitional provisions as the Secretary of State thinks necessary or expedient.

(8) A recognition order may be revoked at the request or with the consent of the recognised body and any such revocation shall not be subject to the restrictions imposed by sub-paragraphs (1) and (2) or the requirements of sub-paragraphs (3) to (5).

(9) On making an order revoking a recognition order the Secretary of State shall give the body written notice of the making of the order, take such steps as he considers reasonably practicable for bringing the making of the order to the attention of members of the body and publish a notice of the making of the order in such manner as he thinks appropriate for bringing it to the attention of any other persons who are in his opinion likely to be affected.

PART II

REQUIREMENTS FOR RECOGNITION

Holding of appropriate qualification

4.—(1) The body must have rules to the effect that a person is not eligible for appointment as a company auditor unless—

(*a*) in the case of an individual, he holds an appropriate qualification;

(*b*) in the case of a firm—

(i) the individuals responsible for company audit work on behalf of the firm hold an appropriate qualification, and

(ii) the firm is controlled by qualified persons (see paragraph 5 below).

(2) This does not prevent the body from imposing more stringent requirements.

(3) A firm which has ceased to comply with the conditions mentioned in sub-paragraph (1)(*b*) may be permitted to remain eligible for appointment as a company auditor for a period of not more than three months.

5.—(1) The following provisions explain what is meant in paragraph 4(1)(*b*)(ii) by a firm being 'controlled by qualified persons'.

(2) For this purpose references to a person being qualified are, in relation to an individual, to his holding an appropriate qualification, and in relation to a firm, to its being eligible for appointment as a company auditor.

(3) A firm shall be treated as controlled by qualified persons if, and only if—

(*a*) a majority of the members of the firm are qualified persons, and

(*b*) where the firm's affairs are managed by a board of directors, committee or other management body, a majority of the members of that body are qualified persons or, if the body consists of two persons only, that at least one of them is a qualified person.

(4) A majority of the members of a firm means—

    (*a*) where under the firm's constitution matters are decided upon by the exercise of voting rights, members holding a majority of the rights to vote on all, or substantially all, matters;

    (*b*) in any other case, members having such rights under the constitution of the firm as enable them to direct its overall policy or alter its constitution.

(5) A majority of the members of the management body of a firm means—

    (*a*) where matters are decided at meetings of the management body by the exercise of voting rights, members holding a majority of the rights to vote on all, or substantially all, matters at such meetings;

    (*b*) in any other case, members having such rights under the constitution of the firm as enable them to direct its overall policy or alter its constitution.

(6) The provisions of paragraphs 5 to 11 of Schedule 10A to the Companies Act 1985 (rights to be taken into account and attribution of rights) apply for the purposes of this paragraph.

Auditors to be fit and proper persons

6.—(1) The body must have adequate rules and practices designed to ensure that the persons eligible under its rules for appointment as a company auditor are fit and proper persons to be so appointed.

(2) The matters which the body may take into account for this purpose in relation to a person must include—

    (*a*) any matter relating to any person who is or will be employed by or associated with him for the purposes of or in connection with company audit work; and

    (*b*) in the case of a body corporate, any matter relating to any director or controller of the body, to any other body corporate in the same group or to any director or controller of any such other body; and

    (*c*) in the case of a partnership, any matter relating to any of the partners, any director or controller of any of the partners, any body corporate in the same group as any of the partners and any director or controller of any such other body.

(3) In sub-paragraph (2)(*b*) and (*c*) 'controller', in relation to a body corporate, means a person who either alone or with any associate or associates is entitled to exercise or control the exercise of 15 per cent or more of the rights to vote on all, or substantially all, matters at general meetings of the body or another body corporate of which it is a subsidiary.

Professional integrity and independence

7.—(1) The body must have adequate rules and practices designed to ensure—

    (*a*) that company audit work is conducted properly and with integrity, and

    (*b*) that persons are not appointed company auditor in circumstances in which they have any interest likely to conflict with the proper conduct of the audit.

(2) The body must also have adequate rules and practices designed to ensure that no firm is eligible under its rules for appointment as a company auditor unless the firm has arrangements to prevent—

    (*a*) individuals who do not hold an appropriate qualification, and

    (*b*) persons who are not members of the firm,

from being able to exert any influence over the way in which an audit is conducted in circumstances in which that influence would be likely to affect the independence or integrity of the audit.

Technical standards

8. The body must have rules and practices as to the technical standards to be applied in company audit work and as to the manner in which those standards are to be applied in practice.

Procedures for maintaining competence

9. The body must have rules and practices designed to ensure that persons eligible under its rules for appointment as a company auditor continue to maintain an appropriate level of competence in the conduct of company audits.

Monitoring and enforcement

10.—(1) The body must have adequate arrangements and resources for the effective monitoring and enforcement of compliance with its rules.

(2) The arrangements for monitoring may make provision for that function to be performed on behalf of the body (and without affecting its responsibility) by any other body or person who is able and willing to perform it.

Membership, eligibility and discipline

11. The rules and practices of the body relating to—

  (*a*) the admission and expulsion of members,
  (*b*) the grant and withdrawal of eligibility for appointment as a company auditor, and
  (*c*) the discipline it exercises over its members,

must be fair and reasonable and include adequate provision for appeals.

Investigation of complaints

12.—(1) The body must have effective arrangements for the investigation of complaints—

  (*a*) against persons who are eligible under its rules to be appointed company auditor, or
  (*b*) against the body in respect of matters arising out of its functions as a supervisory body.

(2) The arrangements may make provision for the whole or part of that function to be performed by and to be the responsibility of a body or person independent of the body itself.

Meeting of claims arising out of audit work

13.—(1) The body must have adequate rules or arrangements designed to ensure that persons eligible under its rules for appointment as a company auditor take such steps as may reasonably be expected of them to secure that they are able to meet claims against them arising out of company audit work.

(2) This may be achieved by professional indemnity insurance or other appropriate arrangements.

Register of auditors and other information to be made available

14. The body must have rules requiring persons eligible under its rules for appointment as a company auditor to comply with any obligations imposed on them by regulations under section 35 or 36.

Taking account of costs of compliance

15. The body must have satisfactory arrangements for taking account, in framing its rules, of the cost to those to whom the rules would apply of complying with those rules and any other controls to which they are subject.

Promotion and maintenance of standards

16. The body must be able and willing to promote and maintain high standards of integrity in the conduct of company audit work and to co-operate, by the sharing of information and otherwise, with the Secretary of State and any other authority, body or person having responsibility in the United Kingdom for the qualification, supervision or regulation of auditors.

SCHEDULE 12

Section 32(4)

RECOGNITION OF PROFESSIONAL QUALIFICATION

PART I

GRANT AND REVOCATION OF RECOGNITION

Application for recognition of professional qualification

1.—(1) A qualifying body may apply to the Secretary of State for an order declaring a qualification offered by it to be a recognised professional qualification for the purposes of this Part of this Act.

(2) Any such application—

  (*a*) shall be made in such manner as the Secretary of State may direct, and
  (*b*) shall be accompanied by such information as the Secretary of State may reasonably require for the purpose of determining the application.

(3) At any time after receiving an application and before determining it the Secretary of State may require the applicant to furnish additional information.

(4) The directions and requirements given or imposed under sub-paragraphs (2) and (3) may differ as between different applications.

(5) Any information to be furnished to the Secretary of State under this section shall, if he so requires, be in such form or verified in such manner as he may specify.

In the case of examination standards, the verification required may include independent moderation of the examinations over such period as the Secretary of State considers necessary.

'6) Every application shall be accompanied by a copy of the applicant's rules and of any guidance issued by it which is intended to have continuing effect and is issued in writing or other legible form.

Grant and refusal of recognition

2.—(1) The Secretary of State may, on an application duly made in accordance with paragraph 1 and after being furnished with all such information as he may require under that paragraph, make or refuse to make an order (a 'recognition order') declaring the qualification in respect of which the application was made to be a recognised professional qualification for the purposes of this Part of this Act.

In this Part of this Act a 'recognised qualifying body' means a qualifying body offering a recognised professional qualification.

(2) The Secretary of State shall not make a recognition order unless it appears to him, from the information furnished by the applicant and having regard to any other information in his possession, that the requirements of Part II of this Schedule are satisfied as respects the qualification.

(3) Where the Secretary of State refuses an application for a recognition order he shall give the applicant a written notice to that effect specifying which requirements, in his opinion, are not satisfied.

(4) A recognition order shall state the date on which it takes effect.

Revocation of recognition

3.—(1) A recognition order may be revoked by a further order made by the Secretary of State if at any time it appears to him—

(a) that any requirement of Part II of this Schedule is not satisfied in relation to the qualification to which the recognition order relates, or

(b) that the qualifying body has failed to comply with any obligation to which it is subject by virtue of this Part of this Act.

(2) An order revoking a recognition order shall state the date on which it takes effect and that date shall not be earlier than three months after the day on which the revocation order is made.

(3) Before revoking a recognition order the Secretary of State shall give written notice of his intention to do so to the qualifying body, take such steps as he considers reasonably practicable for bringing the notice to the attention of persons holding the qualification or in the course of studying for it and publish it in such manner as he thinks appropriate for bringing it to the attention of any other persons who are in his opinion likely to be affected.

(4) A notice under sub-paragraph (3) shall state the reasons for which the Secretary of State proposes to act and give particulars of the rights conferred by sub-paragraph (5).

(5) A body on which a notice is served under sub-paragraph (3), any person holding the qualification or in the course of studying for it and any other person who appears to the Secretary of State to be affected may within three months after the date of service or publication, or within such longer time as the Secretary of State may allow, make written representations to the Secretary of State and, if desired, oral representations to a person appointed for that purpose by the Secretary of State; and the Secretary of State shall have regard to any representations made in accordance with this subsection in determining whether to revoke the recognition order.

(6) If in any case the Secretary of State considers it essential to do so in the public interest he may revoke a recognition order without regard to the restriction imposed by sub-paragraph (2) and notwithstanding that no notice has been given or published under sub-paragraph (3) or that the time for making representations in pursuance of such a notice has not expired.

(7) An order revoking a recognition order may contain such transitional provisions as the Secretary of State thinks necessary or expedient.

(8) A recognition order may be revoked at the request or with the consent of the qualifying body and any such revocation shall not be subject to the restrictions imposed by sub-paragraphs (1) and (2) or the requirements of sub-paragraphs (3) to (5).

(9) On making an order revoking a recognition order the Secretary of State shall give the qualifying body written notice of the making of the order, take such steps as he considers reasonably practicable

for bringing the making of the order to the attention of persons holding the qualification or in the course of studying for it and publish a notice of the making of the order in such manner as he thinks appropriate for bringing it to the attention of any other persons who are in his opinion likely to be affected.

PART II

REQUIREMENTS FOR RECOGNITION

Entry requirements

4.—(1) The qualification must only be open to persons who have attained university entrance level or have a sufficient period of professional experience.

(2) In relation to a person who has not been admitted to a university or other similar establishment in the United Kingdom, attaining university entrance level means—

 (a) being educated to such a standard as would entitle him to be considered for such admission on the basis of—

  (i) academic or professional qualifications obtained in the United Kingdom and recognised by the Secretary of State to be of an appropriate standard, or

  (ii) academic or professional qualifications obtained outside the United Kingdom which the Secretary of State considers to be of an equivalent standard; or

 (b) being assessed on the basis of written tests of a kind appearing to the Secretary of State to be adequate for the purpose, with or without oral examination, as of such a standard of ability as would entitle him to be considered for such admission.

(3) The assessment, tests and oral examination referred to in sub-paragraph (2)(b) may be conducted by the qualifying body or by some other body approved by the Secretary of State.

Course of theoretical instruction

5. The qualification must be restricted to persons who have completed a course of theoretical instruction in the subjects prescribed for the purposes of paragraph 7 or have a sufficient period of professional experience.

Sufficient period of professional experience

6.—(1) The references in paragraphs 4 and 5 to a sufficient period of professional experience are to not less than seven years' experience in a professional capacity in the fields of finance, law and accountancy.

(2) Periods of theoretical instruction in the fields of finance, law and accountancy may be deducted from the required period of professional experience, provided the instruction—

 (a) lasted at least one year, and

 (b) is attested by an examination recognised by the Secretary of State for the purposes of this paragraph;

but the period of professional experience may not be so reduced by more than four years.

(3) The period of professional experience together with the practical training required in the case of persons satisfying the requirement in paragraph 5 by virtue of having a sufficient period of professional experience must not be shorter than the course of theoretical instruction referred to in that paragraph and the practical training required in the case of persons satisfying the requirement of that paragraph by virtue of having completed such a course.

Examination

7.—(1) The qualification must be restricted to persons who have passed an examination (at least part of which is in writing) testing—

 (a) theoretical knowledge of the subjects prescribed for the purposes of this paragraph by regulations made by the Secretary of State, and

 (b) ability to apply that knowledge in practice,

and requiring a standard of attainment at least equivalent to that required to obtain a degree from a university or similar establishment in the United Kingdom.

(2) The qualification may be awarded to a person without his theoretical knowledge of a subject being

tested by examination if he has passed a university or other examination of equivalent standard in that subject or holds a university degree or equivalent qualification in it.

(3) The qualification may be awarded to a person without his ability to apply his theoretical knowledge of a subject in practice being tested by examination if he has received practical training in that subject which is attested by an examination or diploma recognised by the Secretary of State for the purposes of this paragraph.

(4) Regulations under this paragraph shall be made by statutory instrument which shall be subject to annulment in pursuance of a resolution of either House of Parliament.

Practical training

8.—(1) The qualification must be restricted to persons who have completed at least three years' practical training of which—

(a) part was spent being trained in company audit work, and

(b) a substantial part was spent being trained in company audit work or other audit work of a description approved by the Secretary of State as being similar to company audit work.

For this purpose 'company audit work' includes the work of a person appointed as auditor under the Companies (Northern Ireland) Order 1986 or under the law of a country or territory outside the United Kingdom where it appears to the Secretary of State that the law and practice with respect to the audit of company accounts is similar to that in the United Kingdom.

(2) The training must be given by persons approved by the body offering the qualification as persons as to whom the body is satisfied, in the light of undertakings given by them and the supervision to which they are subject (whether by the body itself or some other body or organisation), that they will provide adequate training.

(3) At least two-thirds of the training must be given by a fully-qualified auditor, that is, a person—

(a) eligible in accordance with this Part of this Act to be appointed as a company auditor, or

(b) satisfying the corresponding requirements of the law of Northern Ireland or another member State of the European Economic Community.

The body offering the qualification

9.—(1) The body offering the qualification must have—

(a) rules and arrangements adequate to ensure compliance with the requirements of paragraphs 4 to 8, and

(b) adequate arrangements for the effective monitoring of its continued compliance with those requirements.

(2) The arrangements must include arrangements for monitoring the standard of its examinations and the adequacy of the practical training given by the persons approved by it for that purpose.

SCHEDULE 13

Section 46(6)

SUPPLEMENTARY PROVISIONS WITH RESPECT TO DELEGATION ORDER

Introductory

1. The following provisions have effect in relation to a body established by a delegation order under section 46; and any power to make provision by order is to make provision by order under that section.

Status

2. The body shall not be regarded as acting on behalf of the Crown and its members, officers and employees shall not be regarded as Crown servants.

Name, members and chairman

3.—(1) The body shall be known by such name as may be specified in the delegation order.

(2) The body shall consist of such persons (not being less than eight) as the Secretary of State may appoint after such consultation as he thinks appropriate; and the chairman of the body shall be such person as the Secretary of State may appoint from amongst its members.

(3) The Secretary of State may make provision by order as to the terms on which the members of the

body are to hold and vacate office and as to the terms on which a person appointed as chairman is to hold and vacate the office of chairman.

Financial provisions

4.—(1) The body shall pay to its chairman and members such remuneration, and such allowances in respect of expenses properly incurred by them in the performance of their duties, as the Secretary of State may determine.

(2) As regards any chairman or member in whose case the Secretary of State so determines, the body shall pay or make provision for the payment of—

(a) such pension, allowance or gratuity to or in respect of that person on his retirement or death, or

(b) such contributions or other payment towards the provision of such a pension, allowance or gratuity,

as the Secretary of State may determine.

(3) Where a person ceases to be a member of the body otherwise than on the expiry of his term of office and it appears to the Secretary of State that there are special circumstances which make it right for him to receive compensation, the body shall make a payment to him by way of compensation of such amount as the Secretary of State may determine.

Proceedings

5.—(1) The delegation order may contain such provision as the Secretary of State considers appropriate with respect to the proceedings of the body.

(2) The order may, in particular—

(a) authorise the body to discharge any functions by means of committees consisting wholly or partly of members of the body;

(b) provide that the validity of proceedings of the body, or of any such committee, is not affected by any vacancy among the members or any defect in the appointment of any member.

Fees

6.—(1) The body may retain fees payable to it.

(2) The fees shall be applied for meeting the expenses of the body in discharging its functions and for any purposes incidental to those functions.

(3) Those expenses include any expenses incurred by the body on such staff, accommodation, services and other facilities as appear to it to be necessary or expedient for the proper performance of its functions.

(4) In prescribing the amount of fees in the exercise of the functions transferred to it the body shall prescribe such fees as appear to it sufficient to defray those expenses, taking one year with another.

(5) Any exercise by the body of the power to prescribe fees requires the approval of the Secretary of State; and the Secretary of State may, after consultation with the body, by order vary or revoke any regulations made by it prescribing fees.

Legislative functions

7.—(1) Regulations made by the body in the exercise of the functions transferred to it shall be made by instrument in writing, but not by statutory instrument.

(2) The instrument shall specify the provision of this Part of this Act under which it is made.

(3) The Secretary of State may by order impose such requirements as he thinks necessary or expedient as to the circumstances and manner in which the body must consult on any regulations it proposes to make.

8.—(1) Immediately after an instrument is made it shall be printed and made available to the public with or without payment.

(2) A person shall not be taken to have contravened any regulation if he shows that at the time of the alleged contravention the instrument containing the regulation had not been made available as required by this paragraph.

9.—(1) The production of a printed copy of an instrument purporting to be made by the body on which is endorsed a certificate signed by an officer of the body authorised by it for the purpose and stating—

(a) that the instrument was made by the body,

(b) that the copy is a true copy of the instrument, and

(c) that on a specified date the instrument was made available to the public as required by paragraph 8,

is prima facie evidence or, in Scotland, sufficient evidence of the facts stated in the certificate.

(2) A certificate purporting to be signed as mentioned in sub-paragraph (1) shall be deemed to have been duly signed unless the contrary is shown.

(3) Any person wishing in any legal proceedings to cite an instrument made by the body may require the body to cause a copy of it to be endorsed with such a certificate as is mentioned in this paragraph.

Report and accounts

10.—(1) The body shall at least once in each year for which the delegation order is in force make a report to the Secretary of State on the discharge of the functions transferred to it and on such other matters as the Secretary of State may by order require.

(2) The Secretary of State shall lay before Parliament copies of each report received by him under this paragraph.

(3) The Secretary of State may, with the consent of the Treasury, give directions to the body with respect to its accounts and the audit of its accounts and it is the duty of the body to comply with the directions.

(4) A person shall not be appointed auditor of the body unless he is eligible for appointment as a company auditor under section 25.

Other supplementary provisions

11.—(1) The transfer of a function to a body established by a delegation order does not affect anything previously done in the exercise of the function transferred; and the resumption of a function so transferred does not affect anything previously done in exercise of the function resumed.

(2) The Secretary of State may by order make such transitional and other supplementary provision as he thinks necessary or expedient in relation to the transfer or resumption of a function.

(3) The provision that may be made in connection with the transfer of a function includes, in particular, provision—

(a) for modifying or excluding any provision of this Part of this Act in its application to the function transferred;

(b) for applying to the body established by the delegation order, in connection with the function transferred, any provision applying to the Secretary of State which is contained in or made under any other enactment;

(c) for the transfer of any property, rights or liabilities from the Secretary of State to that body;

(d) for the carrying on and completion by that body of anything in process of being done by the Secretary of State when the order takes effect;

(e) for the substitution of that body for the Secretary of State in any instrument, contract or legal proceedings.

(4) The provision that may be made in connection with the resumption of a function includes, in particular, provision—

(a) for the transfer of any property, rights or liabilities from that body to the Secretary of State;

(b) for the carrying on and completion by the Secretary of State of anything in process of being done by that body when the order takes effect;

(c) for the substitution of the Secretary of State for that body in any instrument, contract or legal proceedings.

12. Where a delegation order is revoked, the Secretary of State may by order make provision—

(a) for the payment of compensation to persons ceasing to be employed by the body established by the delegation order; and

(b) as to the winding up and dissolution of the body.

SCHEDULE 14

SUPERVISORY AND QUALIFYING BODIES: RESTRICTIVE PRACTICES

PART I

PREVENTION OF RESTRICTIVE PRACTICES

Refusal of recognition on grounds related to competition

1.—(1) The Secretary of State shall before deciding whether to make a recognition order in respect of a supervisory body or professional qualification send to the Director General of Fair Trading (in this Schedule referred to as 'the Director') a copy of the rules and of any guidance which the Secretary of State is required to consider in making that decision together with such other information as the Secretary of State considers will assist the Director.

(2) The Director shall consider whether the rules or guidance have, or are intended or likely to have, to any significant extent the effect of restricting, distorting or preventing competition, and shall report to the Secretary of State; and the Secretary of State shall have regard to his report in deciding whether to make a recognition order.

(3) The Secretary of State shall not make a recognition order if it appears to him that the rules and any guidance of which copies are furnished with the application have, or are intended or likely to have, to any significant extent the effect of restricting, distorting or preventing competition, unless it appears to him that the effect is reasonably justifiable having regard to the purposes of this Part of this Act.

Notification of changes to rules or guidance

2.—(1) Where a recognised supervisory or qualifying body amends, revokes or adds to its rules or guidance in a manner which may reasonably be regarded as likely—

    (*a*) to restrict, distort or prevent competition to any significant extent, or

    (*b*) otherwise to affect the question whether the recognition order granted to the body should continue in force,

it shall within seven days give the Secretary of State written notice of the amendment, revocation or addition.

(2) Notice need not be given under sub-paragraph (1) of the revocation of guidance not intended to have continuing effect or issued otherwise than in writing or other legible form, or of any amendment or addition to guidance which does not result in or consist of guidance which is intended to have continuing effect and is issued in writing or other legible form.

Continuing scrutiny by the Director General of Fair Trading

3.—(1) The Director shall keep under review the rules made or guidance issued by a recognised supervisory or qualifying body, and if he is of the opinion that any rules or guidence of such a body have, or are intended or likely to have, to any significant extent the effect of restricting, distorting or preventing competition, he shall report his opinion to the Secretary of State, stating what in his opinion the effect is or is likely to be.

(2) The Secretary of State shall send to the Director copies of any notice received by him under paragraph 2, together with such other information as he considers will assist the Director.

(3) The Director may report to the Secretary of State his opinion that any matter mentioned in such a notice does not have, and is not intended or likely to have, to any significant extent the effect of restricting, distorting or preventing competition.

(4) The Director may from time to time consider whether—

    (*a*) any practices of a recognised supervisory or qualifying body in its capacity as such, or

    (*b*) any relevant practices required or contemplated by the rules or guidance of such a body or otherwise attributable to its conduct in its capacity as such,

have, or are intended or likely to have, to any significant extent the effect of restricting, distorting or preventing competition and, if so, what that effect is or is likely to be; and if he is of that opinion he shall make a report to the Secretary of State stating his opinion and what the effect is or is likely to be.

(5) The practices relevant for the purposes of sub-paragraph (4)(*b*) in the case of a recognised supervisory body are practices engaged in for the purposes of, or in connection with, appointment as a company auditor or the conduct of company audit work by persons who—

    (*a*) are eligible under its rules for appointment as a company auditor, or (*b*) hold an appropriate qualification and are directors or other officers of bodies corporate which are so eligible or partners in, or employees of, partnerships which are so eligible.

(6) The practices relevant for the purposes of sub-paragraph (4)(*b*) in the case of a recognised qualifying body are—

(*a*) practices engaged in by persons in the course of seeking to obtain a recognised professional qualification from that body, and

(*b*) practices engaged in by persons approved by the body for the purposes of giving practical training to persons seeking such a qualification and which relate to such training.

Investigatory powers of the Director

4.—(1) The following powers are exercisable by the Director for the purpose of investigating any matter in connection with his functions under paragraph 1 or 3.

(2) The Director may by a notice in writing require any person to produce, at a time and place specified in the notice, to the Director or to any person appointed by him for the purpose, any documents which are specified or described in the notice and which are documents in his custody or under his control and relating to any matter relevant to the investigation.

(3) The Director may by a notice in writing require any person to furnish to the Director such information as may be specified or described in the notice, and specify the time within which and the manner and form in which any such information is to be furnished.

(4) A person shall not under this paragraph be required to produce any document or disclose any information which he would be entitled to refuse to produce or disclose on grounds of legal professional privilege in proceedings in the High Court or on the grounds of confidentiality as between client and professional legal adviser in proceedings in the Court of Session.

(5) Subsections (6) to (8) of section 85 of the Fair Trading Act 1973 (enforcement provisions) apply in relation to a notice under this paragraph as they apply in relation to a notice under subsection (1) of that section but as if, in subsection (7) of that section, for the words from 'any one' to 'the Commission' there were substituted 'the Director'.

Publication of Director's reports

5.—(1) The Director may, if he thinks fit, publish any report made by him under paragraph 1 or 3.

(2) He shall exclude from a published report, so far as practicable, any matter which relates to the affairs of a particular person (other than the supervisory or qualifying body concerned) the publication of which would or might in his opinion seriously and prejudicially affect the interests of that person.

Powers exercisable by the Secretary of State in consequence of report

6.—(1) The powers conferred by this section are exercisable by the Secretary of State if, having received and considered a report from the Director under paragraph 3(1) or (4), it appears to him that—

(*a*) any rules made or guidance issued by a recognised supervisory or qualifying body, or

(*b*) any such practices as are mentioned in paragraph 3(4),

have, or are intended or likely to have, to any significant extent the effect of restricting, distorting or preventing competition and that that effect is greater than is reasonably justifiable having regard to the purposes of this Part of this Act.

(2) The powers are—

(*a*) to revoke the recognition order granted to the body concerned,

(*b*) to direct it to take specified steps for the purpose of securing that the rules, guidance or practices in question do not have the effect mentioned in sub-paragraph (1), and

(*c*) to make alterations in the rules of the body for that purpose.

(3) The provisions of paragraph 3(2) to (5), (7) and (9) of Schedule 11 or, as the case may be, Schedule 12 have effect in relation to the revocation of a recognition order under sub-paragraph (2)(*a*) above as they have effect in relation to the revocation of such an order under that Schedule.

(4) Before the Secretary of State exercises the power conferred by sub-paragraph (2)(*b*) or (*c*) above he shall—

(*a*) give written notice of his intention to do so to the body concerned and take such steps (whether by publication or otherwise) as he thinks appropriate for bringing the notice to the attention of any other person who in his opinion is likely to be affected by the exercise of the power, and (*b*) have regard to any representation made within such time as he considers reasonable by the body or any such other person.

(5) A notice under sub-paragraph (4) shall give particulars of the manner in which the Secretary of State proposes to exercise the power in question and state the reasons for which he proposes to act; and the statement of reasons may include matters contained in any report received by him under paragraph 4.

Supplementary provisions

7.—(1) A direction under paragraph 6 is, on the application of the Secretary of State, enforceable by injunction or, in Scotland, by an order under section 45 of the Court of Session Act 1988.

(2) The fact that any rules made by a recognised supervisory or qualifying body have been altered by the Secretary of State, or pursuant to a direction of the Secretary of State, under paragraph 6 does not preclude their subsequent alteration or revocation by that body.

(3) In determining for the purposes of this Part of this Schedule whether any guidance has, or is likely to have, any particular effect the Secretary of State and the Director may assume that the persons to whom it is addressed will act in conformity with it.

PART II

CONSEQUENTIAL EXEMPTIONS FROM COMPETITION LAW

Fair Trading Act 1973 (c 41)

8.—(1) For the purpose of determining whether a monopoly situation within the meaning of the Fair Trading Act 1973 exists by reason of the circumstances mentioned in section 7(1)(*c*) of that Act (supply of services by or for group of two or more persons), no account shall be taken of—

(*a*) the rules of or guidance issued by a recognised supervisory or qualifying body, or
(*b*) conduct constituting such a practice as is mentioned in paragraph 3(4) above.

(2) Where a recognition order is revoked there shall be disregarded for the purpose mentioned in sub-paragraph (1) any such conduct as is mentioned in that sub-paragraph which occurred while the order was in force.

(3) Where on a monopoly reference under section 50 or 51 of the Fair Trading Act 1973 falling within section 49 of that Act (monopoly reference not limited to the facts) the Monopolies and Mergers Commission find that a monopoly situation within the meaning of that Act exists and—

(*a*) that the person (or, if more than one, any of the persons) in whose favour it exists is—

(i) a recognised supervisory or qualifying body, or
(ii) a person of a description mentioned in paragraph 3(5) or (6) above, or

(*b*) that any such person's conduct in doing anything to which the rules of such a body relate is subject to guidance issued by the body,

the Commission in making their report on that reference shall exclude from their consideration the question whether the rules or guidance of the body concerned, or the acts or omissions of that body in its capacity as such, operate or may be expected to operate against the public interest.

Restrictive Trade Practices Act 1976 (c 34)

9.—(1) The Restrictive Trade Practices Act 1976 does not apply to an agreement for the constitution of a recognised supervisory or qualifying body in so far as it relates to rules of or guidance issued by the body, and incidental matters connected therewith, including any term deemed to be contained in it by virtue of section 8(2) or 16(3) of that Act.

(2) Nor does that Act apply to an agreement the parties to which consist of or include—

(*a*) a recognised supervisory or qualifying body, or
(*b*) any such person as is mentioned in paragraph 3(5) or (6) above,

by reason that it includes any terms the inclusion of which is required or contemplated by the rules or guidance of that body.

(3) Where an agreement ceases by virtue of this paragraph to be subject to registration—

(*a*) the Director shall remove from the register maintained by him under the Act of 1976 any particulars which are entered or filed in that register in respect of the agreement, and (*b*) any proceedings in respect of the agreement which are pending before the Restrictive Practices Court shall be discontinued.

(4) Where a recognition order is revoked, sub-paragraphs (1) and (2) above shall continue to apply for a period of six months beginning with the day on which the revocation takes effect, as if the order were still in force.

(5) Where an agreement which has been exempt from registration by virtue of this paragraph ceases to be exempt in consequence of the revocation of a recognition order, the time within which particulars of the agreement are to be furnished in accordance with section 24 of and Schedule 2 to the Act of 1976 shall be the period of one month beginning with the day on which the agreement ceased to be exempt from registration.

(6) Where in the case of an agreement registered under the 1976 Act a term ceases to fall within sub-paragraph (2) above in consequence of the revocation of a recognition order and particulars of that terms have not previously been furnished to the Director under section 24 of that Act, those particulars shall be furnished to him within the period of one month beginning with the day on which the term ceased to fall within that sub-paragraph.

Competition Act 1980 (c 21)

10.—(1) No course of conduct constituting any such practice as is mentioned in paragraph 3(4) above shall constitute an anti-competitive practice for the purposes of the Competition Act 1980.

(2) Where a recognition order is revoked there shall not be treated as an anti-competitive practice for the purposes of that Act any such course of conduct as is mentioned in sub-paragraph (1) which occurred while the order was in force.

SCHEDULE 15

Section 105

CHARGES ON PROPERTY OF OVERSEA COMPANIES

The following provisions are inserted in Part XXIII of the Companies Act 1985—

'CHAPTER III

REGISTRATION OF CHARGES

703A Introductory provisions

(1) The provisions of this Chapter have effect for securing the registration in Great Britain of charges on the property of a registered oversea company.

(2) Section 395(2) and (3) (meaning of 'charge' and 'property') have effect for the purposes of this Chapter.

(3) A 'registered oversea company', in relation to England and Wales or Scotland, means an oversea company which has duly delivered documents to the registrar for that part of Great Britain under section 691 and has not subsequently given notice to him under section 696(4) that it has ceased to have an established place of business in that part.

(4) References in this Chapter to the registrar shall be construed in accordance with section 703E below and references to registration, in relation to a charge, are to registration in the register kept by him under this Chapter.

703B Charges requiring registration

(1) The charges requiring registration under this Chapter are those which if created by a company registered in Great Britain would require registration under Part XII of this Act.

(2) Whether a charge is one requiring registration under this Chapter shall be determined—

(*a*) in the case of a charge over property of a company at the date it delivers documents for registration under section 691, as at that date,

(*b*) in the case of a charge created by a registered oversea company, as at the date the charge is created, and

(*c*) in the case of a charge over property acquired by a registered oversea company, as at the date of the acquisition.

(3) In the following provisions of this Chapter references to a charge are, unless the context otherwise requires, to a charge requiring registration under this Chapter.

Where a charge not otherwise requiring registration relates to property by virtue of which it requires to be registered and to other property, the references are to the charge so far as it relates to property of the former description.

703C The register

(1) The registrar shall keep for each registered oversea company a register, in such form as he thinks fit, of charges on property of the company.

(2) The register shall consist of a file containing with respect to each such charge the particulars and other information delivered to the registrar under or by virtue of the following provisions of this Chapter.

(3) Section 397(3) to (5) (registrar's certificate as to date of delivery of particulars) applies in relation to the delivery of any particulars or other information under this Chapter.

703D Company's duty to deliver particulars of charges for registration

(1) If when an oversea company delivers documents for registration under section 691 any of its property is situated in Great Britain and subject to a charge, it is the company's duty at the same time to deliver the prescribed particulars of the charge, in the prescribed form, to the registrar for registration.

(2) Where a registered oversea company—

(a) creates a charge on property situated in Great Britain, or
(b) acquires property which is situated in Great Britain and subject to a charge,

it is the company's duty to deliver the prescribed particulars of the charge, in the prescribed form, to the registrar for registration within 21 days after the date of the charge's creation or, as the case may be, the date of the acquisition.

This subsection does not apply if the property subject to the charge is at the end of that period no longer situated in Great Britain.

(3) Where the preceding subsections do not apply and property of a registered oversea company is for a continuous period of four months situated in Great Britain and subject to a charge, it is the company's duty before the end of that period to deliver the prescribed particulars of the charge, in the prescribed form, to the registrar for registration.

(4) Particulars of a charge required to be delivered under subsections (1), (2) or (3) may be delivered for registration by any person interested in the charge.

(5) If a company fails to comply with subsection (1), (2) or (3), then, unless particulars of the charge have been delivered for registration by another person, the company and every officer of it who is in default is liable to a fine.

(6) Section 398(2), (4) and (5) (recovery of fees paid in connection with registration, filing of particulars in register and sending of copy of particulars filed and note as to date) apply in relation to particulars delivered under this Chapter.

703E Registrar to whom particulars, &c to be delivered

(1) The particulars required to be delivered by section 703D(1) (charges over property of oversea company becoming registered in a part of Great Britain) shall be delivered to the registrar to whom the documents are delivered under section 691.

(2) The particulars required to be delivered by section 703D(2) or (3) (charges over property of registered oversea company) shall be delivered—

(a) if the company is registered in one part of Great Britain and not in the other, to the registrar for the part in which it is registered, and
(b) if the company is registered in both parts of Great Britain but the property subject to the charge is situated in one part of Great Britain only, to the registrar for that part;

and in any other case the particulars shall be delivered to the registrars for both parts of Great Britain.

(3) Other documents required or authorised by virtue of this Chapter to be delivered to the registrar shall be delivered to the registrar or registrars to whom particulars of the charge to which they relate have been, or ought to have been, delivered.

(4) If a company gives notice under section 696(4) that it has ceased to have an established place of business in either part of Great Britain, charges over property of the company shall cease to be

subject to the provisions of this Chapter, as regards registration in that part of Great Britain, as from the date on which notice is so given.

This is without prejudice to rights arising by reason of events occurring before that date.

703F Effect of failure to deliver particulars, late delivery and effect of errors and omissions

(1) The following provisions of Part XII—

(*a*) section 399 (effect of failure to deliver particulars),
(*b*) section 400 (late delivery of particulars), and
(*c*) section 402 (effect of errors and omissions in particulars delivered),

apply, with the following modifications, in relation to a charge created by a registered oversea company of which particulars are required to be delivered under this Chapter.

(2) Those provisions do not apply to a charge of which particulars are required to be delivered under section 703D(1) (charges existing when company delivers documents under section 691).

(3) In relation to a charge of which particulars are required to be delivered under section 703D(3) (charges registrable by virtue of property being within Great Britain for requisite period), the references to the period of 21 days after the charge's creation shall be construed as references to the period of four months referred to in that subsection.

703G Delivery of further particulars or memorandum

Sections 401 and 403 (delivery of further particulars and memorandum of charge ceasing to affect company's property) apply in relation to a charge of which particulars have been delivered under this Chapter.

703H Further provisions with respect to voidness of charges

(1) The following provisions of Part XII apply in relation to the voidness of a charge by virtue of this Chapter—

(*a*) section 404 (exclusion of voidness as against unregistered charges),
(*b*) section 405 (restrictions on cases in which charge is void),
(*c*) section 406 (effect of exercise of power of sale), and
(*d*) section 407 (effect of voidness on obligation secured).

(2) In relation to a charge of which particulars are required to be delivered under section 703D(3) (charges registrable by virtue of property being within Great Britain for requisite period), the reference in section 404 to the period of 21 days after the charge's creation shall be construed as a reference to the period of four months referred to in that subsection.

703I Additional information to be registered

(1) Section 408 (particulars of taking up of issue of debentures) applies in relation to a charge of which particulars have been delivered under this Chapter.

(2) Section 409 (notice of appointment of receiver or manager) applies in relation to the appointment of a receiver or manager of property of a registered oversea company.

(3) Regulations under section 410 (notice of crystallisation of floating charge, &c) may apply in relation to a charge of which particulars have been delivered under this Chapter; but subject to such exceptions, adaptations and modifications as may be specified in the regulations.

703J Copies of instruments and register to be kept by company

(1) Sections 411 and 412 (copies of instruments and register to be kept by company) apply in relation to a registered oversea company and any charge over property of the company situated in Great Britain.

(2) They apply to any charge, whether or not particulars are required to be delivered to the registrar.

(3) In relation to such a company the references to the company's registered office shall be construed as references to its principal place of business in Great Britain.

703K Power to make further provision by regulations

(1) The Secretary of State may by regulations make further provision as to the application of the provisions of this Chapter, or the provisions of Part XII applied by this Chapter, in relation to charges of any description specified in the regulations.

(2) The regulations may apply any provisions of regulations made under section 413 (power to make further provision with respect to application of Part XII) or make any provision which may be made under that section with respect to the application of provisions of Part XII.

703L Provisions as to situation of property

(1) The following provisions apply for determining for the purposes of this Chapter whether a vehicle which is the property of an oversea company is situated in Great Britain—

(*a*) a ship, aircraft or hovercraft shall be regarded as situated in Great Britain if, and only if, it is registered in Great Britain;

(*b*) any other description of vehicle shall be regarded as situated in Great Britain on a day if, and only if, at any time on that day the management of the vehicle is directed from a place of business of the company in Great Britain;

and for the purposes of this Chapter a vehicle shall not be regarded as situated in one part of Great Britain only.

(2) For the purposes of this Chapter as it applies to a charge on future property, the subject-matter of the charge shall be treated as situated in Great Britain unless it relates exclusively to property of a kind which cannot, after being acquired or coming into existence, be situated in Great Britain; and references to property situated in a part of Great Britain shall be similarly construed.

703M Other supplementary provisions

The following provisions of Part XII apply for the purposes of this Chapter—

(*a*) section 414 (construction of references to date of creation of charge),
(*b*) section 415 (prescribed particulars and related expressions),
(*c*) section 416 (notice of matters disclosed on the register),
(*d*) section 417 (power of court to dispense with signature),
(*e*) section 418 (regulations) and
(*f*) section 419 (minor definitions).

703N Index of defined expressions

The following Table shows the provisions of this Chapter and Part XII defining or otherwise explaining expressions used in this Chapter (other than expressions used only in the same section)—

charge	sections 703A(2), 703B(3) and 395(2)
charge requiring registration	sections 703B(1) and 396
creation of charge	sections 703M(*f*) and 419(2)
date of acquisition (of property by a company)	sections 703M(*f*) and 419(3)
date of creation of charge	sections 703M(*a*) and 414
property	sections 703A(2) and 395(2)
registered oversea company	section 703A(3)
registrar and registration in relation to a charge	sections 703A(4) and 703E
situated in Great Britain	
in relation to vehicles	section 703L(1)
in relation to future property	section 703L(2)'.

SCHEDULE 16

Section 107

AMENDMENTS CONSEQUENTIAL ON PART IV

Land Charges Act 1972 (c 61)

1.—(1) Section 3 of the Land Charges Act 1972 (registration of land charges) is amended as follows.

(2) In subsection (7) (registration in companies charges register to have same effect as registration under that Act), for 'any of the enactments mentioned in subsection (8) below' substitute 'Part XII, or Chapter III of Part XXIII, of the Companies Act 1985 (or corresponding earlier enactments)'.

(3) In subsection (8) for 'The enactments' substitute 'The corresponding earlier enactments' and at the end insert 'as originally enacted'.

Companies Act 1985 (c 6)

2.—(1) Schedule 24 to the Companies Act 1985 (punishment of offences) is amended as follows.

(2) For the entries relating to sections 399(3) to 423(3) (offences under Part XII: registration of charges) substitute—

'398(3)	Company failing to deliver particulars of charge to registrar.	1. On indictment. 2. Summary.	A fine. The statutory maximum.
408(3)	Company failing to deliver particulars of taking up of issue of debentures.	Summary.	One-fifth of the statutory maximum.
409(4)	Failure to give notice to registrar of appointment of receiver or manager, or of his ceasing to act.	Summary.	One-fifth of the statutory maximum.
410(4)	Failure to comply with requirements of regulations under s 410.	Summary.	One-fifth of the statutory maximum.
411(4)	Failure to keep copies of charging instruments or register at registered office.	1. On indictment. 2. Summary.	A fine. The statutory maximum.
412(4)	Refusing inspection of charging instrument or register or failing to supply copies.	Summary.	One-fifth of the statutory maximum.'.

(3) After the entry relating to section 703(1) insert—

'703D(5)	Oversea company failing to deliver particulars of charge to registrar.	1. On indictment. 2. Summary.	A fine. The statutory maximum.'.

Insolvency Act 1986 (c 45)

3.—(1) The Insolvency Act 1986 is amended as follows.

(2) In section 9(3) (restrictions on making administration order where administrative receiver has been appointed), in paragraph (*b*) (exceptions) insert—

> '(i) be void against the administrator to any extent by virtue of the provisions of Part XII of the Companies Act 1985 (registration of company charges),';

and renumber the existing sub-paragraphs as (ii) to (iv).

(3) In sections 45(5), 53(2), 54(3) and 62(5) (offences of failing to deliver documents relating to appointment or cessation of appointment of receiver) omit the words 'and, for continued contravention, to a daily default fine'.

Company Directors Disqualification Act 1986 (c 46)

4. In Schedule 1 to the Company Directors Disqualification Act 1986 (matters relevant to determining unfitness of directors), in paragraph 4 (failure of company to comply with certain provisions), for sub-paragraph (*h*) substitute—

> '(*h*) sections 398 and 703D (duty of company to deliver particulars of charges on its property).'.

SCHEDULE 17

Section 130(7)

COMPANY CONTRACTS, SEALS, &C: FURTHER PROVISIONS

Execution of deeds abroad

1.—(1) Section 38 of the Companies Act 1985 (execution of deeds abroad) is amended as follows.

(2) In subsection (1) (appointment of attorney to execute deeds), after 'A company may' insert 'under the law of England and Wales'.

(3) For subsection (2) (effect of deed executed by attorney) substitute—

'(2) A deed executed by such an attorney on behalf of the company has the same effect as if it were executed under the company's common seal.'.

Official seal for use abroad

2.—(1) Section 39 of the Companies Act 1985 (power to have official seal for use abroad) is amended as follows.

(2) In subsection (1), after 'A company' insert 'which has a common seal' and for 'the common seal of the company' substitute 'its common seal'.

(3) For subsection (2) (effect of sealing with official seal) substitute—

'(2) The official seal when duly affixed to a document has the same effect as the company's common seal.'.

(4) In subsection (3) (instrument authorising person to affix official seal), after 'by writing under its common seal' insert 'or, in the case of a company registered in Scotland, subscribed in accordance with section 36B,'.

Official seal for share certificates, &c

3.—(1) Section 40 of the Companies Act 1985 (official seal for share certificates, &c) is amended as follows.

(2) After 'A company' insert 'which has a common seal' and for 'the company's common seal' substitute 'its common seal'.

(3) At the end add—

'The official seal when duly affixed to a document has the same effect as the company's common seal.'.

Authentication of documents

4. In section 41 of the Companies Act 1985 (authentication of documents), for the words from 'may be signed' to the end substitute 'is sufficiently authenticated for the purposes of the law of England and Wales by the signature of a director, secretary or other authorised officer of the company.'.

Share certificate as evidence of title

5. For section 186 of the Companies Act 1985 (certificate to be evidence of title) substitute—

'186 Certificate to be evidence of title

(1) A certificate under the common seal of the company (or, in the case of a company registered in Scotland, subscribed in accordance with section 36B) specifying any shares held by a member is—

(a) in England and Wales, prima facie evidence, and
(b) in Scotland, sufficient evidence unless the contrary is shown,

of his title to the shares.'.

Share warrants to bearer

6. For section 188 of the Companies Act 1985 (issue and effect of share warrant to bearer) substitute—

'188 Issue and effect of share warrant to bearer

(1) A company limited by shares may, if so authorised by its articles, issue with respect to any fully paid shares a warrant (a 'share warrant') stating that the bearer of the warrant is entitled to the shares specified in it.

(2) A share warrant issued under the company's common seal (or, in the case of a company registered in Scotland, subscribed in accordance with section 36B) entitles the bearer to the shares specified in it; and the shares may be transferred by delivery of the warrant.

(3) A company which issues a share warrant may, if so authorised by its articles, provide (by coupons or otherwise) for the payment of the future dividends on the shares included in the warrant.'.

Identification of company on common seal

7. In section 350 of the Companies Act 1985 (identification of company on company seal), for subsection (1) substitute—

'(1) A company which has a common seal shall have its name engraved in legible characters on the seal; and if it fails to comply with this subsection it is liable to a fine.'.

Floating charges under Scots law

8. In section 462 of the Companies Act 1985 (power of company to create floating charge), for subsections (2) and (3) substitute—

'(2) In the case of a company which the Court of Session has jurisdiction to wind up, a floating charge may be created only by a written instrument which is presumed under section 36B to be subscribed by the company.'.

9. In section 466(2) of the Companies Act 1985 (execution of instrument altering floating charge)—

   (*a*) at the beginning of the subsection insert 'Without prejudice to any enactment or rule of law regarding the execution of documents,';
   (*b*) omit paragraph (*a*);
   (*c*) at the end of paragraph (*b*) insert '; or', and
   (*d*) omit paragraph (*d*) and the word 'or' preceding it.

10. In section 53(3) of the Insolvency Act 1986 (execution of instrument appointing receiver), in paragraph (*a*) for 'in accordance with the provisions of section 36 of the Companies Act as if it were a contract' substitute 'in accordance with section 36B of the Companies Act 1985'.

SCHEDULE 18

Section 144(4)

'Subsidiary' and related expressions: consequential amendments and savings

Coal Industry Nationalisation Act 1946 (c 59)

1. In Schedule 2A to the Coal Industry Nationalisation Act 1946 (eligibility for superannuation benefits), in the definition of 'subsidiary' in paragraph 5 of the Table, for 'section 154 of the Companies Act 1948' substitute 'section 736 of the Companies Act 1985'.

Electricity Act 1947 (c 54)

2. In section 67 of the Electricity Act 1947 (interpretation)—

   (*a*) in the definition of 'holding company' for 'the definition contained in the Companies Act 1947' substitute 'section 736 of the Companies Act 1985', and
   (*b*) in the definition of 'subsidiary company' for 'the Companies Act 1947' substitute 'section 736 of the Companies Act 1985'.

Landlord and Tenant Act 1954 (c 56)

3. In section 42 of the Landlord and Tenant Act 1954 (groups of companies), in subsection (1) for 'the same meaning as is assigned to it for the purposes of the Companies Act 1985 by section 736 of that Act' substitute 'the meaning given by section 736 of the Companies Act 1985'.

Transport Act 1962 (c 46)

4. In the Transport Act 1946, in the definition of 'subsidiary' in section 92(1) (interpretation) omit the words '(taking references in that section to a company as being references to a body corporate)'.

Harbours Act 1964 (c 40)

5. In section 57(1) of the Harbours Act 1964 (interpretation), in the definition of 'marine work' for 'section 154 of the Companies Act 1948' substitute 'section 736 of the Companies Act 1985'.

General Rate Act 1967 (c 9)

6. In section 32A of the General Rate Act 1967 (rateable premises of Transport Boards), in the definition of 'subsidiary' in subsection (6) omit the words '(taking references in that section to a company as being references to a body corporate)'.

Transport Act 1968 (c 73)

7. For the purposes of Part V of the Transport Act 1968 (licensing of road haulage operators) as it applies in relation to licences granted before the commencement of section 144(1), the expression 'subsidiary' has the meaning given by section 736 of the Companies Act 1985 as originally enacted.

Post Office Act 1969 (c 48)

8. In section 86 of the Post Office Act 1969 (interpretation), in subsection (2) for '736(5)(*b*)' substitute '736'.

Industry Act 1972 (c 63)

9. In section 10 of the Industry Act 1972 (construction credits), in subsection (9) for 'for the purposes of the Companies Act 1985 by section 736 of that Act' substitute 'by section 736 of the Companies Act 1985'.

Coal Industry Act 1973 (c 8)

10. In section 12(1) of the Coal Industry Act 1973 (interpretation) for the definition of 'subsidiary' and 'wholly-owned subsidiary' substitute—

'"subsidiary" and "wholly-owned subsidiary" have the meanings given by section 736 of the Companies Act 1985;'.

Industry Act 1975 (c 68)

11. In section 37(1) of the Industry Act 1975 (interpretation), in the definition of 'wholly-owned subsidiary' for 'section 736(5)(*b*)' substitute 'section 736'.

Scottish Development Agency Act 1975 (c 69)

12. In section 25(1) of the Scottish Development Agency Act 1975 (interpretation), in the definition of 'wholly-owned subsidiary' for 'section 736(5)(*b*)' substitute 'section 736'.

Welsh Development Agency Act 1975 (c 70)

13. In section 27(1) of the Welsh Development Agency Act 1975 (interpretation), in the definition of 'wholly-owned subsidiary' for 'section 736(5)(*b*)' substitute 'section 736'.

Restrictive Trade Practices Act 1976 (c 41)

14.—(1) This paragraph applies to agreements (within the meaning of the Restrictive Trade Practices Act 1976) made before the commencement of section 144(1); and 'registrable' means subject to registration under that Act.

(2) An agreement which was not registrable before the commencement of section 144(1) shall not be treated as registrable afterwards by reason only of that provision having come into force; and an agreement which was registrable before the commencement of that provision shall not cease to be registrable by reason of that provision coming into force.

Industrial Common Ownership Act 1976 (c 78)

15. In section 2(5) of the Industrial Common Ownership Act 1976 (common ownership and co-operative enterprises) for 'for the purposes of the Companies Act 1985' substitute 'as defined by section 736 of the Companies Act 1985 or for the purposes of'.

Aircraft and Shipbuilding Industries Act 1977 (c 3)

16. In section 56(1) of the Aircraft and Shipbuilding Industries Act 1977 (interpretation), in the definition of 'subsidiary' for 'the same meaning as in' substitute 'the meaning given by section 736 of'.

Nuclear Industry (Finance) Act 1977 (c 7)

17. In section 3 of the Nuclear Industry (Finance) Act 1977 (expenditure on acquisition of shares in National Nuclear Corporation Ltd and subsidiaries), after 'within the meaning of' insert 'section 736 of'.

Coal Industry Act 1977 (c 39)

18. In section 14(1) of the Coal Industry Act 1977 (interpretation), in the definition of 'wholly-owned subsidiary' for 'section 736(5)(*b*)' substitute 'section 736'.

Shipbuilding (Redundancy Payments) Act 1978 (c 11)

19. In section 1(4) of the Shipbuilding (Redundancy Payments) Act 1978 (schemes for payments to redundant workers), for the definitions of 'subsidiary' and 'wholly-owned subsidiary' substitute—

' "subsidiary" and "wholly-owned subsidiary" have the meanings given by section 736 of the Companies Act 1985;'.

Capital Gains Tax Act 1979 (c 14)

20. In section 149 of the Capital Gains Tax Act 1979 (employee trusts), in subsection (7) for 'the same meaning as in' substitute 'the meaning given by section 736 of'.

Crown Agents Act 1979 (c 43)

21. In section 31(1) of the Crown Agents Act 1979 (interpretation), in the definition of 'wholly-owned subsidiary' for 'section 736(5)(*b*)' substitute 'section 736(2)'.

Competition Act 1980 (c 21)

22. In sections 11(3)(*f*) and 12 of the Competition Act 1980 (references relating to public bodies, &c), after 'within the meaning of' insert 'section 736 of'.

British Aerospace Act 1980 (c 26)

23. In section 14(1) of the British Aerospace Act 1980 (interpretation)—
 (*a*) in the definition of 'subsidiary' for 'the same meaning as in', and
 (*b*) in the definition of 'wholly-owned subsidiary' for 'the same meaning as it has for the purposes of section 150 of the Companies Act 1948',
substitute 'the meaning given by section 736 of the Companies Act 1985'.

Local Government, Planning and Land Act 1980 (c 65)

24. In sections 100(1), 141(7) and 170(1)(*d*) and (2) of the Local Government, Planning and Land Act 1980 (which refer to wholly-owned subsidiaries) for 'within the meaning of section 736(5)(*b*)' substitute 'as defined by section 736'.

British Telecommunications Act 1981 (c 38)

25. In section 85 of the British Telecommunications Act 1981 (interpretation), for subsection (2) substitute—

'(2) Any reference in this Act to a subsidiary or wholly-owned subsidiary shall be construed in accordance with section 736 of the Companies Act 1985.'.

Transport Act 1981 (c 56)

26. In section 4(2) of the Transport Act 1981 (interpretation of provisions relating to activities of British Railways Board), for 'section 154 of the Companies Act 1985' substitute 'section 736 of the Companies Act 1985'.

Value Added Tax Act 1983 (c 55)

27. In section 29 of the Value Added Tax Act 1983 (groups of companies), in subsection (8) after 'within the meaning of' insert 'section 736 of'.

Telecommunications Act 1984 (c 12)

28. In section 73(1) of the Telecommunications Act 1984 (interpretation of Part V), for 'the same meaning as in' substitute 'the meaning given by section 736 of'.

London Regional Transport Act 1984 (c 32)

29. In section 68 of the London Regional Transport Act 1984 (interpretation), for the definition of 'subsidiary' substitute—

' "subsidiary' (subject to section 62 of this Act) has the meaning given by section 736 of the Companies Act 1985;'.

Inheritance Tax Act 1984 (c 51)

30.—(1) The Inheritance Tax Act 1984 is amended as follows.

(2) In section 13 (dispositions by close companies for benefit of employees), in the definition of 'subsidiary' in subsection (5) for 'the same meaning as in' substitute 'the meaning given by section 736 of'.

(3) In section 103 (introductory provisions relating to relief for business property), in subsection (2) for 'the same meanings as in' substitute 'the meanings given by section 736 of'.

(4) In section 234 (interest on instalments) in subsection (3) for 'within the meaning of' substitute 'as defined in section 736 of'.

Ordnance Factories and Military Services Act 1984 (c 59)

31. In section 14 of the Ordnance Factories and Military Services Act 1984 (interpretation), for the definitions of 'subsidiary' and 'wholly-owned subsidiary' substitute—

'"subsidiary" and "wholly-owned subsidiary" have the meanings given by section 736 of the Companies Act 1985.'.

Companies Act 1985 (c 6)

32.—(1) The following provisions have effect with respect to the operation of section 23 of the Companies Act 1985 (prohibition on subsidiary being a member of its holding company).

(2) In relation to times, circumstances and purposes before the commencement of section 144(1) of this Act, the references in section 23 to a subsidiary or holding company shall be construed in accordance with section 736 of the Companies Act 1985 as originally enacted.

(3) Where a body corporate becomes or ceases to be a subsidiary of a holding company by reason of section 144(1) coming into force, the prohibition in section 23 of the Companies Act 1985 shall apply (in the absence of exempting circumstances), or cease to apply, accordingly.

33.—(1) Section 153 of the Companies Act 1985 (transactions excepted from prohibition on company giving financial assistance for acquisition of its own shares) is amended as follows.

(2) In subsection (4)(*bb*) (employees' share schemes) for 'a company connected with it' substitute 'a company in the same group'.

(3) For subsection (5) substitute—

'(5) For the purposes of subsection (4)(*bb*) a company is in the same group as another company if it is a holding company or subsidiary of that company, or a subsidiary of a holding company of that company.'.

34. Section 293 of the Companies Act 1985 (age limit for directors) does not apply in relation to a director of a company if—

(*a*) he had attained the age of 70 before the commencement of section 144(1) of this Act, and
(*b*) the company became a subsidiary of a public company by reason only of the commencement of that subsection.

35. Nothing in section 144(1) affects the operation of Part XIIIA of the Companies Act 1985 (takeover offers) in relation to a takeover offer made before the commencement of that subsection.

36. For the purposes of section 719 of the Companies Act 1985 (power to provide for employees on transfer or cessation of business), a company which immediately before the commencement of section 144(1) was a subsidiary of another company shall not be treated as ceasing to be such a subsidiary by reason of that subsection coming into force.

37. For the purposes of section 743 of the Companies Act 1985 (meaning of 'employees' share scheme'), a company which immediately before the commencement of section 144(1) was a subsidiary of another company shall not be treated as ceasing to be such a subsidiary by reason of that subsection coming into force.

38. In Schedule 25 to the Companies Act 1985 'subsidiary' has the meaning given by section 736 of that Act as originally enacted.

Transport Act 1985 (c 67)

39. In section 137(1) of the Transport Act 1985 (interpretation), in the definition of 'subsidiary' for the words from 'as defined' to the end substitute 'within the meaning of section 736 of the Companies Act 1985 as originally enacted (and not as substituted by section 144(1) of the Companies Act 1989);'.

Housing Act 1985 (c 68)

40. In section 622 of the Housing Act 1985 (minor definitions: general), in the definition of 'subsidiary' for 'the same meaning as in' substitute 'the meaning given by section 736 of'.

Housing Associations Act 1985 (c 69)

41. In section 101 of the Housing Associations Act 1985 (minor definitions: Part II), in the definition of 'subsidiary' for 'the same meaning as in' substitute 'the meaning given by section 736 of'.

Atomic Energy Authority Act 1986 (c 3)

42. In section 9 of the Atomic Energy Authority Act 1986 (interpretation), in the definition of 'subsidiary' and 'wholly-owned subsidiary' for 'have the same meaning as in' substitute 'have the meaning given by section 736 of'.

Airports Act 1986 (c 31)

43. In section 82 of the Airports Act 1986 (general interpretation), in the definition of 'subsidiary' for 'has the same meaning as in' substitute 'has the meaning given by section 736 of'.

Gas Act 1986 (c 44)

44. In the Gas Act 1986—

   (*a*) in section 48(1) (interpretation of Part I), in the definitions of 'holding company' and 'subsidiary', and
   (*b*) in section 61(1) (interpretation of Part II), in the definition of 'subsidiary',

for 'has the same meaning as in' substitute 'has the meaning given by section 736 of'.

Building Societies Act 1986 (c 53)

45. In section 119 of the Building Societies Act 1986 (interpretation), in the definition of 'subsidiary' for 'has the same meaning as in' substitute 'has the meaning given by section 736 of'.

Income and Corporation Taxes Act 1988 (c 1)

46. In section 141 of the Income and Corporation Taxes Act 1988 (benefits in kind: non-cash vouchers), in the definition of 'subsidiary' in subsection (7) for 'section 736(5)(*b*)' substitute 'section 736'.

British Steel Act 1988 (c 35)

47. In section 15(1) of the British Steel Act 1988 (interpretation), in the definition of 'subsidiary' for 'has the same meaning as in' substitute 'has the meaning given by section 736 of'.

SCHEDULE 19

Section 145

Minor amendments of the Companies Act 1985

Correction of cross-reference

1. In section 131(1) of the Companies Act 1985 (merger relief) for 'section 132(4)' substitute 'section 132(8)'.

This amendment shall be deemed always to have had effect.

Particulars to be given of directors and secretaries

2.—(1) Section 289 of the Companies Act 1985 (particulars of directors required to be entered in register) is amended as follows.

(2) In subsection (1)(*a*) (particulars of individual directors)—

   (*a*) in sub-paragraph (i) for 'Christian name and surname' and in sub-paragraph (ii) for 'Christian name or surname' substitute 'name', and
   (*b*) for sub-paragraph (vii) substitute—

      '(vii) the date of his birth;'.

(3) In subsection (1)(*b*) (particulars of other directors) after 'corporation' insert 'or Scottish firm' and after 'corporate' insert 'or firm'.

(4) For subsection (2) substitute—

      '(2) In subsection (1)(*a*)—

      (*a*) 'name' means a person's Christian name (or other forename) and surname, except that in the case of a peer, or an individual usually known by a title, the title may be stated instead of his Christian name (or other forename) and surname, or in addition to either or both of them; and

(b) the reference to a former name does not include—

    (i) in the case of a peer, or an individual normally known by a British title, the name by which he was known previous to the adoption of or succession to the title, or

    (ii) in the case of any person, a former name which was changed or disused before he attained the age of 18 years or which has been changed or disused for 20 years or more, or

    (iii) in the case of a married woman, the name by which she was known previous to the marriage.'.

3.—(1) Section 290 of the Companies Act 1985 (particulars of secretaries to be entered in register) is amended as follows.

(2) In subsection (1)(a) (particulars of individuals) for 'Christian name and surname' and 'Christian name or surname' substitute 'name'.

(3) For subsection (3) substitute—

'(3) Section 289(2)(a) and (b) apply for the purposes of the obligation under subsection (1)(a) of this section to state the name or former name of an individual.'.

4.—(1) Section 305 of the Companies Act 1985 (directors' names on company correspondence, &c) is amended as follows.

(2) In subsection (1) for the words from 'the Christian name' onwards substitute 'the name of every director of the company'.

(3) For subsection (4) substitute—

'(4) For the purposes of the obligation under subsection (1) to state the name of every director of the company, a person's 'name' means—

(a) in the case of an individual, his Christian name (or other forename) and surname; and

(b) in the case of a corporation or Scottish firm, its corporate or firm name.

(5) The initial or a recognised abbreviation of a person's Christian name or other forename may be stated instead of the full Christian name or other forename.

(6) In the case of a peer, or an individual usually known by a title, the title may be stated instead of his Christian name (or other forename) and surname or in addition to either or both of them.

(7) In this section 'director' includes a shadow director and the reference in subsection (3) to an 'officer' shall be construed accordingly.'.

5.—(1) Section 686 of the Companies Act 1985 (documents to be delivered to registrar on registration of company not formed under companies legislation) is amended as follows.

(2) In subsection (1) (particulars to be delivered to registrar), for paragraph (b) (particulars of directors and managers) substitute—

'(b) a list showing with respect to each director or manager of the company—

    (i) in the case of an individual, his name, address, occupation and date of birth,

    (ii) in the case of a corporation or Scottish firm, its corporate or firm name and registered or principal office,'.

(3) After that subsection insert—

'(1A) For the purposes of subsection (1)(b)(i) a person's 'name' means his Christian name (or other forename) and surname, except that in the case of a peer, or an individual usually known by a title, the title may be stated instead of his Christian name (or other forename) and surname or in addition to either or both of them.'.

6. In section 691 of the Companies Act 1985 (documents to be delivered to registrar on registration of oversea company), for subsection (2) (particulars of directors and secretary) substitute—

'(2) The list referred to in subsection (1)(b)(i) shall contain the following particulars with respect to each director—

(a) in the case of an individual—

    (i) his name,

    (ii) any former name,

    (iii) his usual residential address,

      (iv) his nationality,

      (v) his business occupation (if any),

      (vi) if he has no business occupation but holds other directorships, particulars of them, and

      (vii) his date of birth;

  (*b*) in the case of a corporation or Scottish firm, its corporate or firm name and registered or principal office.

  (3) The list referred to in subsection (1)(*b*)(i) shall contain the following particulars with respect to the secretary (or, where there are joint secretaries, with respect to each of them)—

  (*a*) in the case of an individual, his name, any former name and his usual residential address;

  (*b*) in the case of a corporation or Scottish firm, its corporate or firm name and registered or principal office.

Where all the partners in a firm are joint secretaries of the company, the name and principal office of the firm may be stated instead of the particulars required by paragraph (*a*).

  (4) In subsections (2)(*a*) and (3)(*a*) above—

  (*a*) 'name' means a person's Christian name (or other forename) and surname, except that in the case of a peer, or an individual usually known by a title, the title may be stated instead of his Christian name (or other forename) and surname, or in addition to either or both of them; and

  (*b*) the reference to a former name does not include—

      (i) in the case of a peer, or an individual normally known by a British title, the name by which he was known previous to the adoption of or succession to the title, or

      (ii) in the case of any person, a former name which was changed or disused before he attained the age of 18 years or which has been changed or disused for 20 years or more, or

      (iii) in the case of a married woman, the name by which she was known previous to the marriage.'.

7.—(1) Schedule 1 to the Companies Act 1985 (particulars of directors and secretaries to be sent to registrar) is amended as follows.

(2) In paragraph 1(*a*) (particulars of individual directors)—

  (*a*) for 'Christian name and surname' and 'Christian name or surname' substitute 'name';

  (*b*) for the words from 'and, in the case' to the end substitute 'and his date of birth'.

(3) In paragraph 1(*b*) (particulars of other directors) after 'corporation' insert 'or Scottish firm' and after 'corporate' insert 'or firm'.

(4) In paragraph 3(1)(*a*) (particulars of individual secretaries) for 'Christian name and surname' (twice) substitute 'name'.

(5) For paragraph 4 substitute—

  '4. In paragraphs 1(*a*) and 3(1)(*a*) above—

  (*a*) 'name' means a person's Christian name (or other forename) and surname, except that in the case of a peer, or an individual usually known by a title, the title may be stated instead of his Christian name (or other forename) and surname or in addition to either or both of them; and

  (*b*) the reference to a former name does not include—

      (i) in the case of a peer, or an individual normally known by a British title, the name by which he was known previous to the adoption of or succession to the title, or

      (ii) in the case of any person, a former name which was changed or disused before he attained the age of 18 years or which has been changed or disused for 20 years or more, or

      (iii) in the case of a married woman, the name by which she was known previous to the marriage.'.

Transactions with directors not requiring authorisation

8. In section 321 of the Companies Act 1985 (exceptions from provisions requiring authorisation for substantial property transactions with directors, &c), after subsection (3) insert—

  '(4) Section 320(1) does not apply to a transaction on a recognised investment exchange which is effected by a director, or a person connected with him, through the agency of a person who in relation to the transaction acts as an independent broker.

For this purpose an 'independent broker' means—

(*a*) in relation to a transaction on behalf of a director, a person who independently of the director selects the person with whom the transaction is to be effected, and

(*b*) in relation to a transaction on behalf of a person connected with a director, a person who independently of that person or the director selects the person with whom the transaction is to be effected;

and 'recognised', in relation to an investment exchange, means recognised under the Financial Services Act 1986.'.

Time limit for holding extraordinary general meeting convened on members' requisition

9. In section 368 of the Companies Act 1985 (extraordinary general meeting on members' requisition), after subsection (7) add—

'(8) The directors are deemed not to have duly convened a meeting if they convene a meeting for a date more than 28 days after the date of the notice convening the meeting.'.

Removal of restriction on transfer of shares

10.—(1) In section 456(3) of the Companies Act 1985 (removal of restrictions by order of court), in paragraph (*b*) (order where shares to be sold)—

(*a*) for 'sold' substitute 'transferred for valuable consideration', and

(*b*) for 'sale' substitute 'transfer'.

(2) In section 454(2) and (3) (which refer to section 456(3)(*b*)) for 'sell' and 'sale' substitute 'transfer'.

Protection of company's members against unfair prejudice

11. In Part XVII of the Companies Act 1985 (protection of company's members against unfair prejudice)—

(*a*) in section 459(1) (application by company member), and

(*b*) in section 460(1)(*b*) (application by Secretary of State),

for 'unfairly prejudicial to the interests of some part of the members' substitute 'unfairly prejudicial to the interests of its members generally or of some part of its members'.

Requirements for registration by joint stock companies

12. In section 684(1) of the Companies Act 1985 (requirements for registration by joint stock companies: documents to be delivered to registrar), in paragraph (*b*) (list of members on specified day) for '(not more than 6 clear days before the day of registration)' substitute '(not more than 28 clear days before the day of registration)'.

Delivery of documents by oversea companies

13. In Chapter I of Part XXIII of the Companies Act 1985 (oversea companies: registration, &c), for section 696 (office where documents to be filed) substitute—

'696 Registrar to whom documents to be delivered

(1) References to the registrar in relation to an oversea company (except references in Chapter III of this Part (registration of charges): see section 703E), shall be construed in accordance with the following provisions.

(2) The documents which an oversea company is required to deliver to the registrar shall be delivered—

(*a*) to the registrar for England and Wales if the company has established a place of business in England and Wales, and

(*b*) to the registrar for Scotland if the company has established a place of business in Scotland;

and if the company has an established place of business in both parts of Great Britain, the documents shall be delivered to both registrars.

(3) If a company ceases to have a place of business in either part of Great Britain, it shall forthwith give notice of that fact to the registrar for that part; and from the date on which notice is so given it is no longer obliged to deliver documents to that registrar.'.

Companies' registered numbers

14. For section 705 of the Companies Act 1985 (companies' registered numbers) substitute—

'705 Companies' registered numbers

(1) The registrar shall allocate to every company a number, which shall be known as the company's registered number.

(2) Companies' registered numbers shall be in such form, consisting of one or more sequences of figures or letters, as the registrar may from time to time determine.

(3) The registrar may upon adopting a new form of registered number make such changes of existing registered numbers as appear to him necessary.

(4) A change of a company's registered number has effect from the date on which the company is notified by the registrar of the change; but for a period of three years beginning with the date on which that notification is sent by the registrar the requirement of section 351(1)(*a*) as to the use of the company's registered number on business letters and order forms is satisfied by the use of either the old number or the new.

(5) In this section 'company' includes—

(*a*) any oversea company which has complied with section 691 (delivery of statutes to registrar, &c), other than a company which appears to the registrar not to have a place of business in Great Britain; and

(*b*) any body to which any provision of this Act applies by virtue of section 718 (unregistered companies).'.

Exemptions from limit of 20 on members of partnership

15.—(1) Section 716 of the Companies Act 1985 (prohibition of formation of company, association or partnership with more than 20 members unless registered as company, &c) is amended as follows.

(2) In subsection (2) (exemptions), after paragraph (*c*) insert—

'(*d*) for any purpose prescribed by regulations (which may include a purpose mentioned above), of a partnership of a description so prescribed.';

and omit the words inserted by paragraph 22 of Schedule 16 to the Financial Services Act 1986.

(3) For subsections (3) and (4) substitute—

'(3) In subsection (2)(*a*) 'solicitor'—

(*a*) in relation to England and Wales, means solicitor of the Supreme Court, and

(*b*) in relation to Scotland, means a person enrolled or deemed enrolled as a solicitor in pursuance of the Solicitors (Scotland) Act 1980.

(4) In subsection (2)(*c*) 'recognised stock exchange' means—

(*a*) The International Stock Exchange of the United Kingdom and the Republic of Ireland Limited, and

(*b*) any other stock exchange for the time being recognised for the purposes of this section by the Secretary of State by order made by statutory instrument.'.

16.—(1) Section 717 of the Companies Act 1985 (limited partnerships: limit on number of members) is amended as follows.

(2) In subsection (1) (exemptions from limit of 20 members under section 4(2) of Limited Partnerships Act 1907), after paragraph (*c*) insert—

'(*d*) to a partnership carrying on business of any description prescribed by regulations (which may include a business of any description mentioned above), of a partnership of a description so prescribed.';

and omit the words inserted by paragraph 22 of Schedule 16 to the Financial Services Act 1986.

(3) For subsections (2) and (3) substitute—

'(2) In subsection (1)(*a*) 'solicitor'—

(*a*) in relation to England and Wales, means solicitor of the Supreme Court, and

(*b*) in relation to Scotland, means a person enrolled or deemed enrolled as a solicitor in pursuance of the Solicitors (Scotland) Act 1980.

(3) In subsection (1)(*c*) 'recognised stock exchange' means—

(*a*) The International Stock Exchange of the United Kingdom and the Republic of Ireland Limited, and (*b*) any other stock exchange for the time being recognised for the purposes of this section by the Secretary of State by order made by statutory instrument.'.

Meaning of 'officer who is in default'

17. In section 730 of the Companies Act 1985 (punishment of offences), in subsection (5) (meaning of 'officer who is in default'), after 'company' (twice) insert 'or other body'.

Offences committed by partnerships and other unincorporated bodies

18. In section 734 of the Companies Act 1985 (criminal proceedings against unincorporated bodies), at the end add—

'(5) Where such an offence committed by a partnership is proved to have been committed with the consent or connivance of, or to be attributable to any neglect on the part of, a partner, he as well as the partnership is guilty of the offence and liable to be proceeded against and punished accordingly.

(6) Where such an offence committed by an unincorporated body (other than a partnership) is proved to have been committed with the consent or connivance of, or to be attributable to any neglect on the part of, any officer of the body or any member of its governing body, he as well as the body is guilty of the offence and liable to be proceeded against and punished accordingly.'.

Meaning of 'office copy' in Scotland

19. In Part XXVI of the Companies Act 1985 (interpretation), after section 743 insert—

'743A Meaning of 'office copy' in Scotland

References in this Act to an office copy of a court order shall be construed, as respects Scotland, as references to a certified copy interlocutor.'.

Index of defined expressions

20. In Part XXVI of the Companies Act 1985 (interpretation), after section 744 insert—

'744A Index of defined expressions

The following Table shows provisions defining or otherwise explaining expressions for the purposes of this Act generally—

accounting reference date, accounting reference period	sections 224 and 742(1)
acquisition (in relation to a non-cash asset)	section 739(2)
agent	section 744
allotment (and related expressions)	section 738
annual accounts	sections 261(2), 262(1) and 742(1)
annual general meeting	section 366
annual return	section 363
articles	section 744
authorised minimum	section 118
balance sheet and balance sheet date	sections 261(2), 262(1) and 742(1)
bank holiday	section 744
banking company	section 744
body corporate	section 740
books and papers, books or papers	section 744
called-up share capital	section 737(1)
capital redemption reserve	secton 170(1)
the Companies Acts	section 744
companies charges register	section 397
company	section 735(1)
the Consequential Provisions Act	section 744
corporation	section 740
the court (in relation to a company)	section 744
current assets	sections 262(1) and 742(1)
debenture	section 744
director	section 741(1)
document	section 744
elective resolution	section 379A

employees' share scheme	section 743
equity share capital	section 744
existing company	section 735(1)
extraordinary general meeting	section 368
extraordinary resolution	section 378(1)
financial year (of a company)	sections 223 and 742(1)
fixed assets	sections 262(1) and 742(1)
floating charge (in Scotland)	section 462
the former Companies Acts	section 735(1)
the Gazette	section 744
hire-purchase agreement	section 744
holding company	section 736
the Insider Dealing Act	section 744
the Insolvency Act	section 735A(1)
insurance company	section744
the Joint Stock Companies Acts	section 735(3)
limited company	section 1(2)
member (of a company)	section 22
memorandum (in relation to a company)	section 744
non-cash asset	section 739(1)
number (in relation to shares)	section 744
office copy (in relation to a court order in Scotland)	section 743A
officer (in relation to a body corporate)	section 744
official seal (in relation to the registrar of companies)	section 744
oversea company	section 744
overseas branch register	section 362
paid up (and related expressions)	section 738
parent company and parent undertaking	sections 258 and 742(1)
place of business	section 744
prescribed	section 744
private company	section 1(3)
profit and loss account	sections 261(2), 262(1) and 742(1)
prospectus	section 744
public company	section 1(3)
realised profits or losses	sections 262(3) and 742(2)
registered number (of a company)	section 705(1)
registered office (of a company)	section 287
registrar and registrar of companies	section 744
resolution for reducing share capital	section 135(3)
shadow director	sections 741(2) and (3)
share	section 744
share premium account	section 130(1)
share warrant	section 188
special notice (in relation to a resolution)	section 379
special resolution	section 378(2)
subsidiary	section 736
subsidiary undertaking	sections 258 and 742(1)
transfer (in relation to a non-cash asset)	section 739(2)
uncalled share capital	section 737(2)
undistributable reserves	section 264(3)
unlimited company	section 1(2)
unregistered company	section 718
wholly-owned subsidiary	section 736(2)'.

Fraudulent trading by unregistered companies

21. In Schedule 22 to the Companies Act 1985 (provisions applying to unregistered companies), at the appropriate place insert—

    'Part XVI   Fraudulent trading by a company   —'.

SCHEDULE 20

AMENDMENTS ABOUT MERGERS AND RELATED MATTERS

Fair Trading Act 1973 (c 41)

1. In section 46 of the Fair Trading Act 1973, subsection (3) is omitted.

2.—(1) In section 60 of that Act—

    (*a*) in subsection (1) for 'the period of three months beginning with the date of the' there is substituted 'such period (not being longer than three months beginning with the date of the reference) as may be specified in the',

    (*b*) in subsection (2) for 'original period of three months' there is substituted 'period specified in the newspaper merger reference', and

    (*c*) in subsection (3) for 'subsection (1)' there is substituted 'the newspaper merger reference'.

(2) This paragraph does not apply in relation to any newspaper merger reference made before the passing of this Act.

3. In section 63(1) of that Act, for 'to 75 of this Act shall have effect in relation to merger references other than' there is substituted 'to 75K of this Act shall not have effect in relation to'.

4. In section 66 of that Act—

    (*a*) in subsections (1) and (3), after 'the Secretary of State' there is inserted 'or the Commission', and

    (*b*) in subsection (4), after 'this section' there is inserted 'and to section 66A of this Act'.

5.—(1) In section 67 of that Act, in subsection (2)(*a*), for the words from 'any enterprise' to the end there is substituted—

    ' (i) any enterprise which remains under the same ownership and control, or

    (ii) if none of the enterprises remains under the same ownership and control, the enterprise having the assets with the highest value, and'.

(2) In subsection (4) of that section—

    (*a*) after 'section 66' there is inserted 'or subsection (1) of section 66A', and

    (*b*) for 'that subsection' there is substituted 'either of those subsections'.

6. In section 68(4) of that Act, after 'the Secretary of State' there is inserted 'or, as the case may be, the Commission'.

7. In section 71 of that Act—

    (*a*) in subsection (1) the words 'made under section 69(4) of this Act', and

    (*b*) subsection (2),

are omitted.

8. In section 74(1) of that Act—

    (*a*) the words 'and does not impose on the Commission a limitation under section 69(4) of this Act' are omitted, and

    (*b*) in paragraph (*d*), for 'paragraph 12' there is substituted 'paragraphs 12 and 12A'.

9. In section 75(4) of that Act—

    (*a*) after 'sections 66' there is inserted '66A', and

    (*b*) for paragraphs (*a*) and (*b*) there is substituted—

    '(*a*) section 66 shall apply, where an event by which any enterprises cease as between themselves to be distinct enterprises will occur if the arrangements are carried into effect, as if the event had occurred immediately before the date of the reference;

    (*aa*) section 66A shall apply, where a transaction falling within subsection (2) of that section will occur if the arrangements are carried into effect, as if the transaction had occurred immediately before the date of the reference;

    (*b*) in section 67(4) the references to subsection (1) of section 66 and subsection (1) of section 66A shall be construed as references to those subsections as modified in accordance with paragraph (*a*) or (*aa*) of this subsection;'.

10. Paragraphs 4 to 9 (and the repeals in Schedule 24 corresponding to paragraphs 7 and 8(*a*)) do not apply in relation to any merger reference made before the passing of this Act.

11. At the end of section 76 of that Act there is added—

    '(2) In exercising his duty under this section the Director shall take into consideration any representations made to him by persons appearing to him to have a substantial interest in any such arrangements or transactions or by bodies appearing to him to represent substantial numbers of persons who have such an interest.'.

12.—(1) In section 83 of that Act, after subsection (3) there is inserted—

'(3A) Without prejudice to subsection (3) above, if the Minister or Ministers to whom any such report is made consider that it would not be in the public interest to disclose—

> (a) any matter contained in the report relating to the private affairs of an individual whose interests would, in the opinion of the Minister or Ministers, be seriously and prejudicially affected by the publication of that matter, or
>
> (b) any matter contained in the report relating specifically to the affairs of a particular person whose interests would, in the opinion of the Minister or Ministers, be seriously and prejudicially affected by the publication of that matter,

the Minister or Ministers shall exclude that matter from the copies of the report as laid before Parliament and from the report as published under this section.'.

(2) This paragraph does not apply in relation to any report made before the passing of this Act.

13.—(1) In section 85 of that Act, for subsection (7) there is substituted—

'(7) If any person (referred to in subsection (7A) of this section as 'the defaulter') refuses or otherwise fails to comply with any notice under subsection (1) of this section, any one of those who, in relation to the investigation in question, are performing the functions of the Commission may certify that fact in writing to the court and the court may enquire into the case.

(7A) If, after hearing any witness who may be produced against or on behalf of the defaulter and any statement which may be offered in defence, the court is satisfied that the defaulter did without reasonable excuse refuse or otherwise fail to comply with the notice, the court may punish the defaulter (and, in the case of a body corporate, any director or officer) in like manner as if the defaulter had been guilty of contempt of court.'.

(2) Subsections (5) and (6)(b) of that section are omitted.

14.—(1) In section 88 of that Act, in subsection (1) for the words from 'if requested' to 'the relevant parties' there is substituted 'to comply with any request of the appropriate Minister or Ministers to consult with any persons mentioned in the request (referred to below in this section as 'the relevant parties')'.

(2) After subsection (2) of that section there is inserted—

'(2A) Where—

> (a) an undertaking is given under this section after the commencement of this subsection, or
> (b) an undertaking given under this section is varied or released after that time,

the Minister to whom the undertaking is or was given shall cause the undertaking or, as the case may be, the variation or release to be published in such manner as the Minister may consider appropriate.'.

(3) In subsection (4) of that section—

> (a) in paragraph (a) for 'it' there is substituted 'the undertaking is no longer appropriate and either the relevant parties (or any of them) can be released from the undertaking or the undertaking', and
>
> (b) in paragraph (b) for 'that it' there is substituted 'that any person can be so released or that an undertaking',

and in subsection (5), after 'varied' (in both places) there is inserted 'or revoked'.

(4) In subsection (6) of that section the words from 'the relevant parties' to the 'and' immediately following paragraph (c) are omitted.

(5) Sub-paragraphs (1) and (4) (and the repeal in Schedule 24 corresponding to sub-paragraph (4)) do not apply in relation to any report made before the passing of this Act.

15.—(1) In section 89 of that Act, in subsection (1), for paragraphs (a) and (b) there is substituted—

'(a) in the circumstances specified in subsection (1) of any of the following sections—

> (i) sections 56, 73 and 75K of this Act, and
> (ii) section 10 of the Competition Act 1980,

the Secretary of State makes, has made, or has under consideration the making of, an order under the section in question exercising any of the powers specified in Schedule 8 to this Act, or (*b*) in the circumstances specified in subsection (1) of section 12 of the Competition Act 1980 the Secretary of State makes, has made, or has under consideration the making of, an order under subsection (5) of that section exercising any of those powers.'.

(2) In subsection (2) of that section, 'Part II of' is omitted.

(3) In subsection (3) of that section, after paragraph (*b*) there is inserted—

    '(*bb*) require any person to furnish any such information to the Director as may be specified or described in the order;'.

(4) The amendments made by sub-paragraphs (1) to (3) have effect in relation to the making of any order under section 89 of the Fair Trading Act 1973 after the passing of this Act, whether the principal order (within the meaning of that section) was made before or after that time.

16.—(1) Section 90 of that Act is amended as follows.

(2) In subsection (1) after 'section 74' there is inserted ', section 75K'.

(3) For subsection (5) there is substituted—

    '(5) Nothing in any order to which this section applies shall have effect so as to—

      (*a*) cancel or modify conditions in licences granted—

        (i) under a patent granted under the Patents Act 1949 or the Patents Act 1977 or a European patent (UK) (within the meaning of the Patents Act 1977), or

        (ii) in respect of a design registered under the Registered Designs Act 1949,

      by the proprietor of the patent or design, or

      (*b*) require an entry to be made in the register of patents or the register of designs to the effect that licences under such a patent or such a design are to be available as of right.'.

17. In section 132(1) of that Act, after '85(6)' there is inserted 'section 93B'.

18.—(1) In Schedule 3 to that Act, in paragraph 16(2) for '75' there is substituted '73'.

(2) This paragraph does not apply in relation to any report made before the passing of this Act.

19.—(1) Schedule 8 to that Act is amended as follows.

(2) After paragraph 9 there is inserted—

    '9A.—(1) An order may require a person supplying goods or services to publish—

      (*a*) any such accounting information in relation to the supply of the goods or services, and

      (*b*) any such information in relation to—

        (i) the quantities of goods or services supplied, or

        (ii) the geographical areas in which they are supplied,

    as may be specified or described in the order.

    (2) In this paragraph 'accounting information', in relation to a supply of goods or services, means information as to—

      (*a*) the costs of the supply, including fixed costs and overheads,

      (*b*) the manner in which fixed costs and overheads are calculated and apportioned for accounting purposes of the supplier, and

      (*c*) the income attributable to the supply.'.

(3) After paragraph 12 there is inserted—

    '12A. An order may require any person to furnish any such information to the Director as may be specified or described in the order.

    12B. An order may require any activities to be carried on separately from any other activities.

    12C. An order may prohibit or restrict the exercise of any right to vote exercisable by virtue of the holding of any shares, stock or securities.'.

20.—(1) In Schedule 9 to that Act, in paragraph 4 the words from 'either' to the end are omitted.

(2) This paragraph has effect in relation to the laying of any draft order under paragraph 4 of Schedule 9 to the Fair Trading Act 1973 after the passing of this Act, whether the notice under that Schedule was published before or after that time.

Competition Act 1980 (c 21)

21. In section 3(8) of the Competition Act 1980—

    (*a*) for '(5)' there is substituted '(6)', and

(*b*) at the end there is inserted 'but as if, in subsection (7) of that section, for the words from "any one" to "the Commission" there were substituted "the Director" '.

22. In section 4(4) of that Act for paragraph (*a*) there is substituted—

'(*a*) to arrange for—

(i) any undertaking accepted by him under this section, and

(ii) any variation or release of such an undertaking after the passing of the Companies Act 1989,

to be published in such manner as appears to him to be appropriate,'.

23. In section 9(4) of that Act—

(*a*) in paragraph (*a*), after 'undertaking' there is inserted 'and of any variation of it after the passing of the Companies Act 1989', and

(*b*) in paragraph (*b*), after 'undertaking' there is inserted 'and any variation or release of it after that time'.

24. In section 29(1)(*a*) of that Act after 'section' there is inserted '75G or'.

Telecommunications Act 1984 (c 12)

25.—(1) In section 13(9) of the Telecommunications Act 1984, after 'Commission)' there is inserted 'together with section 24 of the Competition Act 1980 (modification of provisions about performance of Commission's functions)'.

(2) The Monopolies and Mergers Commission (Performance of Functions) Order 1989 shall have effect as if sub-paragraph (1) above had come into force immediately before the making of the Order.

Financial Services Act 1986 (c 60)

26. In section 123(3) of the Financial Services Act 1986—

(*a*) for '(5)' there is substituted '(6)', and

(*b*) at the end there is inserted 'but as if, in subsection (7) of that section, for the words from "any one" to "the Commission" there were substituted "the Director" '.

SCHEDULE 21

Section 156(1)

ADDITIONAL REQUIREMENTS FOR RECOGNITION

PART I

UK INVESTMENT EXCHANGES

Default rules

1.—(1) The exchange must have default rules which, in the event of a member of the exchange appearing to be unable to meet his obligations in respect of one or more market contracts, enable action to be taken in respect of unsettled market contracts to which he is party.

(2) The rules may authorise the taking of the same or similar action in relation to a member who appears to be likely to become unable to meet his obligations in respect of one or more market contracts.

(3) The rules must enable action to be taken in respect of all unsettled market contracts, other than those entered into by a recognised clearing house for the purposes of or in connection with the provision of clearing services for the exchange.

(4) As regards contracts entered into by the exchange for the purposes of or in connection with the provision of its own clearing services, the rules must contain provision corresponding to that required by paragraphs 9 to 11 below in the case of a UK clearing house.

(5) As regards other contracts the rules must contain provision complying with paragraphs 2 and 3 below.

Content of rules

2.—(1) The rules must provide for all rights and liabilities between those party as principal to unsettled market contracts to which the defaulter is party as principal to be discharged and for there to be paid by one party to the other such sum of money (if any) as may be determined in accordance with the rules.

(2) The rules must further provide—

    (*a*) for the sums so payable in respect of different contracts between the same parties to be aggregated or set off so as to produce a net sum, and

    (*b*) for the certification by or on behalf of the exchange of the net sum payable or, as the case may be, of the fact that no sum is payable.

(3) The rules may make special provision with respect to, or exclude from the provisions required by sub-paragraphs (1) and (2), contracts of any description prescribed for the purposes of this sub-paragraph by regulations made by the Secretary of State.

Notification to other parties affected

3. The exchange must have adequate arrangements for securing that—

    (*a*) parties to unsettled market contracts with a defaulter acting as principal are notified as soon as reasonably practicable of the default and of any decision taken under the rules in relation to contracts to which they are a party; and

    (*b*) parties to unsettled market contracts with a defaulter acting as agent and the defaulter's principals are notified as soon as reasonably practicable of the default and of the identity of the other party to the contract.

Application of default rules to designated non-members

4.—(1) The rules make the same or similar provision in relation to designated non-members as in relation to members of the exchange.

(2) If such provision is made, the exchange must have adequate procedures—

    (*a*) for designating the persons, or descriptions of person, in respect of whom action may be taken,

    (*b*) for keeping under review the question which persons or descriptions of person should be or remain so designated, and

    (*c*) for withdrawing such designation.

(3) The procedures shall be designed to secure that a person is not or does not remain designated if failure by him to meet his obligations in respect of one or more market contracts would be unlikely adversely to affect the operation of the market, and that a description of persons is not or does not remain designated if failure by a person of that description to meet his obligations in respect of one or more market contracts would be unlikely adversely to affect the operation of the market.

(4) The exchange must have adequate arrangements—

    (*a*) for bringing a designation or withdrawal of designation to the attention of the person or description of persons concerned, and

    (*b*) where a description of persons is designated, or the designation of a description of persons is withdrawn, for ascertaining which persons fall within that description.

Delegation of functions in connection with default procedures

5. The rules may make provision for the whole or part of the functions mentioned in paragraphs 1 to 4 to be performed by another body or person on behalf of the exchange.

Co-operation with other authorities

6. The exchange must be able and willing to co-operate, by the sharing of information and otherwise, with the Secretary of State, any relevant office-holder and any other authority or body having responsibility for any matter arising out of, or connected with, the default of a member of the exchange or any designated non-member.

Margin

7. Where the exchange provides its own clearing arrangements and margined transactions are effected, paragraph 14 below applies as it applies in relation to a clearing house.

PART II
UK CLEARING HOUSES

Default rules

8.—(1) The clearing house must have default rules which, in the event of a member of the clearing house appearing to be unable to meet his obligations in respect of one or more market contracts, enable action to be taken to close out his position in relation to all unsettled market contracts to which he is a party.

(2) The rules may authorise the taking of the same or similar action where a member appears to be likely to become unable to meet his obligations in respect of one or more market contracts.

Content of rules

9.—(1) The rules must provide for all rights and liabilities of the defaulter under or in respect of unsettled market contracts to be discharged and for there to be paid by or to the defaulter such sum of money (if any) as may be determined in accordance with the rules.

(2) The rules must further provide—

(a) for the sums so payable by or to the defaulter in respect of different contracts to be aggregated or set off so as to produce a net sum;

(b) for that sum—

(i) if payable by the defaulter to the clearing house, to be set off against any property provided by or on behalf of the defaulter as cover for margin (or the proceeds of realisation of such property) so as to produce a further net sum, and

(ii) if payable by the clearing house to the defaulter to be aggregated with any property provided by the defaulter as cover for margin (or the proceeds of realisation of such property); and

(c) for the certification by or on behalf of the clearing house of the sum finally payable or, as the case may be, of the fact that no sum is payable.

10.—(1) The reference in paragraph 9 to the rights and liabilities of a defaulter under or in respect of an unsettled market contract includes (without prejudice to the generality of that provision) rights and liabilities arising in consequence of action taken under provisions of the rules authorising—

(a) the effecting by the clearing house of corresponding contracts in relation to unsettled market contracts to which the defaulter is a party;

(b) the transfer of the defaulter's position under an unsettled market contract to another member of the clearing house;

(c) the exercise by the clearing house of any option granted by an unsettled market contract.

(2) A 'corresponding contract' means a contract on the same terms (except as to price or premium) as the market contract, but under which the person who is the buyer under the market contract agrees to sell and the person who is the seller under the market contract agrees to buy.

This sub-paragraph applies with any necessary modifications in relation to a market contract which is not an agreement to sell.

(3) The reference in paragraph 9 to the rights and liabilities of a defaulter under or in respect of an unsettled market contract does not include, where he acts as agent, rights or liabilities of his arising our of the relationship of principal and agent.

Notification to other parties affected

11. The clearing house must have adequate arrangements for securing that parties to unsettled market contracts with a defaulter are notified as soon as reasonably practicable of the default and of any decision taken under the rules in relation to contracts to which they are a party.

Delegation of functions in connection with default procedures

12. The rules may make provision for the whole or part of the functions mentioned in paragraphs 8 to 11 to be performed by another body or person on behalf of the clearing house.

Co-operation with other authorities

13. The clearing house must be able and willing to co-operate, by the sharing of information and otherwise, with the Secretary of State, any relevant office-holder and any other authority or body having responsibility for any matter arising out of, or connected with, the default of a member of the clearing house.

Margin

14.—(1) The rules of the clearing house must provide that, in the event of a default, margin provided by the defaulter for his own account is not to be applied to meet a shortfall on a client account.

(2) This is without prejudice to the requirements of any relevant regulations under section 55 of the Financial Services Act 1986 (clients' money).

PART III
OVERSEAS INVESTMENT EXCHANGES AND CLEARING HOUSES

15.—(1) The rules and practices of the body, together with the law of the country in which the body's head office is situated, must be such as to provide adequate procedures for dealing with the default of persons party to market contracts connected with the body.

(2) The reference in sub-paragraph (1) to default is to a person being unable to meet his obligations.

SCHEDULE 22

Section 182(4)

FINANCIAL MARKETS AND INSOLVENCY: PROVISIONS APPLYING TO PRE-COMMENCEMENT CASES

Introductory

1. The provisions of this Schedule have effect for the purpose of safeguarding the operation of certain financial markets—

    (*a*) in the event of the insolvency, winding up or default of a person party to transactions in the market (paragraphs 2 to 8), and

    (*b*) as regards the effectiveness or enforcement of certain charges given to secure obligations in connection with such transactions (paragraphs 9 to 12).

Recognised investment exchanges and clearing houses

2.—(1) This Schedule applies to the following descriptions of contract connected with a recognised investment exchange or recognised clearing house.

    The contracts are referred to in this Schedule as 'market contracts'.

(2) In relation to a recognised investment exchange, this Schedule applies to—

    (*a*) contracts entered into by a member or designated non-member of the exchange which are—

        (i) made on or otherwise subject to the rules of the exchange,

        (ii) on terms expressed to be as traded on the exchange, or

        (iii) on the same terms as those on which an equivalent contract would be made on the exchange; and

    (*b*) contracts subject to the rules of the exchange entered into by the exchange for the purposes of or in connection with the provision of clearing services.

    A 'designated non-member' means a person in respect of whom action may be taken under the default rules of the exchange but who is not a member of the exchange.

(3) In relation to a recognised clearing house, this Schedule applies to contracts subject to the rules of the clearing house entered into by the clearing house for the purposes of or in connection with the provision of clearing services for a recognised investment exchange.

    This includes contracts effected under or in consequence of action taken by the clearing house under its default rules.

3. The general law of insolvency has effect in relation to market contracts, and action taken under the rules of a recognised investment exchange or recognised clearing house with respect to such contracts, subject to the following provisions of this Schedule.

4.—(1) None of the following shall be regarded as to any extent invalid at law on the ground of inconsistency with the law relating to the distribution of the assets of a person on bankruptcy, winding-up or sequestration, or in the administration of an insolvent estate—

    (*a*) a market contract,

    (*b*) the rules of a recognised investment exchange or recognised clearing house as to the settlement of market contracts,

    (*c*) the default rules of a recognised investment exchange or recognised clearing house.

(2) The powers of a relevant office-holder in his capacity as such, and the powers of the court under the Insolvency Act 1986 or the Bankruptcy (Scotland) Act 1985, shall not be exercised in such a way as to prevent or interfere with—

    (*a*) the settlement of a market contract in accordance with the rules of a recognised investment exchange or recognised clearing house,

    (*b*) any action taken under the default rules of such an exchange or clearing house.

(3) Nothing in the following provisions of this Schedule shall be construed as affecting the generality of sub-paragraph (2).

(4) A debt or other liability arising out of a market contract which is the subject of default proceedings may not be proved in a winding up or bankruptcy, or in Scotland claimed in a winding up or sequestration, until the completion of the default proceedings.

    A debt or other liability which by virtue of this sub-paragraph may not be proved or claimed shall not be taken into account for the purposes of any set-off until the completion of the default proceedings.

5.—(1) A liquidator or trustee of a defaulter shall not—

    (*a*) declare or pay any dividend to the creditors, or

    (*b*) return any capital to contributories,

unless he has retained what he reasonably considers to be an adequate reserve in respect of any claims arising as a result of the default proceedings of the exchange or clearing house concerned.

(2) Nothing in section 11(3), 130 or 285 of the Insolvency Act 1986 (which restrict the taking of certain legal proceedings and other steps), and nothing in the Bankruptcy (Scotland) Act 1985, shall affect any action taken by an exchange or clearing house for the purpose of its default proceedings.

6.—(1) The following provisions apply with respect to the net sum certified by a recognised investment exchange or recognised clearing house, upon the completion of proceedings under its default rules, to be payable by or to a defaulter.

(2) If, in England and Wales, a bankruptcy or winding up order has been made, or a resolution for voluntary winding up has been passed, the debt—

    (*a*) is provable in the bankruptcy or winding up or, as the case may be, is payable to the relevant office-holder, and

    (*b*) shall be taken into account, where appropriate, under section 323 of the Insolvency Act 1986 (mutual dealings and set-off) or the corresponding provision applicable in the case of a winding up,

in the same way as a debt due before the commencement of the bankruptcy or winding up.

(3) If, in Scotland, an award of sequestration or a winding-up order has been made, or a resolution for voluntary winding up has been passed, the debt—

    (*a*) may be claimed in the sequestration or winding up or, as the case may be, is payable to the relevant office-holder, and

    (*b*) shall be taken into account for the purposes of any rule of law relating to compensation or set-off applicable in sequestration or winding up,

in the same way as a debt due before the date of sequestration (within the meaning of section 73(1) of the Bankruptcy (Scotland) Act 1985) or the commencement of the winding up.

7.—(1) Sections 178, 186, 315 and 345 of the Insolvency Act 1986 (power to disclaim onerous property and court's power to order rescission of contracts, &c) do not apply in relation to—

    (*a*) a market contract, or

    (*b*) a contract effected by the exchange or clearing house for the purpose of realising property provided as margin in relation to market contracts.

In the application of this sub-paragraph in Scotland, the reference to sections 178 and 315 shall be construed as a reference to any rule of law having the like effect as those sections.

(2) Sections 127 and 284 of the Insolvency Act 1986 (avoidance of property dispositions effected after commencement of winding up or presentation of bankruptcy petition) do not apply to—

    (*a*) a market contract, or any disposition of property in pursuance of such a contract,

    (*b*) the provision of margin in relation to market contracts,

    (*c*) a contract effected by the exchange or clearing house for the purpose of realising property provided as margin in relation to a market contract, or any disposition of property in pursuance of such a contract, or

    (*d*) any disposition of property in accordance with the rules of the exchange or clearing house as to the application of property provided as margin.

(3) However, if a person enters into a market contract knowing that a petition has been presented for the winding up or bankruptcy of the other party to the contract, the value of any profit or benefit to

him arising from the contract is recoverable from him by the relevant office-holder unless the court directs otherwise.

(4) Any sum recoverable by virtue of sub-paragraph (3) has the same priority, in the event of the insolvency of the person from whom it is due, as if it were secured by a fixed charge.

8.—(1) No order shall be made in relation to a market contract under—

    (*a*) section 238 or 339 of the Insolvency Act 1986 (transactions at an under-value),

    (*b*) section 239 or 340 of that Act (preferences), or

    (*c*) section 423 of that Act (transactions defrauding creditors),

unless the court is satisfied that the person in favour of whom the contract was made knew at the time he entered into it that it was at an under-value (within the meaning of the relevant provision) or, as the case may be, that a preference was being given.

(2) As respects Scotland, no decree shall be granted in relation to a market contract—

    (*a*) under section 34 or 36 of the Bankruptcy (Scotland) Act 1985 or section 242 or 243 of the Insolvency Act 1986 (gratuitous alienations and unfair preferences), or

    (*b*) at common law,

unless the court is satisfied that the person with whom the contract was made knew at the time he entered into it that it was challengeable under any of the provisions mentioned in paragraph (*a*) or at common law.

(3) Sub-paragraphs (1) and (2) apply in relation to—

    (*a*) a disposition of property in pursuance of a market contract,

    (*b*) the provision of margin in relation to market contracts,

    (*c*) a contract effected by a recognised investment exchange or recognised clearing house for the purpose of realising property provided as margin, or

    (*d*) a disposition of property in accordance with the rules of the exchange or clearing house as to the application of property provided as margin,

as they apply in relation to the making of a market contract.

Market charges

9.—(1) The charges to which paragraphs 10 to 12 apply are charges, whether fixed or floating, granted—

    (*a*) in favour of a recognised investment exchange, for the purpose of securing debts or liabilities arising in connection with the settlement of market contracts,

    (*b*) in favour of a recognised clearing house, for the purpose of securing debts or liabilities arising in connection with their ensuring the performance of market contracts, or

    (*c*) in favour of a person who agrees to make payments as a result of the transfer of specified securities made through the medium of a computer-based system established by the Bank of England and The Stock Exchange, for the purpose of securing debts or liabilities of the transferee arising in connection with the payments.

Those charges are referred to in this Schedule as 'market charges'.

(2) Where a charge is granted partly for purposes specified in sub-paragraph (1)(*a*), (*b*) or (*c*) and partly for other purposes, paragraphs 10 to 12 apply to it so far as it has effect for the specified purposes; and the expression 'market charge' shall be construed accordingly.

(3) In this paragraph and paragraphs 10 to 12—

    'charge' means any form of security, including a mortgage and, in Scotland, a heritable security; and

    'specified securities' means securities for the time being specified in the list in Schedule 1 to the Stock Transfer Act 1982, and includes any right to such securities.

10. The general law of insolvency has effect in relation to market charges and action taken in enforcing them subject to the following provisions of this Schedule.

11.—(1) Sections 10(1)(*b*) and 11(3)(*c*) of the Insolvency Act 1986 (no enforcement of security while petition for administration order pending or order in force) do not apply to a market charge.

(2) Section 11(2) of that Act (receiver to vacate office when so required by administrator) does not apply to a receiver appointed under a market charge.

(3) Section 15(1) and (2) of that Act (administrator's power to deal with charged property) do not apply to a market charge.

(4) Sections 127 and 284 of that Act (avoidance of property dispositions effected after commencement of winding up or presentation of bankruptcy petition) do not apply to—

(a) a disposition of property as a result of which the property becomes subject to a market charge, or any transaction pursuant to which that disposition is made, or

(b) any disposition of property made in enforcing a market charge.

(5) However, if a person (other than the chargee under the market charge) who is a party to a disposition mentioned in sub-paragraph (4)(a) knows at the time of the disposition that a petition has been presented for the winding up or bankruptcy of the party making the disposition, the value of any profit or benefit to him arising from the disposition is recoverable from him by the relevant office-holder unless the court directs otherwise.

(6) Any sum recoverable by virtue of sub-paragraph (5) has the same priority, in the event of the insolvency of the person from whom it is due, as if it were secured by a fixed charge.

12.—(1) No legal proceedings, execution or other legal process may be commenced or continued, and no distress may be levied against property which is, or becomes, subject to a market charge except with the consent of the person in whose favour the charge was granted or the leave of the court.

(2) The court may give leave subject to such terms as it thinks fit.

(3) Sub-paragraph (1) does not apply to proceedings to enforce any security over, or any equitable interest in, the property.

(4) Sections 10(1)(c), 11(3)(d), 130(3) and 285(3) of the Insolvency Act 1986 (which restrict the taking of certain legal proceedings and other steps) have effect accordingly.

(5) In the application of this paragraph to Scotland, the reference to execution being commenced or continued includes a reference to diligence being carried out or continued, and the reference to distress being levied shall be omitted.

Supplementary provisions

13.—(1) In this Schedule 'default rules' means—

(a) in relation to a recognised investment exchange, rules which provide in the event of a member or designated non-member of the exchange appearing to be unable, or likely to become unable, to meet his obligations in respect of one or more market contracts, for the settlement forthwith of all unsettled market contracts to which he is a party as principal, other than those whose performance is ensured by a recognised clearing house;

(b) in relation to a recognised clearing house, rules which provide in the event of a member of the clearing house appearing to be unable, or likely to become unable, to meet his obligations in respect of any market contract, for the closing out of his position in relation to all market contracts to which he is a party.

(2) References in this Schedule to a 'defaulter' are to a person in respect of whom action has been taken by a recognised investment exchange or recognised clearing house under its default rules, whether by declaring him to be a defaulter or otherwise; and references in this Schedule to 'default' shall be construed accordingly.

(3) In this Schedule 'default proceedings' means proceedings taken by a recognised investment exchange or recognised clearing house under its default rules.

14.—(1) The following are relevant office-holders for the purposes of this Schedule—

(a) the official receiver,

(b) any person acting in relation to a company as its liquidator, provisional liquidator, administrator or administrative receiver,

(c) any person acting in relation to an individual (or, in Scotland, a deceased debtor) as his trustee in bankruptcy or interim receiver of his property or as permanent or interim trustee in the sequestration of his estate,

(d) any person acting as administrator (or, in Scotland, as judicial factor) of an insolvent estate of a deceased person.

(2) Sub-paragraph (1)(c) applies in relation to a partnership, and any debtor within the meaning of the Bankruptcy (Scotland) Act 1985, as it applies in relation to an individual.

(3) In this paragraph—

'administrative receiver' has the meaning given by section 251 of the Insolvency Act 1986;

'company' means a company within the meaning of section 735(1) of the Companies Act 1985 or a company which may be wound up under Part V of the Insolvency Act 1986 (unregistered companies); and 'interim trustee' and 'permanent trustee' have the same meaning as in the Bankruptcy (Scotland) Act 1985.

15.—(1) In this Schedule—

'clearing house' has the same meaning as in the Financial Services Act 1986;

'investment' and 'investment exchange' have the same meaning as in the Financial Services Act 1986;

'recognised' means recognised under the Financial Services Act 1986;

'The Stock Exchange' means The International Stock Exchange of the United Kingdom and the Republic of Ireland Limited.

(2) References in this Schedule to ensuring the performance of a transaction have the same meaning as in the Financial Services Act 1986.

(3) References in this Schedule to a market contract to which a person is a party include, unless the contrary intention appears, contracts to which he is party as agent.

SCHEDULE 23

Section 206(1)

CONSEQUENTIAL AMENDMENTS OF THE FINANCIAL SERVICES ACT 1986

PART I

GENERAL AMENDMENTS

1.—(1) Section 13 of the Financial Services Act 1986 (power to direct alteration of rules of recognised self-regulating organisation) is amended as follows.

(2) Omit subsection (1).

(3) For subsection (2) substitute—

'(2) If at any time it appears to the Secretary of State that—

(*a*) a recognised self-regulating organisation is concerned with two or more kinds of investment business, and

(*b*) the requirement in paragraph 3(1) of Schedule 2 to this Act is not satisfied in respect of investment business of one or more but not all of those kinds,

he may, instead of revoking the recognition order or making an application under section 12 above, direct the organisation to alter, or himself alter, its rules so that they preclude a member from carrying on investment business of a kind in respect of which that requirement is not satisfied, unless he is an authorised person otherwise than by virtue of membership of the organisation or is an exempted person in respect of that business.'.

(4) For subsection (3) substitute—

'(3) A direction under this section is enforceable on the application of the Secretary of State by injunction or, in Scotland, by an order under section 45 of the Court of Session Act 1988.'.

(5) Omit subsections (4) to (6).

2.—(1) Section 48 of the Financial Services Act 1986 (conduct of business rules) is amended as follows.

(2) In subsection (1) omit the words 'members of a recognised self-regulating organisation or' and 'organisation or'.

(3) After subsection (10) insert—

'(11) Section 63A below (application of designated rules) has effect as regards the application of rules under this section to members of recognised self-regulating organisations in respect of investment business in the carrying on of which they are subject to the rules of the organisation.'.

3.—(1) Section 49 of the Financial Services Act 1986 (financial resources rules) is amended as follows.

(2) For subsection (1) substitute—

'(1) The Secretary of State may make rules requiring—

(*a*) a person authorised to carry on investment business by virtue of section 25 or 31 above, or

(*b*) a member of a recognised self-regulating organisation carrying on investment business in the carrying on of which he is subject to the rules of the organisation,

to have and maintain in respect of that business such financial resources as are required by the rules.'.

(3) After subsection (2) insert—

'(3) Section 63A below (application of designated rules) has effect as regards the application of rules under this section to members of recognised self-regulating organisations in respect of investment business in the carrying on of which they are subject to the rules of the organisation.'.

4. In section 50 of the Financial Services Act 1986 (power of Secretary of State to modify conduct of business and financial resources rules for particular cases), after subsection (3) insert—

'(4) The powers conferred by subsection (1) above shall not be exercised in a case where the powers conferred by section 63B below are exercisable (powers of recognised self-regulating organisation in relation to designated rules).'.

5. In section 52 of the Financial Services Act 1986 (notification regulations), in subsection (3) (application to member of recognised self-regulating organisation or professional body), for 'subject to any of the rules made under section 48 above' substitute 'not subject to the rules of that organisation or body'.

6.—(1) Section 55 of the Financial Services Act 1986 (clients' money) is amended as follows.

(2) In subsection (2)(*b*) and (*e*) omit the words 'a member of a recognised self-regulating organisation or' and 'organisation or'.

(3) In subsection (3) omit the words 'organisation or'.

(4) After subsection (5) insert—

'(6) Section 63A below (application of designated regulations) has effect as regards the application of regulations under this section to members of recognised self-regulating organisations in respect of investment business in the carrying on of which they are subject to the rules of the organisation.'.

7. In section 56 of the Financial Services Act 1986 (unsolicited calls), for subsection (7) substitute—

'(7) Section 63A below (application of designation regulations) has effect as regards the application of regulations under this section to members of recognised self-regulating organisations in respect of investment business in the carrying on of which they are subject to the rules of the organisation.

As it applies to such persons in respect of such business the reference in subsection (1) above to conduct permitted by regulations made by the Secretary of State shall be construed—

(*a*) where or to the extent that the regulations do not apply, as a reference to conduct permitted by the rules of the organisation; and

(*b*) where or to the extent that the regulations do apply but are expressed to have effect subject to the rules of the organisation, as a reference to conduct permitted by the regulations together with the rules of the organisation.

(7A) In the application of this section to anything done by a person certified by a recognised professional body in carrying on investment business in the carrying on of which he is subject to the rules of the body, the reference in subsection (1) above to conduct permitted by regulations made by the Secretary of State shall be construed as a reference to conduct permitted by the rules of the body.'.

8. In section 86 of the Financial Services Act 1986 (collective investment schemes constituted in other member States), in subsection (7) (restriction on application of conduct of business rules), at the end add—

'This subsection also applies to statements of principle under section 47A and codes of practice under section 63A so far as they relate to matters falling within the rule-making power in section 48.'.

9. In section 95 of the Financial Services Act 1986 (collective investment schemes: contraventions), after subsection (2) add—

'(3) The disciplinary action which may be taken by virtue of section 47A(3) (failure to comply with statement of principle) includes—

(*a*) the giving of a direction under section 91(2), and

(*b*) the application by the Secretary of State for an order under section 93;

and subsection (6) of section 47A (duty of the Secretary of State as to exercise of powers) has effect accordingly.'.

10.—(1) Section 107 of the Financial Services Act 1986 (appointment of auditors) is amended as follows.

(2) For subsection (1) (power to make rules) substitute—

'(1) The Secretary of State may make rules requiring—

(*a*) a person authorised to carry on investment business by virtue of section 25 or 31 above, or

(*b*) a member of a recognised self-regulating organisation carrying on investment business in the carrying on of which he is subject to the rules of the organisation,

and who, apart from the rules, is not required by or under any enactment to appoint an auditor, to appoint as an auditor a person satisfying such conditions as to qualifications and otherwise as may be specified in or imposed under the rules.'.

(3) After subsection (3) add—

'(4) In its application to members of recognised self-regulating organisations, this section has effect subject to section 107A below.'.

11. After section 107 of the Financial Services Act 1986 insert—

'107A Application of audit rules to members of self-regulating organisations

(1) The Secretary of State may in rules under section 107 designate provisions which apply, to such extent as may be specified, to a member of a recognised self-regulating organisation in respect of investment business in the carrying on of which he is subject to the rules of the organisation.

(2) It may be provided that the designated rules have effect, generally or to such extent as may be specified, subject to the rules of the organisation.

(3) A member of a recognised self-regulating organisation who contravenes a rule applying to him by virtue of that section shall be treated as having contravened the rules of the organisation.

(4) Except as mentioned above, rules made under section 107 do not apply to members of recognised self-regulating organisations in respect of investment business in the carrying on of which they are subject to the rules of the organisation.

(5) A recognised self-regulating organisation may on the application of a member of the organisation—

(*a*) modify a rule designated under this section so as to adapt it to his circumstances or to any particular kind of business carried on by him, or

(*b*) dispense him from compliance with any such rule, generally or in relation to any particular kind of business carried on by him.

(6) The powers conferred by subsection (5) shall not be exercised unless it appears to the organisation—

(*a*) that complaince with the rule in question would be unduly burdensome for the applicant having regard to the benefit which compliance would confer on investors, and

(*b*) that the exercise of those powers will not result in any undue risk to investors.

(7) The powers conferred by subsection (5) may be exercised unconditionally or subject to conditions; and subsection (3) applies in the case of a contravention of a condition as in the case of contravention of a designated rule.

(8) The reference in paragraph 4(1) of Schedule 2 (requirements for recognition of self-regulating organisations) to monitoring and enforcement of compliance with rules includes monitoring and enforcement of compliance with conditions imposed by the organisation under subsection (7).'.

12.—(1) Section 114 of the Financial Services Act 1986 (power to transfer functions to designated agency) is amended as follows.

(2) For subsection (9) substitute—

'(9) The Secretary of State shall not make a delegation order transferring any legislative functions unless—

(*a*) the agency has furnished him with a copy of the instruments it proposes to issue or make in the exercise of those functions, and

(*b*) he is satisfied that those instruments will afford investors an adequate level of protection and, in the case of such provisions as are mentioned in Schedule 8 to this Act, comply with the principles set out in that Schedule.

In this subsection 'legislative functions' means the functions of issuing or making statements of principle, rules, regulations or codes of practice.'.

(3) In subsection (12) for 'rules or regulations made' substitute 'statements of principle, rules, regulations or codes of practice issued or made'.

13.—(1) Section 115 of the Financial Services Act 1986 (resumption of transferred functions) is amended as follows.

(2) For subsection (5) substitute—

'(5) Where the transferred functions consist of or include any legislative functions, an order may be made under subsection (2) above if at any time it appears to the Secretary of State that the instruments issued or made by the agency do not satisfy the requirements of section 114(9)(*b*) above.'.

(3) In subsection (7)—

    (*a*) in the opening words, for 'subsection (2)(*b*) above' substitute 'this section', and

    (*b*) in paragraph (*a*) for 'functions of making rules or regulations' substitute 'functions of issuing or making statements of principle, rules, regulations or codes of practice'.

14.—(1) Section 119 of the Financial Services Act 1986 (competition scrutiny: recognition orders) is amended as follows.

(2) In subsection (1) (considerations relevant to making of recognition order), for paragraphs (*a*) and (*b*) substitute—

    '(*a*) in the case of a self-regulating organisation, the rules and any guidance of which copies are furnished with the application for the order, together with any statements of principle, rules, regulations or codes of practice to which members of the organisation would be subject by virtue of Chapter V of this Part,

    (*b*) in the case of an investment exchange, the rules and any guidance of which copies are furnished with the application for the order, together with any arrangements of which particulars are furnished with the application,

    (*c*) in the case of a clearing house, the rules and any guidance of which copies are furnished with the application for the order,'.

(3) In subsection (2) (circumstances in which powers are exercisable in relation to recognised body), for paragraphs (*a*) to (*c*) substitute—

    '(*a*) in the case of a self-regulating organisation,

        (i) any rules made or guidance issued by the organisation,

        (ii) any practices of the organisation, or

        (iii) any practices of persons who are members of, or otherwise subject to the rules made by, the organisation,

    together with any statements of principle, rules, regulations or codes of practice to which members of the organisation are subject by virtue of Chapter V of this Part,

    (*b*) in the case of a recognised investment exchange—

        (i) any rules made or guidance issued by the exchange,

        (ii) any practices of the exchange, or

        (iii) any practices of persons who are members of, or otherwise subject to the rules made by, the exchange,

    (*c*) in the case of a recognised clearing house—

        (i) any rules made or guidance issued by the clearing house,

        (ii) any practices of the clearing house, or

        (iii) any practices of persons who are members of, or otherwise subject to the rules made by, the clearing house,

    or any clearing arrangements made by the clearing house,'.

(4) In subsection (3) (powers exercisable in relation to recognised body)—

    (*a*) in paragraph (*b*) for 'the rules' substitute 'its rules, or the', and

    (*b*) in paragraph (*c*) for 'the rules' substitute 'its rules'.

(5) In subsection (5) (construction of references to practices)—

    (*a*) for 'paragraph (*b*)' substitute 'paragraph (*a*)(ii), (*b*)(ii) and (*c*)(ii)', and

    (*b*) omit the words from 'and the practices referred to in paragraph (*c*)' to the end.

(6) After that subsection insert—

    '(6) The practices referred to in paragraph (*a*)(iii), (*b*)(iii) and (*c*)(iii) of subsection (2) above are—

        (*a*) in relation to a recognised self-regulating organisation, practices in relation to business in respect of which the persons in question are subject to—

    (i) the rules of the organisation, or

    (ii) statements of principle, rules, regulations or codes of practice to which its members are subject by virtue of Chapter V of this Part,

and which are required or contemplated by the rules of the organisation or by those statements, rules, regulations or codes, or by guidance issued by the organisation,

  (b) in relation to a recognised investment exchange or clearing house, practices in relation to business in respect of which the persons in question are subject to the rules of the exchange or clearing house, and which are required or contemplated by its rules or guidance,

or which are otherwise attributable to the conduct of the organisation, exchange or clearing house as such.'.

15.—(1) Section 121 of the Financial Services Act 1986 (competition scrutiny: designated agencies) is amended as follows.

(2) In subsection (1) for 'rules, regulations' substitute 'statements of principle, rules, regulations, codes of practice'.

(3) In subsection (2)(a) and (c) for 'rules or regulations made' substitute 'statements of principle, rules, regulations or codes of practice issued or made'.

(4) In subsection (3)(b) for 'rules, regulations' substitute 'statements of principle, rules, regulations, codes of practice'.

(5) In subsection (4) for 'rules or regulations' (twice) substitute 'statements of principle, rules, regulations or codes of practice'.

16.—(1) Section 122 of the Financial Services Act 1986 (reports by Director General of Fair Trading) is amended as follows.

(2) In subsection (1) for 'and regulations' substitute ', statements of principle, regulations and codes of practice'.

(3) In subsection (2) for 'regulations,' substitute 'statements of principle, regulations, codes of practice,'.

(4) In subsection (4)—

  (a) in paragraph (a) for 'rules, guidance, arrangements and regulations' substitute 'rules, statements of principle, regulations, codes of practice, guidance and arrangements', and

  (b) in the words following the paragraphs, for 'rules, guidance, arrangements, regulations' substitute 'rules, statements of principle, regulations, codes of practice, guidance, arrangements', and for 'rules, guidance, arrangements or regulations' substitute 'rules, statements of principle, regulations, codes of practice, guidance or arrangements'.

17.—(1) Section 124 of the Financial Services Act 1986 (matters to be left out of account for certain purposes in connection with competition scrutiny) is amended as follows.

(2) In subsection (1) (matters to be left out of account in determining whether monopoly situation exists), in paragraph (c) for 'rules or regulations made or guidance issued' substitute 'statements of principle, rules, regulations, codes of practice or guidance issued or made'.

(3) In subsection (3) (matters to be excluded from consideration where monopoly situation exists)—

  (a) in paragraph (a), for 'rules or regulations made' substitute 'statements of principle, rules, regulations or codes of practice issued or made',

  (b) in paragraph (b), for 'rules or regulations' substitute 'statements of principle, rules, regulations or codes of practice', and

  (c) in the closing words, for 'rules, regulations' substitute 'statements of principle, rules, regulations, codes of practice'.

18. For section 205 of the Financial Services Act 1986 (regulations, rules and orders) substitute—

'205 General power to make regulations

The Secretary of State may make regulations prescribing anything which by this Act is authorised or required to be prescribed.

205A Supplementary provisions with respect to subordinate legislation

(1) The following provisions apply to any power of the Secretary of State under this Act—

  (a) to issue statements of principle,

  (b) to make rules or regulations,

  (c) to make orders (other than such orders as are excepted by subsection (4) below), or (*d*) to issue codes of practice.

(2) Any such power is exercisable by statutory instrument and includes power to make different provision for different cases.

(3) Except as otherwise provided, a statutory instrument containing statements of principle, rules or regulations shall be subject to annulment in pursuance of a resolution of either House of Parliament.

(4) The above provisions do not apply to a recognition order, an order declaring a collective investment scheme to be an authorised unit trust scheme or a recognised scheme or to an order revoking any such order.'.

19. In section 206(1) of the Financial Services Act 1986 (publication of information and advice)—

(*a*) in paragraph (*a*), for 'rules and regulations made' substitute 'statements of principle, rules, regulations and codes of practice issued or made', and

(*b*) in paragraph (*b*) for 'rules or regulations' substitute 'statements of principle, rules, regulations or codes of practice'.

20. In Schedule 2 to the Financial Services Act 1986 (requirements for recognition of self-regulating organisations), in paragraph 4(1) (monitoring and enforcement) for 'rules or regulations' substitute 'statements of principle, rules, regulations or codes of practice'.

21. In Schedule 3 to the Financial Services Act 1986 (requirements for recognition of professional bodies), in paragraph 4(2) (monitoring and enforcement) for 'rules or regulations' substitute 'statements of principle, rules, regulations or codes of practice'.

22. In Schedule 7 to the Financial Services Act 1986 (qualifications of designated agency), in paragraph 2(2) (arrangements for discharge of functions: matters to be decided upon by the governing body) for 'rules or regulations must be made' substitute 'statements of principle, rules, regulations and codes of practice must be issued or made'.

23.—(1) Schedule 8 to the Financial Services Act 1986 (principles applicable to designated agency's rules and regulations) is amended as follows.

(2) In the heading for 'Rules and Regulations' substitute 'Legislative Provisions'.

(3) For paragraph 1, and the cross-heading preceding it, substitute—

'Introduction

1.—(1) In this Schedule 'legislative provisions' means the provisions of statements of principle, rules, regulations and codes of practice issued or made under Part I of this Act.

(2) References in this Schedule to 'conduct of business provisions' are to rules made under section 48 of this Act and statements of principle and codes of practice so far as they relate to matters falling within that rule-making power.

(3) References in this Schedule to provisions made for the purposes of a specified section or Chapter are to rules or regulations made under that section or Chapter and statements of principle and codes of practice so far as they relate to matters falling within that power to make rules or regulations.

Standards

1A. The conduct of business provisions and the other legislative provisions must promote high standards of integrity and fair dealing in the conduct of investment business.'.

(4) In paragraphs 2 to 7, 9, 11 and 12 for 'conduct of business rules' substitute 'conduct of business provisions'.

(5) In paragraph 7 for 'those rules and rules under' substitute 'those provisions and provisions made for the purposes of'.

(6) In paragraph 8 for 'Rules made under' substitute 'Provisions made for the purposes of'.

(7) In paragraph 9 for 'regulations made under' substitute 'provisions made for the purposes of'.

(8) In paragraph 10 for 'Rules made under' substitute 'Provisions made for the purposes of' and for 'under those sections' substitute 'for the purposes of those sections'.

(9) In paragraph 12 for 'rules and regulations made under' substitute 'provisions made for the purposes of'.

24.—(1) Schedule 9 to the Financial Services Act 1986 (designated agency: exercise of transferred functions) is amended as follows.

(2) In paragraph 4(1) (copies of instruments to be sent to Secretary of State), for 'any rules or regulations made' substitute 'any statements of principle, rules, regulations or codes of practice issued or made'.

(3) For paragraphs 5 and 6 substitute—

'5. Paragraphs 6 to 9 below have effect instead of section 205A of this Act in relation to statements of principle, rules, regulations and codes of practice issued or made by a designated agency in the exercise of powers transferred to it by a delegation order.

6. Any such power is exercisable by instrument in writing and includes power to make different provision for different cases.'.

(4) In paragraph 8 (instruments to be printed and made available to public)—

    (*a*) in sub-paragraph (1) for 'is made' substitute 'is issued or made', and

    (*b*) in sub-paragraph (2) for 'rule or regulation' (twice) substitute 'statement of principle, rule, regulation or code of practice'.

(5) In paragraph 9 (proof of instruments), for 'made by the agency' (twice) substitute 'made or issued by the agency'.

(6) For paragraph 12 (consultation) substitute—

'12.—(1) Where a designated agency proposes, in the exercise of powers transferred to it by a delegation order, to issue or make any statements of principle, rules, regulations or codes of practice, it shall publish the proposed instrument in such manner as appears to it best calculated to bring the proposals to the attention of the public, together with a statement that representations about the proposals (and, in particular, representations as to the cost of complying with the proposed provisions) can be made to the agency within a specified time.

(2) Before issuing or making the instrument the agency shall have regard to any representations duly made in accordance with that statement.

(3) The above requirements do not apply—

    (*a*) where the agency considers that the delay involved in complying with them would be prejudicial to the interests of investors;

    (*b*) to the issuing or making of an instrument in the same, or substantially the same, terms as a proposed instrument which was furnished by the agency to the Secretary of State for the purposes of section 114(9) of this Act.'.

25.—(1) Schedule 10 to the Financial Services Act 1986 (application of investment business provisions to regulated insurance companies) is amended as follows.

(2) In paragraph 4 (modification of conduct of business rules), after sub-paragraph (2) insert—

'(2A) Sub-paragraphs (1) and (2) also apply to statements of principle under section 47A and codes of practice under section 63A so far as they relate to matters falling within the rule-making power in section 48.'.

(3) In paragraph 7 (withdrawal of authorisation) after sub-paragraph (2) insert—

'(3) The disciplinary action which may be taken by virtue of section 47A(3) of this Act (failure to comply with statement of principle) includes—

    (*a*) the withdrawal of authorisation under section 11(2)(*a*) of the Insurance Companies Act 1982, and

    (*b*) the giving of a direction under section 13(2A) of that Act;

and subsection (6) of section 47A (duty of the Secretary of State as to exercise of powers) has effect accordingly.'.

PART II

AMENDMENTS RELATING TO FRIENDLY SOCIETIES

26. Schedule 11 to the Financial Services Act 1986 (friendly societies) is amended as follows.

27. In paragraph 3(2) (competition scrutiny: recognition of self-regulating organisation for friendly societies), after 'sent to him under this sub-paragraph' insert ', together with any statements of principle, rules, regulations or codes of practice to which members of the organisation would be subject by virtue of this Schedule,'.

28.—(1) Paragraph 4 (requirements for recognition of self-regulating organisation for friendly societies) is amended as follows.

(2) In sub-paragraph (4)—

    (*a*) in paragraph (*a*) for '22' substitute '22D', and

    (*b*) omit paragraph (*b*).

29. Omit paragraph 7.

30.—(1) Paragraph 10 (competition scrutiny: circumstances in which powers are exercisable in relation to recognised self-regulating organisation for friendly societies) is amended as follows.

(2) In sub-paragraph (1), after paragraph (*c*) insert 'together with any statements of principle, rules, regulations or codes of practice to which members of the organisation are subject by virtue of this Schedule,'.

(3) In sub-paragraph (2)—

    (*a*) in paragraph (*b*), for 'the rules' substitute 'its rules, or the', and

    (*b*) in paragraph (*c*), for 'the rules' substitute 'its rules'.

(4) In sub-paragraph (3) (construction of references to practices), omit the words from 'and the practices referred to in paragraph (*c*)' to the end; and after that sub-paragraph insert—

    '(3A) The practices referred to in paragraph (*c*) of sub-paragraph (1) above are practices in relation to business in respect of which the persons in question are subject to—

        (*a*) the rules of the organisation, or

        (*b*) statements of principle, rules, regulations or codes of practice to which its members are subject by virtue of this Schedule,

and which are required or contemplated by the rules of the organisation or by those statements, rules, regulations or codes, or by guidance issued by the organisation, or which are otherwise attributable to the conduct of the organisation as such.'.

31. In paragraph 13, for 'Paragraphs 14 to 25' substitute 'Paragraphs 13A to 25'.

32. Before paragraph 14 and after the heading '*Conduct of investment business*', insert—

    '13A.—(1) The Registrar may issue statements of principle with respect to the conduct expected of regulated friendly societies.

(2) The conduct expected may include compliance with a code or standard issued by another person, as for the time being in force, and may allow for the exercise of discretion by any person pursuant to any such code or standard.

(3) Failure to comply with a statement of principle under this paragraph is a ground for the taking of disciplinary action or the exercise of powers of intervention, but it does not give rise to any right of action by investors or other persons affected or affect the validity of any transaction.

(4) The disciplinary action which may be taken by virtue of sub-paragraph (3) is—

    (*a*) the making of a public statement under paragraph 21, or

    (*b*) the application by the Registrar for an injunction, interdict or other order under paragraph 22(1), or

    (*c*) any action under paragraph 26 or 27 of this Schedule;

and the reference in that sub-paragraph to powers of intervention is to the powers conferred by Chapter VI of Part I of this Act.

(5) Where a statement of principle relates to compliance with a code or standard issued by another person, the statement of principle may provide—

    (*a*) that failure to comply with the code or standard shall be a ground for the taking of disciplinary action, or the exercise of powers of intervention, only in such cases and to such extent as may be specified; and

    (*b*) that no such action shall be taken, or any such power exercised, except at the request of the person by whom the code or standard in question was issued.

(6) The Registrar shall exercise his powers in such manner as appears to him appropriate to secure compliance with statements of principle under this paragraph.

13B.—(1) The relevant regulatory authority may on the application of a regulated friendly society—

    (*a*) modify a statement of principle issued under paragraph 13A so as to adapt it to the circumstances of the society or to any particular kind of business carried on by it, or

    (*b*) dispense the society from compliance with any such statement of principle, generally or in relation to any particular kind of business carried on by it.

(2) The powers conferred by this paragraph shall not be exercised unless it appears to the relevant regulatory authority—

(a) that compliance with the statement of principle in question would be unduly burdensome for the applicant having regard to the benefit which compliance would confer on investors, and

(b) that the exercise of those powers will not result in any undue risk to investors.

(3) The powers conferred by this paragraph may be exercised unconditionally or subject to conditions; and paragraph 13A(3) applies in the case of failure to comply with a condition as in the case of failure to comply with a statement of principle.

(4) The relevant regulatory authority for the purposes of this paragraph is—

(a) in the case of a member society of a recognised self-regulating organisation for friendly societies, in relation to investment business in the carrying on of which it is subject to the rules of the organisation, that organisation;

(b) in any other case, or in relation to other investment business, the Registrar.

(5) The reference in paragraph 4(1) of Schedule 2 as applied by paragraph 4 above (requirements for recognition of self-regulating organisation for friendly societies) to monitoring and enforcement of compliance with statements of principle includes monitoring and enforcement of compliance with conditions imposed by the organisation under this paragraph.'.

33.—(1) Paragraph 14 (conduct of business rules) is amended as follows.

(2) In sub-paragraph (1), omit the words 'other than a member society'.

(3) After sub-paragraph (2) insert—

'(2A) Paragraph 22B below has effect as regards the application of rules under this paragraph to member societies in respect of investment business in the carrying on of which they are subject to the rules of a recognised self-regulating organisation for friendly societies.'.

(4) In sub-paragraph (3), omit the word 'and' after paragraph (a); and after paragraph (b) insert—

'; and

(c) for the references in subsection (4) to section 63B and a recognised self-regulating organisation there shall be substituted references to paragraph 13B and a recognised self-regulating organisation for friendly societies.'.

34.—(1) Paragraph 19 (clients' money regulations) is amended as follows.

(2) In sub-paragraph (2) for the words from '(but with the substitution' to the end substitute '(but with the substitution for the reference in paragraph (e) of subsection (2) to the Secretary of State of a reference to the Registrar)'.

(3) After that sub-paragraph insert—

'(3) Paragraph 22B below has effect as regards the application of regulations under this paragraph to member societies in respect of investment business in the carrying on of which they are subject to the rules of a recognised self-regulating organisation for friendly societies.'.

35. For paragraph 20 (unsolicited calls) substitute—

'20.—(1) Regulations under section 56(1) of this Act shall not permit anything to be done by a regulated friendly society but that section shall not apply to anything done by such a society in the course of or in consequence of an unsolicited call which, as respects the society, constitutes the carrying on of regulated business, if it is permitted to be done by the society by regulations made by the Registrar with the consent of the Secretary of State.

(2) Paragraph 22B below has effect as regards the application of regulations under this paragraph to member societies in respect of investment business in the carrying on of which they are subject to the rules of a recognised self-regulating organisation for friendly societies.

(3) As it applies to such persons in respect of such business, the reference in sub-paragraph (1) above to conduct permitted by regulations made by the Registrar with the consent of the Secretary of State shall be construed—

(a) where or to the extent that the regulations do not apply, as a reference to conduct permitted by the rules of the organisation; and

(b) where or to the extent that the regulations do apply but are expressed to have effect subject to the rules of the organisation, as a reference to conduct permitted by the regulations together with the rules of the organisation.'.

36. After paragraph 22 (and after the paragraph inserted by section 193(3)) insert—

'22B.—(1) The Registrar may in rules and regulations under—

(a) paragraph 14 (conduct of business rules),
(b) paragraph 19 (clients' money regulations), or
(c) paragraph 20 (regulations as to unsolicited calls),

designate provisions which apply, to such extent as may be specified, to a member society in respect of investment business in the carrying on of which it is subject to the rules of a recognised self-regulating organisation for friendly societies.

(2) It may be provided that the designated rules or regulations have effect, generally or to such extent as may be specified, subject to the rules of the organisation.

(3) A member society which contravenes a rule or regulation applying to it by virtue of this paragraph shall be treated as having contravened the rules of the relevant recognised self-regulating organisation for friendly societies.

(4) It may be provided that, to such extent as may be specified, the designated rules or regulations may not be modified or waived (under paragraph 22C below or section 50) in relation to a member society.

Where such provision is made any modification or waiver previously granted shall cease to have effect, subject to any transitional provision or saving contained in the rules or regulations.

(5) Except as mentioned in sub-paragraph (1), the rules and regulations referred to in that sub-paragraph do not apply to a member society in respect of investment business in the carrying on of which it is subject to the rules of a recognised self-regulating organisation for friendly societies.

22C.—(1) A recognised self-regulating organisation for friendly societies may on the application of a society which is a member of the organisation—

(a) modify a rule or regulation designated under paragraph 22B so as to adapt it to the circumstances of the society or to any particular kind of business carried on by it, or
(b) dispense the society from compliance with any such rule or regulation, generally or in relation to any particular kind of business carried on by it.

(2) The powers conferred by this paragraph shall not be exercised unless it appears to the organisation—

(a) that compliance with the rule or regulation in question would be unduly burdensome for the applicant having regard to the benefit which compliance would confer on investors, and
(b) that the exercise of those powers will not result in any undue risk to investors.

(3) The powers conferred by this paragraph may be exercised unconditionally or subject to conditions; and paragraph 22B(3) applies in the case of a contravention of a condition as in the case of contravention of a designated rule or regulation.

(4) The reference in paragraph 4(1) of Schedule 2 as applied by paragraph 4 above (requirements for recognition of self-regulating organisation for friendly societies) to monitoring and enforcement of compliance with rules and regulations includes monitoring and enforcement of compliance with conditions imposed by the organisation under this paragraph.

22D.—(1) The Registrar may issue codes of practice with respect to any matters dealt with by statements of principle issued under paragraph 13A or by rules or regulations made under any provision of this Schedule.

(2) In determining whether a society has failed to comply with a statement of principle—

(a) a failure by it to comply with any relevant provision of a code of practice may be relied on as tending to establish failure to comply with the statement of principle, and
(b) compliance by it with the relevant provisions of a code of practice may be relied on as tending to negative any such failure.

(3) A contravention of a code of practice with respect to a matter dealt with by rules or regulations shall not of itself give rise to any liability or invalidate any transaction; but in determining whether a society's conduct amounts to contravention of a rule or regulation—

(a) contravention by it of any relevant provision of a code of practice may be relied on as tending to establish liability, and
(b) compliance by it with the relevant provisions of a code of practice may be relied on as tending to negative liability.

(4) Where by virtue of paragraph 22B (application of designated rules and regulations to member societies) rules or regulations—

(*a*) do not apply, to any extent, to a member society of a recognised self-regulating organisation for friendly societies, or

(*b*) apply, to any extent, subject to the rules of the organisation,

a code of practice with respect to a matter dealt with by the rules or regulations may contain provision limiting its application to a corresponding extent.'.

37. For paragraph 29 (transfer of functions of making rules or regulations) substitute—

'29.—(1) The Registrar shall not make a transfer order transferring any legislative functions to a transferee body unless—

(*a*) the body has furnished him and the Secretary of State with a copy of the instruments it proposes to issue or make in the exercise of those functions, and

(*b*) they are both satisfied that those instruments will—

(i) afford investors an adequate level of protection,

(ii) in the case of provisions corresponding to those mentioned in Schedule 8 to this Act, comply with the principles set out in that Schedule, and

(iii) take proper account of the supervision of friendly societies by the Registrar under the enactments relating to friendly societies.

(2) In this paragraph 'legislative functions' means the functions of issuing or making statements of principle, rules, regulations or codes of practice.'.

38. In paragraph 30(2), for 'rules or regulations made' substitute 'statements of principle, rules, regulations or codes of practice issued or made'.

39. In paragraph 31(6)(*c*), for 'as if the reference to section 205(2) were a reference to paragraph 45(1) below' substitute 'as if the reference to section 205A were a reference to paragraph 45(1) and (3) below'.

40. For paragraph 34 substitute—

'34.—(1) A transferee body to which the Registrar has transferred any legislative functions may exercise those functions without the consent of the Secretary of State.

(2) In this paragraph 'legislative functions' means the functions of issuing or making statements of principle, rules, regulations or codes of practice.'.

41. In paragraph 36 (competition scrutiny: transferee bodies) in sub-paragraphs (1) and (3)(*b*) for 'rules, regulations' substitute 'statements of principle, rules, regulations, codes of practice'.

42. In paragraph 38(1) (publication of information and advice)—

(*a*) in paragraph (*a*), for 'rules and regulations made' substitute 'statements of principle, rules, regulations and codes of practice issued or made', and

(*b*) in paragraph (*b*) for 'rules or regulations' substitute 'statements of principle, rules, regulations or codes of practice'.

43. In paragraph 45—

(*a*) in sub-paragraph (1) for 'make regulations, rules or orders' substitute 'issue or make statements of principle, rules, regulations, orders or codes of practice', and

(*b*) in sub-paragraph (3) for 'regulations, rules or orders' substitute 'statements of principle, rules, regulations, orders or codes of practice.'.

SCHEDULE 24

Section 212

REPEALS

Chapter	Short title	Extent of repeal
1964 c 40	Harbours Act 1964	In section 42(6), the words 'required to be attached to a company's balance sheet'.
1973 c 41	Fair Trading Act 1973	Section 46(3). In section 71, in subsection (1) the words 'made under section 69(4) of this Act' and subsection (2).

Chapter	Short title	Extent of repeal
1973 c 41—*cont*	Fair Trading Act 1973—*cont*	In section 74(1), the words from 'and does not' to 'section 69(4) of this Act'. In section 85, subsection (5) and, in subsection (6), paragraph (*b*) and the word 'or' preceding it. In section 88(6), the words from 'the relevant parties' to the 'and' immediately following paragraph (*c*). In section 89(2), the words 'Part II of'. In Schedule 9, in paragraph 4 the words from 'either' to the end.

1985 c 6	Companies Act 1985	Section 160(3).
		In section 169(5), the words from ', during business hours' to 'for inspection)'.
		In section 175(6)(*b*), the words from 'during business hours' to 'period'.
		In section 191—
		  (*a*) in subsection (1), the words from '(but' to 'for inspection)';
		  (*b*) in subsection (3), paragraphs (*a*) and (*b*).
		Section 201.
		In section 202(1), the words '(except where section 201(3) applies)'.
		Section 209(1)(*j*).
		In section 219(1), the words from 'during' to 'for inspection)'.
		In section 288(3), the words from 'during' to 'for inspection)'.
		In section 318(7), the words from 'during' to 'for inspection)'.
		In section 356—
		  (*a*) in subsection (1), the words 'during business hours';
		  (*b*) subsections (2) and (4).
		In section 383—
		  (*a*) in subsection (1), the words 'during business hours';
		  (*b*) subsection (2);
		  (*c*) in subsection (3), the words from 'at a charge' to the end.
		Section 389.
		Section 435.
		Section 440.
		Section 443(4).
		In section 446—
		  (*a*) in subsection (3), paragraph (*b*) and the word 'and' preceding it;
		  (*b*) subsection (7).
		Section 447(1).

Chapter	Short title	Extent of repeal
1985 c 6—*cont*	Companies Act 1985—*cont*	In section 449(1)— (*a*) the words 'or 448'; (*b*) paragraph (*e*). Section 452(1)(*b*). In section 460(1), the words '(inspection of company's books and papers)' and 'under section 440'. In section 464(5), at the end of paragraph (*c*), the word 'and'. In section 466— (*a*) in subsection (2), paragraphs (*a*) and (*d*) and the word 'or' preceding the latter; (*b*) subsections (4) and (5); (*c*) in subsection (6), the words 'falling under subsection (4) of this section'. In section 651(1), the words 'at any time within 2 years of the date of the dissolution'. In section 708(1)(*b*), the words 'or other material'. Sections 712 and 715. In section 716(2), the words following paragraph (*c*). In section 717(1), the words following paragraph (*c*). In section 733(3), the words from 'then' to '216(3)'. In section 735A(1), the words '440, 449(1)(*a*) and (*d*)'. In section 744, the definitions of 'annual return', 'authorised institution', 'authorised minimum', 'expert', 'floating charge', 'joint stock company' and 'undistributable reserves'. In section 746, the words 'Except as provided by section 243(6),'. In Schedule 2— (*a*) in paragraph 1(1), the words 'paragraph 60(2) of Schedule 4 or paragraph 19(3) of Schedule 9'; (*b*) paragraph 1(5); (*c*) in paragraph 2(1), the word '23,'; (*d*) paragraph 2(2); (*e*) in paragraph 3(1), the words 'paragraph 60(2) of Schedule 4 or paragraph 19(3) of Schedule 9'; (*f*) paragraph 3(3); (*g*) in paragraph 4(1), the words '(whether as personal representative or otherwise)';

Chapter	Short title	Extent of repeal
1985 c 6—*cont*	Companies Act 1985—*cont*	(*h*) in paragraph 4(2), the words 'paragraph 60(2) of Schedule 4 or paragraph 19(3) of Schedule 9'. In Schedule 4, paragraphs 50(6), 53(7), 60 to 70, 74, 75, 77 to 81, 87, 90 to 92 and 95. In Schedule 9— (*a*) paragraphs 1, 13(3) and (18), 16, 18(5), 19(3) to (7) and 21 to 26; (*b*) in paragraph 27(4), the words 'of the said Part I'; (*c*) in paragraph 28, in sub-paragraph (1) the words 'to which Part II of the Insurance Companies Act 1982 applies' and in sub-paragraph (2) the words 'of Part I of this Schedule'; (*d*) paragraphs 29 to 31. In Schedule 11— (*a*) paragraph 4(*b*) and (*c*); (*b*) paragraph 5(*b*). In Schedule 13, in paragraph 25, the words from 'during' to 'for inspection)'. Schedule 15. In Schedule 22— (*a*) the entry relating to section 36(4); (*b*) in the entry relating to sections 363 to 365, the words '(with Schedule 15)'; (*c*) in the entry relating to sections 384 to 393, in column 2, the word 'qualifications'. In Schedule 24, the entries relating to sections 245(1), 245(2), 255(5), 260(3), 287(3), 365(3), 384(5), 386(2), 389(10), 390(7), 391(4), 392(2) and 393.
1985 c 65	Insolvency Act 1985	In Schedule 6, paragraphs 7(3), 23 and 45.
1986 c 45	Insolvency Act 1986	In sections 45(5), 53(2), 54(3) and 62(5), the words 'and, for continued contravention, to a daily default fine'. In Schedule 10, the entries in column 5 relating to sections 45(5), 53(2), 54(3) and 62(5). In Part I of Schedule 13, the entries relating to sections 222(4), 225 and 733(3).
1986 c 46	Company Directors Disqualification Act 1986	In section 21(2), the words 'and section 431 (summary proceedings)'.

Chapter	Short title	Extent of repeal
1986 c 53	Building Societies Act 1986	In Schedule 15, in paragraph 3(2)(*b*), the words ', a shadow director'. In Schedule 18, paragraphs 16 and 17.

1986 c 60	Financial Services Act 1986	In section 13—
		  (*a*) subsection (1);
		  (*b*) subsections (4) to (6).
		In section 48(1), the words 'members of a recognised self-regulating organisation or' and 'organisation or'.
		In section 55—
		  (*a*) in subsection (2)(*b*) and (*e*), the words 'a member of a recognised self-regulating organisation or' and 'organisation or';
		  (*b*) in subsection (3), the words 'organisation or'.
		In section 94—
		  (*a*) in subsection (3), the words 'except section 435(1)(*a*) and (*b*) and (2)';
		  (*b*) in subsection (4), the words 'or its affairs', 'and the affairs mentioned in subsection (1) or (2) above' and 'or director'.
		Section 105(7).
		In section 119(5), the words from 'and the practices referred to in paragraph (*c*)' to the end.
		In sections 159(1) and 160(1), the words from the beginning to 'section 161 below'.
		In section 179(3), the word 'and' preceding paragraph (i).
		Section 180(6).
		Section 196(3).
		Section 198(1).
		In section 199(9), the words from 'and, in relation' to the end.
		In Schedule 11—
		  (*a*) paragraph 4(4)(*b*);
		  (*b*) paragraph 7;
		  (*c*) in paragraph 10(3), the words from 'and the practices referred to in paragraph (*c*)' to the end;
		  (*d*) in paragraph 14(1), the words 'other than a member society';
		  (*e*) in paragraph 14(3), the word 'and' after paragraph (*a*).
		In Schedule 16, paragraph 22.

Chapter	Short title	Extent of repeal
1987 c 22	Banking Act 1987	In the Table in section 84(1), the entry relating to persons appointed under section 94, 106 or 177 of the Financial Services Act 1986. Section 90(1). In Schedule 6— (*a*) paragraph 18(1) to (6); (*b*) in paragraph 18(7) the words 'and (1A)'; (*c*) paragraph 18(8) and (9); (*d*) in paragraph 27(3) the words 'and (6)'.
1987 c 41	Criminal Justice (Scotland) Act 1987	Section 55(*a*).
1988 c 1	Income and Corporation Taxes Act 1988	Section 565(6)(*b*).
1988 c 33	Criminal Justice Act 1988	Section 145(*a*).
1988 c 38	Copyright, Designs and Patents Act 1988	In Schedule 7, paragraph 31.

Index

Note: references in this index are to paragraph numbers